SOCIAL CRISES
A Casebook

SOCIAL CRISES

A Casebook

Edited, with introductory essays, by
ROBERT HYBELS
Newton Junior College

tyc THOMAS Y. CROWELL COMPANY
New York   *Established 1834*

Library of Congress Cataloging in Publication Data

HYBELS, ROBERT, comp.
  Social crises: a casebook.

  1. United States—Social conditions—Addresses,
essays, lectures.   2. Social problems—Addresses,
essays, lectures.   I. Title.
HN65.H9   309.1·73′0924   73-18342
ISBN 0-690-00222-X

Manufactured in the United States of America

1   2   3   4   5   6   7   8   9   10

Preface

A crisis is a crucial turning point. In medicine it is a sudden change in the course of a disease—in either direction, for better or for worse. In a story or a drama it is a point of heightened suspense. In political and economic affairs it is an unstable condition arising from impending decisive change.

The term "social crisis" partakes of all of these senses. In the metaphors of social pathology, if society is understood as the patient and social problems as the diseases, a social crisis may be seen as a tangle of chronic social problems grown acute. In other contexts it may be a revolutionary turning point in a nation's social history, or, in the contemporary life of a society, it may be a currently unstable situation whose outcome is in doubt.

In practice the term "crisis" is often loosely used, and sometimes it is recklessly abused, because no synonyms with gradations of meaning exist, and also because some people deliberately inject hyperbole into public discussion out of a conviction that nothing less than a crisis atmosphere can counterbalance other people's inertia and get them to unite and act. In this book, however, its use is restricted to five situations in contemporary American life that seem to fit precisely: (1) the Urban Crisis, involving in particular the social problems of poverty, racial conflict, family and school disorganization, crime, delinquency, and conflict between cities and their suburbs;

(2) the Rural Crisis, involving poverty, malnutrition, poor health, illiteracy, racial conflict, "corporate colonialism," etc.; (3) the Environmental Crisis, involving pollution, depletion of natural resources, misuse of land, etc.; (4) the Spiritual Crisis, a crisis of the American spirit or cultural ethos, involving the black rebellion, women's movement, counterculture (including drug abuse), new left, workers' alienation, populism—together with the backlash against these rebellions; (5) the Crisis of Crises, a new pessimism and sense of tragedy that some call the "national malaise," stemming from the cumulative effects of the other four crises that have shaken our faith in ourselves as a people and forced us to undergo an agonizing reappraisal of the wisdom of our traditional value priorities and the legitimacy of our institutions.

Each of these five social crises is a very complicated set of interlocking social problems aggravated by recent sociocultural change. A social problem may be defined as an intolerable gap as perceived by a significant number of people in a given society between social conditions as they are and as people think they ought to be. Sociocultural change always strains the fabric of society to some extent, but when drastic changes come at explosive speed they can rip that fabric, tough as it is, breaking down traditional roles and institutional controls while simultaneously creating new hopes and anxieties. Since World War II life in the United States has been changing at a pace threatening to rip the fabric. Two of the more basic changes, for example, have been technological progress, ranging all the way from improved gadgets to space spectaculars, and an increasing affluence shared by most—although certainly not all—members of our society. The multitude of social effects flowing from such primary forces has made some social conditions worse, such as pollution and technological unemployment, and raised public expectations of what other social conditions ought to be—stimulating demands for greater equality and liberty, for example—thus building up the pressure in old chronic social problems to a crisis point.

To reduce their complexity to manageable proportions, each of the crises will be described and dissected in an introductory essay, and then a principle as old as Aesop's *Fables* and Plutarch's *Lives* will be employed: to learn about the general look closely at the particular.

An intensive analysis of a particular example is a case study. In contrast to the sample survey, which measures a few characteristics of many units, the case study examines many characteristics of just one unit, such as an individual or a group, a particular place or event. As a teaching technique and research tool it has its limitations, of course. Because it is based on a sample of just one, with the degree of generality unknown, a case study can't prove much. It cannot tell what must happen or what cannot happen; it can show only what did happen within a specific set of circumstances and therefore what is possible under similar circumstances. On the other hand, case studies are often rich in clues for further investigation by other means. They are perhaps best at exploring the beliefs and attitudes that motivate behavior, probing and exposing whatever is subtle and subjective in people's lives. As a teaching device, detailed concrete cases are indispensable to illustrate generalizations and provoke thought and discussion and further reading. At the risk of oversimplifying, carefully selected cases can also dramatize and humanize issues by involving readers' emotions and creating empathy for the victims of social problems.

The case-study technique is especially appropriate for college-level social problems or social psychology courses, since the residual value of such courses probably lies more in the attitudes students carry away than in their mastery of facts and theories.

The primary function of this book is to generate enough curiosity in the reader about the whys of problematic social behavior to motivate him into learning more by further study. Nevertheless, the introductory essays do explain many of the sociological and psychological concepts and theories needed to understand the crises, including the value conflict approach to social problems; how social classes differ in life-style; the effects of rapid, drastic sociocultural change; the causes and effects of migration, invasion, and succession; the main principles of human ecology; the rank-order of basic needs; attitudinal change; relative deprivation; frustrated expectations; the erosion of authority; and coping with grief. The case studies illustrate additional concepts and theories, such as the social factors in personality development and mental health, the causes and effects of group prejudice, social movements, and collective behavior.

Although *Social Crises* can be used as a casebook supplementing a conventional expository textbook, its combination of general, introductory essays followed by many specific examples is designed to be used as a central, organizing text surrounded by ancillary books that explore selected social problems in depth or provide general background or additional cases, such as those listed at the end of this volume (see "To Learn More . . .").

Contents

PART II / THE RURAL CRISIS 79

(Concerning poverty, malnutrition, poor health, illiteracy, unemployment, racial conflict, "corporate colonialism," and the depopulation of rural areas)

PART III / THE ENVIRONMENTAL CRISIS 147

(Concerning pollution and depletion of natural resources, misuse of the land, the ecology movement and the reaction against it)

PART IV / THE SPIRITUAL CRISIS 199

(Concerning rebellions by blacks, women, youth, populists, and workers, countered by a massive backlash)

Contents Arranged by Problems Instead of Crises

II / RACE

III / CRIME AND CORRUPTION

"MAY YOU LIVE IN INTERESTING TIMES"

"May you live in interesting times!" was a curse the ancient Chinese laid on people they disliked. Obviously, somebody doesn't like us, for we certainly live in "interesting" times, full of persistent, vexatious social problems. But if we had a choice, would we really prefer to live in an "era of good feeling" without major domestic crises and conflicts? Paradoxically, some of the young people of Sweden are reported to be bored with their country because the big domestic problems appear to have all been solved by their elders. They have nothing to protest about except that their elders' solutions are too neat to satisfy the human spirit—life is too secure and too predictable and therefore unexciting! Sweden's world-renowned social scientist, Gunnar Myrdal, also finds life in his homeland boring. What excites him instead, he says, are the spectacular struggles being waged with staggering problems in "underdeveloped" countries like the United States.

On the other hand, it is possible that we have an exaggerated notion of how "interesting" these times are. From the point of view of the British, who pride themselves on maintaining a "business as usual" attitude under adversity, we Americans—especially intellectuals—tend to overreact to events. For instance, in the early 1960s a group of social scientists calling themselves the Ad Hoc Committee on the Triple Revolution warned the nation that hooking computers up with automated, self-regulating machinery would create a "cybernetic revolution" in production, out of which would flow new social problems caused by extraordinary leisure and abundance. However, this vision of a comparative utopia proved to be illusory. There was no spectacular jump in productivity; instead, the economy's service sector expanded at the expense of production.

At a point in time which we now realize was near the zenith of the civil rights movement, a sociologist expressed the euphoria that many liberals felt during the early 1960s. The caste system has been broken up throughout the country, he asserted. Prejudice is still a common attitude, but very few people continue to believe in racism as an ideology.

> I venture to predict the end of all formal segregation and discrimination within a decade, and the decline of informal segregation and discrimination so that it [will] be a mere shadow in two decades. The attitude of prejudice might remain indefinitely, but it will be on the minor order of Catholic-Protestant prejudice within three decades.[1]

The hindsight wisdom of the 1980s may judge today's mood of despair to have been equally premature, despite all the signs we see around us recommending pessimism.

---

[1] Arnold Rose, "Introduction" to *An American Dilemma* by Gunnar Myrdal, Anniv. Ed. (New York: Harper & Row, 1964), pp. xliii—xliv.

PART I

THE URBAN CRISIS

3

Introduction:
Migration Headaches

Austin Street, where Catherine Genovese lived, is in a section of Queens known as Kew Gardens. There are two apartment buildings and the rest of the street consists of one-family homes—red-brick, stucco or wood-frame. There are Jews, Catholics and Protestants, a scattering of foreign accents, middle-class incomes.

On the night of March 13, about 3 A.M., Catherine Genovese was returning to her home. She worked late as manager of a bar in Hollis, another part of Queens. She parked her car (a red Fiat) and started to walk to her death.

Lurking near the parking lot was a man. Miss Genovese saw him in the shadows, turned and walked toward a police call box. The man pursued her, stabbed her. She screamed, "Oh my God, he stabbed me! Please help me! Please help me!"

Somebody threw open a window and a man called out: "Let that girl alone!" Other lights turned on, other windows were raised. The attacker got into a car and drove away. A bus passed.

The attacker drove back, got out, searched out Miss Genovese in the back of an apartment building where she had crawled for safety, stabbed her again, drove away again.

The first attack came at 3:15. The first call to the police came at 3:50. Police arrived within two minutes, they say. Miss Genovese was dead.

That night and the next morning the police combed the neighborhood looking for witnesses. They found them, 38.

Two weeks later, when [*The New York Times*] heard of the story, a reporter went knocking, door to door, asking why, why.

Through half-opened doors, they told him. Most of them were neither defiant nor terribly embarrassed nor particularly ashamed. The underlying attitude, or explanation, seemed to be fear of involvement—any kind of involvement.

"I didn't want my husband to get involved," a housewife said.

"We thought it was a lovers' quarrel," said another woman. "I went back to bed."

"I was tired," said a man.

"I don't know," said another man.

"I don't know," said still another.

"I don't know," said others. . . .

Nobody can say why the 38 did not lift the phone while Miss Genovese was being attacked, since they cannot say themselves. It can be assumed, however, that their apathy was indeed of a big-city variety. It is almost a matter of psychological survival, if one is surrounded and pressed by millions of people, to prevent them from constantly impinging on you and the only way to do this is to ignore them as often as possible.

Indifference to one's neighbor and his troubles is a conditioned reflex of life in New York as it is in other big cities.[1]

The thirty-eight witnesses' fear of involvement was a realistic one: it can be dangerous, or costly, to be a good Samaritan. Moreover, accustomed to middle-class norms, they might not have believed that the street crimes associated with the inner city could ever take place where they lived. Whatever occurs in a street late at night, they might have thought, usually happens to vulgar, lower-class people who don't seem to mind very much. Their middle-class life-style may have also inhibited them from taking the law into their own hands, but why, then, didn't they call the police? Probably because each of them assumed that someone else had surely done that. They were unorganized and not in communication with each other. Besides, they were aware of only fragments of an ambiguous situation. And, of course, those who live in physical proximity to each other do not necessarily feel any mutual obligations. At the same time that the logistics of city life crowds people together physically, the psychological pressure of numbers and the effects of heterogeneity and impersonality tend to separate people socially and morally.

In several ways the case of Catherine Genovese symbolizes the Urban Crisis. Our sense of crisis regarding our cities stems essentially from worrying about our personal safety—in the streets, in the schools,

---

[1] A. M. Rosenthal, "Study of the Sickness Called Apathy," *The New York Times Magazine*, 3 May 1964, pp. 24, 70.

and in other public places like the corridors and elevators of apartment buildings—and concern that our cities lie wounded but the suburbs don't seem to care—at least not enough to take any risks.

By themselves most of the social problems peculiar to city life such as traffic congestion and noise, inadequate public transportation, crowded housing, visual ugliness, air and water pollution, waste removal, and the decline of downtown centers, hardly constitute a crisis. What *does* feel like a crisis to most of the people who actually live in the central cities, as opposed to business and political leaders who commute from the suburbs, is the loss of a sense of community at the neighborhood level, that is, the breakdown of standards of proper behavior consistent with—and supportive of—their own life-style, and the resulting collapse of informal social controls. What is so destructive of neighborhood communities is a double migration into and out of the central cities, rivaling in scale the flow from Europe at the turn of the century: an out-migration of families with middle-class values and customs, and an in-migration of families with lower-class values and customs; an out-migration of industries and stores and offices representing thousands of jobs, and an in-migration from depressed areas of the technologically unemployed together with the unskilled and poorly educated; an out-migration of people who can afford to pay for the city services they need, and an in-migration of people whose needs for city services are far beyond their capacity to pay the costs; an out-migration of potential leaders of civic, cultural, and charitable organizations, and an in-migration of people who are inexperienced with urban life and whose natural leaders have rarely been permitted to develop; an out-migration mostly of whites, and an in-migration mostly of blacks.

Atlanta, for example, has lost 60,000 white residents during the past ten years, while gaining 70,000 black residents. Whereas the outgoing white families averaged $14,000 a year income, the incoming blacks earned only $9,000. The city is now more than 50 percent black, and whites are still leaving.

Mattapan, once a predominantly Jewish section of Boston, has been steadily turning black in recent years. Now it is a discordant mixture of synagogues and soul shops, kosher butchers and real estate offices. A Jewish wedding hall has been turned into Elijah Muhammad's Mosque No. 1. FOR SALE signs are burgeoning everywhere.

During the past fifteen years about ten million people, mostly black, have moved from farms and small towns into inner cities, mostly in the North. As a result, blacks have become more urbanized than whites, and more of them now live in the five largest cities of the North than live in the five black-belt states of the South. (Although this migration may be slowing down, population pressures continue to build inside slum-ghettos because the urban black birth rate remains at a high rural level at the same time that the death rate is being drastically cut by urban social services.)

Mass migrations can usually be explained by the sociological formula: pushes + pulls + means. Rural migrants feel pushed by conditions like poverty and unemployment and pulled by urban employment opportunities backed up by welfare programs; they are likely to move if the combined pressures become intolerable—unless they lack the third factor, the means to do so. Urban migrants commonly cite as "pushes" conditions such as congestion, noise, filth, blighted housing, poor schools, street crime, and the expanding black ghetto's threat to their status; as "pulls" the suburbs' high scores in these same categories; and as means their personal prosperity and the new feasibility of commuting.

In combination, these two massive population shifts are responsible for most of the symptoms that generate so much anxiety: housing and stores deteriorating under absentee ownership, property taxes climbing higher and higher to compensate for shrinking real estate values, public schools out of mesh with the lower-class values and customs of their new constituency, crime and delinquency rates rising—our inner cities are approaching social breakdown.

Take, for example, the capital city of this nation, where in just three years' time, recently, all the totals of serious crime doubled—except for robbery, which tripled; where during the decade of the 1960s seven times as many residents were murdered as were killed in action in Vietnam; where many black people who used to feel intimidated by the police now feel still more intimidated by young thugs on the street; where in certain public housing projects nobody dares to live on the ground floor within easy reach of the hoodlum element; where policemen have been assigned to all the junior and senior high schools; where bus drivers no longer dare to carry change and taxi drivers avoid the rougher parts of town; where there are merchants who stay locked up all the time, opening their doors only to customers who don't look dangerous; where uneasy visitors dare leave their hotels only during daylight hours and even then are careful to travel in pairs; where many churches have stopped all evening activities and theaters have shifted their curtain time from 8:30 to 7:30 to cater to the audience's desire to leave downtown early; and where restaurants have lost much of their former after-the-theater trade.

With mounting dismay, the people who at first elected to stay behind in the old familiar neighborhood watch the results of the double migration in and out, and many of them finally decide to move to the suburbs too. Their departure, of course, accelerates the decline that they deplore and starts a vicious circle.

Probably nothing would do more to check the flight to the suburbs than a dramatic improvement in the quality of the inner city's schools, but those in charge are trapped in this same vicious circle. As the reputation of the inner city's school system worsens, more people leave for the suburbs. As more and more of the middle class leave, the inner city is less and less able to maintain academic and disciplinary standards and to finance school improvement; it also feels less pressure to do so because the people most concerned about the schools tend to be the ones who leave.

Unless present trends are reversed or arrested, this is how our centers of commerce, learning, culture, and entertainment may look a few years from now: The central business district, an island of activity during the day, is a deserted enclave by night populated mainly by heavily armed police patrols. During these same night-time hours, the slum-ghetto is a place of terror entirely out of police control. City dwellers with high enough incomes live in residential compounds protected by private guards, dogs, and electronic security devices. Sanitized corridors connect the central city with its suburbs, where ownership of guns is almost universal, and where armed vigilantes in cars supplement inadequate police patrols in neighborhoods on the edges of the central city. Suburbanites commute to work in private cars equipped with unbreakable glass and light armor. On all forms of public transportation armed guards "ride shotgun." Not unnaturally, between the unsafe, decaying central city and the fortress-suburbs there is an ever intensifying hatred and deepening division.

In short, the Urban Crisis is a general anxiety over an impending breakdown of the social order resulting from the geographical polarization of metropolitan areas into three kinds of ghettos: the slums—huge concentrations of people who are not only poor and ignorant but also filled with a sense of injustice; the suburbs—safe and aloof; and the ethnic enclaves in between—full of rebellious reaction. Involved are urban versions of the same chronic maladies that have been sapping the vitality of this nation for generations: poverty and racial conflict, family and school disorganization, crime and delinquency.

One of the most ominous threats to the social structure lies in the signs that many of the slum-ghetto-raised children of the black migration are developing into the same sort of vicious, nihilistic underclass that grew to dangerous proportions at least once before in this country's history, out of the migration from Ireland of impoverished and demoralized peasants whose American-born children turned out to be even wilder. Whenever a peasant family migrates to the city it is likely to be "shook up" by a stripping of gears as the members try to mesh their rural ways with the urban environment. Particularly for adults, migration is an uprooting process, but its effects vary according to how much the new way of life clashes with the old. Most urban Jewish families, for example, emigrating from European to American cities, were able to shift gears smoothly. Likewise, peasant families emigrating from Scandinavian to Midwestern farms experienced few of the cultural shocks suffered in American cities by peasant families from Ireland and Italy in the past or from Mexico and Puerto Rico and the rural South in the present.

What shakes up an immigrant family the most is a reversal of roles and status. Simultaneous emigration and urbanization have the combined effect of canceling out much of the relevance of the parents' past achievements and demoting them below their city-born children, who become in effect their parents' cultural parents. The power vacuum created by the irrelevance of the elders' foreign experience is soon filled by the children's peer groups.

Products of cultural shock, family breakdown, malnutrition, slum life, school failure, and police records; filled with rage by the knowledge that they are not going anywhere because they are not needed or wanted by anybody, while others of their ethnic group are able to take advantage of new opportunities opening up—the Irish underclass was alienated a hundred years ago, and the urban black underclass is alienated today, from the mores and controls, as well as the rewards, of our society.

Besides this worrisome underclass, those left behind in the central cities by the flight of the middle class include most of the working class (especially the working poor), most of the young singles, the intelligentsia, and many of the well-to-do who prefer apartment life. Most important, however, migrants to the suburbs have also left behind legal, political, and financial responsibility for the central city's problems. This loophole in responsibility is the result of the way government is fragmented in metropolitan areas of the United States and the fetish we make of local control. A metropolitan area anywhere is an interrelated complex of cities and towns with a common future, but in this country it is likely to be as uncoordinated as the prehistoric brontosaurus, which was doomed by its lack of a central nervous system. The nation's 228 metropolitan areas are subdivided into 20,745 independent pieces—about 80 in Greater Boston, 1,000 in Chicago, 1,400 in the New York area, and so on, and very few of the residents have a metropolitan point of view—including black separatists who oppose suburban involvement on the suspicion that it is one more trick to keep whites in control of the inner cities.

The cities of London and Toronto have demonstrated that at least technical-political problems such as urban sprawl, traffic congestion, and air and water pollution can be arrested and can even be put into reverse if an inner city's problems are tackled by the surrounding region without regard for the borders of political subdivisions.

The "balkanization" of metropolitan government in the United States, however, may be an excuse rather than the real reason for suburban aloofness from the inner city's plight. Joint efforts could be made without surrendering precious sovereignty if suburbanites were willing to help.

To those who reside in the inner city, all the people in the outer city appear to be selfish "free-loaders" who think it smart business—like tax avoidance—to exploit the inner city for a living and as a center for shopping, higher education, culture, and recreation without paying the full cost. The suburbanites themselves, however, are ambivalent about involvement in the city's problems. Many of them feel like those thirty-eight witnesses of Catherine Genovese's murder, who stared out of their windows, worried, unwilling to act but unable to turn away, feeling their responsibility diffused and diluted by the proximity of so many other people, wanting to do the right thing but paralyzed by dilemmas: "Does she really need help? (Or is she making a fool of me?) Is it my responsibility? (What about those other people who live closer?) If I do get involved, will I get hurt?"

Many suburbanites have bad consciences about running away. They know that the problems the central city needs help with are the same ones they moved out of the city to escape from, and they are aware that their desertion has made things worse. They believe that the relative peace and quiet of the suburbs can exist only if they are rationed, for as soon as they are shared with everybody they disappear. The American ideology makes them feel guilty about their class-consciousness—about not liking most of the people who live in the inner city, feeling they have an inferior life-style. They sense that behind the term "urban crisis" is what would be called a class struggle if it were happening in another country, and they wonder if they are hypocrites. They are torn between loyalties: one to the central city on which their livelihood depends and where they spend their working hours, the other to the community where they reside with their families. They realize that the growth of the suburbs is one of the causes of the core city's decline, that the suburbs have grown by draining away the city's industry and business and leadership without taking a share of its inherited debts and other encumbrances, and they are embarrassed by the question of moral responsibility. They realize that their suburban oasis may turn out to be a mirage, that the suburbs and the central city are in reality "all in the same bag," that the suburbs cannot for long escape being affected by what goes on in the city, and vice versa.

Once there were two young cities, both born in the Midwest around 1900 as single-industry towns—steel in one and oil in the other—attracting a labor force of poorly educated, unskilled immigrants from Europe at first and later black migrants from the South. Both of them grew up to be centers of metropolitan populations roughly the same size, 300,000. From the beginning one developed a national reputation for crime and corruption, whereas the other enjoyed a reputation which was nearly spotless, even though every year the leaders of business and industry in both cities were equally generous in donating their time and know-how and money to public service in their hometowns. The big difference was that the good people of the good city (Tulsa, Oklahoma) chose to live and serve *inside* it, whereas the good people of the bad city (Gary, Indiana) chose to live and serve *outside* it.

Did the bad city first drive out its good people, or did absentee owners first make their city bad?

The case studies that follow illustrate some of the salient points made in the preceding theoretical analysis. The first two, reports from Cleveland and Newark, epitomize what the Urban Crisis is all about: the shattering of a neighborhood's sense of community, polarization according to ethclass (ethnicity plus class), and fear of unpredictable violence from a rebellious underclass. In addition, these two cases expose the friction generated between ethnic groups by processes that sociologists call "invasion" and "succession," borrowing their terminology from ecologists who speak of one kind of plant "invading" an area and spreading until it has shaded out all others and thus "succeeded" to the position of dominance formerly held by another type. The situation in Newark provides a preview of the agony that many other central cities may experience in the near future, as the drive for black power and autonomy turns the screws of the Urban Crisis. (Newark's black mayor enjoys saying, with a bit of local pride mixed in with his anxiety, "Wherever the central cities are going, Newark is going to get there first.")

"Harlem's State of Mind" typifies the response of black people to the simple equation between blacks and crime that whites commonly make. When crime mounted after black people moved in large numbers to the cities, many whites concluded that blacks cause crime. Of course, in reality black residents are just as desperately anxious to flee from crime-ridden neighborhoods as whites, and if they can, they do. Nevertheless, black Americans do commit more crime proportionately than white Americans do, especially crimes involving aggression such as murder, rape, and aggravated assault—most of whose victims tend to be other blacks —and escapist "crimes-without-victims" such as gambling, drug addiction, and drunkenness. White supremacists are quick to explain the racial difference in crime rates as biologically determined by what they believe to be the Negro race's genetic inferiority, despite the lack of scientific evidence to support such a doctrine.

Having learned from over a century of experience since Abolition to distrust the local law and police and courts, whether in the rural and small-town South or in the big-city North, black people habitually respond in the same ways that yesterday's frontiersmen did to similar conditions of anarchy, by relying on concealed weapons for self-protection and by idealizing personal violence.

In recent times a whole new generation of militant blacks has emerged, anxious to demonstrate their masculinity, and determined to break away from the Sambo role by any means within their reach, legal or not, fair or not. Most of the rest of the black community thrills to their exploits as lower-class Englishmen once thrilled to Robin Hood's. To many the cop-killer has become a folk-hero, and, if executed, a martyr. For the black ghettos look like colonial outposts to their residents, with colonial police living off graft and keeping the natives in their place.

The police have learned to expect resistance to arrest in the black ghetto, and the blacks have learned to expect to be roughed up. The reaction of each to what he expects of the other causes the other to behave as expected. In their vain efforts to force respect, the police actually help *produce* crime by escalating minor offenses into bigger ones.

A similar set of self-fulfilling prophecies has been escalating crime in the slum areas of our cities for more than a hundred years. But until recently most of the people feuding with the police have been non-WASP whites carrying on a tradition which started in the old country and was kept alive by the police in the new country living up (or down?) to the immigrants' expectations. Of course, from the point of view of the police they were living up (or down?) to the expectations of the "good people" (i.e., middle-class WASPs), who didn't care how they kept order among low-status peoples like the Slavic and Mediterranean immigrants.

The next three articles show how chronic social problems are being aggravated by what the other social classes see as some of the threatening aspects of the slum-ghetto's life-style: juvenile delinquency ("The 'Rat Packs' of New York"), school disorganization ("Slum-Ghetto Schoolchildren"), and poverty and family disorganization ("The Grim State of Welfare"). What should cities do with people who are surplus—for whom they have no social or economic need or desire? The immediate humane solution has been to keep them alive by putting them on the welfare dole. But the dole was designed to take care of the exceptions—the widowed and the crippled and the aged—not a whole urban underclass plus victims of technological change. As "Slum-Ghetto Schoolchildren" and "The Grim State of Welfare" suggest, there is persuasive evidence that long-term dependence on welfare checks and the well-meant paternalism of caseworkers corrupt welfare recipients and their children, atrophying self-discipline and the will to work, and undermining family life.

"The Battle of the Suburbs," after telling about the political and economic power struggle going on between the residents of the suburbs and the central cities, plus their respective allies, focuses on what stopped the flight of Jews from a section of Philadelphia, in particular their mind-changing realization that *racial* differences are not nearly as relevant to the so-called race problem as *class* differences. (That middle-class black people fear being contaminated by contact with the life-style of the underclass just as much as middle-class whites do is indicated by their resistance to a proposed public housing project in their neighborhood in Cleveland a few years ago. The local housing authority wanted to erect 277 single-family ranch-style houses on vacant land, to rent to low-income families who wished to move out of Hough district slums. "If middle-class Negroes don't let lower-class Negroes in," reproached Carl Stokes, Cleveland's black mayor, "what kind of success do they think we will have in integrating the suburbs?")

The battle of the suburbs, of course, revolves mainly around the issue of segregation in schools and housing, and one of the dilemmas vexing suburbanites is that the double migration has reached such proportions that the inner city's schools cannot be desegregated without a massive transfusion of kids from the suburbs. However, the history of attempts to desegregate central city schools, and also residential areas, demonstrates that as soon as a certain "tipping point" is reached—i.e., that point at which the number of nonwhite children in a school or neighborhood causes white parents to worry about whose life-style is rubbing off on whom—many white parents resegregate by either moving to the suburbs or enrolling their children in independent or parochial schools. What if the issue were clarified as being *socioeconomic* segregation rather than racial? What changes might this bring about in race relations and the battle of the suburbs?

An enormous effort (4,000 schools, $2 million, etc.) was made a few years ago by the U.S. Office of Education under the direction of Professor James S. Coleman to isolate the major factors in pupil achievement. The Coleman Report upset long-held assumptions by finding that one's achievement is largely determined by the social class of one's family and classmates, with school quality a very minor factor. Each class is in fact a subculture or life-style more than an income bracket, with a distinctive pattern of behavior learned by each generation from the preceding one. Many "racial" differences are actually class differences, and what appears to be white racism is mostly consciousness of class.

The underclass (or lower class), for example, tends to be impulsive, improvident, and fatalistic; living for the moment, convinced of the wisdom of immediate gratification; filled with self-contempt, suspicious of others, and resentful of authority; indifferent toward work and any ties with family, ethnic group, neighbors, etc. In contrast, the next higher class in status, the working class, tends to be more future-oriented and respectful of authority and tradition, family and ethnic ties, and work at least to the extent it seems justified by masculinity or tradition. And so on up the social ladder, each life-style being essentially a set of adaptations to the life-situation in which each class finds itself, reflecting in particular its realistic expectations concerning its own future, especially its degree of control over its own destiny.

The Coleman Report, accordingly, recommended that one of the best ways to raise pupil achievement levels is to deliberately distribute lower-class children to schools whose standards and examples are set by children from the working class or higher. So far, Duluth, Minnesota, has been the first city in the United States to consider seriously implementing socioeconomic desegregation. However, soon after initially approving the plan, the local school board regretted its action and postponed it indefinitely. Regardless of whether it is a question of racial or socioeconomic desegregation, it is the tipping point that concerns middle-class parents —the question of whose life-style will rub off on whom.

(Meanwhile, an attempt to achieve socioeconomic integration is being made in England. Convinced that Britain's rigid, sharply defined class system is perpetuated by the practice of segregating children into different schools according to their ability, London's educational authorities have begun mixing a few intellectually able youngsters with average and below-average youngsters. Predictably, parents are resisting the assignment of their children to schools with a reputation for low academic standards and high rates of violence. "You can't make a bad school good just by sending a few bright children to it," they warn anxiously.)

1

As the Blacks
Move In . . .

PAUL WILKES

The signs were there, all right. The little photography studio on the corner of Harvey and 116th Street, where I had looked at the latest brides, their lips retouched deep red and eyebrows dark, was now a karate and judo school. A storefront church, Pilgrim Rest B. C., was on 93d Street near Dickens. Protective grates guarded the front of Rosenbluth's, our local clothing store, whose recorded Santa Claus laugh had scared the patched corduroy pants right off me as a youngster. A public housing project rose from the mud. And in the streets there was a stillness.

As I drove back through my old neighborhood on the East Side of Cleveland last month, there was so little noise. No horns. At 8 o'clock in the evening, there were few cars on the street. There must have been more people walking around, but I remember only a handful at well-lit intersections.

There had been no dinner served on the flight to Cleveland, and as I turned onto Forest Avenue I thought it was just as well. There would be a pot of beef soup bubbling on the stove and huge lengths of garlic-spiced

Source: Paul Wilkes, "As the Blacks Move in, the Ethnics Move out," *New York Times Magazine,* 24 January 1971. © 1971 by The New York Times Company. Reprinted by permission.

kolbasz, the soul food of my ethnic group, the Slovaks. Over such food a son could talk more easily with his father. Over such food it would be more comfortable to talk about the crime that appears to be sweeping this, the peaceful and benign neighborhood where I spent my first 18 years. With hunks of rye bread in our hands and caraway seeds falling softly to the table, we could even talk about *them,* the new immigrants, the blacks who had broken the barrier and swept into this formerly homogeneous area of Cleveland. As the conversation began, though, it was embarrassing for me, always previously eager to shuck the ethnic business and a blue-collar background, to start asking questions about the family and the old neighborhood only because an idea had come to mind and an article had been assigned.

My father—his family name, Vilk, already Americanized to Wilkes—came to Cleveland with my mother and six brothers and sisters a year before I was born in 1938. They left an area that would soon stand for white poverty—Appalachia—and came to one where other Slovaks years before had found work in the factories that spread from the Cuyahoga River up the gentle slopes of streets like Kinsman, Union, Woodland and Buckeye.

They soon bought a house that "wasn't much," my father explained through a wad of Havana Blossom chewing tobacco that remains virtually a part of his anatomy. "There wasn't any sheeting beneath the siding, the floors were wavy, but to your mother it was a mansion." The purchase price was $4,000 and the monthly payments about $35, a third of my father's wages with the W.P.A.

Living on Forest Avenue after the war and through the first half of the nineteen-fifties surely fulfilled all the dreams of the Slovak and Hungarian immigrants and their offspring. There was regular work nearby, the brick streets were clean, lawns were mowed and—except for some home-grown hooligans who might beat you up—it was safe. Blacks? Sure, we knew about blacks. They were a growing mass of look-alikes who flooded in after the war to produce fantastic basketball teams at East Tech. They lived on the crumbling rim of the downtown area seemingly content to wallow in their poverty. They were at once out of mind and a dull pain that would surely trouble us more in days to come.

For the Slovaks, the center of life was St. Benedict's Church, just four blocks from my house, the place where education, religion and social life peacefully coexisted. When asked where I lived in Cleveland, the response was never the East Side, never the 29th Ward. I lived in St. Benedict's Parish.

In its neighborhood of modest older homes the new St. Benedict's Church, completed 17 years ago, is something of a shock. It is a Byzantine mammoth, built at a cost of a million dollars by a blue-collar congregation

that raised more than its share of children. As I rang the bell at the par-
ish-house door, I could hear the chimes within, a long, majestic carillon
whose frequent use would drive any but those with a Higher Calling right
up the wall.

The pastor, Father Michael Jasko, hasn't changed much over the years.
He is 65 now, his hair still regally silver, his voice nasal and high. As he
began to talk about his parish, it was obviously painful. The glory that was
St. Benedict's, the optimism that had built a church with a seating capacity
of 1,100, had faded.

"We had 2,000 families and 8,000 souls when you were here," he
began. "Now it's 1,000 families and 3,000 souls, and most of them are
pensioners. We stopped the Canteen [a weekly dance for teen-agers] 10
years ago and hoped to reopen it, but never did. We made $45,000 in a
big year at the bazaar; last year we got $24,000. Novenas and other
night-time services have been stopped. The old ladies of the church were
getting beaten and robbed on their way to early mass, so we stopped those.
Now the first mass is at 7 o'clock, except in the summer when we have the
5:30. Early this year, we're starting a drive to pay off the $95,000 owing
on the church. If we don't do it now, we'll never be able to.

"We had a lot of trouble with school children being beaten, in fact the
entire baseball team and their coaches were overrun by a gang of 30. I
guess you heard about the eighth-grade girl who was raped by four boys
from Audubon." I had, and Audubon, a public junior high school now almost entirely black though surrounded by a predominantly white neighborhood, was the reason given by many people for the old neighborhood's
current state. "We stopped most of the problem by starting school a half
hour before Audubon and letting out a half hour before them. The children can be safely home before they get out.

"The solution," the pastor said more than once, "is more police protection. My duty in these troubled times is to encourage the souls under my
direction that we are in a changing world. I never mention 'black' from the
pulpit, but I always talk about accepting them. No, we haven't visited the
homes of these new people to ask them to join. They know about the
church; they hear about it from their neighbors. We have a few blacks who
attend." In a neighborhood that is 20 per cent black, with the percentage
rising weekly, one Negro family is on the parish rolls.

A recent event had intensified the resentment in the neighborhood: the
bludgeon slaying of Joe Toke, who was killed during a holdup at the service station he had run for more than 40 years. Had his murder been mentioned from the pulpit? "No, my own judgment tells me it was best not to
mention him," and Father Michael hesitated before saying, with no hint
of expression on his face, "I wouldn't want to pinpoint the problem."

St. Benedict's School, which I had attended through the eighth grade, seemed to have changed little—the walls were still painted bland and restful beige and green, and the Blessed Virgin, who had looked out over us from her second-floor pedestal, was still standing firmly on the writhing serpent, though both he and she had been chipped and gouged over the years. But the appearance was deceptive.

While the 1,100 of us in the student body had been stuffed 50 or 60 to a classroom, there were now only 350 students scattered loosely about the school, and precious space was allotted to an audio-visual room and a library. The student body now includes 25 or 30 non-Catholics—I can't remember a single one in my day—and four blacks.

A lunchroom has been built because even those parents who live only a few blocks away won't allow their children to come home at noon. It is considered too dangerous. A thousand lunches are served free each month, and 400 more go at half price. The total price for those who can pay is 20 cents.

Joe Toke's Sunoco station at Buckeye and E. 111th is one you could easily pass by: nothing fancy, no spinning aluminum or Dayglo disks, no posters proclaiming free glasses or soda pop. But for the neighborhood people there was always Joe, eternally growing bald, a taciturn man whose stern look was a veneer over a heart of gold. His hydraulic lift could be used without charge, credit was extended without a raised eyebrow, kids' bicycle tires were cheerfully filled with free air. Joe had been warned that the neighborhood was changing, that five merchants or property owners had been killed during holdups in the last few years. His response was, "Who would want to hurt me? Anyhow, they can take the money, I'll earn some more."

That night two weeks earlier Marcella Toke had supper on the stove in the simple apartment, made uncomfortably warm by an oil burner in the middle of the living room floor. She saw the lights going out in the gas station next door, but began to wonder what had happened when Joe didn't appear. She found her husband in a pool of blood in the station. His eyes were open, and Marcella Toke thought at first that he was looking at her. His tire gauge had deflected a bullet, but his skull had been crushed in a remorseless beating.

"To people around here, Joe was a fixture, the honest businessman who had made it by hard work," his widow said. "We all knew the neighborhood was changing, but then this. . . . I think of leaving the neighborhood now, but where would I go? Everything I know is here. I just want those killers found, and I want them to get their due."

Each month the parishioners at St. Benedict's receive a copy of The Post, a paper put out by the church's Catholic War Veterans. Frank Stipkala, a 38-year-old bachelor, writes many of the stories and editorials, and he is proud to describe himself as a "superhawk and ultraconservative." Campus protest marches, such pop singers as Janis Joplin, new liturgy and liberal Senators of the Kennedy and Church sort have all drawn his stern rebukes. Frank's rhetoric is still hard to take, but his concern for his nationality group and his love for the neighborhood were far more significant in our conversation.

Frank is an efficient man; he had outlined some things he wanted to tell me. A telephone booth on the corner of his street had been damaged so often that it was removed. A mail box had been burglarized on the day Social Security checks were to come. A doctor had installed a peep hole in his door and had gone to irregular office hours to thwart robbers. A mentally retarded boy whose joy was a paper route had to give it up after his collections were stolen and his papers thrown into the street. Somody's Delicatessen closed between 2:30 and 4 each afternoon to avoid harassment from the Audubon students.

"In everything I've told you," he said, "I've not once mentioned race. It isn't race; it's law and order. We Slovaks are too trusting, too honest, too open. There was never trouble here just because blacks moved in. In Murray Hill, the Italians told the blacks they would kill any who dared to move in. In Sowinski Park, the Polish pointed shotguns at them. That is not our way of life, but look what we are reaping now. Many people thought this neighborhood was a fortress, that we would never have trouble, but how we kidded ourselves. The streets are empty because people are afraid to go out and those that must go out are prey.

"We didn't even know the Hungarians in our neighborhood, and we certainly weren't prejudiced against them. Slovaks come from a country that was a collection of small villages; there was no such a thing as national spirit. Here in America, the center was the church, and our people did everything within that church. The Slovaks have been occupied before, by Russians and Germans, by the Hungarians, and now we are being occupied by the robber, the rapist, the murderer. But this is by far harder to live with, the unknowingness of it all. I see two solutions to help the neighborhood; one is very short-term, the other long: Post a policeman every 150 feet to start. Then go to work on the sociological problems like giving these people a better education."

Frank's sister Ethel stopped by, as she often does. She lived on Manor, several blocks away, and had just sold her house at a $4,000 loss. She planned to move to the suburbs with her husband, a teacher, and their children. She flicked off her knitted cap, and—though she has a son ready to graduate from high school—looked like the lovely, shy, dark-haired girl she was 20 years ago. "One of the turning points for me was when I heard people were buying guns. I asked some of the women on the block and found three of them—just like that—who carry guns in their purses.

Imagine, women who have never fired a gun in their lives carry one to go to the Pick 'n' Pay."

My next stop was at Bill's Grocery, the "corner store" for Forest Avenue and the most crowded store I have ever seen. Bill carries thread, dye, fruit, cough syrup, kites, canned goods, boiled ham, hand-dipped ice cream, socks, two brands of prophylactics (lubricated and plain—both good sellers, he admits) and now items required by his new clientele—canned okra and Jiffy corn-meal mix. He has had some call for chitterlings, but can't bring himself to stock them.

Bill Blissman never married, and it became obvious in our conversation that if he had something, someone to go to, he would close up.

Bill smiles a lot these days. He has been fitted with a good set of uppers and it's a good smile, but beneath all that, he is afraid: "I used to stay open until 8 or so, now I close at 6. I keep the door locked most of the day and look through the window to see if I want to let the person in. Three of them drove up in a car the other day, and I was happy I had the door locked." Bill can see out reasonably well, but seeing in through his window and the labyrinth of key chains, suckers, Kits candy, Dark Shadows Bubble Gum and novelties is impossible.

Bill's complaint was familiar. Things were bad before Mayor Stokes, a black, was elected, but since his election, the situation in the neighborhood had quickly become untenable. Stokes is responsible for encouraging blacks to come up from the South and get on Cleveland's welfare and crime rolls. Stokes has allowed a new permissiveness. The blacks are cocky because one of their own is downtown. It doesn't matter that crime has risen in cities with white mayors. In Cleveland, in the old neighborhood, it is largely Stokes's fault.

Bill and members of my own family had trouble remembering people my age who grew up in the neighborhood and were still there. Joe Kolenic, my buddy through St. Benedict's and Cathedral Latin School, had married and lived in the neighborhood until a few years ago, when, like all of our contemporaries who stayed in Cleveland, he joined the migration to the suburbs. Joe and his wife, Shirley, chose a tri-level tract house in Euclid.

We were sitting in their recreation room, where the Kolenics spend most of their time. Its floor is covered with indoor-outdoor carpeting, and there is a huge color television set and black imitation-leather furniture. Joe has gotten just a little pudgy over the years, but as we talked I saw him as a lean and physically mature eighth grader on the St. Benedict's defensive line. He happily admits to being the stereotype young husband. He wants a safe home for his wife and children, one that he is buying, not renting; a steady job; a winning season for the Browns or Indians, and a good local golf course.

Joe, an accountant, was asked in 1967 to trade his white shirt for khaki and go down into the Hough area with his National Guard unit to quell the disturbance. "You remember our football games at Patrick Henry field; that was a nice neighborhood. And there we were with guns in our arms stepping over garbage in the streets, watching 6- and 7-year-old kids running around in the middle of the night. It was a horror show. Our city. I wasn't a racist then and I'm not one now. But that time in Hough leaves its impression. To be honest, I didn't want to face that possibility every day in the neighborhood, so I left. But I'm not against the blacks. Hough taught me they need an education to help them help themselves. Back in the neighborhood we thought they'd never get across 93d or in from Woodland Hills Park. The dam broke there; it can happen anyplace."

William Ternansky has taught at my high school, Cathedral Latin, for 37 years. His remaining hair is now more gray than black, but otherwise he had changed little since I graduated from Latin in 1956. He still wore a nondescript suit, a V-neck sleeveless sweater beneath, and had a bunch of papers clutched to his chest. He smiled when I told him who I was and why I had come. He remembered me and he smiled—and for both I was immediately happy.

"The neighborhood lived by the Christian ethic of love thy neighbor," he began, "and that pales at the beginning of wrongdoing. The neighborhood is a new ghetto of fear. But for now it is a defensive fear, not an antagonistic fear that ethnic kids have, and that is what is so paralyzing. There is nothing to do but hide and shudder and withdraw with this kind of fear."

Rose Hrutkai is a strong-minded, strong-willed woman of Hungarian stock. She once discouraged a potential robber by going after a broom when he advanced toward her. When real estate agents call—they have been plaguing the neighborhood with panicky lines like "Sell while you can still get your money out"—Rose Hrutkai tells them off. Her house, down the street from mine, is in mint condition, a white double-decker with green trim that looks as though it goes through the weekly wash. Rose Hrutkai is boiling mad at what's happening, so angry she's going to stay in the neighborhood.

Rose sat in her living room in a shapeless cotton dress that didn't dare wrinkle. On her carpeted floor were a half dozen smaller rugs that protected her larger one.

"My husband is a maintenance man, and we've scrimped through all these years, raised two daughters, sent them to Catholic schools and paid off the $15,500 the house cost," she said. "That's about all we could get out of it if we sold it, because we would have to give points so the new people could get the down-payment money. I love this neighborhood, my garden; everything I have is here. My husband will be retiring soon, and we can't take on house payments. And what could we get for $15,500? A tarpaper shack, maybe. Every day you hear about a lady having her purse snatched, a house being broken into. It's that rough stuff coming up from the South. They drive up in a fancy car and even steal bags of groceries out of women's hands. It's sad when women have to pin their key inside their dress and put their grocery money in their shoes."

Her daughter, Mrs. Gloria Town, joined the conversation. Girls Gloria's age—middle twenties—were once commonplace on Forest Avenue, living upstairs in their parents' homes. Now they are a rarity. "We just couldn't face $250 a month in house payments," Gloria said. "I didn't want to live here, but listen, my husband isn't a $15,000-a-year man, not a $10,000-a-year man. I work, too. And we barely make the payments on our car and keep eating. We really wonder if we can ever afford kids. It's tough to just make ends meet, and then the neighborhood has to turn into a jungle. I hate to leave the house any more. But who wants to hear the complaints of the little American? The rich have power, the poor get attention. But we got nobody."

Her mother added: "I've got nothing against the colored that are moving in as long as they live the way we do. But so many of them are so lazy. The houses need paint, the lawns need cutting."

There had been peeling paint before and scrubby lawns. But in earlier years that was the extent of the neighborhood's blight—a few unkempt houses for a few years. Now the people of the neighborhood see it going downhill. These houses were built 50 to 75 years ago in the tradition of Middle Europe, with huge, sloping roofs for the mountain snowfalls that would never come to Cleveland. There were a few fine touches: porch columns might have a scroll on top and bottom or a worked portion in the middle. Leaded glass graced living room windows. Not elegant homes, but big, substantial, ready to house families with many children. That was the appeal to people like my parents and those who had settled here directly from the "Old Country." What appeal do they have to the new immigrants, the people who were alternately received and cursed by the neighborhood?

"At our old place down on 81st and Kinsman, I'd get up in the morning and the smoke from the factories would just about make you sick; all I could see out my windows were chimneys and the filth in the air." Mrs. Mary Owing was talking in the simple gray house an aunt and uncle of mine had owned, diagonally across the street from my old home. "Here I walk out on the porch and the air is so fresh, the birds are chirping and I feel like I'm in paradise. They tell me that tree on the front lawn will blossom so pretty in the spring. I can't wait for that. At the old place, all we had to look forward to was the next rotten building being torn down."

For eight years Mary lived with her husband, a mechanic and competition driver of dune buggies, and their four children in a $50-a-month apartment. Rats and roaches were unwelcome but regular visitors. A husky, good-looking woman with a smoky voice and a warm smile, even though two front teeth are missing, Mary went to school in the Kinsman area, dropped out in the 10th grade and was married at 16. She is a neat housekeeper, but on Kinsman there was a constant battle with the black soot that invaded her house daily. On Forest Avenue she enjoys cleaning the house because the environment doesn't despoil her work.

Her husband replanted some burned-out patches of grass late in the summer and nursed them along so carefully that they look better than the rest of the lawn. He wants to replant the entire lawn this spring. Contrary to what the whites on Forest say, Mary Owing doesn't want the black influx and white outflow to continue indefinitely; she wants a racially mixed neighborhood, and she plans to keep her house up. No neighbors have stopped by to welcome the Owings, but some have said hello as they passed. Still others have stared icily at Mary, who enjoys sitting on a kitchen chair on the front porch. A woman a few doors away found her sidewalk cracked—the work of children with hammers—immediately called the police and told them it was the work of the Owing children. As it turned out, it was not, but the woman sold her house and moved in a few weeks. "I don't want them to move out," Mary says, "because most whites do keep up their houses better than blacks, but what can I do? Tell me and I'll do it."

Across the street from Mary Owing, two doors away from Rose Hrutkai, lives Mrs. Lorainne Gibson. She and her husband, a telephone-panel repairman, and their small daughter were the first blacks to move onto this part of Forest Avenue. They lived before on East 90th Street, off Euclid, where the neighborhood scenery included a house of prostitution across the street and flashily dressed pushers selling to shaky young addicts.

Lorainne was folding her baby's diapers in the living room, absentmindedly watching an afternoon soap opera when I called. She opened the door readily after I introduced myself and told her what I was doing. (In white homes I was viewed with suspicion and forced to ask the first few questions through the pane of a storm door. When I was a boy, even the magazine salesmen were invited in to give their pitch before being turned down.) Lorainne was wearing a bright orange pants suit that seemed strange during the day in a Forest Avenue house; cotton dresses and aprons were the usual attire.

"If it does anything, renting down there makes you appreciate having your own home," she said. "I will never have roaches, I will never have rats here. I saw some roaches down at Bill's Grocery the other day, and I don't go there any more. I go up to Stevie's, a black-owned place; it's cleaner."

Her husband was able to secure a minimum-down-payment G.I. loan for their $18,000 two-family house, on which they pay $150 each month. The upstairs apartment brings $100 a month, and Lorainne supplements her husband's earnings by watching the two children of the woman upstairs, who works and receives child-care public assistance. "No two ways about it," Lorainne says, "we don't want this neighborhood all black; we have an investment to protect. But I'd like to see other young black couples, other white couples, move in because sometimes it gets a little boring around here for the housewife. The only thing wrong with the neighborhood is that there's a generation gap. Crime? The crime rate is going down. Mayor Stokes is doing a beautiful job."

Her attitude was typical. Most of the blacks in the neighborhood have come from high-crime areas, and they see their new homes as relatively safe. The older white residents, who remember when a mugging in the neighborhood was unheard of, feel that the area is crime-riddled and dangerous.

"Mostly," Mrs. Gibson said, "the white neighbors have been nice. One lady brought over a pitcher and glasses as a gift. Mrs. Martin showed me how to plant in the back yard. Then the lady next door buried a piece of rail—you know, like from the railroad—in her lawn, which is right by our driveway. Maybe somebody's car from our driveway ran over the grass a couple of times, but I never even saw a tire print. Now some of our friends have done hundreds of dollars of damage to their cars on the rail. That rail would have never happened if a white family had moved in. Listen, I'm more against all the lazy blacks on welfare than you are. I lived with all that down on East 90th."

I found Mrs. Ollie Slay, my father's next-door neighbor, at home on a Saturday morning. She works as a maid in a hotel during the week, and her husband is a carpenter and general handyman. In the Slays' back yard was a large German shepherd on a length of heavy chain. I can't forget his deep and menacing bark and the grating sound of the chain as it was pulled taut by his lunges.

"I didn't know much about this neighborhood, about all the ethnic business," Ollie said after she turned down the Wes Montgomery record on the stereo. "All I wanted was a place I could live and let live. Down at East 100th, where we lived, we were robbed three times. We bought the dog and started looking for a house. Originally I came from a farm in Loui-

siana; no electricity, no indoor plumbing. So this house, this neighborhood
. . . well, I love it, I just love it.

"Everything we have, we worked for," she says. "Scraping together
$1,500 for a down payment was the toughest thing we've ever done. So
maybe blacks are the cause of crime in this area. But it isn't me out there
bopping old ladies over the head. Talk about law and order—yes, sir, I'm
for law and order. You can put me down as in love with the police."

In the City Council elections last year, the people in my old neighborhood did a strange thing. They elected a Republican—a Republican of
Scottish ancestry, at that. Jayne Muir ordinarily could never have been
elected, regardless of her intent and qualifications. But, by marrying a
Ukranian named Zborowsky, she gained a name as politically potent as
Kennedy, Roosevelt or Taft. She is a former social worker whose constituency is distrustful of change and reform. Father Michael, for instance,
says: "She's pushing the black movement too hard. She should listen more
to the people."

In her storefront office on Buckeye Road, the usual complaints are handled by a group of New Frontier-like college students. The water inspector
will be sent out on Friday to see why Mrs. Kovach's bill was so high. Mrs.
Sterpka's petition for a new streetlight where an elderly woman fell and
broke her hip will be forwarded with a properly irate letter to the illumi-
nating company. But Councilwoman Zborowsky wants to do more than
party pols and hacks have done in the past. One morning while puffing her
way through a half pack of Benson and Hedges and self-consciously trying
to rearrange an uncooperative head of hair, she talked about her area.

"The 29th Ward is a ward in transition. That means whites move out,
blacks move in, businesses close and everybody forgets about it until it's a
slum, then Model Cities is supposed to rejuvenate it. We have 40 per cent
black, a lot of ethnics and a few WASP types on the upper edges, where
we touch on Shaker Heights. We have people who are used to taking care
of things by themselves and of living within their own world. My job is to
bring them together for cooperation and to let them know at the same time
they don't have to go inviting each other over for supper. They can still be
private people with their own traditions, but divided like this, they'll be
eaten alive. Crime is up 25 or 30 per cent, and there's no reason why it
won't go higher. Blacks are suffering, too, but they are used to it. The
press on the ethnics is so strong, they want to kid themselves it's going to
be O.K. tomorrow. So they wait and hope. Useless!"

Realizing that one of the irreparable casualties of "transitional neighborhoods" is often the shopping area, Mrs. Zborowsky—in an effort to
head off the problem in her district—has organized the Buckeye Area

(Cleveland) Development Corporation. "Through it we hope to get foundation money, local, state, Federal money for development of the area that is beyond any businessman. There is no developer—as there would be for a suburban shopping center—ready to fly in here and be our angel." She found that of the 186 business locations in the Buckeye-E. 116th Street area, there were only 11 vacancies, and she wants to be sure that the number won't grow quickly.

The development corporation may or may not get off the ground, and Mrs. Zborowsky knows it, so she continues to work on smaller projects. She compiled a list of the more than 30 real-estate companies working in the area and hopes to coerce them into stopping their scare tactics. She has been instrumental in helping streets organize block organizations. Through her prodding, the abandoned house that was the scene of the gang rape has been torn down.

"I have to avoid the expedient, calling names, placing blame, merely getting more police in. That's what I'm pressured to do. Education is an overused word, but that's my job. The old residents of this ward have always relied on private institutions—their families, churches, clubs, lodges. Now they must be taught to report things to the police and not worry that they will in turn be prosecuted. This neighborhood has fantastic shops for ethnic baked goods, meats, renowned restaurants like Settlers Tavern and the Gypsy Cellar; there is something to be preserved. Right now I'm working to have an Outreach Station funded. It would be manned by an off-duty policeman and be a clearing house for complaints, a place where people could have problems taken care of. The reaction? Mixed. I get complaints like 'You mean I get mugged down on East Boulevard and I have to run up to the station on 116th Street to report it?' It's hard to get a new idea across."

For every optimist like Jayne Muir Zborowsky in the neighborhood, there are 10 nay-sayers. There were nay-sayers when I was a boy, but then the problems were cosmic and removed—like a pigheaded haberdasher named Truman or a war in a strange nation called Korea—or local but containable—like an increase in tax assessments or the placement of a stop sign. Then "bitching and moaning" was a part of ethnic life, our variation on "Nobody Knows the Trouble I've Seen."

On my visit I found people in the neighborhood, knowing that they are the forgotten Americans and no longer relishing the fact, doing two things. First, they leave. This is difficult to watch, but who can blame young families who want both good schools and safe streets for their children? The other reaction is frightening. These second- and third-generation Slovaks and Hungarians are digging in, hardening their attitudes because they are tired of being oppressed.

Take, for instance, one of the young policemen in the old neighborhood. He would talk only after I assured him I would not use his name. He admitted he was a typical Cleveland cop, ethnic, bitter and not afraid to say he was afraid. He feels the old neighborhood is so unsafe that he has opted for the suburbs.

"I was off-duty the other day, and I walked into a bar on Buckeye and kiddingly—you know, like Dodge City or something—I said, 'O.K., you guys, all the hardware on the bar.' There were five guys in there. Four pulled out guns. I'm a bigot and I know it, but arming isn't the way. These people are going to get those guns rammed right up their own butts some day.

"Dope is the big problem beneath it all, and blacks who don't have or don't want work. In the old days, a black man couldn't even ride through the neighborhood without it being a big deal. Now they can move freely because blacks live here. The bad element has found a gold mine, and they're going to work it. The worst thing is that nobody's on the street any more. Those that have to go out are prey for the wolves. Half the crime would stop if more people would be out."

The anxiety and fear in the neighborhood have forged one significant group, the Buckeye Neighborhood Nationalities Civic Association. I attended a B.N.N.C.A. meeting one evening at the First Hungarian Lutheran Church. There were 15 or 20 people there, but two of them dominated the proceedings. Ann Ganda, a woman with sharp features and a high, shrill voice talked about the proposed Outreach Center. "Those two colored kids have Legal Aid after they attacked us [there had been a street assault on an unnamed person], and what do we have? I'm in city housing. They demand tile in the kitchens and they get it. Sliding doors and they get it. We have to demand. We don't want an Outreach Center; we're too kind already. We want more police."

John Palasics, a scholarly looking man with a graying tonsure, three-piece suit and a low, calm voice, took me to the back of the room to display a street map another member had drawn. "This is our battle plan," he began slowly. "We want to have each house with a code number so that our police can get to any house in minutes. The city police won't cover us, so we are willing to give of ourselves. Special Police, Inc., has many people who have taken courses at their own expense to learn crime prevention and first aid, and if we can get the support, we'll have them on the street next year.

"I know people are calling us vigilantes," he said, and it was as if a switch was thrown some place inside him. His eyes widened in their red rims, his voice became louder and his right index finger jabbed at the air. "Anything the blacks say against us is out of ignorance. This neighborhood should be preserved as a national historic monument to mark the contribution of the nationalities. Monuments are WASP or black, nothing for us. We don't want our neighborhood liberated as a slum. And we don't want blacks in our group; we are for the preservation of the nationality way of life."

Words like "liberated" and "slum" came out of his mouth as if he had bitten down on some bitter fruit. "Listen, we know things the F.B.I. doesn't even know yet. When the blacks control this area," he said, sweeping his hand, now trembling, over the map, "they will put up roadblocks to keep the whites out of downtown. We know about all this. A black boy came up to me on the street the other day and said, 'We gonna keel you, whi' man, so get yo'——out NOW.' Let the Anglo-Saxons turn their houses over to them. We demand a right of self-determination."

They are calling my neighborhood transitional, and it is not much fun to go home again. The old formula just doesn't seem to work any more, and there are few people left who want to move along positive lines. So the ethnics continue to abandon the neighborhood, each saying he hates to go and he'll hate to come back in five or ten years when, as many of them say, it will be another Hough. Most major cities must have neighborhoods like it, neighborhoods that are being left to new immigrants who want to believe they have moved to Nirvana.

On a Monday morning I prepared for the trip back to New York, feeling confused and depressed at what I had found. As I walked my dog along Forest Avenue, he did his duty on the lawn of the new black family next door. I moved on, deep in contemplation. A few minutes later, John Slay walked up and, after saying good morning, hesitated. I expected a final plea, a demonstration that the black man wanted to do right by the neighborhood.

All that John Slay asked was, please, and don't take offense, clean off the lawn.

2

The White Niggers of Newark

DAVID K. SHIPLER

On the other side of the city, far from the rotting row houses of the black ghetto with its dropouts and junkies, safe in the sanctuary of the neat, white, working-class neighborhood, there is a grimy poolroom that is lit too brightly. The white kids with long, matted hair squint as they drift in from the night, forming knots around the two ratty little pool tables, their shrill laughter spilling out from under the scalding fluorescent lights onto darkened Bloomfield Avenue. Dropouts. A few junkies. Most are in dungarees, some in Levi jackets, as if it were a uniform. Only two girls are in the crowd, both expertly shooting pool, chewing gum seriously, tough girls in tight sweaters. On the sidewalk, kids flick glowing cigarette butts into the gutter as they lean against the poolroom's two huge storefront windows where the faded red letters from another time can still be seen spelling, "J & J Confectionery." . . .

These kids are part of a dwindling white minority in Newark, New Jersey, where blacks are 54 per cent and Puerto Ricans 13 per cent of the 382,000 people and where, after long decades of powerlessness, blacks

Source: David K. Shipler, "The White Niggers of Newark," *Harper's Magazine* (August 1972). Copyright © 1972 by Harper's Magazine. Reprinted by special permission.

have taken political control. The result has been a new set of angry lines between whites and blacks, drawn as never before in an American city. Black power has been converted into reality with such headiness, and the outside white establishment has applauded the turnabout so vigorously, that many whites in Newark have been left with a corrosive sense of invisibility. Colleges that send recruiters to Newark do so in search of blacks, not working-class whites. Federal programs designed to help youngsters get jobs, keep them off drugs, provide them with recreation, and improve their schooling are aimed at blacks, staffed by blacks, and located in black neighborhoods. They do not reach the white kids who hang out at the J & J Confectionery.

But simple neglect fails to explain completely the difficulties of Newark's poor and working-class whites, just as it never fully summed up the black experience in America. The whites, especially the Italians, are deeply distrusted by many blacks who have attained power, including the city's first black mayor, Kenneth A. Gibson, who sees himself still struggling against the organized crime, corruption, and white racism that gripped the city government under his predecessor, Hugh J. Addonizio. Just before the 1970 election, Addonizio was indicted on sixty-four counts of extortion and conspiracy, along with several city councilmen, former public works directors, and reputed Mafia figures. The indictment, which led to a ten-year federal prison sentence for Addonizio and contributed to his defeat by Gibson, also contaminated all the city's Italians, even those who were disgusted by the corruption, for it reinforced—both to the blacks and to outsiders—a sinister stereotype.

Now, after all the shifts of power, going to Newark is like stepping into a hall of mirrors where familiar images are inverted and twisted into remarkable, confusing shapes that destroy any sense of equilibrium. The familiar American patterns of racism and exploitation dissolve into a mad array of reversals and contradictions. . . .

"We're the niggers now, that's what's happened," said Stephen N. Adubato. "It just is who's on top. The group that's second's gonna catch shit —they're gonna be niggers. This is what this country's really all about." Adubato hunched intently over his desk. "The blacks aren't so sophisticated with their racism. They're just learning what power is about, what America's about. They're more overt, and so are we—we're not sophisticated about our racism as Italians. We're amateurs too." Once a schoolteacher, Adubato is emerging as a political leader in Newark's North Ward, the stronghold of the city's remaining working-class Italian-Americans, who make up most of the city's white population. He spent his younger years fighting for the rights of blacks, and he campaigned for Gibson. But as the power of the blacks grew in the city, and as he discovered that nobody was trying to help the Italians, he turned his attention to his own people. He left teaching and won election as Democratic leader in the North Ward.

"Let me give you this analogy," he said. "I see the Italian community in Newark and the black community in Newark face to face, really in a crowd, lined up in a crowd. And the pressure, the momentum, is with the blacks, and they're pushing us backward, and we're not acting like other whites, 'cause we're fighting back, you know, clawing and punching and kicking in the balls and all the rest. But if you reach up and look beyond that line, that black line, you'll see all of the white liberals and do-gooders and the people who really won't meet the problem, pushing, encouraging, you know, and putting on more pressure. It's a nice picture, you can almost see it. D'ya see it?" He laughed.

"And of course we look bad because we're cursin' and swearin', and we say 'nigger' all the time, and the people in the back always said 'Negro' when that was right and now 'black.' They talk the right way, and they're actually assisting. Someone's got to be hurt, that's what I hear, someone's got to be hurt." . . .

At Barringer high school, white teenagers—who make up about one-fourth of the student body—find themselves engulfed by a whirlwind of blackness: black history, black literature, black culture, black pride, all the components of self-assertion and identity that have been hailed as healthy for a people enslaved and beaten down and brutalized over the centuries. It is not so healthy for the whites. Every morning, "Swahili music" is played over the school's public address system, and some white students find it as offensive and threatening as blacks would find "Dixie." The day after the Board of Education voted to hang the black, red, and green flag of black liberation in every classroom with a majority of black students (a move ultimately barred by the courts), someone got on the PA system and said, "Brothers be cool, sisters be sweet, and others—well, just others."

Whites stay out of the cafeteria, which is black turf; they don't go to basketball games, since the team is black. And just as blacks used to avoid dances at school in Adubato's day, now whites avoid them, taking the cue from the dance posters in the hallways with pictures of black couples cut out of black magazines. "I never saw a sign in the school of a social event that applied to me," said Stephen Mustacchio, an eighteen-year-old senior. "The same thing with the school chorus: 'Brothers and sisters, if you want to find yourself, join the chorus.' I mean, you know, the white people can't join the chorus if they want to?" One boy ventured into a college recruiter's meeting where it had been announced, as usual, that "a representative will be here today to recruit black and Puerto Rican students," and found talk only of black clubs and black studies, "like I didn't belong there," he said. He didn't apply.

In English class, "you have to read black literature," Steve said. "They never give you any white literature to read. You have to read *Black Voices,* there's a book out called *Black Voices,* then we had to read Malcolm X, then there's another one about a black child. We don't have to read anything about a white person."

Most of the teachers at Barringer are white, but they are fearful of the black students declaring them "insensitive," which Adubato noted means insensitive not to Italians or to whites—just to blacks.

The sense of worthlessness and inferiority that has so long afflicted blacks now seems to threaten these white youngsters, many of whom are struggling to get to college, something their parents could not do. They and their parents see themselves in double jeopardy, a minority in their own city, yet too urban and too Italian to be part of the American mainstream, which they characterize as suburban and WASP.

"When you really feel this is like when you get into college," said Lucille Poet, a bright-eyed college sophomore whose father is a foreman in a factory. "You can't get a scholarship because you're not quite poor enough —well, really, you're not black. And you get into college and they look at you, you come from Newark, and you're caught in the middle: you're not rich enough to be really a white person, but you're not poor enough to be a colored person."

When she finished, a roomful of North Ward kids let the silence hang for a long moment.

But the kids fail to see the parallels between their experience and the complaints of blacks about predominantly white schools where no black literature is read and no blacks appear as characters in American history. When the similarity was suggested, Lucille's brother Maurice snapped, "Why should that affect us?" And Steve Mustacchio explained, "When I reached high school my whole attitude changed toward them, 'cause I wasn't really in too much contact with them. I went to a private white grammar school, I hardly spoke about them or anything, but when I got to high school, I had to go to school with them, I grew to hate them. When I got to school, and I saw who they were, I came to hate them."

In their candor, the Barringer kids contrast sharply with another group of white Newark teenagers, who go to Vailsburg High School, the last high school in the city in which whites still constitute the majority, and only 30 per cent of the students are black. Sitting in a circle one evening on the floor of a room belonging to a young divinity student who is trying to help organize the white community, about a dozen white Vailsburg students were asked if they had black friends. "Of course!" they shouted in an annoyed chorus. Pressed for specifics, the kids got tense. Only one girl could name a friend who was black, and her friend went to another school.

The Vailsburg kids have the luxury of fighting very hard to be, or at least to appear, open-minded. The same is often true of North Ward youngsters who have gone to mostly white private high schools. Everyone in that room could list clear differences between his own and his parents' attitudes toward blacks. Always the parents were bigots or racists.

By contrast, the Barringer teenagers generally agree with their parents' anti-black views, and Steve Mustacchio even disputes his mother's liberal attitude that "I work with them and I get along with them." "She works in a candy factory with the older type of people," Steve said. "She don't have to put up with everything." . . .

"It's the same way as white pride has gotten bad," said Frank Don-Diego, who grew up in Newark and now goes to college at Rutgers. "The blacks have gotten their pride, and it started in the beginning really beautiful, but now they've gone into the same white hangups; pride has become a superiority trip." . . .

Even though most teachers, policemen, and firemen are still white, the alleged preference of the city's institutions for blacks is an emotional, hate-filled topic of conversation at the Italian social clubs in the North Ward, where men gather in the evenings to watch ball games on television or shoot pool or drink or play cards or eat huge meals they cook themselves in ancient kitchens laden with enormous pots and greasy stoves. The rhetoric swirls back and forth between fact and myth. . . . "There is no real concept of brotherhood in this city," [Jim Cundari, a twenty-seven-year-old lawyer] said. "We all have our own agendas, for the simple reason that we all have such real problems. The consciousness of who you are and what you are is so rampant in the city, as soon as something becomes identified as yours, that's it. There's no one going into an Italian barbershop and trying to challenge whether they'll cut a black man's hair. There's no one trying to implement busing to bring whites and blacks into closer community. It just doesn't work that way. No one wants it. In a city like this, people would be content with separate but equal facilities, and no one would challenge it."

Newark may be the real truth about America, the nation's subconscious finally stripped of its rationalizations and platitudes. The city wallows in the swath of stinking factories that belch filth from the Jersey flats into the shadow of the Statue of Liberty. It has also tarnished the other symbols of America by making hatred look like honesty, by making old dreams laughable.

3

Harlem's State of Mind

ROSA GUY

"Anyone with half an eye can see that Harlem is dying. Ain't nobody around anymore. All those who could, have moved. Only ones left is those who can't go nowhere." I look around the once impressive little bar. Quartets and small string groups once gigged here on weekends, packing in people from the streets who dug progressive jazz. Now the place seems dingy, hardly able to hold its own. More whisky is served in false-bottom glasses for less money to attract customers, the leather on the seats of the booths is badly worn and even more badly repaired. The owner, an old friend, is not bitter, merely assesses the situation: "Everywhere you look you see boarded-up buildings. People gone. And those left don't drink whisky. They on drugs." . . .

The Kerner Report states: "White institutions created the ghetto, white society condones it." And so, the more Harlem changes, the more Harlem remains the same. Contrary to the belief that the riots of the sixties ran whites out of Harlem, whites are more firmly entrenched than ever. If white landlords have abandoned buildings all over Harlem, it is still the

Source: Rosa Guy, "Black Perspective: On Harlem's State of Mind," *New York Times Magazine*, 16 April 1972. © 1972 by The New York Times Company. Reprinted by permission.

white landlords who are profiting from the new middle-class housing complexes built to accommodate the rising middle class of Harlem. White butchers still sell fourth-grade meat for above-first-grade prices; if the butcher shops are fewer, it is because they have bowed to the white-controlled grocery chain stores which are now everywhere in Harlem. Small black businesses have cropped up all over Harlem. But big businesses are still in the hands of whites: furniture stores, where the poor buy on credit and never finish paying; jewelry stores; shoe stores; theaters; bars, and the big department stores and food centers along 125th Street, Harlem's main artery. If the riots of the sixties changed anything, it was merely to get a few blacks into positions as managers, with whites still quietly hovering in the background.

There is a trend to move away from Harlem, particularly in the lower-income groups. . . .

One of the obvious reasons for leaving is the crumbling buildings, most of them dating from before the turn of the century. And the poor worker cannot afford the new high-rise buildings. One woman I interviewed told me: "I been so used to ice in the faucets and 'air-conditioned' windows in the winter time, I been inhaling so much plaster from these broken-down walls, that I've adapted. I know decent living will kill me, but the minute I can, I'm clearing out."

Another reason is that many of the manufacturing industries that employ unskilled labor are moving into the suburbs and to Puerto Rico. The poor worker must follow or be forced to accept welfare.

Schools are, of course, another reason. Here again, the poor worker and the welfare mother are anxious to get their children out of the grip of the decaying school system before they are of school age, or at least before they get into their teens: "When they get in their teens, they break out like measles."

Another big problem is "crime in the streets." I teach creative writing to fourth and sixth graders, and I asked them the other day to write about their neighborhood. One 11-year-old wrote: "Living in my neighborhood is like living in a bad dream." And another: "My neighborhood is an ordinary neighborhood. It's very typical. In my neighborhood you have typical things like gangs, robbery, murder and other things. . . ." But most of them wrote about heroin. They cannot help being affected by the number of young boys and men nodding along the streets. Beautiful children play around the addicts, adults avert their eyes, policemen walk by with indifference. Everyone is aware that when their "fix" wears off, these men— and women—will stalk the streets like zombies doing the bidding of "the Man."

While junkies stand around nodding, their minds seem to record what matters to them: They know when someone leaves his home—that's the time to burglarize; when someone buys an extra package—that must be his payday, so he's worth mugging; when a relief recipient receives a check or an older person his Social Security benefits. The older person lives in terror more than anyone else. He hates to brave the streets, not knowing what might happen. But it is more than the streets. One retired man told me: "I'm not afraid of the streets, it's going into the house. They run in behind you, they hide behind the steps, they put a knife at your throat. They got me three times in three months." There are certain houses that mailmen refuse to enter, and the people must go to the post office for their mail. One woman, after picking up her welfare check, was mugged on her way home, and when she did get home, she found her apartment had been burglarized. Evening time used to be swinging time in the streets of Harlem. But today, from the Central Park side of 110th Street up to 145th Street—with the possible exception of 125th Street and a few bar areas—the streets are left to the zombies and the cops.

Most blacks believe that the reason drugs found their way into Harlem was a deliberate plan of genocide—that whites want to exterminate blacks. "They get to the kids and the kids get to us and that's the end of their black problem." If this *was* the plan, it certainly backfired, because the white kids got hooked as well. "But even at that, they keep the good drugs and give us the junk," a journalist said, referring to an article by a white student in Forest Hills who wrote about black youths coming to Forest Hills to buy better drugs.

Another important reason for blacks wanting to leave Harlem is the role of the police in perpetuating crime. "The only one surprised by that Knapp Commission testimony was Mr. Knapp himself. Any 5-year-old could have told him that the biggest crooks in the city is the police," says one resident, Mrs. Brown, the mother of five boys, all on drugs. She doesn't want to leave Harlem, though. What can happen here can happen anywhere. "It ain't the people. It's the law." Mrs. Brown has a great sense of humor and laughs at stories that would make other mothers cry. "They sell dope right across the street from me. Everybody knows it. Traffic around here is thicker than on Times Square. And cops going in all the time to get theirs. First time I saw it, my oldest son showed me." Mrs. Brown has been living in the same house for more than 20 years. This happened when her son was 14. "Before then, I used to always try to get my kids to respect the law. But they don't let you. Here comes this car. Pulls up right in front of the house. A black cop and a white cop is inside. And wouldn't you know it, it's the black cop that goes in the house and comes out with a fist full of money. He ain't even have the decency to hide it. I was cussing mad. I didn't know what to say. Then I tell him [her son], 'Now ain't that just downright dishonest?' " Mrs. Brown laughs. "Then I really felt like cussing because that sounded so weak."

Another mother spoke of how a policeman picked up her 12-year-old son for buying wine. The policeman brought him home and told her to be sure that he was in court the next morning to testify against the liquor-store owner. "I told him, sure. And I should've known. The next day my son comes back home and told me that the cop promised him $15 if he would forget the whole thing. He never gave the kid a dime. Then about a week later, my son tells me he's going to the precinct to ask that cop for his money. I told him, 'Fool, don't you know that cop will shoot you and swear that you was reaching for a weapon?' Yes, honey, when I was little, they used to shoot you and say you wouldn't stop running. Today they shoot you and say you was reaching."

Criminal acts against the innocent by policemen seem to be a way of life in the inner cities. And it is not just graft, the sale of drugs or wanton shooting. While visiting a fellow writer in a mixed Spanish-black neighborhood recently, I saw a police car pull up and two white policemen get out to enter the basement of the brownstone building next door. "Yeah," my friend said when I mentioned it to him. "They arrested an old Puerto Rican guy about two weeks ago, and they've been coming back ever since. Sometimes two cars at a time." He deliberately waited for me to ask why, before saying, "The man left his 11-year-old daughter behind." Neighbors were standing at windows and stoops all around looking toward that building. Wasn't anyone going to do something? "Look," he said. "Those cats leave their cars and hitch up that big gun bulge on their hips. They run down into that apartment, they stay about one-half hour. They come out and hitch that bulge again before they get in their cars. They know as long as they hitch that bulge they got us. Those cats are *serious* about their law-and-order thing." . . .

Speaking with a group of men at a bar near The Amsterdam News offices, I was led outside by some of them. "Now show me," one thick-chested man bellowed loud enough to flicker the eyes of the junkies nodding on that corner, "just show me one of these kids who make a million dollars off stuff. Not one. And none of the slick pushers riding their Cadillac cars around here neither. I'll tell you where to find them. Up there in Government, that's where. Or else hiding out in Forest Hills. Talking about they don't want poor folks living in Forest Hills because of crime. *They* the criminals!"

"Yeah, they the criminals," his friend agreed. "Right there in Forest Hills. That's why their kids are on dope. Because they know how criminal their parents are. Their children's on dope and they stay quiet about it. They'll see all of their kids dead before they do without their diamonds and mink." . . .

"Look," one young dancer said, "the man that sells us rotten meat, the cop that's on the take, the racketeer that sells us junk, the landlord who exploits us, all take our money and run to hide in Forest Hills. They think our money makes them untouchable. Well, I've got news for them." Even more depressing than this general hostility is that blacks feel there is a pattern of genocide and that *all* whites, not only the "silent majority," give their silent endorsement. . . .

The lack of power is frustrating to every group I spoke to, but most frustrating of all to the young militants. I am talking here mainly about the poor young dropouts who came out of the harsh realities of the crumbling cities but did not succumb to the drug culture. Those I spoke to were bright. They had still been very young when Malcolm X was killed, when Martin Luther King was killed and when white liberals copped out after the call for Black Power. They came into maturity with the jailings of Huey Newton, Bobby Seale and Angela Davis, and they reached a fuller maturity with the killing of George Jackson and the massacre at Attica. These young militants have no faith in whites; they believe they are marked for genocide. Malcolm X and George Jackson are their heroes, because "they were dropouts who went through the fire and came out brilliant." They have no faith in government, less even in black politicians because "if they black and they politicians, then they tools of the Establishment." When asked about Congressman Charles Rangel, they talk about press publicity over the cost of Rangel's Harlem home. "It just shows that he is like white folks. All he want is money and anybody who just want money can't work for black folks because black folks ain't got none." . . .

Very typical of Harlem's attitude is that of Lewis Micheaux, who was the proprietor of the oldest and largest bookstore in Harlem. The store was razed to make way for the New York State Office Building, but it is still a neighborhood institution at its temporary location on 125th Street near Lenox Avenue. Mr. Micheaux has seen every movement around Harlem, from the Garvey movement to the Black Panthers. And he agrees: "Power is the thing. They do everything they want with us because they have power and we don't. The trouble is, the black man is too honest. Never mind all this talk about crime. Everybody know the white man is the criminal. The white man know it! These young punks around here stealing and carrying on, they victims. We are the victims of the victims. Just look out on the street. See cops giving out parking tickets like tickets going out of style. And all the while a pusher leaning up against him and he pretend he don't see. That's power! He better not see!"

4

The "Rat Packs" of New York

SHANE STEVENS

The air was quiet as the couple walked westward along 110th Street, at Central Park's northern end. People sat noiselessly on benches set against the park's low stone wall, some talking, others apparently dozing. A radio blared music from a stoop across the street, while a little girl moved rhythmically on the sidewalk. Down the block, two men were washing a car.

Steven Schleifer and his companion might have felt a bit apprehensive. They were walking on the cutting edge of Harlem, that invisible line that changes its name from 110th Street to Central Park North to Cathedral Parkway as it slashes west to Broadway and the white enclaves around Columbia University. Yet the night was young, and at 7 o'clock there was still light in the western sky. And people around.

Steven fingered the yarmulke in his pocket. An Orthodox Jew, he was supposed to be wearing the symbol of his orthodoxy on this holiday— Shemini Atsereth, a celebration immediately following Succoth. But to-night he had removed the skullcap while still on Fifth Avenue. He had heard stories of assaults on Jews in the area. And his own younger

Source: Shane Stevens, "The 'Rat Packs' of New York," *New York Times Maga-zine*, 28 November 1971. © 1971 by the New York Times Company. Reprinted by permission.

brother, wearing a yarmulke, had been beaten and verbally abused just the year before.

A taxi slowed ahead of them. Riding in a public conveyance was forbidden in the Orthodox observance of such holidays, so he couldn't even take the 110th Street crosstown bus. To pass the time on their walk, Steven and his companion, Debbie Tannebaum, a fellow medical student, talked of their studies at Mt. Sinai School of Medicine. Steven, at 21, was in his first year. Though his parents had tried to talk him out of going to Mt. Sinai because it was "in a dangerous area," he liked the school and liked living on West 114th Street by Columbia University and Riverside Drive. He was, it seemed, finally in med school; he was going to be married in a few months, and he was now going home to relax after a hard day. As he walked toward the junction of Central Park West and Eighth Avenue at Frederick Douglass Circle, with the sounds and smells of two gas stations exploding upon his consciousness, Steven's prospects in life could not have seemed too bad to him—so long as his luck held out.

"Gimme a quarter, man."

Steven didn't notice the youths until they were just about on top of him. Lost in talk and thought, less than 50 feet from the corner, in a bus stop where nobody waited, across the street from clusters of unseeing people involved in their own activities, Steven Schleifer's luck ran out.

"Gimme a quarter, man."

One of them wore a chino jacket with a big J running up the back. A second had on a jacket with a corduroy collar. Someone's face had a white bandage plastered on the forehead. And one of them wore his hair braided, much like little girls do it.

"Give us some money, you mother————."

Steven didn't reply. There was nothing to say. He had no money on him, not a cent, nothing. He was an Orthodox Jew and was observing another holiday rule of not carrying any money.

"Where you got it, man?"

Steven kept on walking, Debbie by his side.

"This boy don't talk."

"Maybe he talk now."

"Why don't you shoot him, man?"

"Shoot him, shoot him, shoot him!"

The zip gun was clumsy, homemade. Debbie saw it. She screamed.

"No!"

"Shoot him!"

BANG.

As Steven Schleifer slumped to the ground, Lieut. James Motherway sat in an unmarked police car with Patrolman Dominick Cammarata, who was just pulling away from the curb diagonally across the wide thoroughfare. They were working the night shift out of the Taxi-Truck Surveillance Unit. Hearing the shot, Cammarata drove across the intersection into the bus stop. While he ran after the youths, all of whom had scrambled eastward along the park's edge, Motherway bent over Steven.

"Are you shot?"

"I don't know. I think I'm paralyzed."

Feeling for the wound, Motherway found it on the upper back near the spine. It was serious.

"Lay there, and don't move."

He turned to the gathering crowd, several of whom were trying to comfort Steven's hysterical companion. "Somebody call an ambulance."

Patrolman Cammarata, up the block, hailed a passing Volkswagen and the driver sped into the Seventh Avenue park entrance after the fleeing youths. Several of them had jumped over the wall. Motherway, now running up the block, jumped over the wall in pursuit. On the path running parallel to the sidewalk he collared two of the youths, while Cammarata captured another two. A quick search turned up a zip gun and knife, police later said. Motherway held the four as Cammarata continued his search. A few moments later he found another youth whom a passerby identified as one of those in flight.

All the youths lived in the neighborhood and were high school or junior high students. A few of them were identified by a young girl as the boys who had robbed her at gunpoint earlier in the day. A few had juvenile records. Two were 16 years old and the next day were arraigned in Manhattan Criminal Court on charges of attempted murder and robbery. The others—ages 13, 14 and 15, all legally juveniles—were charged with juvenile delinquency.

Steven was taken to Metropolitan Hospital where he underwent surgery to remove the bullet from his back. At the request of Mt. Sinai officials, he was later transferred to that hospital's famed Klingenstein Pavilion.

His luck had not failed him completely. As of Oct. 10 there had been 81 murders this year in Harlem's 28th Precinct, which encompasses the Central Park North area. Steven Schleifer was not to be the 82d. He survived.

The big days of the big fighting gangs are over. Gone are the glories of such adolescent armies as the Egyptian Kings, the Golden Warriors and the Stompers; each with its many dozens—in some spectacular instances, hundreds—of fighters (leg men), spies (shadows), camp followers (debs) and untouchables (coolies); each with its rigid organizational structure of president, vice president, war counselor and weapons commander; each with its own territory (turf), rules (sets) and dress (vines); and finally, each with its own reasons for fighting (bopping) and killing (wasting). What has taken their place may not be any better.

The big gangs grew out of social fragmentation following World War II. Springing up in the late nineteen-forties, they flourished in the early fifties, capturing the public imagination and winning attention in the media. Their successive dynasties, reigning until the mid-sixties, achieved enough success to have this period regarded as the Consciousness I phase of urban juvenile delinquency.

Con II began emerging in the mid-sixties as hard drugs increasingly decimated the gang ranks. Where drugs appear, organization disappears. Increasing, too, was the availability of cheap handguns, homemade and foreign. Three youths could now do more damage to an enemy than a whole gang could heretofore. Accordingly, gangs decreased to groups, territory from a block to a candy store, or pool hall, or a playground. Instead of "bopping," there was "japping." Sometimes by car, often by dark, the "jap," a sneak attack—whether with a gun, knife or even dynamite— would be swift and deadly. If the gang era was a time of pitched battles, the group age featured squads hunting for specific enemies.

We are now in the Consciousness III stage of urban juvenile delinquency. Its philosophy is money, its geography is anywhere, its enemy is— you. It "rips off" (steals), "bangs over" (assaults), "blows away" (kills). Its members sometimes kill when provoked, and sometimes kill when unprovoked.

The old gangs and groups, for all their murderous fury, fought mostly among themselves. While race (or nationality) was often involved, it was a *de facto* racism brought about by the neighborhood boundaries. The struggle was localized and though money was often an issue, it was "revolving" money, neighborhood money stolen or extorted and kept in local circulation.

By the start of the seventies, the country's racial rupture and economic inequalities had filtered through to consciousness in the minds of the youthful poor. Black Power—and the White Power backlash, especially among the frightened poor whites in the cities—set color as the determinant of one's enemies. The depressed economy meant even less money in the slums, and the young, as always, were the first to feel the crunch. Spending money had to be got from outside, and so the whole city became the arena. Rip offs were to be done anywhere, to anybody—preferably to a member of another race, religion, nationality or culture, but basically anyone with money. Violence became an accident of time and place.

The phenomenon is now seemingly endemic to large cities. In New York, as might be expected, it involves predominantly those youths who have the least opportunity and the most grievances—largely, but far from exclusively, black and Spanish-speaking residents. While the gangs and groups of the past fed on their own, today's rat packs, formed along racial lines—all white or Puerto Rican or black—feed on everybody else. For them, the city is one big cheese wheel.

Jumper is 16 and very cool. He has three friends he hangs around with. They're cool too. Johnny Apartment is 15, Wolfie and Chester are 14. They all go to the same junior high school in Central Harlem where they live. They like to play cards on a stoop, or maybe drink a little wine in a basement. Sometimes they go to the park with a girl or to throw a ball around. Most times they just hang out.

Sometimes they go downtown. "Just funnin' around, you know, man." A free ride on the subway and they're at a carnival. Times Square, Penn Station, Grand Central, East Side, West Side, all around the town— downtown, where the action is. They look and listen, watch and wait. Sometimes they pounce.

"Naw, we don't have no trouble with whites 'cause we don't have nothin' to do with them."

Wolfie laughs. "Yeah, that's right. 'Cept when we rip off something."

To get money to survive, Jumper and Johnny Apartment and Wolfie and Chester (their names and certain other data have been changed as part of the terms of their cooperation) might rip off a stray white on a side street, or in Central Park, or even on a subway platform. A purse or hand-bag, a shoulder bag, a wallet or billfold, whatever they can get away with fast.

"You ask me why. You must be crazy to ask me that. We need money and white means money. That's it." No pretense at any racism here. Just an economic fact of life.

Sometimes assault is involved. If they hurt the victim that's his grief. Or hers. But they're not looking to hurt anybody: "We ain't into the kill thing. Anybody on that junk is workin' out of a fruit and nuts bag. We just want the money, like anybody else."

Just business as usual. But what about emotion? No hate there?

Johnny Apartment talks in a whisper, low and savage: "Hate? You wanna talk hate? Listen, Jim, I'll talk hate to you. I'm living with rats, man. Now you know and I know why I'm living like that; 'cause the white man put me there, and 'cause the white man keep me there."

"Say something slick for the Man."

"You wanna talk hate, I'll tell you somethin' about hate, Jim. The best way to hate whitey is to hate him before you born. That way you got a jump on the game."

"Dig it."

"Am I jiving on you?"

"Hey man, are we live or on tape?"

Jumper and the others don't think of themselves as a gang. They don't have any turf to protect, they have the whole city. And they don't need to fight other boys to prove their manhood. Quite the opposite: "Any man feeds off his own ain't got it together. He ain't behind it all." If they're not a gang they're not even a group. They have no special meeting place, no store, or club, or playground. No friends to defend, or enemies to defeat. No power and no feeling for power. They're floaters, here today, there tomorrow. Moving easy, sometimes on the spur of the moment, sometimes meeting with other strays for a day or a night. No pattern, moving haphazardly, perhaps meeting a white somewhere by chance and pulling a rip off if the circumstances are right.

What kind of life is this for a 14-year-old like Wolfie?

"Man, I been on the outlaw trail most all my life. Can't help it. What else you got for me?" How about school, maybe getting an education? "The best thing I like about school is after school." What about the real world out there? "The only real world is what I got in my hand. Everything else is make up."

Chester is 14 and he feels the same way. "The human race stinks, man. I'm glad I ain't in it."

But, of course, he *is* in it. And so are all of them, just as much involved with life as anybody else. Wolfie lives with his married sister, who is a nurse. Parents both dead, killed in a car crash when he was 6. Chester's mother, separated from his father, is on welfare and takes care of five younger children besides Chester. Only three years in New York, Chester's family came north from Louisiana. Both Wolfie and Chester have been left alone for much of their lives, and both are footloose.

Jumper's people fight a lot. His father, sick from some debilitating disease, drinks too much and his mother is always tired from her night job as a cleaning woman in a government building. He has an older brother who is doing time in a California state penitentiary. Jumper doesn't spend much time at home, using it mostly just for sleeping. He likes to keep moving and gets nervous when confined in any way.

Johnny Apartment has nobody. Mother dead, father unknown. A retarded sister is in a state institution. There might be other sisters he doesn't talk about. He was once in a city shelter and "a few times" in a detention facility. He sleeps in parked or abandoned cars, in basements or in friends' homes. For purposes of school, he is listed as living with a kindly building superintendent. He does have a small room there but doesn't often use it because the super is always drunk and there are too many rats.

This kind of existence is not untypical of the life style of many slum youth. For boys like these, life has little meaning and holds less promise. There is no sense of planning, no continuity. Talent and brains may well be there, but lack of opportunity and expression soon stifle ambition. Disorder becomes the rule.

If they're not interested in any kind of organization, Jumper and the others are even less interested in politics or the black struggle. They laugh at the line, "Black Power is prune juice." They have no heroes except Malcolm X. "He was the baddest," they say in admiration. For them, there is no race struggle because the white man already has the game. Their job is to survive in a rip-off world they didn't make. If they cross the police or the courts they'll use their mother wit to get by.

"Man, it took me a long time to see that with the mother—— whites the whole thing is honesty. Once you can fake that, you got it made with them."

In one respect, they are the least racist of all. They don't like any leaders and don't trust any leaders, in or out of Harlem. They instinctively suspect anybody—white or black—who would lead them, or "save" them, or even tell them what is right and wrong with them. All black leaders are put down the same way: "They all eat watermelon." About the only thing that is not scorned is the hustle for the dollar.

"What you got, man?"

"I'm tapped, man."

"Me too."

Jumper is 5 feet 11, medium frame. There's a hardness to him. Maybe he doesn't know all the angles, maybe he won't be around long enough to learn them, but he's playing with what he's got. Trying to survive.

"Let's take a walk 'round the park down there."

Through the gate before anyone spots them and down the stairs two at a time. Subway down to 59th Street. People look warily at the four of them, turn quickly away. They all wear the regulation uniform. White high-top Keds, blue jeans, denim jackets cut Western-style, sweat shirts or T-shirts underneath. Jumper and Wolfie have on their blue porkpie hats, soft, the brim pushed up all around. Johnny Apartment wears a racing cap, brown suede. Smooth.

Into the park by the pond, throwing pebbles at the ducks, badmouthing a few obvious homosexuals. Over to the zoo to look at the lions. "Man, I wouldn't mess with that mother. Lookit them feet he got."

"Them's paws he got on."

"Mean mothers whatever they is."

Deeper into the park. It's early still, people walking, sitting. Past the statues and down to the lake with the rowboats. Chester urinates on the grass.

"*Damn,* I just love this park. I love it 'cause the trees are close together and the people far 'part."

"Ain't far 'part enough for me."

" 'Special when you got some action, ain't that right, man?"

"Only action he get is with his hand."

"What you talkin' about, man? I got chicks comin' outta my ear."

Jumper laughs. "Listen to this stud. And he ain't even half the man his mama is."

"Yeah, but his mama just nigger-struck is what she is."

Wolfie doesn't like that. "You sounding me, man?"

"He just runnin' his tongue, man."

"Yeah, stay loose, man."

A business suit walks by, paunchy, balding. Jumper goes up to him. "Hey, man, front me a quarter." The suit looks at him, sees the others. His right hand slips into his jacket.

In three hours of clowning around, knifing trees, verbally abusing some girls and stealing a radio from an elderly woman dozing on a bench, they make another half-dozen taps on people for change. As they leave the park a cop stands by the wall, watching them.

"Lookit that, man."

"I see him."

"Why he lookin' at us?"

"Maybe he jus' likes your Afro."

"And he a brother too."

"He got some white in him—lookin' like that."

"More'n that, man. He's just a whitey that come out the wrong color."

Sgt. William McCarthy, 15 years a policeman in Harlem, the last three as unit commander of the Youth Aid Division (Y.A.D.) in Central Harlem's sixth division, describes the rat pack's characteristic style:

"These kids lead a nomadic existence. They're like desert wanderers, roaming the city and committing crimes. They sometimes band together on the spur of the moment to go downtown for some action."

How far downtown?

"Penn Station, Times Square, the Upper East Side—anywhere they think there's money."

What about the Schleifer shooting on 110th Street? "That's the borderline going south. We're getting increasing trouble in that whole area, mostly from juveniles. And much of it is violent crime. Schleifer was probably picked on the spur of the moment because he was white, and to a lot of these kids white means money." But how can they be called desert wanderers on 110th Street? "So this one was on the edge. But if Schleifer were 50 blocks downtown they might've jumped him or someone like him. The point is that they're mobile, they can appear anywhere."

Like wanderers in a desert. Or maybe a Disneyland. Where they can touch things they see on TV and know they will never have. Where they can rip off an executive because they'll never be one. Where they can cop a woman's handbag because they'll never be given credit cards and charge plates like she has. And where they can blow away a white man who put them where they are, and keeps them there.

"The Black Panthers and other black nationalist groups have told the kids that it's the white man who keeps them in the ghetto, and the only way to get him off their back is to go after him." McCarthy looks around his dismal office on the third floor of the 28th Precinct house, built in 1912. His eyes, stopping at a battered old school desk, seem to shrug. "If the white man has that kind of power then he's got the money to back it up, so he's a natural target," the sergeant says. He smiles. "Then, too, there's the practical matter of anonymity. Nobody knows them in any other areas."

Can anything be done? "It's got to start in the home, long before it gets to the streets and the police. There's no family supervision today. When nobody cares about a kid, everything goes wrong. Youth crime is increasing. Sometimes I think maybe we're losing the war, all of us." *

Statistics bear this out. In the last 20 years reported juvenile incidents involving the police have increased more than 300 per cent in New York City. In McCarthy's division, taking in much of Central Harlem, the number of such incidents has doubled in the past decade; in 1970 alone, there were 297 arrests of juveniles (those under 16) for felonies and 3,401 "referrals" (which become part of a juvenile's record) for lesser offenses. City-wide the figures for last year were 17,944 arrests, of which more than 10,000 were for felonies, and 49,000 referrals. The 1970 figures for adolescents (those between 16 and 20) were just as dismal.

As a more recent example, in the first eight months of this year there were almost 800 reported robberies and a total of 1,135 felonies in Central Park. Both figures indicate a 20 per cent rise over 1970 and a still larger increase over 1969. Police attribute much of this crime to city youths who roam the park, sometimes in packs of six or more, seeking victims. The growing use of drugs and increased migration of unskilled men and boys from the South and from Puerto Rico are the two major reasons cited for the escalation in criminal activity in the park.

But criminal activity is heavy in all areas of the city, and the rise in vio-

---

* The Y.A.D. in Central Harlem has 20 people patrolling and investigating; each of the other 16 divisions in the city has about the same number. Acting as liaison between police and school, and police and family, the Y.A.D. concerns itself with juveniles. Legally, a juvenile delinquent is any youth over 7 and under 16 who does something which, if done by an adult, would be a crime. What crimes? A felony, any offense for which the sentence is more than one year, or a serious misdemeanor, such as unauthorized possession of a dangerous weapon, sex offenses or possession of dangerous drugs.

lent crime by youths is part of the picture. There has also been an increase in such crimes in other cities. Recently, an editorial in *The Times* noted that "reports from across the country confirm the dismal trend." But the real situation is even worse than statistics reveal, because many crimes of a semiviolent nature (such as purse snatching, which could lead to assault) are not reported unless the victim is injured.

There is no way to arrive at an estimate of how many city youths run in rat packs. The groups are amorphous, changing constantly, with no structure to them, no shape. There's no hard-core element, no criminal control, no Mafia management, no Fagin directing things. There's no common denominator among these youths beyond the desperate need for money. Some do it once and get scared. Some do it twice and get caught. Some move on to other things. Some just move. It's a childish kind of activity, grabbing a bag, hustling a wallet. Unfortunately, oftentimes children can hurt and even kill. But it's not man's work, it's not professional. It is, as one retired professional thief put it, "something for junkies and punks."

Punks. Most of them are living at home with parents or relatives; most attend school. On any school day hundreds of thousands of youngsters are traveling to different areas of an open city. Many rip offs are done on the way home from school. A rip off, almost by definition, is a spontaneous act done at a given moment because of favorable circumstances.

Under other circumstances, they might not do it. If they didn't need money, they might not. If they had some hope for the future, they might not. If they had a sense of responsibility, they might not. If family and community life were not deteriorating, they might not. Maybe, finally, if anyone cared, they might not.

In the matter of the ethnic background of rat packs, it is again impossible to arrive at any figure. Official juvenile statistics are hard to come by, since the law seems to guard them more zealously than adult figures. For instance, when asked for the percentages of white, black and Spanish-speaking juveniles arrested in 1970, the official police answer was, "This information is not available." In any case, economic need is color blind and there are slums in every corner of the city. And rat packs in all of them.

The public feels a wide-spread unease, a fear that something is radically wrong, a dread that "crime in the streets" may be getting out of control. The phrase means exactly that. Not crime committed by professionals but street rip offs committed largely by drug addicts and alienated elements of society, of which the roving packs of youngsters are a part.

Where will it end? "I don't know," said the young white man from the Lower East Side, a veteran rip-off artist at 18, "but long as you got your foot up my ass, I'm gonna have my knife at your throat."

"Yeah," said his 17-year-old friend, "and if that ain't enough, a gun at your head."

She was a model. Tall, sinewy; with long black hair reaching down over a tan jump jacket, framing a Pola Negri face. Her right hand held the model's black portfolio, proof of her identity. On her left shoulder hung a large beige bag, her fingers cupped around the wide strap. A big yellow "happy-face" button was pinned to the bag's flap. Black seamless stockings curved down to short Pucci boots with block heel and buckle buttons.

Walking south on Lexington Avenue and 85th Street, a slight wind teasing her hair, she seemed poised and confident. It was early, and she might well have been on her way to an important assignment on this bright autumn afternoon.

Chester saw her first. Coming around a corner, he spotted her across the street and motioned to Jumper and Wolfie. Jumper called over to Johnny Apartment, idling in front of a store. One look was enough for him. "Easy rider," he said softly. And started across the street, the others following.

She did not see them. Crossing behind her, keeping their distance, walking quietly, they caused no alarm or suspicion in the people on the street. If anyone noticed them in their sneakers and jeans, they were probably considered school kids going home or somewhere. What with all this school busing these days, you know. . . .

She was mid-block now. The sun's rays, warming the other side of Lexington Avenue, seemed to catch a sudden movement at the edge of shadow. A brief blurring of light as Wolfie ran up behind her and punched her with closed fist in the small of the back.

Involuntarily reacting to the blow, her arms opening in surprise much as a sea gull in startled flight, she dropped her portfolio just as her shoulder bag slipped to the sidewalk. With one quick scoop Jumper grabbed the bag, while Johnny Apartment reached for a ring on her outstretched hand. In a matter of seconds they were at the corner and around it, headed toward Third Avenue. After two blocks they split up, each to get home, with Jumper holding the money. The shoulder bag and its contents had already been tossed under a parked car. Like American merchants of an earlier time, only cash was acceptable. At least in a daylight rip off in enemy country where capture was always a possibility. And getting rid of evidence was a necessity.

The life of a nomad is never easy. With far horizons comes the burden of getting home safely. With the advantage of anonymity in a strange land comes the disadvantage of not knowing the terrain. Jumper and the others are aware of the dangers. They are also aware that, being minority youths, they could be stopped at any time by cops "vamping everybody in sight," who might put them "upside a wall and frisk our ass off." Normally they would be all right, but in a rip off their one goal is to get home fast or, if not that, to some other area. For this they need swift transportation.

The subway is their magic carpet. It takes them where they want to go, and away from where they don't want to be. It is a lifeline of sorts, providing both speed and anonymity. Small wonder that many rip offs occur near subway stations. Of course, in an area such as midtown Manhattan almost anywhere is near a subway station. One wonders what would happen to the rip-off rate of rat packs if the subways were closed at night.

Are youths like Jumper and Wolfie and Chester and Johnny Apartment worried about the possible consequences of getting caught? Not overly, apparently.

"First thing is, dig it. You gotta do some real wild-man stuff for them to come down on you. Most times they let you go home with your people right there."

"If you don't got too many raps on the sheet [juvenile record]."

"Yeah, that too. But if they keep you, then the judge'll let you go."

"That the God truth, man. I was there onct and that judge talkin' to me till I was catchin' a headache. Talk my ear clean off 'fore they let me go."

"Like I know some men they was sent somewhere and inside two weeks they back home."

"Sure, everybody know that."

For offenses that are not felonies or serious misdemeanors, a juvenile may either be held in custody for an appearance in Family Court or released to parents until the court appearance. This decision is made by the desk officer in the precinct. About 90 per cent of such juveniles are so released, according to a high police official. The remaining 10 per cent usually have a growing juvenile record. (A referral form—the YD1—is made out by the Y.A.D. for juveniles and is, in effect, a record.)

If youths under 16 are considered juveniles and often let go with a referral and a verbal "spanking" or short-term detention, what of those over 16?

"That's a whole other thing, man. That's why a lotta men you see, they got papers on 'em saying they under 16. They could be 50, but they under 16. Am I jiving on you, man?"

"No, man, that's just the way it is."

"That's 'cause if you over 16 they come down on you like you was King Kong. 'Special if you doing the heavy work [armed robbery, homicide with a gun]. Then they kick ass."

In New York adolescents between 16 and 20 are treated as adults under the Penal Code. That is, they are arraigned in Criminal Court, held in custody if bail is not set or posted, bound over to State Supreme Court if a grand jury hands down an indictment, tried in court and, if convicted, sentenced to prison. They are, however, separated from adult inmates.

Jumper, who just turned 16, isn't worried because "I got no record worth nothing. Long's I don't use a gun everything's cool." What about a knife? "Most times I don't even carry a blade. But if something goes wrong you can always throw it away fast."

What if a knife can't be thrown away fast enough?

"The thing is, we just grabbin' the stuff and run. That way nobody gets hurt. Nothin' can go real wrong."

But even if something does go "real wrong"—short of homicide, perhaps—a youth of 16 or 17 or even 18 with no prior felony conviction could still come out all right. If he were judged a "youthful offender," he would stand a chance of being put on probation or even receiving a conditional discharge (conditional on his behaving himself). And his record of conviction would be sealed; in effect, he would have no criminal record.

Popeye, an 18-year-old Puerto Rican punchman (one who punches a passing woman full in the face and then runs off with her bag) from the Lower East Side, was tried as a youthful offender and got probation on a Class B felony. "My woman, she rode me somethin' awful at night. She'd look me straight up the eye and she'd say, 'I need this' and 'I need that,' so I hadda get it for her."

His court-appointed lawyer ("If I listened to him I'd be talking to myself now") told him he'd be lucky to get five years, but instead he got a Y.O. and probation. "Not only that but now I got no record or nothin'. And all I hadda do was promise to go straight." Popeye laughs. "But you know, man, my woman is still there on my ear so I gotta go back to work. Only now I'm exter careful."

What if they found out he broke his word? It could mean prison.

That doesn't worry Popeye; he's a realist. "I didn't break my word, man, I just changed my mind. They understand."

Times Square is the watering hole of the jungle. Everybody who's anything in the nothing world of the hustle makes the scene sooner or later. The prossies walk their beat, early on Eighth Avenue, late on Broadway, their pimps sitting in little luncheonettes along Eighth in the 40's. Jockers and queens stand in front of sex bookstores on 42d Street or lounge in the back of cafeterias. Sharks and Murphy men patrol the bars near the bus terminal, while grifters of every shade work the side streets between Sixth and Eighth Avenues in the mid-40's. It's after 8 o'clock and the hustle is on, along with the bright lights of the neon jungle.*

---

* A "jocker" is the aggressive partner in a homosexual relationship. A "Murphy man" accosts men in the street and tries to sell them a prostitute who he says is waiting in an apartment nearby; after receiving the money, he enters the building— telling the customer to wait while he makes preparations—then disappears, usually making his exit via the roof. A "grifter" is any kind of street hustler (the word is related to "graft").

Jumper and Johnny Apartment walk down Broadway, Wolfie and Chester trailing by a few steps. They like Times Square, the variety, the crazies, the quick ways to spend a buck. They come down at least once a week when they have the money. Movies, fast food, sometimes clothing and assorted junk.

"It's where to spend it. We don't mess 'round there 'cause it's too open, too many people. The whole place is leaking sounds."

For possible rip offs they go where it's not so noisy. Down to the Penn Station area or even farther, to 23d Street. Across town, west to east, all those blocks mostly quiet after business hours. The East 20's and 30's along Third and Second Avenues. Then around Grand Central and the U.N., working their way north through the moneyed 50's and 60's. The rich parks along the East River. The Upper East Side, going home. Baghdad on the subway. Or the bus.

Tonight they go to a 42d Street movie, eat at Nathan's ("Gimme ketchup on everything." "It's over there, pal") then walk around Broadway for a while. Wolfie's handwriting, analyzed, reveals that he "will make a lot of money in the near future." Chester, feeling sick from eating too much, turns salty. "I didn't eat too much, I was overserved."

As a goof, Jumper puts the make on a whore at 50th Street, but she turns away. Everybody laughs. "What she say, man?" Jumper shakes his head. "Says she only eats white bread."

"That's 'cause you didn't front no money."

"Make no difference. She don't burn no coal."

"Hell, when a whore talking under her clothes she take any money."

"Not from me she don't."

"Ain't worth it, man."

"No woman worth the money."

" 'Special no whore."

"And a ugly old whore like that."

"Right on there, man."

It's well past midnight as the four of them move down Seventh Avenue. The street is dark. At 36th, a car's alarm system suddenly starts up by itself. They break into a run down the block, cursing the car, fearful that they'll be blamed. Into Penn Station, down the stairs, franks and Cokes at a stand, walk about a bit, then back outside.

On 33d Street a man headed toward the station is suddenly confronted by four youths who come upon him halfway up the deserted block. As they pass, Johnny Apartment turns quickly and shoves the tip of his blade into the man's back, up high on the shoulder, where it does little damage. The man, in pain, flails his arms, trying to reach the hurt. Jumper's hand is already inside the man's jacket, while Wolfie and Chester cut out his pants pockets with razors. Within 30 seconds they are away and racing for the corner. Once out of sight they will slow to a walk and immediately throw away everything but cash. Wallets and keys go down a sewer or basement. Checkbooks, credit cards, all go into the gutter unless there is no chance of being picked up by the cops. In which case they'll sell the cards, since there is no way they would ever be able to use them.

A walk to the next subway station, this time buying tokens so they cause no suspicion, and home. Just a night of fun and profit on the nomad circuit in the big city.

Is there any future in it?

Jumper doesn't think much about the future. Neither do the others. They find the present bad enough—or good enough, depending on their mood of the moment. Like many youngsters, they seek instant gratification and cannot readily handle long-term considerations. They don't like school and don't especially like to read. They know little about world affairs and couldn't care less. Yet they are infinitely more sophisticated than the gang members of years ago. They have been around the city, they have seen many things. They are aware of their rights and of society's wrongs. It would be hard to cheat them out of anything.

Only Johnny Apartment has a plan for the future. He's going to become a top pimp and "make plenty." He likes the way pimps dress, and the cars they drive, and how they handle their women. Most of all, he likes the idea of making it big. The point is not that he intends to be a pimp but that he's got all the ambition and drive and determination to rise to the top of his chosen profession, and that's just what every red-blooded American boy is supposed to have.

Johnny Apartment is lucky, at least he knows what he wants. All Jumper and the others know is what they don't want. Which is more of the same they've had all their lives.

"What future?"

"I'm trying to forget my future."

Boys like Jumper and Johnny Apartment and Wolfie and Chester— thousands of them in rat packs all over the city, coming from every economic slum—ordinarily are not addicted to hard drugs. Those who do use drugs normally restrict themselves to snorting nonaddictive cocaine, when available. A longtime junkie does not have the coordination for the street rip off. Speed, steadiness, above all, control are needed. When a junkie does make the attempt, it is usually a more desperate—and for the victim, more dangerous—situation. A junkie often will use a gun, invariably one of the $10 "Saturday night specials." If not a gun, then a long knife held at the victim's throat or belly. Unfortunately, compliance is no guarantee of safety. Junkies are notoriously unpredictable.

The rat packs generally do not carry guns. They rely on surprise and speed, though knives are often shown for effect. If they use a weapon at times, it is a razor blade or the tip of a pocketknife, which distracts the victim momentarily. When guns are shown, it somehow changes the complexion, the "feel" of the crime from thievery to armed robbery, and places it in another, more premeditated category. Even then, the gun is seldom used. Those instances in which a victim is shot are usually the result of an act of bravado by the one holding the gun, who is perhaps challenged beyond the point of return by his companions.

In a time of social unrest and economic deprivation, lots of things go wrong. The emergence of rat packs is one of them. It is a problem for the city and for society, but even more of a problem for the youths themselves. Acts of hostility against anyone who crosses their path will in the long run destroy them. Cumulative degeneration is never pleasant to watch. Individual suicide is oftentimes tragic, but mass suicide, especially of the young, is always a national tragedy.

What can be done? Short of social evolution or biological revolution, perhaps nothing. Robbery—and violence—are increasing in every big city in the country, regardless of how much police officials like to pretend to the contrary. Based on the evidence, on statistics, on the rates of recidivism, nobody—not the police, not the courts, not the correction departments, and certainly not the prison systems—is taking care of its business. Rehabilitation is still in its infancy, community treatment has not yet even been born, and the concept of crime *prevention* rather than crime detection is still just a dream.

Albert Seedman, Chief of Detectives in New York, was recently quoted as saying: "Robbery grows out of social unrest, out of poverty and out of a society that is in flux. We can't do much about these root causes of robbery, but we can arrest more of the robbers."

That is an answer. It is not a solution.

What's going on? Maybe Jumper had it right after all. "Every turkey has its Thanksgiving, man."

On Saturday, Oct. 23, I retrace the walk westward that had ended in disaster for Steven Schleifer. It is warm, a beautiful day for late October in New York. To set a mood for myself, I start at 86th Street and Fifth Avenue, walking north past rows of elegant apartment houses smelling of money and guarded by watchful doormen, past the Guggenheim Museum with its Liquid Theatre sessions sold out, past the Jewish Museum at 92d Street, the National Audubon Society headquarters at 94th and the Klingenstein Pavilion at 100th. Steven had lain in the Pavilion for eight days with a bullet wound less than an inch from his spinal cord (he was not paralyzed).

At 101st Street, midway between Fifth and Madison Avenues, the Mt. Sinai School of Medicine of the City University of New York is in front of me. The time is 6:30. At about 6:30 on a Monday 12 days earlier, Steven Schleifer, with a companion, had begun the longest journey of his young life.

The stretch between the school and 110th Street seems somehow devoid of life, lined as it is with institutional buildings such as the New York Medical College, Flower and Fifth Avenue Hospitals. I reach Frawley Circle at Fifth Avenue and 110th Street, and stand in front of a sprawling gas station. The street sign above my head reads Central Park North, but I am not fooled. Central Park South means money and Central Park West means success, but Central Park North only means 110th Street. Harlem. The southern boundary.

I look uptown, thinking of the years I lived in Harlem, white sheep in wolf's clothing but lean and hungry. Just about a mile from here at 128th Street and Park Avenue. But from where I started a little while ago, at 86th and Fifth, my old block's way uptown in another world.

A shudder ripples the street. An earthquake, or perhaps the sensation one is supposed to feel in private moments of love. But no, I'd recognize that sound anywhere. I turn my face east toward Park Avenue as the train goes tomcatting past my ear on its elevated paws. Old horrors rip through my mind and I quickly cross the street to the park side. Thomas Wolfe was right: You can't go home again. And perhaps for most of us, it's just as well.

I walk into the park, a momentary digression from Steven's route. Ahead of me are a dozen groups of youngsters, some of whom stare intently at the calm water. The lake itself stretches before me like a piece of a jigsaw puzzle incongruously set on a checkerboard, its irregular shape not quite fitting its linear surroundings. Yet there it is. I walk along the edge, pebbles kicking at my heels. Night is near. No matter. Everything is peaceful in this oasis in the city. My soul breathes.

"Got a nickel, mister?"

Three of them. Couldn't be more than 11 or 12 years old. One has a tree branch in his hand. Another smokes a cigarette, standing about 10 feet away. The third one, empty-handed, is next to me. I stop, turn toward him. He has a nice smile, and very big eyes and a hole in the arm of his sweat shirt.

"Got a nickel?"

I look at him. A nickel, what the hell can you do with a nickel? I fish out a quarter and put it in his hand. He cups it and moves off; the others follow. They start laughing in what sounds like boyish good spirits.

I stand there, not laughing. My throat is tight, my arms ache. I check myself. Why did I think this might be a rip off? Because they're black?

No. I feel the same way when groups of white kids hit on me for change in lonely places. So it wasn't racist, it was instinct. You can't tell a rat pack from an ordinary group until it's too late. Trust no one. New York paranoia says every tree twig is a branch and thus a weapon. Every boy who smokes is a killer. Every group is robber-rapist. Everybody under 20 is out to get you.

What a way to live.

By the time I semicircle the lake I'm approached twice more by youngsters for money. The third time it's not a question but a demand: "Gimme some change, man. I need it." I tell him no, I need it more. There's some cursing at my back but their mouths aren't really into it. Score: no violence, no hits, no errors, and one man left off base. I walk back up the down stairs and out of the park.

Moving along the park's edge, following Steven's route homeward, I cross Lenox Avenue, one of Harlem's great streets, and continue west toward Seventh. Midway down the block a car passes and someone shouts, "Get outta town, whitey." I look around. Many of the benches next to the stone wall are occupied. I don't see anybody white. I move on.

It is just about 7 o'clock as I approach the spot where Steven was shot. Ahead is Frederick Douglass Circle and the end of Central Park. Nearby, a woman walks her dog, a man sits in a car, its motor running, and two men talk softly on a bench. Nothing out of the ordinary. I cross the street and talk to a young man in the gas station. He sees nothing, hears nothing, knows nothing. "Do you work on Mondays about this time?" He doesn't know. I thank him and walk away.

"That white boy die?" he shouts after me.

I shake my head. Now he knows something.

If Steven had been allowed to finish his journey, he would have ended it at his home on 114th Street between Broadway and Riverside Drive. I continue west on 110th, which now becomes Cathedral Parkway, and finally reach Columbia University, a neighborhood that was once part of his world of safety and security (Steven was graduated from Columbia). Yet, of course, there are no longer any areas of absolute safety and security; violence, the sudden and often senseless attack, can strike anybody, anywhere.

I turn into Steven's block, past the Papyrus bookstore on the corner, the Xerox copyquick sign on the apartment house, the row of rocks and Ming trees fenced in next door, past once-fashionable apartment buildings and a still-fashionable residential area. On a stoop a young man sits with large boxes of household furnishings. A rented truck is double-parked. I ask him why he is moving. "Not me, I don't live here. It's my girl friend."

His girl friend was attacked the week before, around the corner. Knocked down and kicked, threatened with death, handbag stolen. Now she was scared enough to move. Where to? "Down to the Village to stay with some girls she knows," the young man says. "It's safe there. I'm over in the dorms or I'd get out myself."

As we talk his girl friend comes out of the building, a beautiful black girl in her early 20's. I wish them luck. Good-by and good luck.

5

Slum-Ghetto Schoolchildren

MARY FRANCES GREENE and ORLETTA RYAN

Mr. Rowby

Stair wall: "Mr. Rowby has a big banana and he can't get enough of Betty Jane's ass (6-A)."

Under thirty. Round, pale face, defeated eyes. When you enter, you know his room is supplied out of his own pocket with many maps, colored chalks, and the like, but the class—this was Mr. Zimmer's class last year; it was in order—this year is a zoo. He believes in one-to-one contact, in trying to reach them all. But being a nice guy is equated with soft. A kid steals money off Rowby's desk. Rowby: "Why did you steal it? I'd have given it to you."

Mrs. Weiss: "He wants to be liked. He has a scene going showing fishes he's brought in, writing instructions on the board, or watering plants but doesn't know what he *should* be doing. I said, 'If children have a seat, they must be in it. I taught fifth grade here last year. I had children who never,

Source: Mary Frances Greene and Orletta Ryan, *The Schoolchildren* (New York: Random House, 1966), pp. 73–75, 121, 155–156, 166–167, 171–172, 194–196. Copyright © 1964, 1965, 1966 by Mary Frances Greene and Orletta Ryan. Reprinted by permission of Pantheon Books, a Division of Random House.

58

not once, swore at me.' He said, 'But all children do.' I said, 'No, they do in your room because you permit it. . . .' "

Children: "The kids in Mr. Rowby's room be warring *everybody,* because they don't know what to do with theirselves. They war so bad, even they gets wore out!"

Mrs. Arnheim

Mr. Rowby's opposite, teaching a top sixth grade. An intense and disciplined person. Young, under thirty, but dedicated to her vocation. Her children show it.

On her own time last summer, she tutored a little girl who'd failed her class in June; arranged for Rhonda to be re-examined at summer's end, and the child passed at grade level. (Rhonda's mother had come out of prison, and promised to visit the child each week while on parole but didn't.) The tutoring, a daily two or three hours in the park, may have made all the difference.

Mrs. Arnheim goes to NYU classes at night; she's getting her M.A. in elementary teaching. She does psychological testing with children on her own time. She lunches with two or three children downstairs each day. In her top fifth-grade room is a bright library table, with new books each week; a science display she and children have cooperatively prepared. Her children learn quietly and steadily. On Assembly day, they appear with starched clean blouses and walk with their heads up.

Thanksgiving approaches. Mr. Rowby grows pale, seems ill, but stays in school; other teachers absent. Double number of substitutes, and assistant principals taking over classes on every floor. By Wednesday the building is turning over. Guys tumbling in and out of washrooms, "Shi' man, don't push this door," fights, rushes on girls' washrooms, girls' screams. A girl is grabbed, carried halfway down the hall, her friends pile out and rescue her; they get back in the washroom, more screams. Boards in the door slip. Water floods and fights. Mr. Rodgers, the janitor, scrubs new outbursts of signs from stair walls, some in red Magic Marker: "Mr. Pressman so busy gettin pusy he don't have time to give out homework." . . .

Some teachers give little parties in their rooms. All say they never will again. Mr. Saltz sent a notice around, "All parties to start at 1:30 but not before." Most rooms are parties all day. Mrs. Weiss saw the 'Tarded Teacher hauling two great bags of Horn & Hardart goodies at 8:30 A.M. from the subway station. "When she came in the door the children flew on her from every direction in their eagerness to begin the party. Everybody grabbed his food away from her, and each had his own party in his own corner. Food was going everywhere, up to the ceilings and down throats. The party was over at ten past nine."

Harold remains after school for remedial reading at primer level and, leaving him for a few minutes, on the way to the washroom I pass Mr. Rowby's room. Some tall boys—sixth grade? his own boys? Jefferson [Junior High]? —are hanging around the open door calling in to him. Rowby's got their friend inside.

—Wheee, Mr. Roowby, you a homosexual, Mr. Rooobey! Shi', man, when you go down that aisle you think you so hot, Mr. Rowby, that tail of you wave back and forth!

—I tell you, Rowby, if Waldon here, *he* take and smash you butt, only Waldon don't go here no more.

—You such a faggot, Mr. Row-by, you a homosex-ual! you keepin that boy in there for nothin, you faggot, cause Waldon ain't around.

(Rowby was inside leaning over his table; he looked as though he would burst out crying or fall, but didn't close the door. He couldn't; they'd kick it in.) . . .

In the three months since school began, several teachers have quit. (The school had a 70 per cent opening list in June.) One was the first science teacher, a young woman in English tweeds and walking shoes and long brown hair, who entered a fourth grade to give a lesson on magnets. The children threw the magnets out the window, she left and was replaced after many weeks by Mr. Wilcox. Another was a girl with a face like a line drawing and somber eyes. She'd asked for a Harlem school but got a low fifth grade; her gentle personality began to suffer from the all-day attacks and senseless violence. The day before Halloween, she brought in whipped-cream cakes for a party. The kids blew the whipped cream through the centers of cakes, plastered it on walls, ceiling, each other. She went out to get rags and did the cleaning-up herself, but then nothing happened the rest of the morning. In fact, the room grew very quiet just at noon. When she went into the coatroom, she found the pockets of her cashmere coat had been defecated in, and left within that hour. . . .

Iris. Survival

A quiet lady who can read. Shy. Speaks only when she's called on (it is the Curtises who get attention in any class) but for all the trouble at home with her stepfather, manages to report on a book each Monday morning. Until Claude, she was the only recent Deep South in class.

"Pickles, the Fiah-House Cay-ht.

"Pickle, he were a *fiah*-house cay-ht. . . . Fiah-mens gonna git 'im a hel-mut; cause he tuk an' *save* that baby kitten! Cah-ied that kitten home. Lady called Miz Goodkin', she say, 'Pickles don' raht-ly b-*lonng* in a fiah-house—' "

Iris is very dark, her body beginning to develop, as tall as I. "Big Feet," they call her, and "Eyeball Shoes." Wears her birthday dress with bows in the back on Assembly days. Her size is her painful existence. A fight is boiling outside—Jefferson [Junior High] boys. "Shut up, I'll get my cousin." "Your cousin ain't nothin to me." "Okay, I'm ready for you. Come on. I'll knock the black off you." Iris comes back from the doorway into the room and stands trembling beside the blackboard. I go over to her: "What is the matter, honey?" She says to one side in her faint voice, "Miss Buh'ke, Jeff'son boys they talks to me at night, say they goan rake me some night." I cannot calm her. Her slender neck with its Adam's apple (her gesture of touching her long hand to her neck) and little head are trembling. "Miss Buh'ke, they say they goan, and I don't got a broken bottle with me tonight." She will not leave the building alone without Cassie any afternoon they stay after school.

In this neighborhood, little girls walk with their eyes down. Jefferson boys and sixth-graders torment them, go at even littler girls with fingers in a V stabbing at legs, and early in the term I had to help find and identify a boy who had "done something" to a first-grade child. The little girl was dissolved in whispers and tears, couldn't look to see which boy when we entered the sixth-grade room. The mother, a thin, poorly dressed woman, stood angrily in the doorway, hugging herself with arms that had big slash marks on them, her eyes darting around the room. "I'm lookin for the light-skin one that touch my baby. Get him, or." . . .

On Wednesday afternoon, a child in the back of Mrs. Hervine's room raised his hand to read. She didn't know who he was. "But Albert, you'll have to go back to your room. Who's your teacher?" "We don't got one; we got subs every day and the one today slams chairs." He'd found himself a nice room—hers. She says, "I can't get him to leave. He slips in every day and I don't notice him; he sits in different places. He's in a third grade. He cries, then I let him stay. He says, 'I get sick to my stomach it's so nutty down there and she goes Eeeagh all day; I hates her voice!' No one's missed him yet." . . .

The first day I was out with the flu, a young man substituted. Children: "He was really be-yewtiful, and he had jello hair. But he say he kick us in the ass and butt if we didn't sit down and stop throwing stuff."

To Harold he said, "Where'd you get the clothes, kid, out of a ragbag?" At noon he told the children he was going out to plan a nice program for them, but never came back.

The second day was a fat middle-aged man who kept crossing himself and saying little prayers.

Vernon. Wanted us to stay in our seats.

Cassandra. Cross himself and keep sayin his prayers, and call, "One, two three! Where should we all be?" And said he would give everyone a quatuh that was quiet. Give some quatuhs to the boys, and say he gonna get some more change at noon. But when he come back, still had only eight more quatuhs. I was quiet but he never did give my my quatuh. He was a *liah,* Miss Buh'ke. . . .

I put a problem on the board—a rather long one—turn around, and two children are bleeding, three are on top of them, fingers stabbing at eyes. The whole thing has been completely silent. Pieces of skin ripped off a cheek. A little girl is crying with her coat over her head.

Choking guttural noises outside—not loud. In the corridor a third-grade girl, low-slung, stocky, is slugging a fifth-grade boy. Her eyes are cloudy; she drives her fists at him, "Fuck off, buddy," but he gets her head and beats it against the wall. My kids rush to the door behind me, Reggie's eyes gleaming. But for once it looks so deadly, most kids are scared. The boy and girl are ringed. A boy says, *"She turnin him on,* let her get what he give her. She gotta learn to defend herself." The boy is socking her in the throat. . . .

There are teachers who have been attacked days after an incident with a kid. No one wants to break up the fights in halls. Mr. Pressman knows of sixth-grade boys who are laying for him. He gets in his car and drives off fast in the afternoon.

A new teacher in her early twenties, just back from her honeymoon in Honolulu, is waiting for the bus after a bad day. She looks at her purse, drawing a heavy sigh. Her hands tremble. She says, "I go home from here with pains in my legs and nausea. I can't cope with what I see all day. I try to tell my husband, and he says, 'They're ten years old, why can't you control them?' I called my mother last night, and she said, 'You're a college graduate with a degree, what's the problem?' I went to bed at eight-thirty last night; I didn't want to wake up this morning. No one will listen to me." . . .

One afternoon, weeks after the truant reports had gone out on Curtis and Ernie, I was in the back of the room where a fight was raging. Some-one had snatched someone else's sandwich at noon. "Your teeth so rotten they're crumbly and flaky, and so's your mother's. Your mother's teeth, they're almost not there." "Double for *your* mother's teeth. Your mother's an addic'." "Well, yours's a whore, and she wears iron drawers with barb wire trimmins." More. Then a sudden silence fell on the room. The fight stopped. Leanore, who has been taking mornings off again lately, dropped quietly in her seat.

The truant officer had entered, and when I'd returned to my desk we talked for a few minutes. He kept the children under his eye, and they stared back at his stickpin in a dark tie with whorls running in it, the cut of his suit, his cuff links. They do not often see a Negro man like this. I said, "I'm sorry I had to send out so many notices. But too much work has been put into these boys. Miss Myles, Mrs. Weiss, myself. Not to pick them up now would be like dropping them in a sewer."

"Oh no, I'm glad you did. As you see, I can't keep up with my truant notices. We always have a backlog of months. I've been to see Curtis and Ernie since last night. Neither place answered the bell."

Vernon: "Hey, I'll take you where Ernie *really* lives! He's back at his mother's! But we gotta go there *real* late, she ain't there till late. Ernie neither."

The officer continued, "Donald's mother was to escort him to school today—oh, she didn't? Well, we can have her in court. Once he's back we'll put a special officer on him to see there's no deviation. Curtis?"

"Curtis just goes home, into a pocket. For him, it's better than being in school. His mother doesn't care."

"Today I've had three mothers lie to me for their kids: measles, hospital, measles. No father, any of the three. I wish there were more of us. But we're just machinery. The State can't replace parents." . . .

The officer then talked to William and Leanore, bending down beside each of them. They squirmed but listened. "Have you been in court before? This jig-jag course leads you to the court. I'm not here to intimidate you or make you fearful. But the law says you must be in school. That's what you must understand. Your place is not at home doing laundry or watching babies, but here. Tell your mothers you can only do home chores after three o'clock. Each day in this room follows up what you did yesterday. You must be here, doing your best."

6

The Grim State of Welfare

JULIUS HORWITZ

What really happens in the public-assistance world of New York City? No one can possibly know without taking the black notebook of a social investigator under his arm and walking into the rotting ghettos of New York, blocks so horrible that they would have awed the missionaries of the 19th century. The black notebook has become a symbol of living death to tens of thousands of New Yorkers. It lists the families for whom simple words like love, home, work, father are devoid of meaning. It lists families whom the rest of us have ruthlessly dumped into oblivion, to be hidden from our sight and banished from our thoughts.

These are the families who fall early prey to the drug pushers, the addicts, the muggers, the purse snatchers, the elevator thieves, the psychologically castrated men whose only proof of manhood is an out-of-wedlock baby, and the morally castrated drifters who have brought panic to New York, a panic that pulses through thousands of brownstone blocks, where white, Negro, and Puerto Rican families plot escapes with the same inner frenzy that infected Londoners during the bubonic plague.

For seven years, I carried the black notebook. There are many names in

Source: Julius Horwitz, "The Grim State of Welfare," *Look Magazine,* 26 March 1963, pp. 72, 77–78, 80. Reprinted by permission.

it. The names used in this article are not from my notebook. They are ficti-
tious. The situations are not. They are composites of actual case histories.
The black notebook is immediately recognized on the stoops of the sprawling slums. That notebook brims with requests for beds, shoes, teeth, eye
appointments, winter coats and contraceptives.

That notebook has spawned the special "landlords" who swarm into the
welfare offal like the worms that five-year-old Paula Rivera saw crawling
into the mouth of a Mr. Clark during the three days he lay dead "in the
single-room occupancy" brownstone owned by a Mr. Sheck. Paula's
mother took her screaming out of the building; they slept on a friend's
floor in East Harlem rather than return to Mr. Sheck's building.

You must walk through the buildings to know what it's like to have Mr.
Sheck for your landlord.

I've known Mr. Sheck as long as I've carried the black notebook. He
owns five buildings. The five hold a total of over 200 families, if you count
as a family any single, unattached person with one or more children. All
the people in his houses are on welfare, except for an occasional tenant
unable or unwilling to move. . . .

Who would pay $30 a week for two rooms chopped out of a railroad
flat, with broken walls, vermin, furniture that belongs in an incinerator, a
front door through which rats enter as freely as the swarming children?
Who would pay $30 a week, $65 semimonthly, $130 a month? The City
of New York would and does. Why? The landlords know the answer. And
the answer makes them inviolate. One of them said, "I run a pigsty for the
City of New York. We're partners. See? The city pays me to keep these
people off the street and out of everybody's sight, period. They aren't people. They're drunken, filthy, baby-producing pigs, and as soon as they die
off, there are more to take their places. Nobody in City Hall would dare
mention 'birth control.' They might lose votes, but they don't care about
losing the whole city to these pigs. Nobody down there knows how these
people live, because if they did, they would scream in their sleep. Me? I
sleep, because I'm doing everybody a favor. I give the pigs four walls, and
the city appreciates it, or, instead of paying me so well, they'd close me
down tomorrow, just like they close down bookie joints and hustlers. But
they won't, because there's no place else to put the 150 babies I've got uri-
nating in my halls."

Slums are not a new story in New York. As soon as it took shape, the
city became a massive slum. But the institutionalized slum, the publicly
supported, high-rental slum, the slum that houses only welfare families, the
slum that a child cannot forget, not in sleep, not in the ping of heroin, not
in Rockland State Hospital, this is the new social-welfare slum.

Wilma Gilbort is one of Mr. Sheck's tenants. Open the door to Mrs.
Gilbort's two rooms. You squeeze between the edge of the door and the

edge of the stove and enter a dark hall that is a bedroom for five children, whose faces look at you with shattered innocence. Leonard, William and Thomas sleep in the three-quarter bed. Deborah and Judy sleep in the single bed. Deborah has asthma. William is retarded. Thomas screams in his classroom. Leonard is in a PS 600 school, a kind of educational stopgap for children who are apt to fling themselves at our throats. The living room, where Roberta sleeps on a cot, hasn't seen sunlight since 1905.

Roberta is 14, and pregnant. Mrs. Gilbort is 41 and pregnant. This is Roberta's first pregnancy. It is Mrs. Gilbort's 16th. Her ten living children (one, Louis, is in prison) had seven different fathers—all with whereabouts unknown, except for George Williams in Pilgrim State Hospital and John Green in Manhattan State Hospital.

"I got caught this time, Mr. Horwitz," said Mrs. Gilbort. "I didn't mean to let it go this far."

I could see her stomach pushing out of the skirt held together by a diaper pin, a stomach that has heard 16 human monologues, five silenced by the probing of a clothespin.

"Generally I get rid of them, Mr. Horwitz, you know that from my old record. I don't see any reason for bringing more of them into the world."

"Where are you going to put this one? There's no room left for a second crib."

"In the dresser drawer. She'll grow up all right."

I opened my black notebook. "Who's the father?"

Mrs. Gilbort looked at me, trying to remember. Her mind strained for a name, a presence, a real man. She didn't remember, or she didn't know.

Roberta spoke up. Her slipper scraped on the floor. I thought it was the scratching of a rat. I did see a rat run under the crib. Charles saw the rat and smiled secretly at me. Charles is six.

"You know it was that super's helper on West 103rd Street," Roberta told her mother.

"Yes, I'm sure it was him," Mrs. Gilbort told me, relieved.

"Who's him? I need a name."

"He didn't have much of a name. They called him Pim. But that's not his real name. He's from Jersey. I don't know anything about him except that he was a super's helper."

"Did he actually work as a super's helper, or did he just sleep in the basement?"

"I think he just slept there more of the time."

"Did you tell him you were pregnant?"

"He wasn't around when I knew for sure."

"All right, we'll put the baby on the budget when it comes." . . .

I went upstairs, up the green hallway, newly painted for the housing inspectors, past the children rushing down into the street. Were they children? Every girl in Sheck's building over the age of 13 was pregnant, or had delivered a baby, or was imminently in the process of initiation. Like little girls playing with dolls everywhere, they believed their babies were real. The babies weren't real! The babies were hunks of flesh, laid down in dark rooms to age like meat, to be eaten when their taste appealed to rats, sodomites, drug pushers. And if they survived to the age of 18, they could expect to receive their own crisp IBM-processed public-assistance check, payable with the proper yellow identification card.

Mrs. Ringate lives on the first floor. Her door opens right into her toilet. The kitchen is a dark hole with a tiny refrigerator and a makeshift sink drained by leaking rubber hoses. Her two rooms hold five beds and two cribs, and cost $135 a month. The two cribs hold two babies born seven months ago on the 5th and 15th. Mrs. Ringate had her baby on the 5th. Her daughter Gloria had hers on the 15th. Gloria is 17. Mrs. Ringate is 37. Gloria "graduated" from a training school. Mrs. Ringate's oldest son Lawrence is in Dannemora prison. He threw a bottle of lye at his mother; it ate into her face and blinded her in one eye, almost blotting out her vision of him. I looked at Gloria and saw that she was pregnant again.

"Who this time?" I asked Gloria. The father of the first baby was Juan Martinez. He signed the form 384b admitting paternity, then vanished into the brownstones. Gloria told me that she wouldn't go looking for him, because she had heard he was pushing dope on West 88th Street. I could tell by Gloria's eyes that she heard only about every fifth word I uttered, and probably understood about as many as a well-trained cocker spaniel.

"I need a name for the record," I said to Gloria.

"Put down any name this time, Mr. Horwitz. I don't know his name for sure, and that's a fact. And it doesn't make any difference who's the father as long as you give me the checks." Gloria went into the toilet to comb her hair.

Mrs. Ringate showed me the letter from Dannemora advising her that her son would be discharged as soon as he was no longer capable of throwing lye in his mother's face.

"Will they let Lawrence out for real, Mr. Horwitz?"

"They might if they find the right pills."

"What do I do then?"

"Call the police and get an order restricting him from coming to your house."

"You know that won't keep him away. He'll come up the fire escape. He kicked the door in one time. One time, when I had the door blocked with the crib, he started to break in the wall. He'll do it again."

"Why?"

"You must know, Mr. Horwitz, you must know. I think if they let Lawrence out of that hospital, I'm going to take him South and show him his father's grave. Then at least he'll know he had a father once. He's a sick boy. I guessed that when I first saw him laying next to me. His eyes just looked like he shouldn't be looking out on this world. His eyes didn't have the surprise of a new baby. This is no place for him, not this world. He'll get shot in the head by the police or beaten to death in a street fight if they let him out. And if they keep him, then they've got to feed him all those years and watch him to see that he doesn't kill anyone in that hospital. Just send the checks, Mr. Horwitz, as Gloria says. She hasn't the good sense of a three-year-old baby, but she knows about the checks, your checks. Do you know what she told me last night? I tried to talk to her about what she was going to do with her first baby and the coming baby, because she can't stay here—there's no room for us to breathe or for all of us to sit down and eat at the same time. Do you know what Gloria told me? 'Shut up, you pig. I'm getting my own check, ain't I?' "

Mrs. Ringate spoke in a whisper, as though she believed her other children might survive if they didn't hear, but they lay on their beds, stiff, silent, straining, and they already knew.

I went into Anna Domingo's room. Her mother, Rosa, lives in 2F. Anna lives in 4D. Her mother is a drug addict who has managed to fill two Department of Welfare case folders in eight years. Anna had to quit school. She had her first baby at 16 and now has a second baby. Her room is big enough to hold two cribs, a single bed, one chair, a table. The cooking is done in the community kitchen, and her babies' food is carried through trash-strewn corridors. Anna's brother lives with her mother in 2F. He sleeps with his mother. Incest would be the least of his mother's preoccupations.

"When are you going to get out of here?" I asked Anna.

"I look, Mr. Horwitz."

"I said, 'When are you going to get out of here?' You'll have another baby in ten months."

"I won't have any more."

"How do you know?"

"I'll go to church and tell God that I won't have any more babies. I'll tell Him that I'm not His seed any more."

"But you still have to get out of here."

"I will, Mr. Horwitz. If I get to be like my mother, I'm going to stick my head in an oven."

"Is she sleeping with your brother?"

"I don't know. I don't know what she does. She's high as soon as the check comes on the first and the 16th. I try to feed her after that. I don't know how she lives. I only know she's my mother because we used to be on the same welfare budget. I want to get off the budget. Mr. Horwitz, that's what I want to do more than anything else in the world. I hate being on welfare. I know I can't prove it to you now, but that's what I want to do, and that's what I *will* do. I'm looking for someone to take care of my babies. If I find someone, I can go out and work like the other people I see on the street."

"But, in the meantime, you're in this damn building."

"On check day, I'll move. I'll take my check before the landlord cashes it. He always takes his rent money first. He always says I owe him money for extra days. Why does he need *more* money from me, if the money I get is only enough to feed me and my babies for 15 days? I'll move on check day. I'll run."

I watched Anna "run" from Apt. 4D to Apt. 3C.

How do you stop the institutionalized welfare slums, the slums that turn New York's classrooms into bedlam, the slums that turn [thousands of] children into potential criminals and their teachers into terrorized bureaucrats? How do you fight the institutionalized welfare slums frequently disguised as Broadway hotels? What do you do with welfare slums hidden in blocks of crumbling, hacked-up, emasculated apartment houses, when they are protected by the guilt and fear of the Department of Welfare? A few sacrificial blocks and separate houses have been fed to the bulldozers. But what do you do when the shiny, vertical replacements are almost immediately befouled by the same forces that poisoned the tenements? What do you do when the cancer of welfare slums spreads to nursing homes, turning them into charnel houses? What do you do with the welfare slums that breed schizophrenia in children faster than the slums of the 19th century bred tuberculosis? And what of the welfare slums that are burgeoning all over the American urban landscape?

7

The Battle of the Suburbs

NEWSWEEK

She was a pretty woman, brunette, thirtyish and discernibly nervous at the prospect of addressing even so small a crowd as the twenty-odd residents who assembled in the tiny American Legion clubhouse just outside the affluent Los Angeles suburb of Woodland Hills, Calif. The atmosphere was already emotionally charged and now, as the woman rose, the tension became almost palpable. But once she had risen, the words came easily— soft, steady and with no trace of a falter.

"As a housewife," said Mrs. Carleen Zawocki, "I do not fear low-income housing in our community. I'm not afraid of having black and poor people move in. I just don't see what's so frightening about this."

With that, the room seemed to explode with fury. Shouts and epithets rang out. Several persons had to be sternly reprimanded by the hearing officer after they had jumped up to hurl personal insults at the speaker. One woman shrilly accused Mrs. Zawocki of having brought her eight-month-old baby with her to the meeting solely to create sympathy for her stand.

This outburst set the tone. In tumultuous weeks that followed, few fam-

Source: *Newsweek,* "The Battle of the Suburbs," and "A Suburb That Struck a Truce," 15 November 1971, pp. 61–64, 69, 70. Condensed from *Newsweek.* Copyright Newsweek, 1971, reprinted by permission.

ilies in Woodland Hills were left unaffected. Cookouts and Kaffeeklatsches were transformed into acrid encounter sessions. Neighbor turned against neighbor. At one point, a young stockbroker offered a calm and candid summation of the position of those who, like himself, were fighting Mrs. Zawocki and her allies.

"Low-income housing," he said, "represents all of the problems I moved here to the San Fernando Valley to get away from. If we allowed it to be built, Woodland Hills could turn into a suburban slum. To be frank, I believe we should simply close the gates." And in the end, that is exactly what Woodland Hills did—but only by the narrowest of margins. The proposal to rezone the community to permit multiple-unit, low-income housing was defeated by the Los Angeles city council by a vote of 8 to 7. But to the proponents of open-door housing, this came as much less of a shock than the sheer emotionalism that the issue had precipitated in the first place.

"I just didn't expect people who are so much like myself to get so violent about this," Mrs. Zawocki recalls in troubled puzzlement. "But now I know that even these people can be terrible when they're afraid—and people here are afraid of any kind of poor people moving into the community."

None of the participants in Woodland Hills' drama stands alone. Each has his counterparts, thousands strong in hundreds of other town halls and zoning-commission chambers from one end of the nation to the other. Collectively, these ordinary U.S. citizens are the protagonists in what looms as the major domestic social and political battle of the decade ahead —a battle whose outcome will be of enormous importance in determining the structure of U.S. society for many years to come.

Urban experts call this confrontation "The Battle of the Suburbs," and already it has become the kind of close-to-home domestic war whose headlines regularly dwarf all others in local newspapers. No corner of the nation is unaffected by the strife. . . .

Like most of the other great domestic issues that have come to the fore in recent years, the battle of the suburbs is both cause and symptom of the tremendous force for change that seems to be at work today at virtually every level of U.S. society—a force that is simultaneously social, political, moral (particularly with respect to racial issues) and, above all, economic.

There is no lack of hard, statistical documentation for both the extent and the rate of change that is at work on U.S. suburbs. Now, for the first time in history, more Americans (a total of 76 million) live in the suburbs than either in the great urban enclaves (which are home to 59 million) or in the predominantly rural regions outside the metropolitan areas (total population: 71 million).

Nor is there any dispute among the experts as to the original cause of this phenomenon: it is the rapidly accelerating flight by the middle class from the decaying central cities, with their slums, their ghettos, their increasingly bereft and bewildered populations of the poor, the black and the elderly. But now this flight has been joined by a massive new exodus. For in city after city, hundreds of major corporations have packed up and moved their plants from urban to suburban addresses. This corporate migration has created a vast, new blue-collar job market in the suburbs—but one that is, for the moment, physically inaccessible to the urban blue-collar workers the corporations have left behind them. This is because the corporate émigrés have fled to communities where restrictive zoning laws ban the sort of federally subsidized housing that would permit the urban poor to settle near their old jobs. The New York City region provides a striking example. In the New York suburbs, it is estimated that 150,000 of the 750,000 new jobs created during the last decade were blue-collar jobs. But the number of blue-collar workers who found homes in the New York metropolitan area suburbs during the same period increased by only 50,000.

To the pessimists, who seem to outnumber the optimists by a substantial majority, one possible outcome of the cities vs. suburbs struggle has already been limned in lurid and frightening detail. Some, echoing the 1968 Kerner commission's report on civil disorders, see the fight developing for the most part along racial lines, with the central city of tomorrow looming as a kind of concentration camp for Negroes and other nonwhite minorities, while the white middle class guards the ramparts of suburbia, possibly with arms. "The great irony of current history," says New York University sociologist Richard Sennett, "may someday appear to be that this generation, seeking to avoid the disorder of city life, succeeded only in creating warring camps that had no way of communicating—other than through violence."

The pessimists may yet be proved right. Meanwhile such hope as can be said to exist seems to lie in the prospect that the struggle over the suburbs may unfold in such a way that the combatants will finally realize that it need not be fought to the bitter end. But before anything like that can be brought about, a number of myths remain to be dispelled and a number of new realities faced up to and accepted.

First on the list of the new realities is the proposition that most of the nation's suburbs simply aren't the suburbs any more. The older suburbs have grown so fast and so dynamically in recent years that most of them have long since become cities themselves. These are the areas that urban planners call "spread cities" or the "slurbs," and while some have deteriorated badly others are holding their own; a few, like Philadelphia's Wynnefield section, have actually reversed the trend to decay and set about resolutely trying to establish a community where white and black, poor and moderately affluent can live together in relative amity.

Partly for this reason, the older suburbs do not rank as a prime strategical objective in the battle of the suburbs. The real objective of the rather fluid coalition of white liberals, blacks and other social activists, moderate and radical alike, who are the vanguard in the fight for open housing, is farther away from the city. The goal is the suburbs whose defenders see them as a kind of second-defense perimeter around the cancer of the megalopolis. They are the more affluent suburbs of Chicago, New York, Los Angeles, St. Louis and other big cities—leafy enclaves with neatly manicured lawns and rigorously enforced zoning regulations that prohibit the construction of either small-plot (a quarter acre or less) single-family units or any multiple-unit housing at all. Federally subsidized low-income housing is generally taboo in these areas, and the emotional climate in many is such that newcomers who do not fit established economic and racial standards are about as welcome as Dutch elm disease. . . .

Like similar struggles, the battle of the suburbs has already produced its own particular version of the fog of war. One graphic demonstration of how subtly the propaganda machines are working still may be found on a campaign billboard in Jefferson Parish, La., currently the scene of a heated dispute over the construction of low- and middle-income housing. The billboard, erected by a slate of candidates, shows a typically American family in silhouette and reads: "Jefferson: It's the good life. Let's keep it that way."

At this level, there is no scant question that "keeping it that way" means maintaining suburbia's racial barriers. "The fear as always is that low-income housing means black people," says Celia Zager, chairman of the San Fernando Valley Fair Housing Council. Interestingly enough, however, the 1970 census figures on the over-all exodus from the cities offers at least some signs that racial barriers are slowly being chipped away in some parts of suburbia. These figures show that while the white population of the suburbs registered an increase of 29 per cent during the preceding decade, the nonwhite population of the suburbs rose by 37 per cent. Extrapolating from these figures, the experts estimate that some 200,000 blacks are leaving the city ghettos each year—not, to be sure, to settle in Grosse Pointe, Beverly Hills or Old Greenwich, but at least to travel the first stage of the long, difficult trek from the ruined central cities to the green and leafy expanses beyond.

There are also some further, faint signs that the racial issue may not in the long run prove as decisive as it looms at present. A growing body of evidence suggests that what is really at the heart of the struggle is income and class rather than color—and the fact is that some vigorous opposition to federally subsidized low-income housing in suburbia now comes from the black middle class itself. A dramatic demonstration of this attitude recently occurred in the New York City suburb of South Hempstead. There black homeowners bitterly challenged a proposal to erect a group of prefabricated ranch houses that were to be rented to tenants of a largely black, public-housing project in the city. In the face of the black homeowners' organized resistance, town officials finally abandoned the plan. "People who rent houses don't keep them up," one of the Negroes who fought the proposal explained to housing expert Joseph Fried. Then his gaze locked on a painting of Martin Luther King on his living-room wall. "Maybe what I'm saying would be contrary to what Dr. King would say," he added. "But this is my opinion."

For the moment, suburban opponents of low-income housing command an imposing arsenal of stratagems to help them keep the lower classes out. Thus besides raising the prices of developing land, many suburbs impose so-called "Cadillac requirements." For example, building codes may call for relatively expensive housing materials, thus barring cheaper, factory-produced units; or they may require the construction of costly sidewalks, water lines and sewers before a house or apartment can be built. But the ultimate weapon of the exclusionists is what the open-door forces call "snob zoning." These are ordinances that permit only single-family homes to be built—and then only on relatively large 1- or 2-acre plots; low-cost, multi-unit buildings are thereby effectively precluded.

In defense of these practices, suburban leaders argue accurately enough that even a modest influx of low-income families usually places an intolerable burden on already strained services. Certainly, as Fried demonstrates in his definitive book, "Housing Crisis U.S.A.," there is no denying that even federally subsidized low-cost housing rarely "pays its way" in suburbia. First, it fails notably to enlarge the property tax base; then, since low-cost housing is usually inhabited by families with more children than the norm, it invariably requires higher public expenditures for schools— an item that already composes the largest chunk of most communities' budgets. Another argument that resounds forcefully at most rezoning hearings is that exclusive zoning helps preserve a suburb's "quality of life"—in other words, that higher population densities invariably produce higher rates of crime, welfare and pollution.

For their part, the open-housing activists readily acknowledge that more low-income families invariably require more public services. The solution they propose is the equalization of property taxes throughout a county or state, with dozens of communities sharing the same tax-revenue pool to pay for their schools, police departments and recreational facilities. Thus a community with a tax base that could not support an influx of the poor would be sustained by neighboring communities with more solid tax bases and few low-income families. . . .

Another contention put forward by the zoning reformers is that the federally subsidized housing program—which currently accounts for more than a fourth of all housing units produced annually in the U.S.—is undergoing a radical transformation as it thrusts toward suburbia. The reformers say that the sterile, high-rise urban monsters that are the stereotype of such housing are being discarded now in favor of the low-density, "cluster" concept popularized by such new, planned communities as Reston, Va., and Columbia, Md. These low-income dwellings would resemble garden apartments and be built on open land along with more expensive homes—perhaps town houses and split-levels ringing a common, village-style green. "If the open land in the suburbs is made available to low-income housing, there is absolutely no reason why it can't be built for human needs and to human scale," says Paul Davidoff, co-director of the Suburban Action Institute, a nonprofit organization that is emerging as the most activist open-door champion.

Another development that the activists see as working in their favor is that while many suburban governments seem more than willing to rezone to accommodate relocating urban corporations and thus acquire additional tax revenues, they are balking at rezoning to permit the construction of housing for the firms' working-class employees. One of the most bitter engagements over this zoning double standard is unfolding in suburban Mahwah, N.J. (population: 10,440). Mahwah officials readily welcomed the Ford Motor Co. when it decided to relocate an assembly plant from Camden, N.J. But it next became apparent that only one in five of the plant's 5,000 employees could afford to live in predominantly middle-class Mahwah. At this point, protesting civil-rights groups found themselves joined by a somewhat unlikely ally—Local 906 of the United Auto Workers. The UAW's regional nonprofit housing corporation had planned to construct a low-income housing complex near the plant, a move that would require considerable loosening of the residential laws. Mahwah residents quickly sent up a roar of indignation. . . .

What . . . [Federal] officials see as the best long-term solution is gradually to create metropolis-wide housing agencies, composed of representatives from all the communities, that would choose the sites for future subsidized, low-cost units by majority vote. The suburbs thus selected would then receive Federal grants to help pay for the extra services required by their new, low-income residents. . . .

"It may look like we're passing the buck," admits one HUD hand, summing up what seems to be Washington's view of the battle of the suburbs, "but a system like this just might help get across the idea that the fates of the cities and the suburbs are basically intertwined."

A Suburb That Struck a Truce

There was a time, back in a crueler day, when the Wynnefield section of Philadelphia was known derisively as "Kike's Peak." But for the thousands of Jews who migrated there from the city's ghettos in the 1920s and '30s, a Wynnefield address was a sure sign of having arrived. Located just inside city limits, yet cut off from other neighborhoods by the main-line railroad tracks and Fairmont Park, Wynnefield had all the feel of a suburban fastness only fifteen minutes from downtown. Its houses ranged from substantial pillared dwellings set back on manicured lawns to well-kept row houses along streets lined with maples and sycamores. Its public schools turned out more children who ended up with doctorates than any other area in the city. And Wynnefield's Har Zion synagogue, with a Conservative congregation of 1,700 families, soon became one of the largest and most powerful in all the Delaware Valley. "Wynnefield was brand-new, clean, green, spacious and had status," says lawyer Stanton Kratzok who has lived in Wynnefield for 50 years. "It was a gilded ghetto without walls. It had a heterogeneous pocketbook but a homogeneous attitude— everybody felt middle-class."

Then in 1963 or 1964—no one is quite sure when—a house for sale in the heart of Wynnefield eluded the protective custody of local real-estate agents and went out on an open listing to brokers all over the city. The man who finally bought it was a retired Army colonel turned schoolteacher from West Philadelphia. He also turned out to be black.

At first, the reaction among Wynnefield whites was one of confusion and a vague feeling of alarm. Then, like cider turning sour, the community began to decay. Real-estate blockbusters moved in and spread fear with postcards warning homeowners to sell while they still had time. Blacks were hustled into cheaper housing in lower Wynnefield and For Sale signs sprouted like dandelions in the plusher environs of upper Wynnefield as well. Stores along 54th Street began boarding up their windows and moving out. Juvenile crime shot up.

And as a final blow, Wynnefield's most prized possession—its school system—deteriorated rapidly. Parents started fearing for their children's safety. "The whole character changed," complained one PTA activist who solved her family's problem by moving to another suburb. By 1970, the black incursion into Wynnefield had reached about 50 per cent, and many residents felt the complete turnover was only a matter of time.

But then, almost miraculously, or so it seemed, the tide began to turn. In the past year, even some of the For Sale signs have started coming down. Alarm was replaced first by caution, sometimes by optimism, and some whites are buying alongside blacks. And in the process of apparently holding the line, Wynnefield residents feel they have learned some bitter lessons that may serve other suburbs similarly besieged.

For one thing, the whites discovered soon after their initial fright that the real problem facing them was more one of class than of race. The first wave of newcomers, for instance, was largely made up of "Ebony readers," middle-class blacks as bourgeois in their attitudes toward education and appearances as the whites they replaced. "They considered Wynnefield as an escape from the jungles of West Philadelphia," says Kratzok, "just as the Jews found it a refuge in the 1920s." They were more than eager to join crusades to keep out bars, laundermats and the other potential hangouts for young people who might prove to be troublemakers. "You work all your life to come to a place like this," says George Howe, a 48-year-old black carpenter who works for the Philadelphia transit authority, "and you don't want the rough element around."

Some Wynnefield residents responded to this realization with alacrity. A Wynnefield Residents Association was formed to bring lawsuits against blockbusters and campaign for integration. The Jewish Community Relations Council held block meetings to encourage whites to stay put. "They were told they shouldn't leave unless something drastic happened," says Rabbi Henry Cohen of the Beth David synagogue. "And that the only thing drastic that could happen would be if they left."

Next, some of the whites discovered that they couldn't afford to move even if they wanted to. "My home is worth $25,000," says Martin Piltch, an executive for an electronics company and former president of WRA. "If you moved it four blocks over the city line, it would cost me $50,000." So homeowners dug in for the duration. "Now I don't feel tension among my friends," says Rabbi Cohen, whose congregation has taken to sponsoring bicultural Sunday school for black and Jewish children. "We have to do the whole bit—floodlights on the house, locks, alarm systems. Our wives don't walk out at night more than a couple of houses away. OK, there are certain things we accept. Big deal. Within this, we feel secure. We're not sacrificing anything; we're comfortable."

So far, perhaps the biggest threat to Wynnefield's stability has come from within its white ranks—specifically at the time two years ago when officials of the Har Zion synagogue started making noises about moving the whole congregation out of the community. "The oligarchy of the synagogue was made up of very practical business people," says sociologist Samuel Klausner of the University of Pennsylvania. "As they saw it, Wynnefield was going to be all-black, and they should simply reinvest elsewhere." To cover its tracks, however, Har Zion hired Klausner to make a study of the community, which the synagogue elders hoped would provide enough evidence of Jewish emigration to justify their evacuation. What they got, however, was hardly to their liking. Instead of offering up a rationale for flight, Klausner's study found that the Wynnefield area was not likely to become all-black in the foreseeable future. And even if more Jews did flee the community, Klausner concluded, they would all scatter to different suburbs, thus failing to provide Har Zion with a big enough congregation in any one town to justify a new temple.

After voting to reject Klausner's conclusions, Har Zion reluctantly decided to stay put—for the time being. Over at Beth David, however, a firm decision was made seven years ago. Not only did the Reform synagogue decide to stay in Wynnefield, but since then it has added to the congregation many Jews who live across the city line in Lower Merion. "Once you get across the city line, it's very easy for the wall to go up," says Rabbi Cohen. "There's a psychological value in having suburbanites maintain contact with integration and all the problems of take-over. Today, it's Wynnefield. Tomorrow it could be anywhere."

PART II

THE RURAL CRISIS

79

Introduction:
Poverty for Export

If you had to choose between being poor in the city and poor in the country, which would you prefer? If you chose the farm under the impression that there you would always have something to eat, or at least be able to enjoy the fresh air and the pretty scenery, you might be making a big mistake.

Picture this: a frame house of skimpy proportions, two stories high with a shaky, narrow porch along one side, built of second-hand lumber and covered with tar shingles pressed to look like yellow brick. It's on a dirt road pocked with ruts and stones—dust in August, a slough in March and a mad toboggan-slide in December; two cars cannot pass. It's more than a mile to the nearest paved road, and three miles more to the nearest general store and post office and school. The view is magnificent: a thousand feet below and miles away is a winding river lined with rich black farms where the land is as carefully utilized as it is in France. In the distance there are lavender hills, and in the winter moonlight, blue snow and black trees. Inside the kitchen door hangs the only light bulb in the whole house. Last year there was electricity for the first time in the area but there was only enough credit to wire the one room. You go to the "bathroom" and up to bed by candlelight, which makes for an atmosphere not of romance but of melancholy, and the mother of small children is ever on the alert for disaster. There is neither radio nor telephone. In the summertime the cooking is done on a kerosene stove that smokes and stinks if it is not carefully tended and expertly used; in the winter there is a kitchen range. If cash and credit are relatively adequate there is the luxury of coal, usually bought by the hundred-weight, which is more expensive than by the ton. And when things get really difficult the derelict barn gives a few more boards, and these are sawed up by hand.

The poor, both rural and urban, are forced to live constantly in extravagant debt: they must buy cheap shoes that wear out quickly, cheap foods that do not keep the body in top form, cheap tools that break and are inefficient, second-hand, broken down, wasteful cars that bad roads soon tear up completely. The result is exhaustion that permits no rest, no growth, and little joy at the bright vistas in the fertile valleys below. There is only weary dragging on from day to day, almost a guilt-sense of failure at such poverty in the midst of the nation's storied progress recorded in much expensive color in the shiny magazines each week.

Here there is no fieldstone pumphouse with cedar shingles snugly housing a plump tank of cold and sweet artesian water; there is only the shallow spring that drools the water through for half the year; when the trickle stops, water must be fetched in buckets down the road, starting in the summertime when all the fields in the valley below are being worked by men who cannot spend their time carting water in a bucket; they're out producing. Here the fields are full of wild flowers, with only patches cultivated for the sake of quaint, small fruit that makes one say, "Well, it's not worth it, cheaper to buy it in town."

At one time this land was cleared of trees and made to yield some fruit, support some families. Up the road there is still the heaped-up wreckage of a one-room schoolhouse that served a score of families until sometime between 1918 and 1939. Now the trees are growing back, along with untidy brambles and black-eyed Susans, thistles and grape vines that run wild. Little foxes scoot across the road, and the dog barks on the leash. The children stand in the mud near the postbox in their thin clothes waiting for the school bus moving carefully in the November weather. They do not come home again until it is almost dark.

There is no hot water in the house except for what can be heated on the stove in a bucket so, except in warm weather, there are mostly sponge baths in the kitchen. There is an outhouse, frigid in winter and alive with flies and stench and foraging rats in the summer, a sweatbox under the slow-moving sun. In winter the house is a cave of draughts because everything is fitted poorly.

Discouragement and fatigue and loss of vision line the face of rural poverty. It is difficult to see beyond the muddy dooryard in the grey morning, and the mood lasts all day. No one comes and no one goes. A longing sets in for a little escape from the water-stained walls and unmended furniture, the cracked saucer and the wrinkled housedress. The supreme objective becomes the capture of a moment of spice, covered with spangles and filled with bubbles; a jukebox, a movie, a glass of lemon and lime or a comic book for the children, a permanent wave—which are wasteful as the thrifty and virtuous know. And there is always alcohol.[1]

Now, to this burden of chronic poverty, illiteracy, bad health, and mental depression (plus racial discrimination if you happen to be black), add a last straw that is transforming agriculture from a way of life to a business and a science: a technological and economic revolution that means prosperity for a few but unemployment for many. Whereas fifty years ago one farmer grew enough food and fiber for ten people, nowadays he produces enough for himself and forty-five others. In the Deep South and Southwest, using chemical weed killers and tractor-drawn harvesting equipment, three men now operate a plantation that used to employ forty *families* of men, women, and children to hoe and pick the cotton and tobacco by hand. The owners of large-scale farming operations in California and the Midwest have also been busy displacing field hands with recently invented machines and chemicals. The brutal result is that most farmers are not really needed any more. Items:

> since 1940, more than 3 million farms have folded, and farms continue to fold at the rate of 2,000 a week
> the number of black farm operators fell from 272,541 in 1959 to 98,-000 in 1970
> 14 million rural Americans exist below a poverty income, with millions more clinging just on the edge of poverty
> 2.5 million substandard houses are occupied by rural families; that is 60 percent of the bad housing in America
> since 1940, 30 million people have left their rural homes for urban areas, and this migration continues at a rate of 800,000 a year
> entire rural communities are being abandoned
> independent, small-town businesses are closing at a rate of more than 16,000 a year
> more than 73 percent of the American people live now on less than two percent of the land [2]

Behind the Urban Crisis is a rural one that must be subdued before the core cities can begin to cope, since the amount of poverty available

---

[1] John Stanley, "Poverty on the Land," *The Commonweal,* 18 November 1955, pp. 162–63.

[2] Jim Hightower, *Hard Tomatoes, Hard Times* (Washington: Agribusiness Accountability Project, 1972), p. 4. Condensed and rearranged.

for export from rural areas is nearly unlimited. People who reside in metropolitan areas tend to associate poverty with black people in slum-ghettos, and indeed about one-third of the nation's blacks do live below the official poverty line, in contrast to only 10 percent of the whites, but, numerically, most of the nation's poverty-stricken are white and live either out in the countryside or in small towns.

Figuratively speaking, for over three decades the rural areas and small towns of America have been hemorrhaging. "Laissez-faire demography," one secretary of agriculture called it—a voluntary, unplanned population drift. But is this exodus really so voluntary and unplanned? And are the people who benefit from it really so innocent?

As usual, one's definition of the situation depends on one's personal perspective—a mixture of social position, vested interests, ideology, etc. Many of the rural migrants themselves feel that they have been pushed off the land not by an act of god—the god Technology—but instead by scheming landowners, corporations, and politicians, for whom the new machinery's capacity to displace people is its main attraction, rather than a regretted side effect. These suspicions have recently been supported by charges from a nonprofit, public-interest-minded research organization that a very powerful sponsor of the agricultural revolution is a "land-grant complex" resembling the "military-industrial complex" in the field of armaments production. According to its report, a complex of tax-supported organizations—schools of agriculture, experiment stations, and state extension services—devotes perhaps as much as $1 billion a year of public money to projects that work to the profit of large corporations involved in agriculture—at tremendous social cost—while practically ignoring the problems of small farmers, farm workers, and rural communities—let alone the needs and desires of consumers—with the result that hundreds of thousands of people are annually turned into "waste products" who dump themselves into the cities, creating the Urban Crisis.

> The land grant complex has been eager to work with farm machinery manufacturers and with well-capitalized farming operations to mechanize all agricultural labor, but it has accepted no responsibility for the farm laborer who is put out of work by the machine. The complex has worked hand in hand with seed companies to develop high-yield seed strains, but it has not noticed that rural America is yielding up practically all of its young people. The complex has been available day and night to help nonfarming corporations develop schemes of vertical integration, while offering independent, family farmers little more comfort than "adapt or die." The complex has devoted hours to create adequate water systems for fruit and vegetable processors and canners, but 30,000 rural communities still have no central water system for their people. The complex has tampered with the gene structure of tomatoes, strawberries, asparagus, and other foods to prepare them for the steel grasp of the me-

chanical harvestors, but it has sat still while the American food supply has been liberally laced with carcinogenic substances. . . .

In 1966, USDA [U.S. Dept. of Agriculture] and land grant spokesmen said: "It is generally agreed that it is neither socially desirable nor economically feasible to try to arrest or even slow down this trend [of a steadily declining farm population]." Who "generally agreed" on this? Did they check with the one million more farmers expected by USDA to fold between now and 1980? What about tens of thousands of small-town businessmen who will have to board up their stores as those farmers pull out? There would not likely be general agreement among the residents of the rural towns that will wither and die, nor by the millions of people who will be rural refugees in alien cities.

Yet, no one in a position of leadership questioned this basic assumption of land grant college policy. In the five years since that statement, half a million farms have gone out of business and some three to four million people have migrated from their rural homes. But the land grant college complex apparently does not perceive this as a crisis. If those four million people leaving rural America had been four million corn-borers entering rural America, the land grant community would have rung all alarms, scurried into the labs and rushed out with an emergency program to meet the "crisis." [3]

Some years ago, a rural crisis of a different sort did alarm the land-grant complex. As a result of the new efficiency of corporate farming, the United States produced more than even worldwide markets could absorb and, accordingly, prices fell. The Federal Government came to the rescue of the politically powerful big landowners with a system of subsidies and crop allotments. But for the thousands of small farmers and tenants already living in a marginal state, their assigned share of the allowed production was too small to maintain a family above an animal level of life. If a tenant lived on a plantation that "kept" five families, for instance, and the allotment cut production 20 percent, the landowner solved his problem by "letting" one of the families go. Allotments continued to be reduced to compensate for the increasing production that big landowners achieved by investing even more money in labor-saving (i.e., people-displacing) machinery and chemicals, and so still more families were "let go."

In brief, the government's farm program set in motion a vicious circle that only the rich could afford to ride. New machinery and chemicals were responsible for overproduction, which then required a system of allotments to which big farmers reacted by investing in more machinery and chemicals, which in turn aggravated the problem of overproduction, and around and around everybody went, except the small farmers and tenants who were soon squeezed out of the game.

[3] Ibid., pp. 8–10.

But isn't there a farm program to meet the needs of small farmers and tenants? There is, but it is administered locally by committees of large landowners who are biased in favor of their own upper class and white race. Theoretically, a small farmer may get a loan from the Farmers Home Administration, but he has to be certified as a good credit risk by a committee of three local farmers—an obstacle few blacks can hurdle. Moreover, the Extension Service of the U. S. Department of Agriculture generally fails to make the same effort to give its free advice to black farmers and their wives as it does to whites, such crucially important advice as which crops to grow and how to cultivate them (e.g., the advantage of switching from cotton and tobacco to vegetables), how to keep records, the fundamentals of nutrition, and how cash-crop farmers can help themselves by growing more of their own food.

In many parts of the rural South, most poor homes, black and white, have no vegetable gardens, partly because landowners have a vested interest in forcing workers and sharecroppers to buy at the company store; thus they insist that their people grow cotton and tobacco right up to the front door of their shack.[4]

As experiments in resolving group conflict have demonstrated, harmony and respect between groups depend largely on the extent to which the groups need each other in order to reach goals which neither can achieve without the other. By making it possible for white landowners to realize their goals without the help of black workers, the agricultural revolution has worsened race relations in the South. The civil rights movement, of course, has also contributed to the status of blacks as personae non gratae. Many white Southerners want to decrease the number of black residents before they learn to organize politically and become a major power bloc: "We don't get them out, we're going to have a colored boy for governor." Add to these hostile pressures the traditional "redneck" jealousy of any black person who starts to rise above poor whites, and one can understand why so many of the uprooted rural people who have reluctantly ended up in the middle of big cities feel that the South offered them no other choice but to leave.

During much of the time that unemployed black Southerners have been pouring into Northern cities looking for work, the South has enjoyed an industrial boom stimulated in large part by its success in luring industry out of some of those same Northern cities. However, because of racial discrimination practiced by labor unions as well as management, on top of the effects of discrimination previously practiced by the schools— approximately one-third of adult black Southerners are functionally illiterate—few of these new jobs have been accessible to black people pushed off the land.

[4] Roger Beardwood, "The Southern Roots of the Urban Crisis," *Fortune*, August 1968, p. 87.

Undoubtedly, the notorious difference between Southern and Northern welfare standards has pressured many of the unemployed into drifting north with the expectation that if the men can't find work the women and children, at least, will be taken care of by a relatively bounteous welfare system. However, many of the rural poor have been denied *any* public assistance at all by local officials, north and south, either too proud to admit that anybody in their county could be that poor, or ideologically opposed to antipoverty programs as "federal interference," or determined to force unwanted people into moving out. There is hypocrisy here: several hundred of the counties that have deliberately excluded their poor people from federal handouts have at the same time seen nothing shameful about distributing federal checks to *affluent* farmers who agree not to grow anything on a portion of their land.

There is irony, too, in a nation that, while rather ostentatiously giving away "surplus" food to foreigners in distress and taking steps to boost food prices by creating scarcity, discovers millions of hungry and malnourished people within its own borders. Six doctors who investigated the living conditions of rural blacks in Mississippi in 1967 reported that they had seen children who were "suffering from hunger and disease and directly or indirectly they are dying from them—which is exactly what 'starvation' means."

> We saw homes with children who are lucky to eat one meal a day —and that one inadequate so far as vitamins, minerals, or protein is concerned. We saw children who don't get to drink milk, don't get to eat fruit, green vegetables, or meat. They live on starches— grits, bread, Kool Aid. Their parents may be declared ineligible for commodities, ineligible for the food-stamp program, even though they have literally nothing. We saw children fed communally—that is, by neighbors who give scraps of food to children whose own parents have nothing to give them.[5]

The next year, a blue-ribbon citizens' panel published similarly appalling findings from its nationwide study. Although initially greeted by a chorus of disbelief, the discoveries of both groups have since been confirmed. Some of the evidence is in the incidence of nutritional diseases, such as goiter, scurvy, and rickets, widely assumed to have been eradicated decades ago. Many Americans were found to be resorting to eating laundry starch and clay to make their stomachs feel full. Alone among Western nations, the United States has cases of kwashiorkor, a disease caused by extreme protein deficiency, associated with Africa and Asia, as well as rates of parasitic infection ranking with Egypt and parts of Central America. In its rate of infant mortality the nation as a whole ranks 13th— behind most of Europe and Japan—and some parts of the country rate

[5] Citizens' Board of Inquiry into Hunger and Malnutrition in the United States, *Hunger, U.S.A.* (Boston: Beacon, 1968), p. 13.

no better than most of Asia. A cycle of malnutrition-induced brain damage may partially explain the life history of families trapped for several generations in "permanent poverty," because conclusive evidence—ending a long dispute among scientists—has finally been found linking serious malnutrition during pregnancy and infancy with irreversible mental retardation.

Close examination of the Rural Crisis behind the urban one reveals that none of its component social problems are new; they include poverty, illiteracy, bad health, racial conflict, and economic and political exploitation by what might be called "corporate colonialism"; and they have been brought to a crisis stage by the social effects of a new phase of the continuing agricultural revolution. If rural migrants are considered ill-equipped for urban life and cities equally unready to cope with them, the nation might better be served by giving the Rural Crisis a higher priority than even the cities' woes. This might involve, for example, putting the preservation of family farming as a way of life ahead of public assistance to corporate agribusiness; land distribution via long-term, low interest loans; crop diversification; job retraining; or perhaps a social reform movement like the "folk school" movement that began rejuvenating rural life in Denmark a hundred years ago. A start on such a movement might be made by community health centers like the one pioneered in the Mississippi Delta by Dr. H. Jack Geiger, sponsored by Tufts University but funded by a federal antipoverty agency, to combat parasites and malnutrition by teaching not only proper sanitation and nutrition but also how poor people can compete successfully with corporations by farming cooperatively.

When it comes to the question of how to develop rural areas while at the same time preserving the values of family farming and small town life, an "underdeveloped" nation like the United States might do well to take a few lessons from the Chinese island of Taiwan (i.e., Formosa). Taiwan chose not to follow the conventional road to development, that is, concentrating on industrialization with the expectation that while an urban elite was being enriched benefits would trickle down to the rural poor who form the majority of the population. Instead, Taiwanese officials invested American aid in (1) land reform: breaking up large landholdings and redistributing land to the peasants; (2) a system of cooperatives to provide the credit and marketing facilities formerly supplied by landlords; (3) rural elementary schools, rather than secondary and higher education for a relative handful of managers and technicians; (4) the training of paramedics to work at raising health standards in rural areas; and (5) labor-intensive projects, i.e., those employing large numbers of people rather than machines. Primarily as a result of these value priorities, during the past two decades, the island's economy has been growing at a rate of 10 percent per year, the income level of the poorest fifth of the population has risen over 200 percent, and the average small farmer's real income has more than trebled. The literacy rate has been raised to 85 percent and life expectancy to 68 years, while the birth rate has been lowered to 2.2 percent and unemployment reduced to 4 percent.

No one doubts our capacity to bring all our rural areas up to Taiwanese standards; the question is, Do we want to?

Several aspects of the Rural Crisis are illustrated by the case studies that follow. A sample of the appalling evidence that hunger and malnutrition and ignorance are prevalent in many rural pockets of this nation is provided by "Let Us Now Praise Dr. Gatch." The living conditions of migrant farm workers, who move with the season and are "always goin' someplace, but . . . never get noplace," are described in "Slaves for Rent." To further explain the exodus from the rural South, "The Black Immigrants" suggests what kinds of personal situations precipitate the fateful decision to move.

An example of how corporate exploitation of people and their land may be a major cause of rural troubles is provided by Harry Caudill's comparison between eastern Kentucky and Switzerland. Eastern Kentucky is but a small part of a huge patch of mountains and concentrated rural misery called Appalachia, stretching from a corner of Mississippi to a corner of Maine and taking in parts of fifteen states, where more than one-third of the population in some counties is chronically unemployed, three-fourths of the children drop out of school before completing the twelfth grade, and high rates of tuberculosis, silicosis, and infant mortality are endemic. Typical signs of these conditions are visible at its northern end, off the tourist routes in Maine: decaying old mill towns straddling heavily polluted rivers, hundreds of trailer homes and thousands of tin-roofed, tar-paper shacks with rusting car hulks out back, and, in the worst-hit county, a quarter of the people existing on the dole and 60 percent living in "substandard" housing. Appalachia is now raising its third generation on welfare. Why has an affluent and idealistic society allowed such living conditions to persist so long? Maybe because our national integrity is compromised by a conflict of interests, as Peter Schrag suggests:

> The vested Appalachian interests in the status quo—coal companies, railroads, banks, local bar associations, insurance agencies, politicians—are so vast that they represent a fair cross section of American society itself. Their stockholders and beneficiaries live all over the nation; they help sustain our affluence. If Appalachia hasn't changed, it may be in part because too many are dependent on it as it now is.[6]

A fifth article features an agribusiness executive and an oil corporation's farming subsidiary as examples of the latest developments in the century-old economic and technological revolution that are primarily responsible for old rural complaints escalating into a crisis.

The last of this series of case studies, Peter Schrag's close inspec-

[6] Peter Schrag, "Appalachia: Again the Forgotten Land," *Saturday Review,* 27 January 1968, p. 18.

tion of the warts on Mason City, Iowa, may act as both a foil for contrasting the troubles of big and little cities and as an example of how the depopulation of rural areas spells economic stagnation for small towns that have traditionally served farmers as shopping and service centers, consequently driving a few more million people, especially the youth, to seek their fortunes in a metropolis.

8

Let Us Now
Praise Dr. Gatch

BYNUM SHAW

Almost ten years ago the telephone rang in the office of a young doctor
who had just set up practice in the small coastal community of Bluffton
(pop. 356), near Beaufort, South Carolina. The call was a plea for help:
on Daufuskie Island, a remote Gullah settlement accessible only by boat
an old woman lay in unconscious limbo. Her family could not tell whether
she was dead or alive.

Dr. Donald E. Gatch, then not yet thirty, slipped a flashlight into his
medical bag and set out on his errand without a second thought. There was
no money on Daufuskie, but there was need. He paid $20 for the thirty-
mile round-trip ride, and from a public landing he hiked to a sea-weath-
ered shanty where the old Negress lay on a rude bed. There was no light
in the house, and when Gatch called the patient's name there was no response. Automatically, he took up her wrist to check for pulse. As he
lifted her arm the skin came away in his hand.

"I knew she was not dead," he recalls. "The skin felt alive in my fingers." He reached in his bag, took out the flashlight and played its beam

Source: Bynum Shaw, "Let Us Now Praise Dr. Gatch," *Esquire Magazine* (June
1968). First published in *Esquire Magazine.* © 1968 by Esquire, Inc. Reprinted by
permission of the author and the author's agents, Scott Meredith Literary Agency,
Inc., 580 Fifth Avenue, New York, New York 10036.

on the bed. As a general practitioner he was already hardened to the sight of the many forms of disease, but in this case, as his eyes adjusted to the spray of light, he could not repress a shocked gasp. "Her arms, her legs— her entire body was full of maggots. Medical books don't cover that condition, not the complete infestation of the body. How do you treat maggots?"

The patient died, and Dr. Gatch believed then and he believes now that although the immediate cause of death might have been listed as some "acceptable" disease like pneumonia, the real cause of death was plain hunger. That pathetic case made a profound impression on the young doctor, and in the intervening decade he has been seeking out and doing battle with the hunger and parasites of Beaufort County. In the war thus far, the worms have been winning.

It has been, of course, a war in which there have been few allies, for it has been waged on the level of the dirt-poor outcasts of the Great Society. Beaufort County, ideally located and wonderfully warmed, has been striving with considerable success to build a tourist trade. It has a rich patina of history and is mightily endowed with the mossy legacy of the plantation South. Talk of intestinal parasites tends to blight the charm of live oaks, cypress knees, wisteria and sailing regattas. But the *Ascaris lumbricoides* (roundworm) and *Trichuris trichiura* (whipworm) are there, along with the *Tillandsia usneoides* (Spanish moss).

Dr. Gatch established that, beyond doubt, six years ago. With a team of doctors from the Public Health Service's National Institute of Allergy and Infectious Diseases at Columbia, S.C., he conducted stool tests of two hundred twelve residents mainly along Goethe (pronounced goatie) Lane in Bluffton. The findings . . . showed that 7.8 percent had one or more species of worms. More than eighty percent of children under five were infected. Those figures, comparable to rates found in Columbia, Egypt, South Africa and the Cook Islands, suggested to the researchers that tidewater South Carolina might "represent one of the areas of highest endemicity for the continental United States." Health authorities in Beaufort County accepted the study as valid, deplored the condition aloud and for the most part went on about their business.

Only Gatch kept talking and agitating and relating worms to malnutrition. Gatch is not the ordinary member of the medical profession; he abhors the fraternal society; not a Southerner, he regards even the poor or illegitimate Negro as a human being; he reads books and listens to music of every beat; and gradually he came to be regarded as a medical troublemaker, tolerable only as long as his voice echoed meaninglessly across the forsaken rice paddies that encircle Bluffton. . . .

On a day after a rare January freeze he stopped on a dismal lane near Bluffton and pointed to a backlot shanty shivering in the wind. "Woman lives there with five children," he said. "All illegitimate. All got worms."

He walked through the field to the shack. Two boys, three or four years old, sat listlessly on the decaying log step. He patted them on the head and a spindle-legged woman came to the open door. Behind her wood burned in a rusting, thin-gauge stove that was used for both heating and cooking. Gatch pointed to her legs, so bent that she was pygmied. "Rickets," he said. He turned to the woman and asked, "What'd you give these kids for breakfast?"

"I give 'em grits."

"What you gonna give 'em for lunch?"

"I doan know."

"For supper?"

"I doan know."

"You got anything to eat in the house?"

"No, suh."

In an alcove a month-old baby lay under a tattered blanket on a broken bed. The walls were papered with the sports section of the Savannah *Morning News,* and torn cardboard sagged over the broken panes of the only window. The baby pulled at a soiled bottle filled with blue milk. "Where'd that milk come from?" Gatch asked.

"Dat baby's daddy, he take care a him."

"Who takes care of the others?"

"Doan nobody."

"You get any welfare?"

"No, suh."

Gatch turned to leave. "Dammit, dammit, dammit," he said. "You see, they are punishing illegitimacy. This woman has illegitimate children, so she is denied help. You see who they're punishing? Those boys." He stopped over one of the children and pulled up a torn shirt to expose a bloated belly. "That's worms," he said. "These boys ever pass worms?"

The woman nodded dejectedly. "Dey did when you give 'em dat medicine."

"You got a privy?"

"No."

"Where you go?"

"Nex' doah."

"All the time?"

"No."

"You go to the woods, don't you?"

The woman nodded.

Gatch started back to the car. "That's one of the problems," he said. "Sanitation. To get the worms is easy, but the kids get reinfected immediately. It takes two years, with treatment every three months. That way the eggs die in the soil. People say to me, 'Your patients got worms? Why don't you treat them?' Well, I'm one man. What we need in here is a whole task force, with time and equipment and money. And people say, 'Worms? What's so bad about that? Everybody has worms, one time or another.' Sure they do. Treated, worms are no problem. White kids, kids in families with just a little money, get treatment. The kids I'm talking about don't get treated. Or the adults. And nobody knows how many there are, and nobody's trying to find out."

He got in the car and started the motor. His horn-rimmed glasses had slipped down on his nose, and he reached to straighten them. The earpiece was gone. "I got to get over to Savannah some day and get that fixed," he said. "Let me tell you about that woman there. One Monday she brought her nine-year-old daughter to my office. Same legs like that. A dwarf. The kid's appendix had been ruptured for two days. We took her over to Beaufort Memorial, and when we were doing the appendectomy we found some roundworms. The surgeon said, 'Of course, in these colored children the closer we get to the ilium in the stomach the more worms we'll find, because these kids don't have much to eat.' And that's where they head. *The worms get the food before the kids do.*"

On the way to another stop Gatch told about a woman who had brought her baby to his office with symptoms of asthma. "It *was* a kind of asthma, an allergy. It was caused by worms migrating through the lungs. When the worms were eliminated the asthma cleared up. It's related to all kinds of things: pneumonia, anemia. I get kids in my office with a hemoglobin count of six to eight. Normal's twelve to sixteen. Most places you'd put a kid like that in the hospital. I just give 'em some iron. I haven't lost one of 'em yet."

Asked whether he had ever attempted to get a foundation grant for research, Gatch replied, "I've tried them all. National Institutes of Health. Big foundations. Most of them think giving money to a small country doctor is throwing it away. They either want to work it through a university, or they want you to be in Africa. If I were in Africa, I could get plenty of money. But this isn't Africa."

He stopped the car again in front of a shack which had broken in the middle. The center was resting on the ground. Over the window crude wooden shutters had been nailed to keep out the cold. An old woman answered Gatch's knock and set the door aside. It had not known hinges for a long time. Inside, the house was dark. Light of any kind was too expensive. Except daylight, which was too cold. The floor on both sides of the house rolled uphill on an angle, and in the close air there was a sickening smell of urine and feces. In one dark room an old woman lay bedridden, completely crippled by arthritis.

"How are you?" Gatch asked.

"Can't complain," she groaned.

"What'd you have for breakfast?"

"Liddle bit a grits 'n' peas."

"What you gonna have for lunch?"

"Grits 'n' peas."

"You get welfare?"

"Yes, suh!"

"How much?"

"I doan know."

"She really doesn't know," Gatch explained. "Somebody else has to cash her check for her. That's another one of the problems down here. Illiteracy. People don't know how to get help, whether they're entitled to it, how to apply for it. If we could just start something for the bottom one percent." Beaufort County has a population approaching 58,000, of which around 22,000 are Negroes. At most, Gatch thus is projecting a total rehabilitation program which would involve no more than six hundred people. "Just for a change, let's start at the bottom and work up," he said. "If we could start something here, some pilot endeavor, we might by extension assist the entire South. And not just the South. These are not isolated conditions. In some degree, they exist all over the country."

The old arthritic woman turned his thoughts to drugs. "We're doing ourselves a great disservice in this country in our attitude toward some of the psychedelic drugs. LSD. Marijuana. I'm not talking about kicks, now. I mean ethical medicine. No telling what we might be able to accomplish in psychiatry or cancer with some of these things. Even aphrodisiacs are important medically. There's one drug—it's psychedelic—which can be bought for about a dollar a gallon. It's a great pain-killer, and it's ingested through the skin. With a gallon of that stuff that old woman back there could swab herself every day. She'd be a lot more comfortable and a lot happier. But it would be against the law for her to have it. The medicine she can have costs her $15 a month, and she can't afford it. That's crazy."

At another stop at a rotting, drafty hovel like so many others around Bluffton, a teen-aged girl had stayed home from school to care for eight younger brothers and sisters. "Some of these kids should be in school," Gatch said, "but they don't have proper clothing. At night they pile four or five of 'em in a bed. Or sleep them on the floor." He stamped on the floor, and the dust flew.

"Where's your mother?" Gatch asked the girl.

"She at wuk."

"Where she work?"

"At the factory."

Gatch explained. "The woman is an oyster shucker. In a good week, in season, she'll make $15. Not much to take care of all these kids."

Asked how the family would survive, the doctor said, "Some of these kids won't. They'll die. Of pneumonia. Something like that. If they had decent food and decent shelter they wouldn't get pneumonia. And that's what I mean when I say people down here are starving to death. Only the hardiest survive. The statistics call me a liar. 'Not a single case of starvation.' I call the statistics a liar."

He spoke to the girl again. "You got an inside bathroom?"

"No."

"A privy?"

"No."

"Running water?"

"No."

"Electricity?"

"No."

Gatch spoke another aside. "They don't all have two cars and a television set, but that's the popular belief."

On one such excursion through the wormlands, Gatch picked up an unexpected convert. Wilton Graves, a fifty-two-year-old Hilton Head Island motel operator who has represented Beaufort County in the State Legislature for fourteen years, was one of the few members of the power structure willing to be shown. A tough businessman who came up through the ranks of poverty himself, Graves was a skeptic. But he had one priceless asset: an open mind. After a trip through the Gatch nightmare, he was visibly shaken.

"I thought I knew what poverty was," he said, "but I never saw anything like this. I honestly did not know conditions like these existed in Beaufort County."

Graves asked school officials to develop information on the bedrock poor. Mrs. Vallie Connor, who works with the federal school-aid program, came up with some shocking findings. She talked to principals whose food resources were so meager that they could provide free lunches only on alternate days. On one day half the hungry ate; the next day the other half had their turn.

Further evidence of hunger was supplied by John Gadson, a bright young Negro educator who testified that on many occasions he had had to take Negro high-school students home because their stomachs ached from lack of food. (The Negro school dropout rate is eighty percent.)

Graves persuaded Senator James M. Waddell Jr., and Representative W. Brantley Harvey Jr., the other members of the Beaufort legislative delegation, to provide the leadership needed for a study of county poverty. "There are no votes in this," Graves said, "but somebody has to take a stand."

"Well, I've been in the Legislature long enough," Waddell said.

Graves's team then offered to do what no white authority in Beaufort County had yet dared to undertake: to meet with the leaders of G.R.I.P., the Negro organization, and to look at anything the Negroes wanted to show.

The tour, although covering a wider area than Gatch's beat, confirmed his allegations. An old woman on Wassau Island lived in a hut, without income of any kind. She knew nothing of welfare or Social Security benefits. In the Burton section a family of eight subsisted on $44 a month; in a tumbling shack nearby a family of fifteen fought a constant battle with starvation. In the Dale community there were fifteen children in one house, representing several generations; the family's total income: $40 a week.

After the inspection, Senator Waddell said publicly that "there is no doubt that there are cases of dire poverty, bad housing, lack of proper sanitary facilities and good water supplies in the county." Gatch had broken through the wall of complacency, because no other official agency in Beaufort County had been willing to go quite that far.

In a concurrent development, the Penn Community Services, a highly respected century-old private social agency at Frogmore, near Beaufort, presented to the County Health Department a parasite study which substantially confirmed Gatch's assertions regarding infection. With the help of Lieutenant Mack Bonner, a Marine Corps doctor at Parris Island, Penn ran stool tests on fifty-five preschool children in Big Estate and Pritchardville, at opposite ends of Beaufort County. Of the children tested, thirty, or 54.5 percent, showed "a high intensity" of roundworm and whipworms.

Penn said that because its study was conducted in haste, it had found no conclusive evidence of gross malnutrition, but in a warning note it set words to Gatch's ten-year-old refrain:

"The seriousness of worm infection," Penn said, "is not always realized. Members of the County Board of Health without medical training should understand what takes place in the process of becoming infected with worms. The eggs are taken into the body through the mouth. They go to the stomach, where they enter the circulatory system as if they were food. Eventually the eggs end up in the lungs, where they are incubated. While these eggs are developing in the lungs there is a danger of pneumonia. As the developing worms grow, they cause irritation and are usually coughed up and are then swallowed to return to the stomach. There they grow and thrive on the food which would otherwise be used by the body. This causes nutritional problems, loss of weight, listlessness and even bowel restriction. If left to thrive in a person's body, worms can cause death."

The Penn report, which placed highest priority on eradication of parasite infection, did not receive enthusiastic endorsement at the Health Department. On the day it was issued, the department asserted stubbornly that "illegitimacy and poor housing are our greatest health problems." Without question, they are serious problems in Beaufort, and neither Gatch nor G.R.I.P. denies it. In January the Health Department had sixteen Negro mothers under prenatal care. Of the sixteen, ten were unwed.

One of the married mothers was having her fifteenth child; the concept of birth control is almost impossible to spread, because illiteracy (forty-six percent of Beaufort's Negroes over 25 are "functionally illiterate") and superstition combine to prevent its acceptance. The uneducated poor suspect that birth-control pills cause cancer, and that intrauterine rings are dangerous.

It is hinted that Gatch opposes birth control. "It's a damned lie," he retorted. "I was the first doctor in Beaufort County to insert intrauterine rings, and some of my colleagues removed them under the mistaken supposition that the rings cause changes that might lead to cancer."

Although the case for Gatch is building up, the effort to destroy him not only as a doctor but also as a man persists. When his charges began to appear supportable, a cruelly scurrilous whisper campaign began. It was suggested behind the hand that Gatch was a moral degenerate who has no right to speak for ethical medicine. The smirking reference is to an incident of three years ago when Dr. Gatch was arrested and lodged in jail on a charge of sodomy. It made a big splash in the Beaufort area papers. It made no splash at all, however, when Gatch insisted on a speedy trial and when the complaining witness, a teen-aged boy, could give no coherent evidence on the witness stand. The charge against Gatch was thrown out of court, and the doctor has in his possession an affidavit from the complainant admitting that the charge was fabricated.

The real case against Gatch is that he is a loner who speaks his mind. He does not radiate the accepted image of the doctor. To the company of his colleagues he prefers the company of Savannah nonprofessionals, and in Beaufort his social life has been constricted to a circle of Negro friends. That relationship, however, has given him a keen insight into black thought and, as a philosophical question, race relations concern him.

"The white people here—and for that matter all over the country—do not realize how deeply resentful the Negroes are. The young ones leave home and go North. They may prosper, but they can't forget how underprivileged and oppressed their people back home are. Their resentment is expressed in contempt for all whites, and there is enough of that resentment to breed revolution. The whites just don't understand that."

Over a beer one evening when the strain in Beaufort was at its worst, Gatch tried to summarize what his thirty-eight years had taught him. When the words came he spoke not as a man of medicine but as a student of philosophy, for what he said concerned eternal verity. "I used to think truth was like a flash of lightning. You couldn't mistake it." He took a sip of beer and packed his pipe with his favorite tobacco, H. Sutliff's Mixture No. 79. "I don't believe that anymore. Truth is like a hippopotamus. You've got to keep prodding it, or it won't move."

Gatch is still prodding the hippopotamus. And he won't shut up.

9

Slaves
for Rent

TRUMAN MOORE

Each year when the harvest begins, thousands of buses haul thousands of crews to fields across America as millions of migrant workers hit the road. They ride in flatbed trucks or old condemned school buses patched together for just one more season. They go by car: Hudson bombers with engines knocking, laying a smoke screen of oil; pre-war Fords packed with bags, bundles, pots and pans, children crying. They go in pickups made into mobile tents—a home for the season. They ride the rods of the "friendly" Southern Pacific.

They come from farms in the Black Belt, from closed mines in the mountains of Kentucky and West Virginia, from wherever men are desperate for work. They come by whatever means they can find. These are the migrants—the gasoline gypsies, the rubber tramps—crossing and recrossing America, scouring the countryside in a land where the season never ends. There's always a harvest somewhere.

From Florida to Oregon the fruit tramp pursues the orchards. From Texas to Michigan the berry migrants work from field to field. Two mil-

Source: Truman Moore, "Slaves for Rent," *Atlantic Monthly* (May 1965). Reprinted by permission of the author. Condensed from the article "Slaves for Rent," published in the Atlantic Monthly, May 1965. Copyright © 1965, by Truman Moore.

lion men, women, and children invade every state of the Union to pick fruit, to chop cotton, to scrap beans, to top onions, to bunch carrots, to pull corn, to fill their hampers with the richest harvest earth ever yielded to man.

Across America there are tens of thousands of migrant camps. They are in the valleys and in the fields, on the edges of cities and towns. Some are half deserted. Some are behind barbed wire and even patrolled by armed guards. Migrant camps are within commuting distance of Times Square, under the vapor trails of Cape Kennedy, and surrounded by missile sites in the Southwest. They have names like Tin Top, Tin Town, Black Cat Row, Cardboard City, Mexico City, The Bottoms, Osceola (for whites), Okeechobee (for blacks), and Griffings Path.

Let us look at a typical migrant camp which we will call Shacktown. Shacktown is owned by a corporate farm, one of whose foremen is in charge of the camp. "But mostly," he says, "we just turn it over to the people to run for themselves." In other words, no one collects garbage or maintains the camp in any way. The camp is built on the grower's sprawling farm. It cannot be reached without trespassing, and several signs along the road remind the visitor of this fact. Even finding it is difficult. Local residents are suspicious of outsiders who are interested in migrant camps. Requests for directions are met with icy stares.

Shacktown was built about fifteen years ago. No repairs to speak of have been made since then. Most of the screen doors are gone. The floors sag. The roofs leak. The Johnsons, a Shacktown family, have a six-month-old baby and five older children. "When it rains," says Mr. Johnson, "it leaks on our bed and all over the room. At night when it rains, we have to stand up with the baby so he don't get wet and catch pneumonia."

All the rooms in Shacktown are the same size, eight feet by sixteen. When the Johnsons moved in, they found they needed much more space. They sawed through the wall, a single thickness of one by six inch pine, and made a door to the next cabin, which was not occupied. The exterior walls are unpainted and uninsulated. They keep out neither wind nor rain, sight nor sound. Cracks between the boards are big enough to put your hand through. There is no privacy, and the Johnsons, like most Shacktown families, have learned to live without it. The windows are simple cutouts with a hatch propped open from the bottom. Some have a piece of cloth-like screening tacked on.

The only touch of the twentieth century in the Johnsons' cabin is a drop cord that hangs down from the ceiling. It burns a single light bulb, plays a small worn radio, and when it works, an ancient television set that Mr. Johnson bought for ten dollars, through which they get their only glimpse of urban, affluent America.

Although there are trees nearby, the camp is built on a barren red-clay hill, baked by a blazing summer sun. There are four barrack-type frame buildings, divided into single rooms. Behind the barracks are two privies, both four-seaters. The door to the women's privy is missing, but the rank growth of weeds serves as a screen. There are no lights, and no one uses the toilets after dark. The Johnsons use a slop jar at night. It is kept in the kitchen and used for garbage, too.

There is virtually no hope of keeping out the flies that swarm around the privies. But one county health inspector found an unusual way of getting the growers interested in the problem. The inspector would drop by the grower's house just before lunch and ask to see the migrant camp. When they came to the privy, the inspector would throw a handful of flour over the seats, which invariably swarmed with flies. On the way back to the house, the inspector would manage to get invited to stay for lunch. At the table he would remark, "Well, I'm sure glad you asked us all to lunch." And there crawling around on the fried chicken would be a floured, white-backed privy fly.

During most of the season in Shacktown there will be several full- or part-time whores. The going price is $3.00. Prostitution thrives behind open doors. Venereal diseases are sometimes epidemic.

There are two hasps on the Johnsons' door in Shacktown. One is for the family to use. The other is for the grower. If the rent is not paid, the family will find when they return from the field that they have been locked out.

The Johnsons, like most Shacktown families, do their own cooking. But grocery shopping is not easy. There is a small cracker-barrel store near the camp, run by the grower, but the prices are a third higher than in town. "We got a ten-cent raise," says Mr. Johnson, "and everything in the store went up a quarter. He wants us to buy from him or move out. It don't seem right."

Cooking is done on a small, open-flame, unvented kerosene stove which serves as a heater in the cold weather. Fires and explosions are not uncommon. The cabins are not wired for electric heaters; natural gas is not available. Bottled gas requires a deposit and an installation fee. Asked if the tenants didn't suffer from the cold nights, the camp manager replied, "Oh, heat's no problem. You'd be surprised how hot it gets in one of them little cabins with so many people."

For most of the year the cabins are miserably hot. Refrigeration is nonexistent, and perishable foods seldom find their way to the migrant's table. The baby's milk sours quickly, and he is given warm Coke. Good water is always scarce in Shacktown. Between the long buildings there is a single cold-water tap. The faucet leaks, and there is no drainage. A small pond has developed, and the faucet is reached by a footbridge made of boards propped on rocks. This is the only water in camp.

Just keeping clean is a struggle. Water must be carried in from the spigot, heated over the kerosene stove, and poured into the washtub. In the evening, the oldest children are sent out with buckets to stand in line for water. Sometimes when the line is too long, the Johnsons buy their water from a water dealer, who sells it by the bucket. "We get some of our water down the road about five miles," says Mrs. Johnson. "Sometimes I get so tired I'd just like to go in and die. We have to boil the water and then take it to the tub to wash the clothes. We have to boil water for washing dishes. The last camp we was in had a shower, but you had to stand in line for it half a day, especially in the summer."

The Children of Harvest

The man put down his hamper. "It sure looks like rain," he said. The skies were a bright crystal blue, with only a trace of clouds to the east. The crew kept working, but a few looked up and saw the three men coming down the row. One was the grower, who seldom came around. The other was the crew leader. The third man was a stranger. He carried a brown leather case and a clipboard. The men just nodded as they passed.

They went up and down the rows, the first two walking easily. The third man, the stranger, stumbled now and then—a city man used to flat sidewalks. They crossed the red-clay road and went into the south field. A woman looked up as they came past the stacks of empty crates. Before they were close enough to hear, she turned to the busy crew. "Sure looks like rain." Two small pickers dropped their boxes and darted through the vines and ran into the woods. Someone on the next row passed the word. "Sure looks like rain." Two more children ducked into the vines and ran.

The children hid beyond the road in a small clearing in a clump of scrub oaks. From here they could see the man leave. It was their favorite game. Hiding from the inspector was about the only thing that broke up the long hours in the field. In the camp they played hide and seek this way. When you were "it" you were the inspector. But it was more fun when there was a real inspector.

Luis at twelve was the oldest of the children. He had been to school off and on since he was six, but he was only in the fourth grade. If he ever went back he would be in the fifth grade, because he was older and bigger now. But Luis didn't want to go back. He wanted to run away. He had been around the country a lot. Last year his family went to California and Oregon. One year they went to Arkansas. Once long ago—he was too young to remember when—his father took them to Florida for the winter citrus harvest. Luis was an ageless child. He had a way of taking a deep weary drag on a cigarette, and after a long while letting the smoke curve slowly out of his nostrils. His face was wrinkled, marked with a tiny network of fragile lines at the corners of his eyes and deeper lines across his forehead.

Still a child, he liked to play games. He enjoyed the gaiety at the Christmas feast. But at the end of the working day, he would stand stooped over slightly with his hands stuck flat into his back pockets. From behind he looked like a dwarf, a tiny old man whose bones had dried up and warped with age.

Billy was the youngest of the children. He was not quite five but old enough to do a little work. He didn't earn much, but it was better, his father said, than having him sit around the day-care center costing them $.75 every single day. His mother kept the money he earned in a mason jar. When fall came, he'd get a pair of shoes if there was enough money. He could start school, if there was one nearby, in new shoes.

His brother lay beside him in the clearing. John was ten. In the years that separated Billy and John, a brother and sister had died, unnamed, a day after birth. John kept them alive in his imagination. There were few playmates in the camps and fields that he ever got to know.

"I got two brothers and a sister," he would say. "And they's all in heaven but Billy there."

Robert was almost as old as Luis. He had been on the season for two years. His father came from the sawmill one day and said, "They don't need me any more. They hired a machine." His father had tried to make a joke of it, but late at night Robert could hear his mother crying. He knew it wasn't a joke about the machine being hired. They sold their house and packed everything into the car. Robert left school, and now they lived in one camp after another. Sometimes they slept in the car.

The man with the clipboard left. The children came out of the bushes, picked up their boxes. They bent over in silence and began to pluck at the vines. These are the children of harvest. "The kids that don't count" they are sometimes called. "The here-today-gone-tomorrow kids." . . .

The migrant child may never develop any idea of home. His family is never in any place long enough, and home to him is wherever he happens to be. He seldom sees a doctor. It is almost certain that he will have pinworms and diarrhea. Other common ailments untreated are contagious skin infections, acute febrile tonsillitis, asthma, iron deficiency anemia, and disabling physical handicaps. A poor diet condemns the child from the start. A report on a camp in Mathis, Texas, showed that 96 percent of the children had not drunk milk in six months. Their diet consisted mainly of cornmeal and rice. A doctor commenting on the report said there was evidence of ordinary starvation. The migrant child is prone to scurvy, rickets, and kwashiorkor—a severe protein deficiency. Some reports have put the incidence of dental abnormalities at 95 percent, and others said that bad teeth were universal.

10

The Black Immigrants

BEN H. BAGDIKIAN

. . . Walter Austin, who had lived for almost half a century within 60 miles of the Mississippi, [was seeing] the river for the first time. Still wearing his four-dollar overalls, he was sitting in the back seat of an automobile, jammed in with four other members of his family, crossing a high bridge. His eyes were red with the fatigue of the last 38 sleepless hours. But he stared down through the dusk at the aluminum reflection of the greatest body of water he had ever seen, and he said the same thing that rose out of him earlier when someone told him that in New York City there is a building 102 stories high: a low, slow, "Good gracious!" The car moved across the bridge, its occupants turning to keep in sight the massive river that had been the source of life and of suffering for five generations of Austin families. And then the river was gone, and they turned forward again to look uncertainly into the darkness ahead.

It was the most momentous crossing of their lives. From that time on their experiences would be like nothing they or their ancestors had ever known. That morning they had been just another impoverished Negro fam-

Source: Ben H. Bagdikian, "The Black Immigrants," *Saturday Evening Post,* 15 July 1967. Copyright © 1967 by Ben Bagdikian. Reprinted by permission of The Sterling Lord Agency Inc.

ily working the fields on a remote Mississippi plantation. But at noon, with hardly a backward glance, they had slammed the doors of the two cars driven by a relative and a friend and headed north for a new life in the city. They carried all they could from the last hog they would ever butcher —the salted jaw, a slab of salt pork, two hams, 100 pounds of lard— stashed in the car like sacred objects. Riding with them as well was a new and confusing collection of hopes and fears.

That day the Austins—father, mother, five children aged 17 to 6, and one grandchild—added their eight lives to a flow of Americans that is one of the great unsung sagas of human history. It is an uprooting of more people in a shorter period of time than almost any peacetime migration known to man, a vast transfer that is changing America. . . .

This exodus of southern Negroes is one of the most dramatic demographic events of the mid-century, yet it is a clandestine operation. When the Negro goes, he goes suddenly and secretly, because he is afraid of the white man. Generally, the Negro is a sharecropper, living in a feudal, non-cash economy—his plantation owner provides him land and credit. When the harvest is over, the plantation owner announces that, after deducting the cost of food, fuel, seed, fertilizer and other things the sharecropper has obtained on credit, the sharecropper's profit is such and such. Or, much more likely, the owner tells him he owes the plantation as much as $100 or $500.

To the Negro this kind of debt is so astronomical that no one, laborer or landlord, expects that it will ever be paid off in cash. Only by working off the debt can the Negro family be clear. As manual farm work gives way to huge machines, the means of paying back the debt disappears. When that happens, most plantation owners are resigned to seeing their tenants leave.

Even so, there is often a question of who gets the paid-for television or kitchen range, in light of the debt, the landlord or the departing family's friends and relatives? And the rural Negro has been taught in the harshest way never to make an important decision without the approval of his landlord. So when he moves North, the Negro usually goes unannounced, a final gesture of rebellion and fear.

The families themselves seldom know when they will go until the moment comes. Moving vans are unknown to the dirt roads of the rural South, and departure frequently depends on the car of a visiting relative. Thus the times of greatest population loss in the South are the holidays—Christmas, New Year's, Memorial Day, July 4, Labor Day, any long weekend when city relatives can make the long trip down from the North. And at funerals. The South loses more than the dead at funerals. A brother from Chicago who comes down for the ceremony, having driven the 12 hours since work let out on Friday, arrives Saturday morning before dawn, and suddenly some of the youngsters, or the whole family, decide to go back with him.

Sometimes the mail arrives with the awaited passport: bus tickets sent by older children in the city. The next day the younger children drop out of school, and after dark that night the family heads for the station, carrying in their hands everything with which they will start their new life.

Or a mother takes the youngest children to "visit my sick aunty in the city," where she gets a job and sends the tickets back for her husband and the older children, and the next Saturday night the husband pays a neighbor $1.50 to drive him and his children and their suitcases to the station. Morning on the plantation finds the shack abandoned, and another rural family has entered the central mass of an American metropolis. . . .

"I don't want to leave Mississippi," Austin said. "I never been out of Mississippi except one time in my whole life, and that was only one week. . . . I never been in no kind of trouble, never paid a fine, never been to court. I'll peck on wood"—he reached over the torn leatherette arm of the chair in his living room and rapped the bare wood floor of the shack with his knuckles—"I've been just plain Walter all my life."

We had spent hours talking country-versus-city, and there wasn't much doubt where he stood, given a free choice and enough food.

"I likes to farm. I loves it. I can raise my chickens, raise my hog. I have my garden with peas and beans and potatoes and squash and cucumbers and onions and greens. You can't do that in town. You can't raise a hog in town. I'm just a home child. I just don't want to leave home unless I have to. I'll be frank with you, I like the country."

He lifted his leather cap and scratched his hair.

"I know in the city you's supposed to have an education. If you got me a job in the morning and I was supposed to separate the salt from the sugar, I couldn't do it, not if they was in the same kind of bag. I couldn't do it, Cap'n, because I can't read."

His wife, with a soft face drawn with worry, and a blurry right eye blinded by a stroke seven years ago, told about a visit she made once to Chicago.

"I stayed with my husband's brother. I didn't even walk on the outside. That's all I know, what I saw from his place. I just couldn't stand that noise.

"I'd be satisfied working right here. If we had work. If I had enough to live on and be comfortable, oh, I'd stay. I'd stay."

What did she mean, "comfortable"?

"Nothing extra. You come into this world with nothing, and when you leave you can't carry anything away. I need some covers—quilts, you know—comfortable mattresses, some beds don't need to be propped up. I would like some clothes."

She thought for a moment and then worried that I might misunderstand her desire for clothes. She didn't mean for herself (she bought her last dress [ten years ago], her husband had never bought a suit and limited his new clothes to a four-dollar pair of overalls each year).

"I mean for the children. And nothing fancy, just not all sewed up. Not half-priced or leftovers but good common clothes, you know? Not eight-dollar dresses, just good three-dollar dresses. What I need most is extra underclothes and socks. We have enough outerclothes so the kids can wear clean things to school, but the children have to wash their underwear and socks every night so they'll be clean in the morning. If they had extra sets they wouldn't have to wash them every night." . . .

To Mrs. Austin the prospect of the city held out the deadly danger that the children would learn to drink. Walter Austin would miss his farming and would no longer experience the pride of running and repairing a large combine. But the children had different thoughts. Frances, 17, whose formal, bland expression masked a quick and taunting wit, was fatalistic—"I think things would be just the same whether I go or stay"—but she looked excited when she described how well-dressed her girl friends and relatives were when they returned from the city. David, 14, also wore an outer mask of solemnity, but his black-cloth visor cap worn at a rakish angle hinted at the adolescent itch. "I just don't want to farm. No, suh. I just don't want to be a farmer." Hearing about the city, Bessie simply glowed wordlessly. Her younger sister, Zettie Mae, 8, and brother, Wendell, 6, looked bewildered and polite.

But their parents kept reminding themselves how much better off they are now than they were in their youth. Neither of them had ever lived in so good a house as this one. It had a tight roof, the five rooms were lined with wallboard. There was a cold-water faucet in the kitchen and a privy out back (some plantation shacks lack even a privy). Three open gas grates heated the place in winter, and they had some chairs, bedsteads, and from a few good years in the early 1960's a television set and a freezer, all paid for.

"My mother's house back in Holmes County," Walter Austin said, "you could see the chickens through the floor and the blue sky through the roof. And when I was a kid, what I had to eat for the whole day was one slice of hog jaw and corn bread with flour gravy, sometimes not even that.

"Now here's David here, fourteen years old and he's in—what grade is it? Eighth—yes, the eighth grade. When I was seven years old I was trying to go to school but, Lordy, I just had to work. When I was seven years old I had to walk three miles before sunup, get a mule and feed it and then work that mule in the fields until dark, all of that for only eight dollars a month.

"I married Bessie, here, the only wife I've ever known, when we were both seventeen, and the day we got married we ate corn bread and flour gravy. We started with an old wood stove, a bed, a pig and a calf my mother-in-law give me."

The family worked for 20 years on a plantation in Holmes County. At the end of that time, Austin was driving a tractor for $4.50 a day, during the season and when weather was good. Mrs. Austin and the children did sharecropping for the same plantation, planting, chopping (weeding) and picking a cotton crop. They provided the labor and the landlord provided the land and their rent-free house. The landlord also gave them credit for their share of the cost of their seed and fertilizer and lent them $40 a month for food until the crop was harvested and sold.

"The four kids and I," Mrs. Austin said, "that last year, did twenty-six bales. We had to keep the kids out of school to do it. But I got tired, just tired going with the crops, weighing my own cotton, tromping it, putting it on the trailer. I got so tired. As a woman, I couldn't farm no more." At that time she had seven living children, ages 19 to 4, the older ones working in the field, the younger ones brought out in boxes to play all day near the cotton rows. Two infants died early, and a daughter later died of leukemia at the age of 16. "And all we got for that year and twenty-six bales of cotton was a hundred and fifty dollars. The four kids and I, from May to October. When I told the boss man I just couldn't sharecrop with the four kids no more, he told us we'd have to move. That's when we come down here."

(The average price farmers received for cotton [that year] . . . was $152 a bale, so the Austins' half share apparently was $1,976, minus $480 lent for food and their share of seed and fertilizer; neither they nor anyone they knew ever saw an accounting.)

Walter's brother heard of an empty house in Bolivar County, and they moved, and though they loved Holmes County better than anyplace else on earth, they considered themselves much improved. People had a little bit more. In Holmes, median income for the rural Negro family was $895 a year; in Bolivar it was $1,198. The Austins didn't know that, but they sensed it, and they sensed that their new plantation owner and agent were more benign. And the house was better.

Life was not easy, of course. They had more children. Their daughter, Jean, had leukemia and spent the last six weeks of her life in University Hospital in Jackson, 100 miles away, where her father lived, penniless, in a chair in her room, fed by compassionate nurses. After she died, he returned home to find that his daughter, Bessie, had been born, and his wife was back in another hospital with the shock that blinded her right eye. But, then, life had never been easy, and their family kept its strong bonds and Walter Austin his mastery within the family.

The world of the Austins in Mississippi was simultaneously enormous and tiny. Their little home was a dot in the Mississippi delta, a flat ocean of land made from the silt of centuries of flooding, land as rich as any on earth. Square mile after square mile of cotton fields stretch out, in the winter a rusty sea with here and there a scrap of windblown paper snagged on a dry stalk like a whitecap. The huge landscape is punctuated by an occasional small town, a cotton gin, a stand of oaks, and the clusters of Negro shacks in the fields. Like most southern rural Negroes, the Austins lived on a dirt road without a name, in a house without a number. But though the view seems endless, their neighbors were few, their life concentrated around their own family. . . .

Before he knew he would go, Walter Austin had uppermost in his mind the improvements he had seen since his youth and all the things he liked in the country and feared in the city. He was genuinely undecided. The plantation owner had told him there would be no guaranteed work the next year because their cotton acreage was being rented to a big agricultural operator. But the owner held out the possibility of a job in a machine shop in a nearby town, or, at least, some days of casual labor in the fields.

The pressure increased, especially during the winter, when work ceases in the delta fields. Merchants knew at once that Austin had been put in the doubtful category. Where credit for food, bottled gas and doctors had once been immediate, everyone wanted cash. Families around them were going away. Ten years earlier 50 families worked and lived on that plantation. Now there were six. Within the last year the two houses on either side of the Austins had been vacated and torn down, and the skies of the delta now were regularly streaked with smoke from empty shanties being burned down to clear the ground for growing. The smoke got thicker after a one-dollar-an-hour wages-and-hours law for agricultural workers began last winter. When motorists stopped one day to watch a spectacular fire consuming a plantation shack, the agent in charge called out, "Wages and hours got that one."

Yet the Austins hung on. He was a good worker. His plantation agent, within the limits of feudalistic white supremacy, was a decent man. Each day Austin rose at 4, went to the plantation headquarters at 7. If there was work, he returned after dark, $10-minus-debts the richer. If there was no work, as was most often the case, he went home and worked in his yard and garden.

Mrs. Austin rose at 5:30 to start breakfast of sausage and corn bread, if they had it. The children rose at 6 and got ready for the 7:20 school bus, if they all had shoes. After school they played with the children of the few remaining neighbors, did homework, had supper of greens and salt pork, and were in bed around 8.

The end of the week was different. On a typical Saturday, David lighted a fire in the backyard under an ancient iron pot and heated water for the washing. Frances did the wash in a round, wringer-style washing machine on the back stoop and hung it on the "clothesline"—two strands, one old electrical cable, the other old barbed wire. David helped his father clean up the backyard. The hog grunted, and Walter Austin rubbed its head with his glove—"Baby, you want your breakfast?"—and told David to fetch the slops. Instantly at the trough were the pig, three puppies, two cats, four kittens and two roosters.

The three younger children, bundled in bright donated clothes, played hopscotch on packed earth at the end of some cotton rows, tiny scarlet figures under a huge sky, chased by their puppies, Frisco, Fuzzy and Alaska.

In the evening they look at television. "I cain't read," Walter Austin explained, "so I have to get the news and weather on the TV."

And they sang, Bessie leading and her mother and the others following. . . .

Later there were baths, in a galvanized washtub put in Frances's room, the most private one, with a heater.

During the evenings the Austins constantly churned over their view of the future. "I wants to stay, I wants to stay." Walter Austin said. "If I could just get that machine-shop job or work in the boss man's pig farm where they works rain or shine. But how in the world am I going to feed eight kids on fifteen dollars a week?"

Periodically he'd resign himself to moving. "But after the snow is off up there. I is naked here, and up north I'm going to freeze." . . .

As the cars moved rapidly northward, one could almost feel the arguments for staying sinking out of sight and the ones for going coming to the top. Before, the need for food and money had dominated conversation. Now, deeper things, long repressed, came to the surface. I asked if he had any fear of facing the strange life in the city at his age.

"Well, I guess so. But it had to come. It had to come. Back in Mississippi I was forty-eight years old, but I was still like a child. I needed the white man for protection. If the colored man had that he could keep out of lots of trouble. He could get credit. He could do lots of things, lots of things. But he just had to have that protection. If you didn't have that protection all kinds of things could happen, all *kinds* of things, just like could happen to a child without a daddy."

His eyes were red and tired, but he talked on.

"You'd get up every morning, and you'd ask the boss man what to do, and every morning he'd tell you, just like you was a child. When you got your pay, he'd take out of it what he wanted for what you owed. He didn't ask you. Now I had a good boss man, for Mississippi, and if I had something special now and then, I could ask him to let me have all my pay, and he'd let me have it. But usual thing, he'd take out what he wanted. He handled most of your bills.

"Now I figure in the North one man pays you, and then you got to take care of your bills yourself. I know a man can get into a mess of trouble handling his own bills, but I reckon that ought to be up to him, to learn and decide himself. But not on a Mississippi plantation. They figured I was a child."

11

Appalachia:
The Case of
Eastern Kentucky

HARRY M. CAUDILL

Let us look at eastern Kentucky. Here we have a territory the size of Switzerland. Like Switzerland, it is mountainous. Both regions embrace about 15,000 square miles. Each is scenically beautiful. Each contains extensive brine beds. But here the comparison ends. Switzerland is almost certainly the richest region in the world. Some 5.5 million Swiss live in their little corner on the housetop of Europe. Their banks are immense. The Swiss taxpayers support twenty-two great institutions of higher learning, including seven world-famous universities and five great medical colleges. The little republic is so desirable a place to live in that it has to enforce the world's strictest emigration laws.

The Swiss earth, by contrast, is remarkably poor; 24 per cent of the surface is barren and incapable of growing anything; about one-fourth will grow timber, though the varieties are exceedingly limited. Very little of the

Source: This article combines excerpts from two sources. Harry M. Caudill, "Appalachia: The Dismal Land," in Jeremy Larner and Irving Howe (eds.), *Poverty: Views from the Left* (New York: William Morrow & Company, 1968). Reprinted by permission of William Morrow & Company. Copyright © 1967 by Dissent Publishing Assn. Harry M. Caudill, *My Land Is Dying* (New York: E. P. Dutton, 1971), pp. 30–32, 58–66, 68–69, 72–73, 103–7, 141–42. Copyright © 1971 by Harry M. Caudill. Reprinted with permission.

country is warm enough for really good crops. Yet, the Swiss have become a remarkably rich, strong, and self-reliant people, despite their poor land.

We, in eastern Kentucky, proceeding in the usual Appalachian fashion, have done precisely the opposite, though the Kentucky mountains are superbly rich in minerals. Originally, the coal fields contained some 35 billion tons of coal; approximately 32 billion tons remain under the hills. There are important deposits of high-grade petroleum, beds of natural gas, and immense strata of limestone and silica-rich sandstone.

The surface of this eastern Kentucky mountain earth is also abundantly endowed. It is rich in timber types and has more strains of oak than there are timber trees of all varieties in Europe. It is blessed with 45 inches of rainfall annually and has no barren land. There is probably not an acre of land in eastern Kentucky that, in its natural state, cannot grow something of utility and beauty.

But the Swiss miracle has not been repeated in Kentucky. The Swiss had confidence in their government and used it as a beneficial tool. They created an equitable tax system and collected the adequate revenues which are the lifeblood of civilization. They built schools, libraries, universities, and hospitals, and these institutions enriched the people in a creative, upward-moving spiral.

Our Kentuckians followed another road. We did not levy such taxes. We did not build the schools, libraries, universities, and hospitals. We neglected the one great resource that overshadows and outweighs all others in importance—the people. Consequently, we are a people in flight. Hundreds of thousands of mountaineers have moved away. While Switzerland fences people out, Appalachia sustains the greatest out-migration since the Irish exodus of the nineteenth century. In fact, central Appalachia is threatened with virtually complete depopulation within another decade or two unless we find a way to stop the present ruinous process.

By comparison with Switzerland's 5.5 million, there are only 800,000 people left in eastern Kentucky. Its counties operate 40 per cent of the nation's remaining one-room schools. One quarter of the white adults are functional illiterates. Its rainfall, shed on denuded hillsides and unchecked by dams, rushes away in ever more frequent floods. Thus water—one of the region's great assets—has become its scourge.

We and our forebears had an opportunity to build a vigorous society, but we have opted for a low-key society instead, a society that places little emphasis on human development—on skills, competence, and inquisitiveness—and the result has been the enlargement of incompetence and dependency. A quarter of the dwindling population is on public assistance. Like most of the Appalachian South, the region has been turned into a pale-face reservation.

Sadly, the experience of Kentucky's eastern counties is in no sense unique. Its failure may have been greater in some respects than those of its kindred regions—southwestern Virginia, West Virginia, eastern Tennessee, western Maryland, and southern Pennsylvania; but in the main its tragic tale has been repeated: a backwoods people has moved into a primordial forest. They began decimating their timber to obtain "new grounds" which they wore out without replenishing them with cover crops. Failing to educate their descendants, the generations perpetuated a lack of understanding of the land and its capacities. When the region was rediscovered after the Civil War the people practically gave away its great riches, effectually disinheriting their children and their children's children. Some of the mineral tracts sold for as little as 10 ¢ an acre. The vast natural wealth passed into the hands of land companies organized by speculators with offices in Philadelphia, Pittsburgh, New York, and Baltimore.

For more than 50 years mountaineers have sat supinely and quietly by and allowed their land, kinsmen, and institutions to be exploited by people who have neither affection nor respect for Appalachia—whose only concern is to plunder it.

My Land Is Dying

In a sense, with the building of the first crude cabins the land began to die. Like the Indians before them, the settlers began by digging up the wild cane and planting corn in its place. Thenceforward, however, a settler when he was not hunting was clearing the ground for ever larger fields of corn and of beans and potatoes. But instead of frugally collecting dead branches for firewood, these pioneers systematically killed the trees by girdling the bark with an ax. They brought in cattle and razorback swine, turning them loose to browse and trample the cornfields after the crop had ripened, thus paving the way for devastating erosion. For thirty years, a steady stream of new immigrants poured into the wooded hills and valleys of the Cumberlands. The birthrate was high, and the wilderness was looked upon as an adversary to be conquered. The Indians had inhabited the region; the white man promptly began to use it up. Within two or three generations the pressures on the land began visibly to take their toll.

In the early years, hunting was a source of income. So many deer were taken that deerskin became the equivalent of cloth, and the hides were so widely used for barter that they took the place of money—a practice that has left behind the word "buck" as slang for "dollar." Around 1810, Napoleon Bonaparte sent a purchasing agent to the village of Louisa, on the Big Sandy River, in search of black bear pelts for use by the Grand Armée. In many districts, the mountaineers hunted the bears to extinction, seeking them out in the caves where they hibernated and killing them by the dozen before they could awaken from their winter sleep. The skins went to France, and most of them probably were lost somewhere in the snows of the Russian winter.

Inexorably, the game began to disappear. As their numbers multiplied, the settlers found that the land they had cleared could no longer support them and provide fodder for their horses and cattle. These wielders of ax and rifle knew nothing of cover-cropping to preserve the soil's fertility and prevent erosion. As generations passed, their isolation deepened. There were no roads and hardly any schools. Without industry, skills, or profitable crafts, they could only cling to their primitive agriculture. Trapped in a descending cycle of toil, poverty, and futility, they turned to clearing the hillside coves as their fathers had cleared the bottomlands. But their labor with ax and plow could not keep pace with their needs. By the middle of the Civil War, the people of the Cumberlands were starving. The final blow had come as bushwhackers and foragers for the contending armies plundered the corncribs and smokehouses of the mountaineers. Abraham Lincoln became the first President to order relief, in the form of food, for the poor of Appalachia.

After the war, a building boom sent timber purchasers into the Cumberlands, and great "log runs" carried millions of felled trees downriver to the sawmills. In some areas, narrow-gauge railroads were built, and the chugging locomotives mingled with the whine of saws and the crash of falling trees. The village of Louisa now expanded into the world's largest outlet for hardwood lumber—a distinction it was to hold for thirty years. In a prolonged orgy of felling and hauling, the finest trees were the first to be cut. Then came those of lower quality. Lumber from virgin groves of Appalachia went into the building of houses and ships, into cooperage for whiskey and hogsheads for tobacco. No seed trees were left except by accident or, occasionally, because of inaccessibility. A region of immeasurable antiquity, where once for miles no tree had been felled, no stream had been sullied, no furrow cut—a region whose huge and ancient trees, whose caves, cliffs, and wind-carved arches had been regarded with veneration by the Indians—had been so altered that for us its primeval majesty is all but impossible to imagine.

By the 1880s, with the recognition that title to the coal beds could open the way to a profitable operation, land-buying agents began coming into the Appalachian region with offers of gold and greenbacks for land. The people they found there had now been isolated by the lack of roads for nearly a century. Few of the men, and almost none of the women, had ever traveled as far from home as the county seat. Schools were so few that only about 10 percent could write their names, and perhaps half of those were functionally illiterate.

The ordinary mountaineer lived in a one- or two-room cabin and worked the soil for subsistence, eating salt pork, cornmeal, beans, and whatever eggs and milk a few chickens and a cow or two were able to provide. Often he operated a still somewhere in the woods, and some of the potent moonshine he made was sold downriver at a profit. He cut logs for timber, and occasionally dug ginseng or other herbs for sale. Money was scarce in any event. The reports that a railroad might one day be built into the Appalachians were generally dismissed as a tale not to be believed.

So, when the agents came, the mountain people signed the deeds. Few of them consulted a lawyer beforehand; of those available, most were already in the employ of the purchasing agents. Literally thousands of signatures were affixed to deeds by persons who could not read a word, let alone the pages of fine print in covenants that bound the sellers and their "heirs, successors and assigns forever." The price per acre generally ran from ten cents to half a dollar.

Sometimes title to the land was bought in fee. Sometimes the deed conveyed title to "all coal, oil, gas, stone, salt and salt water, iron, ores and all minerals and metallic substances whatsoever," reserving to the seller the right to continue to use—and pay taxes on—its surface. But the astute Philadelphia lawyers who drafted the deeds that the agents carried in their saddlebags also inserted a clause vesting the buyer and his successors in title with the right to do "any and all things necessary, or by him deemed necessary or convenient in mining and removing the coal" and other minerals. Just to be safe, a further clause granted the owner of the minerals immunity from lawsuits for damages arising out of the extractive process. By the time the last of the deeds had been executed, all but about 6 percent of the mineral wealth of the region was the property of corporations headquartered in New York, Philadelphia, Pittsburgh, Baltimore, Cincinnati—and London. That meager 6 percent was, moreover, of inferior quality and inaccessibly located. Thus it was that the builders of major American corporations—and of vast private fortunes, notably that of the Mellon family—made eastern Kentucky and the coal regions of six neighboring states into a vast colonial preserve. Without fear of illegality, the boards of directors could proceed to exploit the central Appalachians with the same ruthless drive for profit as was being done by other U.S. corporations in Asia, Africa, and Latin America. By the beginning of World War I, the Appalachian highlanders had allowed the control of their destiny to slip into the hands of outsiders. What remained to them was a choice of alternatives: they could stay on as wage slaves to the owners of the mines, or they could emigrate. Many thousands chose the second only after enduring the first.

During World War II, the federal government subsidized the laying of natural-gas pipelines from the South and Southwest to the fuel-short cities of the Northeast. After the war ended, utility companies continued the expansion of the pipelines, and with astonishing rapidity the long-established monopoly of coal on the space-heating market was broken. During the war the government had also subsidized the development of relatively light and compact oil-burning diesel engines to power ships and electrical installations; soon after the war ended, these engines began to displace the old coal-burning, steam-driven railway locomotives. Oil and gas cornered still other markets while the coal mines were being shut down by a recurring series of nationwide strikes aimed at improving the working conditions and salaries of the miners. By 1952 the coal market had shrunk so drastically that the Appalachian mining companies were in the midst of a depression.

This time, the depression was local rather than nationwide. In the cities, an expanding prosperity meant more jobs, and between 1950 and 1960 entire communities in Appalachia were all but depopulated as men, women, and children climbed into their old cars and headed for a new life in Indianapolis, Cleveland, Detroit, or Chicago. The population of Leslie County, Kentucky, fell from twenty thousand to ten thousand in those ten years; in Harlan County, it dropped from seventy-six thousand to thirty-five thousand. Few of the young men or women ever returned. The exodus of the educated young was nearly total. Suddenly, nearly all the people left in the hills were the old and disabled, the helpless and hopeless.

The consequences of this draining away of the young and strong were political as well as social. Among those who remained out of the thousands of families made idle by the mechanization of a dwindling coal industry, the proportion who could or would not fend for themselves amounted to a third of the entire remaining population. Welfare rolls, commodity food doles, and makeshift public works became the prime support of these unfortunates. Having ceased to be self-supporting, they were now the wards of bureaucrats and the pawns of increasingly ruthless political machines. Independence counted for little at the polls among those who feared that a wrong vote might bring loss of subsistence—and the machines that delivered the vote were, not surprisingly, more finely attuned to the concerns of the mine operators and the land companies whose holdings they worked than to the needs of the voters whose lives they controlled.

The men whom the machines sent to the state legislature were likewise attuned to the interests of the mining industry. They constructed a revenue system that had no scruples about ordinary citizens but that tenderly exempted the purchases of the coal companies. Thus, for example, a 5 percent retail sales tax was passed that applied to a dental drill but not to a coal auger, to a miner's shovel but not to a twenty-ton mechanical loader capable of lifting more than fifty shovelsful at one swoop and priced at $100,000.

Even more oppressive, if less direct, was what happened to the judiciary, on whom the example was clearly not lost. In the earlier days of the mining industry, a population that had learned to be suspicious had also learned the uses of litigation. Hundreds of suits had reached Kentucky's highest tribunal, the Court of Appeals of Frankfort, calling in question the legal authority of the mining corporations to withdraw the coal from the hills by means injurious to the surface and to the inhabitants of the land. The actions involved the piling of shale and other waste in culm heaps, the polluting and diversion of subterranean and surface waters, the pollution of the air from the burning of culm heaps, and the subsidence of the ground in the wake of mining operations. While the mountaineers were still relatively numerous and assertive, judges and legislators had taken note of their claims, and the decisions brought at least a rough approximation of justice.

State judges in Kentucky, as in nearly all state courts, are elected by popular vote. Thus, by the nature of things, they tend to be politicians first and arbiters of justice after that. Appellate judges in seven of the state's districts are elected to office; in order to remain there, they tend to write opinions consonant with the interests and prejudices of a majority of the voters. This being so, there is little wonder that up until the end of World War II the justices consistently showed some concern for the citizens of the coal-bearing regions of the state.

Thus, for example, the general rule was observed that the owner of mining rights had no authority to impose more damage on the surface than was "reasonable" in the mining and marketing of minerals underlying it. Similarly the court ruled that where copperas-polluted water escaping from a mine had been carried by a stream onto a farm, the farmer could recover damages even without proof of negligence. Thus the mining firms were made insurers against such mishap. Again, it was declared to be the supreme law of the state that the owner of the surface had an "absolute" right to enjoy his land without subsidence brought on by the removal of coal pillars. The owner of the minerals was held liable in damages for such harm to the overlying fields and forests even if the actual mining had been done by another company. The bench sought, as well, to protect the lives of citizens with rulings that failure to protect the mouth of a shaft with safety gates rendered the company liable to persons injured while on the premises. Tailings and debris from mines had to be scattered across various surface tracts in reduced heaps so as to minimize injury to any one owner, as a matter of "ordinary and common convenience."

But in the years after World War II, a new and pitiless line of decisions followed the introduction of large-scale strip mining. The first such case was Russell Fork Coal vs. Hawkins, brought up on appeal from the Circuit Court of Pike County. After the operator had ripped all the vegetation from twelve acres of extremely steep land at the head of a creek, a flash flood—a common phenomenon in the Appalachians—tumbled a mass of mining spoil into the swollen stream. Though by a miracle no lives were lost, the flood swept all the houses in the valley before it. A number of suits for damages brought substantial verdicts in favor of the victims, whereupon the company took its case to the more sympathetic tribunal at Frankfort. The decision of the state judges in effect declared that the masses of soil, the uprooted trees, and the slabs of rock and slate had been harmless until set in motion by the force of water. It was nature that had unleashed the water; thus the damage to the plaintiffs was solemnly declared to be an act of God—for which no coal operator, God-fearing or otherwise, could be held responsible. The ruling absolved the stripper of all damages and sent his hapless victims onto the welfare rolls.

A year after the Russell Fork Coal Company had been adjudged blameless, the same court took up the complaint of a farmer that the stream flowing through his property had been contaminated by a discharge of waste petroleum from an oil well. According to its finding, no "material damage" had been done to the farmer, since the discharge merely increased the flow of water in the stream; moreover, it was noted, an injunction against such drainage would have caused "substantial injury" to the oil driller. The case was dismissed, and the costs were borne by the farmer.

As late as the year 1946, the Kentucky state court strongly implied that strip mining was so devastating to the surface that it could not legally be employed if another method of recovering the coal was feasible. Seven years later, the court had evidently had a change of heart. In Buchanan vs. Watson the court dealt squarely for the first time with the conflict between the mineral-owning company and its strip-mining lessee, on the one hand, and the owner of the surface who wanted his property left undisturbed, on the other. The trial judge ruled that the company, since it owned the coal, had the right to extract its property by any means it might choose, but was bound to pay in full for the damage to the surface. The company appealed, seeking authority to ruin the surface without incurring liability—an authority no one but a robber or a coal baron would expect to obtain. The justices handed down an opinion sustaining the claim of the farmer to just remuneration for his loss. The company then petitioned for a rehearing; and during the weeks that followed, in the words of one statehouse watcher, "coal company and railroad lawyers and lobbyists were as thick around the Capitol as horseflies on a mule's back." The buzzing of this swarm had its effect, and the original opinion was withdrawn. The astonishing new conclusion, that the owner of the surface had no grounds for complaint when bulldozers uprooted trees, plowed up pastures, or demolished fences on his property, was based on two considerations, neither of which would appear to have any connection with law or equity; first, that the land destroyed was of relatively little value, and second, that since the coal industry was not unduly prosperous at the time, a decision against the company "would create great confusion and much hardship in a segment of an industry that can ill afford such a blow."

Thus the highest court of the State of Kentucky boldly and arrogantly based a landmark decision on considerations that were patently economic. The implications of that decision for the bituminous coal industry, and no less for the people and the land of the coal-bearing mountain region, were profound. Having thus been given sanction, stripping flourished as never before. Subterranean mine operators could not compete with the strippers, and as their operations were abandoned, the miners who had lost their jobs became part of the exodus to the cities. Farmers driven off their land moved into the coal towns vacated by the miners, and the relief rolls grew. The one cheerful note in all the gloom was that, thanks to the strippers, cheap coal flooded the market, and the price remained stable for a decade. Nor were the strip miners the only beneficiaries; there were also the electric power companies, and above all there was the TVA.

[As part of the New Deal, the Tennessee Valley Authority had originated as] a sweeping program of conservation and reform measures, both political and social, aimed at rescuing a broad subregion out of its self-perpetuating squalor and poverty. The series of dams to be constructed under the Authority would rein the unmanageable Tennessee and its tributaries, at the same time providing vast quantities of hydroelectric power. These installations, together with the nitrate plants, would take advantage of cheap and abundant labor in making available cheap fertilizer along with cheap power and an abundance of water to the stricken valley. In its early years, the project fulfilled the expectations of those who designed it and who managed it—including Arthur Morgan, the Authority's first chairman, and his successor David Lilienthal. The valley prospered as one after another of the great dams and their generators were completed. The river was indeed tamed, and the eroded hills were reclaimed and made green and fertile once again. Capital from the East and from abroad went into the building of plants for the manufacture of textiles, synthetic fibers, paper, and furniture, among scores of other products. Within a decade the valley of the Tennessee had become the showpiece of the nation.

During World War II, the TVA's massive generators made possible the secret research at the Oak Ridge Gaseous Diffusion Plant that played an important role in producing the atomic bomb.

By the time the war ended, it was evident that the cycle of rejuvenation launched by the Authority had succeeded almost too well. Coal and oil furnaces were junked as more and more homeowners switched to electric heat. As electrical appliances, from refrigerators to hair dryers, became commonplace in more and more households, and new factories proliferated in the vicinity of Kingsport, Knoxville, and Nashville, the Authority discovered that it had opened up a demand for electricity greater than it had waterpower to supply. So, as a supplemental source of power, it turned to coal.

"Cheap power" was now an obsession with the TVA. One after another, ten coal-fired generators were built to produce it. Of the ninety-nine billion kilowatt hours produced annually by the agency, at a value of $388 million, 80 percent are now derived from coal. As the nation's largest single consumer of coal, in 1968 it burned about 5.5 percent of the country's entire output, amounting to one thousand six hundred carloads a day. Half of this amount comes from strip mines. Inevitably, for good or ill, TVA now controls the fate of the coal-bearing regions of Appalachia—setting market trends, changing or fixing prices, controlling the development of mining technology, and in effect prescribing the standards to which a whole spectrum of industries is to adhere. In eastern Kentucky, as elsewhere in central Appalachia, its role has been nothing short of disastrous. The same cheap fuel that made possible an era of prosperity in the TVA region has wrecked the coalfields, impoverished entire communities, and forced thousands of mountain people to desert the place of their birth.

Strip mines multiplied as "TVA companies," whose dependence on the agency was virtually total, acquired leases from the holding companies and began dismembering mountains for the coal they contained. They were hardly even mining concerns, except in the loosest meaning of the word. In actuality, rather, they were earthmovers with all the huge and sophisticated machinery of road building at their disposal. The deep miner, even when equipped with the latest electrical devices, simply could not compete with them in the race for output and profit.

Year by year, the proportion of strip-mined coal used by the onetime "conservation" agency rose. By 1961, the TVA's suppliers were digging 122 million tons a year, of which 18.5 million tons were bought by the agency and another 56 million by other power producers. Already twenty-five thousand acres had been stripped for the benefit of TVA. In the same year, taking note of a rising chorus of complaints by conservationists, its board of directors began preparing what they modestly described as "an appraisal of Coal Strip Mining." Issued in 1963, it conceded that stream pollution and soil erosion did follow the bulldozers, that stripping lowered land values and made the landscape "unsightly"—but argued that the land itself was of little value, bringing only a few dollars an acre when offered for sale, producing an annual growth of timber worth a mere $8.50 per acre, whereas the same land might yield coal valued at $9,000 to the acre when given over to the shovels and draglines of the strippers. Thus, it was explained, we must simply accept stripping as a part of our national experience.

This is the way they work: the scene is a forested ridge, rising a thousand feet above the glistening creek that winds in and out, defining the terrain; at its crest is a "razorback" or sharply exposed rock. Two-thirds of the way up, the forest is composed of second-growth hardwoods interspersed here and there with a few pines. The old "cleared line" is evident where the ancient growth of gnarled oaks, beeches, and gums, standing among moss-grown boulders, replaces the younger trees. On the eroded lower slopes, a remarkable amount of humus has been restored by the annual leaf fall from the tulip trees and other species that make up the second growth. The original complex community—rodents, lizards, hawks and owls, swarms of bees and whole empires of insect societies, the bacteria and the fungi—still carries on the multitudinous self-renewing processes of decay and rebirth.

An echo of the bulldozer's roar reverberates from other hills as the huge blade shears the topsoil, bringing an upheaval of the underlayer of clay and crumbly particles of carbon—the "bloom" from the vein of coal. As the treads of the huge earthmover cut deeper into the ground, the topsoil is flung up in a wave a yard deep. Now the first tree—a fifteen-year-old poplar with a diameter of eight inches, its bark unblemished along a thirty-foot trunk—trembles before the assault. Its roots break up through the soil in a taut yet delicate network of snapping strands. For a second or two the uprooted tree appears poised like a startled animal; then it crashes, splintering as it falls, flailing downward through trees of the same generation, snapping off their branches with a crackle that sounds like gunfire.

The D-9 bulldozer is the largest built by the Caterpillar Tractor Corporation. It weighs some forty-eight tons and is priced at $108,000. With a blade that weighs five thousand pounds, rising five feet and curved like some monstrous scimitar, it shears away not only soil and trees but a thousand other things—grapevines, briars, ferns, toadstools, wild garlic, plantain, dandelions, moss, a colony of pink ladyslippers, fragmented slate, an ancient plow point, a nest of squeaking field mice—and sends them hurtling down the slope, an avalanche of the organic and the inorganic, the living and the dead. The larger trees that stand in the path of the bulldozer—persimmons, walnuts, mulberries, oaks, and butternuts—meet the same fate. Toppled, they are crushed and buried in the tide of rubble.

As the days pass, the immense gaping wound crawls ever farther along the ridge, and the flat or "bench" continues to widen. Eventually—as on parts of Big Black Mountain—the sheer, manmade cliff or "highwall" may tower in a raw escarpment of rock, soil, and slate to a height of ninety feet, and the cut into the hill may open an expanse as much as seventy-five feet wide. In the wake of the advancing bulldozers, explosions will be detonated to loosen the coal; then power shovels will lift it into huge Mack trucks, whose twenty-five-ton loads will cause the mountain to tremble once again as they move off with a roar.

The mountain does not yield easily to the machines; its treasure is encased in a ledge of tough sandstone that must be blasted away. The explosives pile the shattered cap rock in towering heaps of spoil along the outer edge of the cut, or send it thundering down the dead flank of the hill. Whole communities tremble as the strings of explosive charges are set off in a process known to the industry as "casting the overburden."

As the stripping continues at one level after another, the entire forest cover vanishes into the rubble. Here and there, miraculously, a little island of green may escape the plunging boulders and the cascades of sliding soil. Where they linger, the trees lean precipitously, perhaps to be finally dislodged by a landslide that catapults them, still upright, onto the valley floor.

Sometimes—though not always—the shovels are followed by augers that drill into the sheer face of the seam, pulling out the shattered coal by the same action as a brace and bit that sends shavings flying as it bores into a plank. These drilling machines are priced at more than $150,000; the exact figure is determined by the size of the bit, which may be as much as six feet in diameter and may be extended, section by section, to a depth of 170 feet. Diesel powered, they are a match for bulldozers and dynamite in sheer violence as well as noise—a shrieking reverberation that deafens while it tumbles out a gush of black fragments that can fill a truck in a minute or less. For an auger of the largest gauge, working an eight-hour shift without interruption, the output can be prodigious—as much as one thousand, five hundred tons per man employed in the operation.

Sometimes contour stripping is used simply to get at the outcrop, the narrow outer remnant of a coal vein that cannot be reached by conventional underground procedures. For this greedy operation the surface of an entire hillside may be dismantled. On the other hand, the coal veins in a hill may be "virgin"—which is to say that no mining has ever taken place there. When the coal is "faced up" and augered, less than 20 percent of the total content can be obtained. The rest is generally beyond the deepest penetration of the huge bit. Deep mining, if it is to be practiced later on, can take place only where a solid wall of undisturbed coal from twenty-five to fifty feet wide has been left as a barrier around the auger holes. The need for stability in the roof of the mine and for the conservation of air make this necessary. As a result, the working area is so restricted that tunneling is usually dismissed as unprofitable. Thus a sizable deposit of coal is lost unless there is a later decision simply to blast away the mountain, layer after layer, from the top downward. When this is done, the rubble that gathers on the valley floor creeps upward as the mountain is sliced away, until the entire range is obliterated. In its place is a wasteland of displaced soil, slabs of rock and slate, and shattered residues of coal and sulfur. All that is left of what was once a tree-covered, living ridge is a vast mesa where nothing moves except the clouds of dust on dry, windy days, or the sluicing autumn rains that carve new creekbeds across its dead surface. It has become an Appalachian Carthage, the beginning of a New World Sahara.

The impact of rain on strip-mined land is immediate and catastrophic. Without leaves or branches to impede its fall, each drop strikes like a whiplash. Enormous gullies are cut into the slopes, and sheets of soil are carried away from more nearly level surfaces. Streams that had run clear for thousands of years are now mud, "too thin to plow and too thick to drink."

Eventually, in compliance with the plan for so-called reclamation on file at the state capital, the seeds of fescue and lespedeza will be strewn over the wrecked surface. If the mining operator is really "concerned," he may plant a few hundred pine seedlings to each acre. Patches of spindly grass will take root, and some stunted pines will go on struggling to survive among the gullied spoil heaps. This done, the bonds will be duly released, and the land officially described as having been "reclaimed." And, while the cocktail-party discussion of how our environment is deteriorating goes on and on, the mess that has been left will likewise continue to be ignored.

In Appalachia, streams that have been killed by industry and that are patently useless for any other purpose are being turned into open dumps. The abundant rainfall of the region travels seaward and into the nation's reservoirs through a jumble of privy wastes, rusting tin cans, discarded mattresses, abandoned cars, dead animals, bottles, cardboard boxes, broken toys, rotting table garbage such as was once used to fatten hogs, dishwater, soapsuds, animal manure, and unnameable varieties of filth. In the heartland of a region where the Shenandoah, the Rappahannock, the James, the Roanoke—streams whose very names are intertwined with the nation's heritage—have their rise, pollution holds sway. And every day that pollution widens, hastened by bulldozers—a spreading cancer that may one day engulf a continent.

In England, Germany, and Czechoslovakia, total reclamation of mined areas is a matter of course; but a reasonable discretion is also exercised in deciding which areas are to be mined. Where circumstances permit stripping to be followed by restoration, the strata are mechanically separated as the earth is peeled away. First the topsoil is scraped back and saved. Next comes the subsoil, which is heaped separately. Next come the rock and slate. Once the underlying coal has been removed, the rock and slate are shoved into the bottom of the pit. The subsoil follows and is compacted with heavy rollers. Then the original topsoil is spread in place and treated with limestone and fertilizers. Seeds are sown and trees are planted. Within five years the scars are healed. Such an outcome is not possible, obviously, on steep, rain-lashed, timbered slopes, or on the sheer sides of a region such as Black Mesa. It could be practiced with ease, on the other hand, in the fields of Iowa, the lignite prairies of the Dakotas, and the ore-bearing regions of Minnesota and Texas. Unfortunately, the process costs huge sums of money. In Britain, the National Coal Board has found the cost to be from a dollar to $1.15 per ton mined—and whereas the British assume that cost, American mining companies are reluctant to spend as much as ten cents a ton, though they have been known to spend lavishly when it comes to opposing reclamation. (A campaign in West Virginia by the Surface Mining Association was reported to have spent $100,000 on advertising its point of view.) As a consequence, mines in Britain and Germany close and U.S. exports soar.

[As *The New York Times* pointed out in a recent editorial,] "in the 1930's the Federal Government undertook numerous and costly soil conservation programs when windstorms turned the prairies into a dust bowl. Yet the Government today stands by, silently, impotently, as coal operators lay waste the land and scatter topsoil as recklessly as the dust storms ever did. Why the contrast? The answer can only be that nobody made money out of the dust storms, but the Consolidation Coal Company, the TVA and other private and public entrepreneurs are profiting from the rape of the land."

12

How Fred Andrew
Tills the Soil
with a Computer

DICK HUBERT and PETER HAUCK

Fred Andrew is forty-six years old, solidly built, and has neatly trimmed, graying hair. He rises about 5:30 every morning in his four-bedroom ranch-style house near a country-club golf course, does twenty minutes of exercise—running in place, pushups—eats a large breakfast, and then drives his company Mercury to his office.

There, in a walnut-paneled room on a small reddish-yellow sea of wall-to-wall acrylic carpeting, at an immaculately uncluttered teakwood desk, flanked by family photographs, two telephones, a radio-telephone and an intercom, Andrew reads the *Wall Street Journal* and then launches into his day's work. This amounts largely to more reading—of reports from his department heads, computer printouts, technical journals, etc.—and to attending meetings and conferring on his telephones. Occasionally he will drive out to his nearest production areas; once every week or ten days he boards the company twin-engine Beechcraft Duke turboprop to visit a distant subsidiary.

Such are the routines, paraphernalia, and philosophy of the modern manager, and quite unextraordinary—except that Fred Andrew embodies a venerable heritage that in popular mythology could not be further from the modern manager: He is a farmer.

If Andrew looks and acts more like a businessman—and he decidedly does—it is because today's farmer is becoming more and more business-like. The farmer as independent yeoman, more or less self-sufficient, tilling the soil, reaping the harvest, at peace with his God, at home in his white clapboard farmhouse, this persistent folk hero of a persistent pastoral legendry, is rapidly fading from the countryside and is being replaced by Fred Andrew—farmer as agribusinessman.

Andrew himself is the president of the Superior Farming Company, a wholly owned subsidiary of the Superior Oil Company of Houston, Texas. Andrew's "farm" resembles the farm of popular idealization no more than Andrew does the farmer. It is better described as an agricultural enterprise. Its fields and orchards are scattered over some 700 miles and two states. Most of its holdings lie near either Fresno or Bakersfield in California's San Joaquin Valley, which runs between the Pacific Coast Range to the west and the Sierra Nevada to the east and which is probably the world's most fecund area. (Farm land sells here for real estate developer prices of up to $5,000 an acre.) Other Superior Farming Company land lies farther south beyond the Tehachapi Mountains, which form the southern end of the San Joaquin Valley. Superior also owns an experimental agricultural operation in Tucson.

On these scattered holdings Superior produces twenty-six different crops, most of them fruit—almonds, apples, apricots, avocados, a variety of citrus fruits, figs, grapes (for both eating and making wine), kiwis, nectarines, olives, peaches, pistachios, plums, and prunes. In addition, the company is one of the country's main suppliers of nursery stock for wine grapes. To help plant, tend, and harvest its production, Superior maintains a fleet of fifteen radio-equipped automobiles, fifty-eight pick-up trucks, and no fewer than seventy-one tractors, and it employs some of the most sophisticated irrigation methods in the world, including watering systems controlled out of centralized electronic consoles. To help run its operations, Superior employs some 387 men and women full time (they get Blue Cross and paid vacations) and up to 650 at peak seasons.

In gross dimensions the company embraces some 15,000 acres and is worth upwards of $40 million in land and equipment, dimensions that place Superior very much in the forefront of American agriculture. For the average-sized farm in the United States has more than doubled in the last three decades, from 167 acres to close to 400, and the number of farms has shrunk in the same period, from 6.3 million to less than half that number. And this trend toward bigger and fewer farms is expected to continue apace and even intensify in the years ahead. A recent study done at Iowa State University estimates that around 700,000 farms, mostly smaller ones, will disappear over the next seven years and of those that remain, a third will account for nearly 90 per cent of all farm income by 1980; average net incomes of better than $55,000 per farm are seen as possible.

At least as significant as increasing size is increasing mechanization and rationalization down on the American farm—the application to agriculture of the elegant technologies and managerial systems and principles that have come to characterize nearly all other American industries. Fred Andrew and Superior Farming, we found during recent visits, very much epitomize these developments, too; they unquestionably represent the wave of agriculture's wondrous future or—in some eyes—are participating in the mournful burial of its Jeffersonian past.

Andrew's and Superior's headquarters is housed in a low, Southern California modern, cement- and stucco-sided, metal-roofed structure bearing the company colors—dune-beige and burnt orange. The headquarters is located on a typical southwestern industrial boulevard, flat and dusty, not far from the Pizza Villas and Howdy Houses and the one- and two-story pastel buildings that make up downtown Bakersfield, California. The offices are, significantly, twenty miles from Superior's nearest fields. While farm offices have traditionally been located on the farms themselves, often consisting of little more than a corner of the farm owner's home, there is no more reason for an operation like Superior's to have its headquarters where its production is than does, say, a cement manufacturer. In fact, there is good reason for not having its offices in the agricultural areas, Andrew explains; being closer to town makes it easier to hire and hold on to clerical workers, upon whom the new agriculture depends as much as it does on field hands.

Fred Andrew—he introduces himself with a firm handshake—is tall and tieless. He wears a short-sleeved white shirt, corduroy trousers, and clean, well-polished boots. His hands are large and wrinkled, his thin face ruddy, weathered. He carries the imprint of a life spent largely in the outdoor West. But Andrew has a certain urbanity about him, too, and considering that most farmers have probably been the sons of farmers, it was interesting—and probably significant in terms of the new agriculture—to find later that Andrew's father and grandfather, far from being progenitors of the soil, were both New York attorneys and that Andrew himself grew up in Great Neck, Long Island.

"Today's farm is a sophisticated factory, more so than most of the production factories in the United States," Fred Andrew explains, in what is evidently a well-rehearsed catechism of the new agriculture. "Our farms are run as businesses, and we're producing food on a field assembly line." Andrew gave us tours, first of the business side, later of the assembly lines.

In the company conference room, Andrew pointed out Superior land on a relief map that covered most of one wall. The company's holdings are marked by white pinheads, with the main cluster along Interstate 99 north of Bakersfield. Each of the pins represents a "ranch," as farms are generally called west of the Rockies. The ranches range up to 1,000 acres in size, and each is headed by a "foreman," who answers to a "superintendent," who oversees a number of ranches and answers to Andrew's production chief, who answers to Andrew. The ranches all have numbers— "Twenty-eight," "Fourteen," "Sixty-five" are domains of the new agriculture. The numbers are headings, too, on computer readouts that come out of the parent company's IBM 370 in Houston, which is fed by a console in Bakersfield. Every month, Andrew explains, a computerized report is drawn up analyzing variables by ranch and also, in a separate set of calculations, by crop. One sheet that Andrew shows contains a bewildering array of figures for such factors as fertilization, irrigation, cultivation, tree replacement, insect control, equipment costs, and harvesting and hulling.

The new agriculture—Andrew asserts it several times—clearly differs from the old in the large amount of planning and analysis that goes into it, and as a tool for these broadening managerial functions the computer has become as vital to modern, large-scale farming as the plow. "The computer," he says, "is the only way I can operate. There's no way I can keep the vast amount of information I need in my head." At one point in our discussions Andrew speaks of a large parcel of land that he is considering buying part of and says that basic to his pondering is a computer analysis of the costs and returns that he can expect. Another product of the computerizing and rationalizing of his operations is the twenty-year projections that Superior has been using to guide its operations since its formation. "Traditionally, most farmers could hardly plan two days ahead, never mind a season ahead," Andrew says. "Well, we're working twenty years ahead." He won't reveal any details of Superior's twenty-year projections for its own future except to say that the company has exceeded the pace of its projections already. For the future of agriculture generally, Andrew says, his projections show food consumption soaring along with world population figures.

Hand in hand with computerized analysis and planning there exists a high degree of specialization in agriculture's metamorphosis into agribusiness. One wing of Superior's headquarters houses administrative services (which handles personnel matters as well as land acquisition) and the production division; accountants and the company comptroller occupy most of another section of the building; marketing specialists another.

Superior's most specialized division—occupying rooms 13 through 21—is styled "technical services" and is headed by Dr. Henry Chavez, a 36-year-old veteran of agricultural research for government and industry who holds a Ph.D. in plant pathology. ("Chavez eats grapes," says a sign in his office, a bit of wryness inspired by farm labor organizer Cesar Chavez's boycott of non-union grapes. Dr. Chavez is no relation to organizer Chavez and, like most farmers, Superior's managers find little that is amusing about the militant labor leader.) Chavez heads a staff of subspecialists, including an agricultural engineer who concerns himself primarily with irrigation design and installation, an entomologist (who doubles as both bug and weed expert), and a horticulturist—all with master's degrees. "We feel that our technical specialists are necessary in order to ensure the maximum utilization of our resources," Chavez explains. In large measure it is a matter of having experts with the company's interests foremost in mind who can evaluate the increasingly arcane flood of technical and scientific information that is related to the growing of food. "Because we have a fulltime entomologist," Chavez explains, for example, "we don't have to rely on a chemical salesman for pesticide information." . . .

Agricultural technology has traditionally lagged behind industrial technology in its rate of change, but part of the business of agribusiness is to systematically push forward the design and application of new approaches, chemicals, and equipment—to supplant, in effect, the hoary wisdom and instincts of the farmer, and much of his labor, with the tools of the technician. Superior is very much part of this process. Andrew himself feels that one of Superior's competitive advantages is its ability and willingness to experiment with new technologies and to implement these rapidly.

Andrew's almond orchards are one of his prides and joys in terms of agricultural technology, and he pointed them out to us as we drove with him into Superior ranch land north of Bakersfield. Three workers can harvest an entire orchard, he says. The almonds are never touched until a consumer puts one in his mouth. They are harvested from trees by machines that literally grasp a tree's trunk and shake the nuts onto the ground. Other machines sweep up the almonds, and then they go to the hulling and packing plants.

The company's technical advances take simpler forms, as well, which have more to do with thinking than mechanics. For instance, Andrew figures he has saved thousands of dollars on minimizing frost damage largely by determining the last possible moment for turning on the large and costly-to-run heaters that stand guard on the upwind flanks of his citrus orchards. Many citrus growers simply turn the things on as soon as the thermometer drops below 32, and they will leave them on all night. Andrew and his technicians have carefully studied how much below-freezing weather their fruit can take before there is any permanent damage, and by using thermometers that measure the temperature inside the fruit and not just in the surrounding air, they are able more effectively to determine critical temperature stages. At the same time Andrew has worked out a system for starting up the heaters for 160 acres in thirty-five minutes. The result has been a cutting in half of usual frost-fighting costs.

Unquestionably, the company's most impressive technology—and, even more fundamental, the most impressive evidence of its ability to incorporate new technology swiftly and decisively—lies in its "drippers."

As in any agricultural operation, water is one of the principal raw materials that go into Superior's farming, and supplying water to its crops is one of the company's main expenses. The cost of water, if anything, is exceptionally high in the San Joaquin Valley, because much of it comes from deep wells and requires expensive pumping equipment as well as extensive ground-level storage reservoirs.

The standard methods of irrigation used in the valley are intermittent flooding of crop areas and sprinkling—both of which use vast amounts of high-priced water. In arid Israel, however, an acute scarcity of water has led to the development of a technique that makes plants grow as well as or even better than traditional irrigation methods do but uses considerably less water because practically none goes into non-producing soil or is lost to evaporation. The water is fed, in effect, through a tap or number of taps near the base of the plant or tree. These taps provide a small trickle—one to two gallons an hour—and over a long period this trickle spreads out to feed the plant's roots amply.

Superior's people heard of the dripper three years ago from a San Diego County farm adviser who had been visiting Israel. Andrew was skeptical about the technique's virtue to begin with. Still, the company began experimenting with the dripper on a small scale, the drip-fed plants thrived, the experiment was broadened to take in two twenty-acre plots. These also did well, and Andrew was convinced to go into drippers fullscale—at a time when most farmers were only dimly aware of the technique. . . .

Dripper systems eventually can effect substantial savings in water costs and in labor costs that are involved in other forms of irrigation, but initially the systems require heavy capital outlays for piping water to every single plant or tree to be irrigated, and for the attendant equipment needed. Touring the fields with Andrew, we could see some evidence of the investment involved—in little drippers lying near the bases of trees or vines and a tractor and work crew that were laying down flexible piping to feed yet more drippers. We also visited a concrete shed that housed one of the consoles that controlled the dripper system for a particular ranch, a wonderfully futuristic contraption—designed specifically for Superior— with a maze of dials and knobs, topped off by an illuminated map that indicates what fields are currently being watered. The panels can be programmed for six days in advance to feed different amounts of water to different twenty-acre sectors over 800 acres of fields. The cost of one electronic regulator alone runs around $40,000, and the pro-rated cost of the drip irrigation comes to about $500 an acre. Do the arithmetic for 4,500 acres, and the result is upwards of $2.2 million for the new dripper irrigation systems alone. Add to that Superior's fleets of cars, trucks, and tractors, its wind machines (for blowing the layers of warmer air that hovers over orchards back into the trees—another frost-fighting method), its tree shakers, etc., and some sense of how big a business agribusiness has become is evident. And if you calculate, as Andrew does, that these investments more than pay for themselves in the long run, then some indications are apparent of the financial disadvantage of traditional small farms that cannot begin to afford massive capital outlays—cannot, in effect, afford the long run. . . .

. . . Andrew envisions the day when the agricultural assembly line will be virtually indistinguishable from its industrial counterpart, and, indeed, Superior has been experimenting with something very close to that already. An ultimate in factory-like farming is represented by Superior's tomato-growing operation in Tucson. There, inside of giant, polyethylene-topped greenhouses, a Superior Farming subsidiary, Environmental Farms, Inc., is growing 10.8 acres of tomatoes under circumstances in which every agronomic variable is meticulously controllable. The resulting crops are eight times as large as they would be for equivalent field acreage.

Andrew explains with pride how within a few days the old stems and roots of a tomato crop that has borne its fruit are mechanically swept up and a new crop of young plants plunked down, and how every stage of a crop's growth is regulated—immune from the vagaries of nature that have plagued farmers forever. "It's just like a factory," he exults. "That's what it is, a tomato-growing factory." And this, he says, "is the agriculture of the future. There's going to be one big greenhouse on your hundred-acre field where you control the gases, the temperature, humidity, control everything."

There are still many Americans who do not believe and do not want to believe that Fred Andrew and Superior Farming represent the agriculture of the future, that ever-bigger, more businesslike, and more factory-like farming operations are inevitable. It is good politics as well as tried romanticism to affirm the eternity of the small farm. Thus, even Secretary of Agriculture Earl Butz, who has been accused of being a friend of agribusiness, has asserted: "We're always going to remain a nation of family farms."

Loosely speaking, there may be something to that. But our farms are likely to be family farms in the same sense that DuPont is a family business. Whether farms are owned by impersonal corporations or by families, they are bound to get bigger and more businesslike—unless government should step in and forcefully resist the trend. Many people, including many small farmers, feel that government should do so, in order to preserve an invaluable realm of America's heritage, "the promoter of its virtue," a morally desirable way of life as well as an industry. Don Paarlberg, director of agricultural economics for the Agriculture Department, asked in a speech a while back whether we should "sacrifice a form of agricultural production that has produced good people as well as good crops and livestock." The question, he pointed out, was "social and political as well as economic."

Andrew appears to be aware of the political and social aspects of what he is doing and advocating, but he stresses the economic: America cannot afford the inefficiencies of small farming units, he says, unless it wants to pay a lot more for its food. As for government stepping in to ensure the continuation of small farms, he compares this abhorrently to the government's breaking up General Motors into a lot of small car companies. He feels that the government has no business doing either. . . .

. . . At his neat teakwood desk with his two telephones, radio, and intercom, the president of the Superior Farming Company was asked whether he would still like to be running his own farm if it were economically feasible. Sure, he said. "Most of the fun in farming is doing it all yourself." But it is a way of the past, he said. And for better or worse he is most likely right.

13

What Happened to Main Street?

PETER SCHRAG

MASON CITY, IOWA. Pop. 32,642. Meat packing, Portland cement, brick and tile, beet sugar, dairy products, commercial feeds, soybean oil and meal, thermopane windows and mobile homes. At the intersection of Highways 18 and 65, 135 miles south of Minneapolis, 125 miles north of Des Moines. Three major railroads. Ozark Airlines. Daily newspaper, one local television station. Library, art museum.

Among the most difficult things in any small American town is to stay more than a few days and remain an outsider. There seems to be a common feeling that anyone—even a writer from New York—is, somewhere in his heart, a small-town boy come home. The light but unceasing stream of traffic which moves through Main Street—Federal Avenue in Mason City—north to Minneapolis and beyond, south to Des Moines, reinforces

Source: Peter Schrag, "What Happened to Main Street?" in *Out of Place in America* (New York: Random House, 1970), pp. 52–73. Copyright © 1970 by Peter Schrag. Reprinted by permission of Random House, Inc.

the belief that this flat, open place is part of a great American continuity extending through other Main Streets, across the fields of corn and beets, past tractor depots and filling stations, past grain elevators and loading pens to the very limits of the national imagination. It must make it difficult to conceive of anyone as a total stranger, for being here—local pride notwithstanding—cannot seem very different from being anywhere else.

They take you in, absorb you, soak you up; they know whom you've seen, where you've been, what you've done. In Mississippi hamlets the sheriff follows you around; here it is The Word. *Small towns co-opt (you tell yourself) and nice small towns co-opt absolutely.* But it is not just them, it's you. The things that you bring with you—your sense of yourself as a friendly sort, the wish to believe that the claims of small-town virtue are valid, and your particular kind of chauvinism—all these make you a willing collaborator. So maybe they're right. *Maybe we're all just small-town boys come home.* Yes, you're willing to come to dinner, to visit the Club, to suspend the suspicion that all this is some sort of do-it-yourself Chamber of Commerce trick. Later perhaps (says the Inner Voice of Reason) you will be able to sort things out, to distinguish Main Street from the fantasies that you and a lot of other people from New York have invented for it. Later.

You have come here to see what is happening to the heart of this country. . . . Is there something here that can survive in New York and Chicago, is there an Americanism that will endure, or will it perish with the farm and the small town? What, you ask, is happening to Main Street? Later. For the moment you are simply in it, listening to them worry about a proposed civic center, about the construction of a mall, about taxes and industrial development, and about something called "the traffic problem" which, by even the more placid standards of New York, seems more imagined than real.

There are ghosts in this country—local ghosts, and ghosts that you bring with you, that refuse to stay behind: shades of brawling railroad workers and dispossessed farmers; frontiersmen and Babbitts; the old remembered tales of reaction and America First, of capital *R* Republicanism and the Ku Klux Klan; the romance of Jefferson and Frederick Jackson Turner, the yeoman farmer and the self-made man. As a place of literary irony, Middle America is celebrating its golden anniversary. "Main Street," wrote Sinclair Lewis in 1920, "is the climax of civilization. That this Ford car might stand in front of the Bon Ton Store, Hannibal invaded Rome and Erasmus wrote in Oxford cloisters. What Ole Jensen the grocer says to Ezra Stowbody the banker is the new law for London, Prague and the unprofitable isles of the sea; whatsoever Ezra does not know and sanction, that thing is heresy, worthless for knowing and wicked to consider." But that irony, too, may be a ghost—now as much myth, perhaps, as the self-flattering cultural propositions invented to answer it. ("Right here in Mason City," someone tells you, "we sell three hundred tickets each year for the Metropolitan Opera tour performances in Minneapolis.") The life of Babbittry, you tell yourself, follows the life (and art) of others. But the models are no longer clear. Main Street once insisted on rising from Perfection (rural) to Progress (urban): Sauk Centre and Zenith were trying to do Chicago's Thing, but what does Chicago have to offer now? The Main Street boosters are still there, hanging signs across the road proclaiming "A Community on the March," but their days are numbered. How would Lewis have portrayed the three hundred marchers of the Vietnam moratorium in Mason City? How would he deal with the growing number of long-haired pot-smoking kids? Here, too, Mason City follows New York and Chicago. (The Mafia, you are told, controls the floating dice games that occasionally rumble through the back rooms of a local saloon.) The certainty of Lewis's kind of irony was directed to the provincial insularity that war, technology, and television are rendering obsolete. Main Street lives modern not in its dishwashers and combines—not even in Huntley-Brinkley and Walter Cronkite—but in its growing ambivalence about the America that creates them, the America that crosses the seas of beets and corn—and therefore about itself.

It is not a simple place, and perhaps never was. You see what you expect, and then begin to see (or imagine) what you did not. Standard America, yes: the Civil War monument in the Square; the First National Bank; Osco's Self-Service Drugs; the shoe store and movie theaters; Damon's and Younkers' ("Satisfaction Always"); Maizes's and Penney's; Sears and Monkey Ward. Middle America the way it was supposed to be; the farmers come to shop on Saturday afternoon; the hunting and fishing; the high school football game Friday night; the swimming and sailing at Clear Lake, a small resort nine miles to the west. You cannot pass through town without being told that Mason City is a good place to raise a family, without hearing praise for the schools, and without incessant reminders that Meredith Willson's musical play *The Music Man* was *about* Mason City, that Willson was born here, and that the town was almost renamed River City because of it. (There *is* a river, the Winnebago, which makes itself known only at times of flood.) Mr. Toot, the figure of a trombone-blowing bandsman (says a man at the Chamber of Commerce), is now the town symbol. "We hope," says the man, "that we can make our band festival into a major event." Someday, you imagine, this could be the band capital of the nation, and maybe the whole wicked universe.

Mason City, they tell you, is a stable community: steady population, little unemployment, no race problem (there are, at most, 300 Negroes in town), clean water and, with some huffy qualifications (dust from one of the cement plants, odor from the packing house), clean air. A cliché. In the

Globe Gazette, the editor, Bob Spiegel, suggests that the problems and resources of the large cities be dispersed to all the Mason Cities in America.
A Jeffersonian, Mr. Spiegel, and a nice guy: "The smaller communities
need the plants and the people that are polluting the urban centers—not in
large doses, but steadily, surely . . . The small communities are geared
up. They have comprehensive plans. They know they can't stand still or
they will be passed by." Stable, perhaps, but what is stable in a relativistic
universe? The very thing that Spiegel proposes seems to be happening in
reverse. The community is becoming less pluralistic: it has fewer Negroes,
fewer Jews, and fewer members of other minorities than it had twenty
years ago. "After the war," said Nate Levinson, an attorney, who is president of the synagogue, "we had eighty Jewish families. Now we have forty.
We can't afford a rabbi any more." On the few occasions that Mason City
has tried to attract Negro professionals, they refused to come or to stay.
There is nobody to keep them company, and the subtle forms of
discrimination—in housing and employment—are pervasive enough to
discourage pioneers. ("My maid says if she hears any more about Black
Power she'll scream . . . I wouldn't mind one living next door, if he
mowed the grass and kept the place neat.") The brighter kids—black and
white—move away, off to college, off to the cities, and beneath that migration one can sense the fear that the city's declining agricultural base
will not be replaced by enough industrial jobs to maintain even the stability which now exists.

Mason City is not a depressed town, although in its stagnating downtown shopping area it often looks like one. (Shopping centers are thriving
on the periphery: the farmers come in to shop, but not all the way.) The
city shares many of the attributes of other small Middle Western communities, competing with them for industry, counting, each week, another farm
family which is selling out or giving up, counting the abandoned houses
around the county, counting the number of acres (now exceeding two
hundred) required for efficient agricultural operation. An acre of land
costs $500, a four-row combine $24,000. If you stop in places like Plym-
outh, a town of 400, nine miles from Mason City, you hear the cadences
of compromise and decline: men who have become part-time farmers who
make ends meet, at $2.25 an hour, by working in the sugar mill in Mason
City. Independence becomes, ever more, a hopeful illusion belied by abandoned shops and boarded windows, and by tales of success set in other
places: an engineer in California, a chemist in Detroit, a teacher in Oregon.

Iowa, you realize, not just from statistics, but from faces, is a state of
old people: "What do the kids here want to do? What do the kids in
Mason City want to do? What do the kids in Iowa want to do? They want
to get out. I'd get out, go to California if I could." There is a double mi-

gration, from farms into towns, from the towns into the cities, and out of
state. More than 10 percent of Mason City's work force is employed at the
Decker Packing Plant on the north side of town. (The plant is a division of
Armour and Co.) At the moment the plant is prosperous; it pays good
wages. (A hamboner—who does piece work—can make $6 to $7 an
hour.) But what would happen, said one of the city's corporate managers,
if the place should succumb to the increasing efficiency of smaller plants?
"What'll we do the day—and don't quote me—when the place has to shut
down?"

It is the fashion to worry slow, worry with a drawl. Urgency and crisis
are not the style. Through most of its history, Mason City was dominated
by a few families, and to some extent it still is, not because they are so
powerful, but because Federal Avenue once thought they were. Small
towns create their own patriarchs, tall men who look even taller against
the flatness of history, producing, inevitably, a belief that civic motion and
inertia are the subtle work of Big Men—bankers, real estate operators and
corporate managers. Mason City still talks about the General, Hanford
MacNider (banking, cement, real estate), who was an assistant secretary of
war under Coolidge, ambassador to Canada, an aspirant for the 1940 Republican nomination for president, and, for a time, a supporter of America
First. (In Mason City, MacNider was *Secretary* of War and barely missed
becoming president.) The MacNiders gave the city land for parks, for the
public library and for a museum. (The General was also a founder of the
Euchre and Cycle Club, a lunch-and-dinner club—all the best people—
which still has no Jewish members, and he is remembered, among other
things, as the man who did not lower his flag for thirty days after John F.
Kennedy was killed.) "My father," said Jack MacNider, now president of
the Northwestern States Portland Cement Co., "was quite a guy. Some
people thought he was tough. To some he was a patron saint. You should
have known him."

The General's shadow survived him, and there are still people who are
persuaded that nothing of major consequence can be accomplished in
Mason City against the opposition of the family. Is that true, you ask Jack,
sitting in his second-story office overlooking Federal Avenue. (There is a
picture of the General, in full uniform, behind Jack's desk). "I'm flat-
tered," he answers, not defensively, but with some amusement, saying
more between the lines than on the record, telling you—you imagine—
that the MacNiders take the rap for a lot of small-town inertia they can't
control, and that they suffer (or enjoy) a visibility for which they haven't
asked. At this very moment a young lawyer named Tom Jolas, a second-
generation Greek, is challenging the Establishment (such as it is) in his
campaign for mayor; you both know that Jolas is likely to win (on November 4 he did win, handily) and that the city's style and mood is now deter-

mined as much by younger businessmen and professionals—and by hundreds of packing-house workers and cement workers—as it is by the old families. "This must be a fishbowl for the MacNiders," you say, and Jack offers no argument. And when you speak about prejudice in Mason City, Jack agrees—yes, there is—but you can't be sure whether he means against Catholics, Jews and Negroes (or Greeks and Chicanos) or also against the MacNiders. The shadow is still there, but the General is dead.

Mason City's traditional style of politics and political behavior was nicely represented by sixty-five-year-old George Mendon, who was mayor for sixteen years until Jolas beat him. Small towns always create the illusion of responsiveness—you can call any public official, any corporate manager, with little interference from secretaries who ask your business, your name, and your pedigree—and you thus can walk into Mendon's office unannounced and receive an audience. But you are never sure that, once in, you have really arrived anywhere. The action must be someplace else. The room is almost bare, the desk virtually clean, the man without visible passion. Yes, jobs and industrial development are a problem, and Mason City has done pretty well, but there are twenty thousand other towns trying to attract industry and, you know, these things take time. Yes, they would like to hire some Negroes for the police force, but none have been qualified. Yes, the MacNiders had been good to the city—all that land they'd given (and all those tax deductions?) but . . . When Mendon was challenged during the campaign about operating an underpaid and undertrained police force, he answered that the city had the most modern equipment, including riot guns, mace, and bulletproof vests. What are they for, you ask, and Mendon, rattling the change in his pocket, identifies himself. "Our colored population is peaceful," he said. "They wouldn't riot. But you never know when people from the outside might come in and try to start something." Mason City is prepared for Watts and Newark, and somewhere in its open heart there lurks an edge of apprehension that the fire next time might burn even here. But when Mendon spoke about his riot guns at an open meeting, the general response was tempered by considerable facetious amusement, and the people who were amused went out to vote against him, and beat him.

There is no single current running against the old style of politics, or against the Mendons and the Establishment they are supposed to represent. . . . "The issue here," said Bud Stewart, who runs a music store and worked for Jolas, "is generational," implying that whatever was young and progressive supported the challenger against the older Establishment. Jolas campaigned under the slogan "Time for a Change," including, among other things, concern for public housing (which the city does not have but desperately needs), more attention to the problems of youth, and the creation of a modern police force that could meet what he called the rising rate of crime. (And which meant, I was told, getting rid of the reactionary police chief who had bought all the riot junk.) But what Jolas said was clearly not as important as what he is: young, energetic and, beneath it all, ambiguously liberal and unambiguously decent. "I had my hair long and wore sideburns," he tells you (two years ago, he managed a teen-age rock band), "but my friends said I couldn't win with it, so I cut it short. But maybe after the election I might get a notion and let it grow again."

Jolas's great political achievement before he ran for mayor was to force the State to re-route a projected interstate highway so that it would pass within a few miles of Mason City, but it was undoubtedly personality rather than politics that elected him. ("You know what they're saying about me," he mused one day toward the end of the campaign. "They're saying that if I'm elected the Greeks and the niggers are going to take over Mason City. I even had someone charge that I belong to the Mafia, the Greek Mafia.") More than anything else, Jolas seems to have a sense of concern about youth—not a program but an awakening awareness of how kids are shortchanged by schools, politicians, by adults. ("He knows," I write in my notes, "that the world screws kids.")

What Jolas can achieve is doubtful. He will not have a sympathetic city council, or perhaps even a sympathetic community, and his commitment to a downtown Civic Center and mall as a means of restoring the vitality of the central business area may be more the tokens of modernism than the substance of progress, yet it is clear that Jolas received the support and represented the aspirations of whatever liberalism (black, labor, professional) that the city could muster. If you sit in his storefront headquarters long enough you learn how far Main Street has come from Babbittry. You meet Mary Dresser, the recently widowed wife of a lawyer, who, as president of the Iowa League of Women Voters, carried a reapportionment fight through the legislature and who speaks of how, when their son decided to grow a mustache, she and her husband decided to back him up against the school authorities and how, eventually, they won; Jean Beatty, the wife of a psychologist, answering phone calls and stuffing Jolas envelopes, and shuttling between meetings of the League and the local branch of the NAACP, knowing that the organization should be run by black people but knowing also that its precariously weak membership cannot sustain it without help; or Jim Shannon, the County Democratic chairman, who has worked for the Milwaukee Railroad all his life and who has gone back to the local community college (working nights, studying economics during the day), speaking in his soft, laconic, infinitely American cadences about the campaign for Bobby Kennedy in 1968, about a decade of legislative fights, reminding you, without meaning to or even mentioning it, that liberalism wasn't invented in New York, that the Phil Harts, the

Frank Churches, the Fred Harrises and the George McGoverns weren't elected by professors.

If that were all—if one could merely say that Mason City and Middle America are going modern—it would all be easy, but they are not. (What, after all, is modern, uniquely modern, after you've dispensed with the technology?) The national culture is there, mass cult, high, middle and low, mod and trad: Bud Stewart in the Edwardian double-breasted suits which he orders from advertisements through the local stores; the elite trooping off to Minneapolis to hear the Met when it comes on tour, or to Ames to catch the New York Philharmonic (mostly, say the cynics, to be conspicuous, not for love of music); the rock on the radio and in the jukes . . . the long hair and the short skirts, the drugs and the booze. (At the same time, beer, rather than pot, seems still to be the preponderant, though not the exclusive, form of adolescent sin.) But somehow what Mason City receives through the box and the tube, and from its trips to Minneapolis and Des Moines, where some of the ladies do almost weekly shopping, it seems to shape and reshape into its own forms. There is a tendency to mute the decibels of public controversy and social friction, perhaps because people are more tolerant and relaxed, perhaps because they are simply less crowded. There is talk about crime and violence, but the most common local examples seem usually to involve the theft of bicycles and the destruction of Halloween pumpkins. (Another way of staking a claim on the modern?) If you ask long enough, you can get some of the blue-collar workers to speak about their resentment against welfare, taxes, and student demonstrators (not at Harvard, mind you, but at the State University of Iowa), but it is commonly only television and the newspapers that produce the talk—and so it tends to be dispassionate, distant, and somewhat abstract. Bumper stickers and decals are scarce; you rarely see American flags on the rear windows of automobiles because, one might assume, there aren't many people at whom to wave them, not many devils to exorcise. The silent majority here is an abstraction, a collage of minorities, except when it comes to the normalcy of the ladies' study clubs and bridge clubs, the football, the hunting and fishing, and the trip to the lake. And every two years they go back, most of them, and vote for [the conservative Congressman] H. R. Gross. . . .

Given the reputation of the average small town in America, the greatest surprise is the school system which, under Rod Bickert, the superintendent, and John Pattswald, the high school principal, has managed to move well beyond the expected, even in the conventional modern suburb. Mason City has abandoned dress codes in its high school, has instituted flexible-modular scheduling (meaning that students have only a limited number of formal lecture classes, and can do their own thing—in "skill" and study centers, in the library or the cafeteria—as they will) and has begun to experiment, in the high school, with an "open mike" where any student can talk to the entire school on anything he pleases. There are no bells, no monitors. As you walk through the halls (modern, sprawling, corporate style), Pattswald, a Minnesotan, explains that he first came to the school as a disciplinarian. "It was a conservative school and I ran a tight ship." When he became principal he turned things around. "We're something of an island, and when some of the parents first heard about it they thought it was chaos. We had an open meeting—parents and students—to explain the flex-mod schedule, but most of the parents wanted to know about dress. (You know, we have everything here, including girls in miniskirts and pants suits.) The students helped us carry it. They know that some sort of uproar could blow this thing right out of the water, but I think they can do the job."

Every day Pattswald spends a couple of hours visiting classes, asking students irreverent questions that are, at least tangentially, directed to the teachers. "I ask them why they're doing what they're doing; what's the significance of this, why study it at all? Sure, we have some weak teachers, but now when I hire people I role-play with them a little, I want to see how they take pressure. In the classroom it's too easy for the teachers always to be the last resort and to put the screws down. That's no way to improve the climate of learning." The conversation is frequently interrupted while Pattswald stops to talk with students (he knows many by name), and later to tell you about them. "Kids are my life," he says, rounding a corner after a brief encounter with two boys. "The whole point is to get them to appreciate the worth of an individual. We have to reach the ones who are overlooked, like one boy they were taunting and who talked about himself as 'a ball that they always kick around.' Those are the ones we have to reach. But I think we're coming."

The militant students seek you out. Mason City is still a confining place, and they find the visitor from New York, the outsider, walking through the hall alone: the organizers of the moratorium, the editors of the mimeographed paper, the *Bitter End* (not quite underground, not quite official), the activists, sons and daughters of the affluent lawyers and doctors, all local people, not carpetbaggers from the East. The school, they say, is divided between "pointy heads like us" and "the animals." (A group passes through the hall after school and the pointy heads, through a glass door, follow the herd with "Moo-moo," "Oink-oink.") The radicals still see the school as a fraud. "There is no way to get a decent education in a public school. Everybody's too uptight." Like what? "Like being allowed to leave school during your unstructured time to make a movie. You can get a release to dish hamburgers at McDonald's, so why not to make movies?" One of them gets threatening letters for his part in the peace movement, another loses his allowance because he won't cut his hair. Their lives are no different, nor are their parents', from those of similar people in Scarsdale or Shaker Heights or Winnetka. (Some of them, said Pattswald, "have told their parents to go to hell.") What is surprising is that, although they are a lonely minority, they are in Mason City (bands, football, cheerleaders, Toot)—that they are in this community at all.

For the majority of the young, the concerns are universal: cars, dances, sports. You hear them in Vic's ("Real Dago Pizza"): "It's a '65 Chevvy. I traded it for that car that was sitting in the grass by the Hub . . . paid three hundred and fifty dollars and put a new engine in it and it runs great." They want to go to college, to get jobs—more than half the high school students work—so they can maintain those automobiles, get married. The modest dream is to become an airline stewardess; "if I'm not too clumsy," to enlist in the Army; to learn a trade. On Friday nights they cruise up and down Federal, shuttling from a root-beer stand at the south end to a drive-in at the other. There is some talk about establishing a teen center, a place Where Kids Can Go, but the proposal draws little enthusiasm from adults and less from the kids. . . .

The young are slowly becoming mediators of the culture, they receive the signals from the outside and interpret the messages for adults. And that's new for all America, not just for Mason City. "The kids are having an effect on their parents," said a mental-health worker, one of the few clinicians in town, apparently, that the adolescents are willing to trust. "People here are friendly and uptight at the same time. Many of them take the attitude that the children should have their fun, that eventually they'll come around to their parents' view. But people have been jarred—by TV and by their own children, and they know, some of them at least, that they've got to listen. They're trying to become looser."

But becoming looser is still a struggle and, given the conditions of life, an imperative that can be deferred. ("I'm *not* going to send my son to Harvard," says a Harvard graduate. "An eighteen-year-old is not mature enough to handle SDS and all that other garbage.") The space, the land, the weather, the incessant reminders of physical normalcy make it possible to defer almost anything. Church on Sunday, football on Friday and the cycle of parties, dinners, and cookouts remain more visible (not to say comprehensible) than the subtleties of cultural change or social injustice. If the churches and their ministers are losing some of their influence among the young (and if the call for psychiatrists is increasing), they are still holding their members, and if the Catholic Monsignor, Arthur Breen, has to schedule a folk mass at Holy Family every Sunday (in addition to four other masses) he nonetheless continues to pack them in.

What you see most of all (see is not a good word—feel, maybe) is a faith in the capacity of people and institutions to be responsive, the belief that, finally, things are pretty much what they seem, that Things Work. "This is just a big farm town," said a Mason City businessman. "You don't check people's credit here; you just assume they'll pay their bills. In Waterloo, which is really an industrial city, even though it isn't very big, you check everybody out." The answer to an economic problem is to work harder, to take a second job, or to send your wife to work, usually as a clerk or a waitress. (Wages for women are extremely low.) On the radio, Junior Achievement makes its peace with modernism by setting its jingle to "Get With It" to a rock beat, but the message of adolescent enterprise (Babbittry?) is the same, and around the lunch tables at the Green Mill Restaurant or the bar at Tom MacNider's Chart House it is difficult to convince anyone that sometimes even people with the normal quota of ambition can't make it.

The advantages of that faith are obvious, but their price is high. "This is a nice town as long as you don't rock the boat," said Willis Haddix, a meat packer who is president of the struggling Mason City chapter of NAACP. "What's wrong here is in the secret places": in subtle discrimination in housing and jobs; in the out-of-sight dilapidated frame houses at the north and south ends of town, buildings surrounded with little piles of old lumber, rusting metal chairs, decaying junk cars once slated for repair; in the lingering aroma of personal defeat; and in the cross between arrogance and apathy that declares "there are no poor people in this area." On Sundays, while most people are packing their campers for the trip home, or making the transition between Church and television football, the old, who have little to do, wander into the Park Inn for lunch (hot roast-beef sandwiches for $1.25), and talk about medicare. And against theirs you hear other voices: Murray Lawson, for example, a civilized, compassionate man who represents Mason City in the legislature, saying, "We've been generous with education, but not so generous with the old; we've had a rough time with nursing homes"; Jim Shannon who supports his wife and seven children on the salary of a railroad clerk and janitor, describing the effects of a regressive sales tax that victimizes the small man but makes little impact on the rich; the official of the local OEO poverty agency talking about the county's third welfare generation and reflecting that "an admission of poverty is an admission of failure, and people here don't do that"; Tom Jolas describing Mason City's enthusiasm for the New York Mets when they won the World Series after a ninth-place finish in 1968 because "people believe in coming off the bottom."

And then you learn something else—about yourself, and about the phenomenon you choose to call Main Street. You hear them complain about Eastern urban provincialism, people who cannot believe that Mason City has television ("You must get it from the West Coast"), let alone an art museum, a decent library, or a couple of go-go joints (or that you can buy

Philip Roth, Malcolm X and Henry Miller in the bookstore), and you begin to understand, almost by suggestion, what the barriers of comprehension are all about. Is it really surprising that Main Street cannot fully comprehend talk about police brutality, police rigidity, or social disillusionment? If the system works here, why doesn't it work everywhere else?

Main Street's uniquely provincial vice lies in its excessive, unquestioning belief in the Protestant ethic—hard work, honesty—and conventional politics; New York's in the conviction that most of the time nothing may make much difference, that institutions and public life are by their very nature unresponsive. And if New York has come to doubt the values and the beliefs of tradition, it still hasn't invented anything to replace them. The anger of the blue-collar worker—at welfare, students, Negroes—is rooted in the frustrated ethic of Main Street, frustrated not only in its encounters with urban problems and technology but also in the growing doubt of the Best People—Wallace's pointy heads, Agnew's effete impudent snobs—that it still has merit. Among the characteristic excesses of rural populism (whether expressed by William Jennings Bryan, Joe McCarthy or Spiro Agnew) was a paranoia about Them: the Bankers, the railroads, the Eastern Establishmment, the Communists in government. But paranoia is surely also one of the characteristic defenses of almost every other inhabitant of New York. (If you try to explain the vicissitudes of dealing with Con Edison or the New York Telephone Company, most people in Mason City stare at you in disbelief; if you speak about rents and housing they're certain you've gone mad.) Every rural or small-town vote against some proposal for the alleviation of a problem in New York or Chicago or Cleveland is not merely an act of self-interest (keeping taxes low, protecting the farmers) but also a gesture of disbelief that Main Street's ethic and tactics—if they were really applied—would be ineffective in the Big City.

At the end, sitting in the waiting room at the municipal airport (all flights from Chicago are late, naturally), you detach yourself. You hear, still, one of the Federal Avenue lawyers saying. "This town is solid; it's solid as a commercial center and as a medical and cultural center for a large region." You see his nearly bare office—the brown wood furniture, the linoleum floors, and the fluorescent lights—see his partner, in a sleeveless gray pullover, walking through the outer office (Clarence Darrow?), and hear the trucks stopping for the red light at the intersection below. You hear Jack MacNider speaking about the gradual movement of the "iron triangle," the Midwestern industrial region, into north central Iowa, speaking about the ultimate industrialization of the area around the city. You see the high school homecoming queen, fragile and uncomfortable in the back of an open convertible in the wind-chilled stadium; see the wide residential streets with their maples and time-threatened elms, the section of magnificent houses by Prairie School architects, one of them by Frank Lloyd Wright, and the crumbling streets at the south end, near the Brick and Tile, and you hear, in that same neighborhood, two NAACP ladies, one white, one Negro, discussing the phrasing of a letter to the school board politely protesting the use of *Little Black Sambo* in the elementary grades. And then, finally, you hear again all those people speaking about how good Mason City is for raising a family, and you wonder what kind of society it is that must separate growing up and the rearing of children from the places where most of its business is transacted, its ideas discussed and its policies determined. And then you wonder, too, what would happen if something ever came seriously to disturb Main Street's normalcy, if direct demands were ever made, if the letters ceased being polite, if the dark places—the discrimination and disregard—were probed and, for the first time, tested. Small towns do co-opt, you think, not by what they do, not by their hospitality, but by what we wish they were—because all of us, big city boys and small, *want* to believe. And yet, when Ozark 974 rises from the runway, off to Dubuque, over the corn and beets, over the Mississippi, off to Chicago, you know that you can't go home again, that the world is elsewhere, and that every moment the distances grow not smaller but greater. Main Street is far away.

PART III

THE ENVIRONMENTAL CRISIS

Introduction: "We Have Met the Enemy..."

Familiar landmarks in several of the western states are huge piles of "tailings"—fine gray sand left over from the processing of uranium. For nearly two decades the mills and the Atomic Energy Commission permitted people to help themselves to the sand, free of charge. Consequently, many builders used it as a base for laying concrete basements and slabs for private homes and schools. In 1971 the residents of Grand Junction, Colorado, woke up to the possibility that the tailings may be dangerously radioactive.

Radioactive readings in some homes in Grand Junction have reached levels well beyond those permitted in uranium mines. . . .

Rooms with high radioactivity counts don't smell strangely. There is no eerie glow from the walls. Residents have not yet been told of the exact count at their homes and offices, though a few have been advised to install fans or ventilating equipment to clear the air in basement rooms.

So most of them just sit tight and wait to see what the state and Federal governments will decide to do. Some talk of selling their homes, but as one man pointed out: "Who would buy it?" [1]

[1] *New York Times*, 3 October 1971, sec. 4, p. 2.

Buried just below the surface of the ground at Hanford, Washington, lie 140 huge steel and concrete tanks containing millions of gallons of concentrated radioactive waste, the by-product of plutonium manufactured for nuclear weapons.

So intensely hot is this waste that it boils by itself for years, will be violently toxic for tens of thousands of years, and is so nasty that a few gallons released in a city's watershed might contaminate it for the indefinite future.

It seems that some of these tanks leak a little, and there have been a few instances of near-rupture. Since they are situated only 240 feet above the water table of the Columbia River, the possibility of a Really Big Show is always imminent. In addition, the chance of tank ruptures at Hanford is enhanced by the fact that it is in a seismically unstable area that is part of the earthquake belt that rings the Pacific, the one responsible for chronic temblors in Alaska, California, South America and Japan. Some geologists have theorized that an offshoot of a major fault runs underneath the atomic facilities and it is known that there was an earthquake in the general area as little as 52 years ago.

Though a quake might not damage the tanks themselves, it could harm the elaborate cooling and stirring systems that keep the tanks from developing hot spots. A breakdown might burst the seams and release radioactive gases into the air. If atmospheric conditions were right, these gases could blanket an extremely large territory like a killer smog, only far more virulent—yea, the havoc could prove worse than that wrought by the atomic bomb over Hiroshima.[2]

"Spent fuel" is transported from nuclear reactors to reprocessing centers in steel canisters aboard trucks and trains. Recently, in spite of elaborate precautions, a canister fell off a truck in Tennessee and for a while lay dented, but tight, in an open field.

A couple of years ago, a thirty-foot wave of "gob" slopped suddenly through a narrow valley in West Virginia, burying a dozen hamlets of Buffalo Creek and killing at least 125 persons. The "gob" had been released by the collapse of a mountainous slag heap behind which a four-teen-acre lake had collected "like a pool of gravy in a mound of mashed potato." The mining waste had been deposited by a subsidiary of the Pittston Company, the nation's fourth largest coal producer.

For years Pittston blithely disregarded state and federal laws prohibiting discharge of industrial wastes into navigable streams

---

[2] Richard Curtis and Dave Fisher, "The Seven Wonders of the Polluted World," *New York Times,* 26 September 1971, sec. 10, p. 15. In a recent incident a massive rupture of one of the tanks went unnoticed for a period of six weeks.

and "tributaries thereof" and proceeded to rid itself of slate, shale, coal, and sludge simply by dumping them into a hollow. The company also flouted regulations issued by the Bureau of Mines under the 1969 Coal Mine Health and Safety Act, which declare that "refuse piles shall not be constructed so as to impede drainage or impound water." The peril posed by the slag heap and the lake of poisonous water glistening on its top had been discovered long before the prolonged rainfall in late February. In 1966 then Interior Secretary Stewart Udall ordered the U.S. Geological Survey and the Bureau of Mines to make a study of mine-waste dumps in the coal fields. Among thirty-eight singled out as hazardous in West Virginia, an immense pile on Buffalo Creek drew the special attention of USGS geologist William Davies. . . .

Because of Davies's report federal officials knew of the existence of the gob pile, that it was unstable, that the northeast corner of the dam was weak, and that in a "hurricane-type" rainfall it would break and fill the valley. They knew that such rains would come to wet Appalachia—as one did for several sodden days in late February. But no action was taken. Udall sent a warning letter to the state's representatives and two senators and then governor, Hulett Smith. The letter proposed a requirement that the angle of the bank slopes be reduced and that adequate spillways be installed. The companies ignored the suggestions, the officials ignored the warning, and the Bureau of Mines ignored Udall's pledge "to continue to observe mine dumps for possible critical situations." No one did any costly boat rocking. In 1971 Pittston's profits soared to $44.4 million, a husky 16 percent of income.[3]

Following the disaster, in response to a study rating over 130 impoundments as dangerous, the West Virginia legislature authorized action against the coal companies and emergency repairs to the dams, but appropriated no funds to carry out its wishes.

Along the southern shore of Lake Michigan, just east of Chicago, there is a fifteen-mile stretch that seems to contain nothing but long, gray steel mills and rows of squat storage tanks belonging to oil refineries. Approaching this area from Chicago:

You drive only five minutes out of the Loop on the Chicago Skyway before the huge, gray, flame-flecked cloud mushrooms into view to the southeast. Then the sulphuric fumes hit, overriding the stench from the Chicago stockyards, forcing you to hastily wind up all windows. "Welcome to Gary, Ind.—City on the Move" proclaims the grimy green sign off Exit 2. Dingy, three-story buildings slide by, each coated with a curious rusty tinge. . . .

[3] Harry M. Caudill, "Buffalo Creek Aftermath," *Saturday Review,* 26 August 1972, pp. 16–17.

There are no especially well-dressed people on the streets of downtown Gary; wearing good clothes is as impractical as hanging a clean wash on a backyard line. New cars become old not long after arrival. The aging agent is the same encrusted grime that forces homeowners to paint their dwellings at least once a year. Outdoor recreation? "There ain't a decent beach or fishing hole left," says one steelworker, who in summer inflates a plastic backyard pool—and skims the scum off it daily. "The most frightening thing," says a young lawyer, "is how you don't notice how bad things are as long as you can see a few feet ahead. Then you go somewhere else for a vacation and it suddenly hits you. My God, I've been living in a fog! And then you finally ask yourself . . . Why do I stay?" [4]

A few years ago, it seemed to have suddenly hit many people all over the nation that they had been living in a deadly fog—in more ways than one—without noticing it, and they began asking, "Why do we put up with it?"

Officials from the U.S. Department of the Interior were conducting an inquiry into the pollution of Maine's Penobscot Bay by chicken-packing plants and pulp mills, when the testimony of the head of a local poultry firm was interrupted by anguished pleas from a man introducing himself as a lobster fisherman and clam man who had lived in the bay region all his life:

I have dragged scallops away out and have your entrails from your chicken plant on my scallop wire, which is 1,200 feet long, and I have caught lobsters out there, and I fished for cod and haddock with Gloucester fishermen over the years down in our bay, which is all gone now due to pollution. We have lost a million dollars worth of scallops. We have lost our recreation. We have lost everything due to pollution.

Now as president of Penobscot Poultry—and you are a very fine man, without any question, and I think I talked with you years ago—now, why for God's sake, can't we clean up this mess? . . .

We can't go down the shore any more. Our shores are littered. We slip and slide on the grease. My shores are littered from A to Z. I can't go down to my shore on a picnic any more.

What are we going to do?

I mean, I am right at the point of committing suicide. Now, that's honest to God.

I have worked all my life. I've got seven grandchildren. Wouldn't I love to see the day when I can go down and see my grandchildren swimming again on the shore?

---

[4] Harry Waters, "Gary: A Game of Pin the Blame," *Newsweek,* 26 January 1970, p. 38.

I know I am interrupting this meeting. I have put my foot right in it, but I've got to speak my piece, because if somebody doesn't do it, how are we going to get it cleaned up? . . .

I told my wife, I said, "Belle, if you will move up with me to Nova Scotia, we'll go up there and settle up there," and get out and let you, the Penobscot Poultry and Maplewood, have the city, but it isn't necessary.

All we ask of you, will you please work with us and help us clean up? That is all we ask. There is room enough for everybody. . . .

So you, as head of Penobscot Poultry, a nice man—you're a nice company; you are doing a wonderful thing for the State of Maine—but will you work with us and clean up this mess, please? . . .

How are you going to pound it through to the average man how many thousands of dollars he is losing by neglect? This has been on my mind. I am going crazy. In fact, I'm a crazy man now. You could probably put me right up in a strait jacket as far as I am concerned. But I spoke my piece.[5]

The widespread public concern over the environment that suddenly welled up in this country and others back in 1969 took most people by surprise. For, after all, the problems posed by smog and noise, impure water and accumulated rubbish, eroded and exhausted soil, and abandoned mines are not new, and one might expect people to have grown accustomed to their sights, smells, and sounds by this time. Indeed, there had been many early warning signals that things were getting worse, but to the general public they appeared to be unrelated, so there seemed to be no cause for alarm.

Easily within the memory of middle-aged people, for example, was an eco-catastrophe that occurred not just once but twice in the same area, the "Dust Bowl" in the middle of the American continent. Ignoring warnings from meteorologists that the high plains on both sides of the 102nd meridian were subject to periodic droughts, having been deceived by the wet phase of the weather cycle and tempted by the high price of wheat and the new tractor-technology of their day, American farmers during the early 1900s had plowed up millions of acres of natural grassland. (Today, conservationists refer to this operation as "the rape of the plains.") The inevitable dry spell came in the early 1930s. The plow-pulverized topsoil, no longer held together by a network of grass roots, turned into a fine powder that either blew away or drifted like dry, fluffy snow in the fields and streets, remorselessly seeping through cracks around doors and windows. Roads and pasturelands and ponds disappeared under shifting dunes of silt. Great expanses of wheat were either uprooted or smothered. Thousands of wells ran dry. The violent wind-

---

[5] "The Lobsterman's Lament," *American Forests*, April 1968, pp. 6, 47.

storms that came regularly every winter and spring became "black blizzards" during which visibility sometimes fell to zero and all traffic ceased, while farmers and townspeople sought shelter; mudballs formed over the eyes of cattle; wild geese fell dead, their throats blocked with dirt; and the sky over Chicago, 600 miles away, turned an eerie shade of yellow-brown.

In combination with the Great Depression, the Dust Bowl caused the mass flight to California that John Steinbeck described so movingly in *The Grapes of Wrath.*

By the time the drought lifted a decade later, much of the area had become a barren desert, its rich humus gone, its hardpan subsoil now gullied by the long-awaited rain. The remaining acreage was "mined" by "suitcase farmers" who lived in nearby cities and commuted to their farms just enough to plant for a maximum yield and a quick profit protected by the Federal Government's crop insurance program. During the early 1950s the rains stayed away again, and, like a volcano, the Dust Bowl was reactivated.

Another early warning of the social costs of mismanaging our environment was the disaster at Donora, Pennsylvania, in 1948, in which at least twenty people were killed and nearly 6,000 (more than one-third of the city's population in those days) were made ill by breathing the outdoor air. With the wisdom of hindsight, some of the survivors recognized that everybody should have seen such a calamity coming. For thirty years preceding, fumes from a zinc smelter and sulfuric-acid plant had killed practically all the vegetation in the city and its immediate vicinity, making everything as desolate-looking as a moonscape.

(In view of Donora's experience, how should New Yorkers react to the news that Cleopatra's Needle, a granite obelisk whose hieroglyphic characters, carved deeply into all four of its sides, were plainly visible when it arrived after 3500 years in Egypt, has been literally eaten smooth on two sides by only ninety years' exposure to chemicals in the air of Central Park?)

The Donora temperature inversion was overshadowed four years later by a killer smog in London that still holds the world's record for casualties and damage.

It began like an ordinary English fog—the kind that makes London indescribably lovely. Toward twilight the city is veiled in a silvery-gold mist through which you can see about a hundred yards. All the lights have halos; from the Embankment the massive buildings along the Strand have all the mystery of Oriental palaces, their outlines softened and shadowy. "The whole city hangs in the heavens," Whistler said.

On the afternoon of Thursday, December 4, 1952, there was nothing to indicate that this would be the Fog of the Century—that it would kill about 4000 persons, cause property damage of many millions of dollars and bring the activities of the great metropolis almost to a halt.

By Friday morning a heavy, wet blanket had closed down. You could just see your own feet. The streets were a queer, unfamiliar world. As you groped along the sidewalk, blurred faces without bodies floated past you. Sounds were curiously muffled: motorcar horns, grinding brakes, the warning cries of pedestrians trying to avoid the traffic and one another. This was a real "peasouper," a "London particular."

The main arteries leading into the center of town were clogged with buses moving at two miles an hour. The conductors walked ahead, calling directions to the drivers.

Private cars formed convoys, 15 or 20 in line. Sometimes a driver got impatient, tried to get ahead—usually with disastrous results. Cars got hopelessly lost. Police were powerless to untangle the traffic snarls that developed at converging streets. Drivers abandoned their cars, further blocking traffic. . . .

At London airport a few planes made instrument landings. One pilot, after landing, got lost trying to taxi to the passenger terminal. After half an hour a search party went out to look for him. But it got lost too. Soon all air traffic was suspended. . . .

As the day went on, the fog changed color. In the early morning it had been a dirty white. When a million chimneys began to pour coal smoke into the air it became light brown, dark brown, black. It got into your nose, your throat, your lungs. By afternoon all London was coughing.

Even yet most Londoners weren't seriously worried—except the weather forecasters. Fog occurs when a body of moist air is cooled and condenses into tiny droplets, which attract and hold particles of soot and smoke. Ordinarily fog is dissipated by wind— the lightest current of air is enough; or the fog rises into the cooler layers of air that usually lie above it.

Now there was no wind, and no promise of any. Worse, the layer of air above the fog was not cooler but warmer. Meteorologists call this rare occurrence an "inversion roof." The upper, warmer layer acts as a lid, holding the fog down. And hour by hour its content of smoke and soot grows denser.

Saturday morning thousands of Londoners began to be frightened. They were those persons, mostly over 50, who had a tendency to bronchitis or asthma. In a long black fog such people are in acute distress. Their lungs burn, their hearts labor, they gasp for breath. They feel as if they are choking to death—and sometimes they do.

By Saturday noon all the doctors in London were on the run. Even with transportation normal they couldn't have reached all the patients who needed them. Some of them stayed in their offices and tried to help sufferers by phone. But there wasn't much to suggest— except to try to get to an oxygen tent. All hospitals were overworked. A mounting number of deaths was reported. . . .

On Sunday morning the fog was thicker than ever. At times visibility got down to 11 inches: literally you couldn't see your hand held out in front of your face. All over London middle-aged and elderly persons were choking their lives away.

The city grew very quiet. Nearly all traffic had come to a halt. The only thing to be heard was the muffled sound of church bells, and the bells of ambulances groping their way toward victims of the fog.

It was cold that day. On the outskirts of town men and women, lost in the murk, sat down—and later were found dead of exposure. In South London 50 bodies were taken to one mortuary.

Toward noon on Monday the fog lifted a little, then came down again. Then it rose a little more. Finally all was clear.

Londoners rubbed the soot out of their eyes and saw a city covered with dirt. Every piece of furniture had a slimy, black film. Curtains were so encrusted with soot that when they were cleaned they went to pieces. Blonde women became brunettes. It was weeks before the hairdressers and laundries and cleaners caught up with their work. . . .

How to prevent its happening again? London will always have fogs. To prevent a white fog from turning black and killing people you need to reduce the volume of smoke that is poured into the air. But in London the factories are not the chief cause of the killing black fog. Rather it is the domestic hearth, the open fireplace burning soft coal that heats most English homes. In London's population of eight million there are probably two million such fires going every cold day, each one rolling out its cloud of black smoke. Open soft-coal fires are inefficient. They produce more smoke and less heat than any other heating method.

Then why not change? Because Englishmen like open fires and insist on having them. For 800 years they have been burning coal in their fires—sea coal, it used to be called. It has always been the only fuel most people could afford. And for 800 years the Englishman's rulers have been trying to make him stop burning soft coal. It is recorded that Queen Elizabeth I "findeth hersealfe greately greved and annoyed by the taste and smoake of the sea coales." She tried to stop it, as did the Stuarts and many later governments. In the winter of 1879–80 there were almost continuous black fogs for four months and deaths in London were 10,000 above the average. But efforts to abolish the soft-coal open hearth failed.

And so it is today. Some houses in London have converted to central heating and to oil; many new homes have modern methods of heating. But far more of them, new and old, stick to the old open hearth. More than a question of cost, it is the Englishman's stubborn insistence on his fireside.[6]

[6] Edwin Muller, "The Great London Fog," *Reader's Digest*, May 1953, pp. 25–28.

(The above was written too soon after the event to measure its impact on the romance between the Englishman and his fireplace. It often takes a catastrophe to turn people's attitudes around; that's what happened in this case. In 1956 Parliament passed a clean air act, forcing everyone in certain areas to convert to smokeless solid fuels or gas and electric heaters. The results have been dramatic. Londoners have not seen a soupy, sulfurous fog since 1964, and smoke concentrations have been reduced by about 80 percent.)

Most Americans tended to pass off the killing smogs of Donora and London as freakish accidents of nature, irrelevant to their lives. While the Dust Bowl was making news again during the 1950s, its lesson in the interrelated complexity of the environment was ignored, along with other signs that human beings were recklessly fouling their own nest. The fallout from nuclear bomb tests in the upper atmosphere, instead of remaining in the stratosphere and decaying over a period of years, as our scientists expected, was coming down after only a few months, still highly radioactive, and spreading all over the globe, poisoning everybody's milk and vegetables with cancer-producing strontium 90. The construction of the St. Lawrence Seaway not only opened up the Great Lakes to ocean-going ships but also to ocean-going pirates like the sea lamprey. In a short time, lake trout were on the verge of extinction and the commercial fishing industry was ruined. Abroad, while the Aswan Dam built by Soviet engineers on the Upper Nile in Egypt created a huge lake for irrigating the desert, it also stopped the flow of silt which used to offset the natural erosion of the Nile's delta, possibly resulting in a net loss of productive land rather than a gain, besides a drastic reduction in commercial fishing also dependent on the nutrient-rich silt. In the meantime, back in this country, Lake Erie, a huge inland sea, began to "die" of unnatural causes, and hardly anybody noticed. In parts of the lake, industrial wastes and household detergents killed just about every form of animal life except sludge worms and a carp mutant adapted to living off poison.

Further evidence mounted in the 1960s of the unforeseen social costs of environmental abuse and reliance on specialists whose training blinded them to the big picture. At the time it was published in 1962, Rachel Carson's *Silent Spring,* which warned about the damage being done by pesticides, was a voice crying in the wilderness. Nevertheless, public awareness did begin to build up across the nation, as the embryo of a social movement gradually took shape alongside several others spawned by the general social unrest of that decade. Old expectations that a society couldn't have too much technological progress and economic growth were being questioned. The spread of affluence and middle-class standards, combined with a rise in educational levels and the acceleration of social contagion made possible by the mass media, had created new expectations regarding the quality of the life that would now be within reach if it were not for increasing pollution and scarcity of natural resources. Thwarted expectations—whether new or old—tend to generate rebelliousness.

In 1966 New York City was trapped under an inversion layer of warm air that kept fumes from rising; the smog killed over a hundred elderly people with respiratory troubles. In response, the mayor appointed a Task Force on Air Pollution, which advised him after a six-month study that if present trends were not checked New York City could become uninhabitable within seven to ten years. Many people were startled when "the only body of water ever classified as a fire hazard," the chocolate-brown Cuyahoga River, which oozes through Cleveland on its way to Lake Erie, full of volatile industrial waste, caught fire and burned two railroad trestles. However, the one event that probably helped more than any other to precipitate a crisis atmosphere was a mammoth oil spill in 1969 along the California coast at Santa Barbara. An oil well being drilled in the publicly owned ocean floor, under a lease from the federal government, suddenly "blew wild." Thousands of gallons of black, tarry goo gushed out of control and covered the ocean surface with an oil slick for more than 800 square miles, fouling thirty miles of beaches and killing thousands of birds and fish, and ruining the commercial fishing and tourist trade for months.

At last, events fell into place and a pattern was widely discerned. Public health specialists, social scientists, and political leaders began to see the outlines of the big picture visible in the past only to ecologists. A nationwide crusade to save the environment was launched. Media journalists began alerting the general public to the teachings of ecology, which, up to that time, was a mystery to most people. It is the scientific study of the intricate web of relationships between living organisms and their surroundings—both living and nonliving. For the layman, its chief lesson is that, in spite of his vaunted technology, man is still utterly dependent on nature's ecosystems (oceans, coastal estuaries, forests, grasslands, etc.), which in turn are interdependent. Each ecosystem is a chain of life consisting of four primary links: (1) nonliving materials such as soil, water, air, and sunlight; (2) plants for producing; (3) animals for consuming; and (4) tiny creatures like bacteria and fungi for decomposing. Modern man is caught in a fateful conflict between, on the one hand, his innate biological role as a subsidiary participant in these ecosystems, and, on the other hand, the social role he has acquired as an exploiter and master of them. Essentially, the Environmental Crisis is a new awareness that affluent, technologically advanced societies like ours are on a collision course with the environment. Involved is far more than cleaning up and beautification. By upsetting stable ecosystems we are courting disaster; we may be on the brink of making our land uninhabitable. Some experts say that we have only thirty-five years left. The optimists among them estimate that some human beings will still be alive a hundred years from now even at the present rate of resource abuse.

Barry Commoner believes that the relatively new science of ecology has already accumulated a number of generalizations worth organizing into an informal set of "laws":

1. *Everything is connected to everything else.* [Basic to ecological thinking is the assumption that every effect is also a cause, and, when they are linked together, causes and effects form long chains that eventually circle back to where they started:] an animal's waste becomes food for soil bacteria; what bacteria excrete nourishes plants; animals eat the plants. [Ecologists worry that we may have gone too far toward breaking] out of the circle of life, converting its endless cycles into man-made, linear events: oil is taken from the ground, distilled into fuel, burned in an engine, converted thereby into noxious fumes, which are emitted into the air. At the end of the line is smog.

2. *Everything must go somewhere.* . . . In nature there is no such thing as "waste." In every natural system, what is excreted by one organism as waste is taken up by another as food.

3. *Nature knows best.* . . . Any major man-made change in a natural system is likely to be *detrimental* to that system. . . . Living things accumulate a complex organization of compatible parts; those possible arrangements that are not compatible with the whole are screened out over the long course of evolution. Thus, the structure of a present living thing or the organization of a current natural ecosystem is likely to be "best" in the sense that it has been so heavily screened for disadvantageous components that any new one is very likely to be worse than the present ones. . . . One of the striking facts about the chemistry of living systems is that for every organic substance produced by a living organism, there exists, somewhere in nature, an enzyme capable of breaking that substance down. In effect, no organic substance is synthesized unless there is provision for its degradation; recycling is thus enforced. Thus, when a new man-made organic substance is synthesized with a molecular structure that departs significantly from the types which occur in nature, it is probable that no degradative enzyme exists, and the material tends to accumulate. . . .

4. *There is no such thing as a free lunch.* . . . Every gain is won at some cost. In a way, this ecological law embodies the previous three laws. Because the global ecosystem is a connected whole, in which nothing can be gained or lost and which is not subject to over-all improvement, anything extracted from it by human effort must be replaced. Payment of this price cannot be avoided; it can only be delayed. The present environmental crisis is a warning that we have delayed nearly too long.[7]

Most of the damage to the American environment has happened during only the past twenty-five years. The principal villain has been the

[7] Barry Commoner, *The Closing Circle* (New York: Knopf, 1971), pp. 11–46 passim.

postwar development of new technologies that break out of natural ecological cycles: synthetic products (such as plastic, nylon, aluminum al-
loys, detergents, DDT, and chemical fertilizers) which nature cannot re-
cycle because they are nondegradable; and new techniques that destroy
in minutes what nature took hundreds of years to build (such as strip-
mining, described in "Appalachia: The Case of Eastern Kentucky" in the
preceding section on the Rural Crisis). The environmental and social
costs of the new technologies have been multiplied several times since
World War II by exponential growth in this country's population and general affluence, and made acute in some places by the increasing mobility
of people and their crowding into metropolises. Current population
projections show a need to duplicate the whole paraphernalia of our way
of life during the next thirty years—equivalent to all the houses, schools,
roads, etc., built by the United States in the last three hundred. Our rising
levels of consumption and increasing reliance on the new technologies
provoke many environmentalists into concluding that the central problem
is "popullution," because "in terms of polluting the environment and
using up the Earth's resources the United States is one of the most *overpopulated* countries in the world. Nowhere [else] is there more pollution
per person." [8] Nor more consumption per person. Although numbering
less than six percent of the world's population, the American people con-
sume nearly thirty percent of its total raw-materials production.

Furthermore, the U.S. is critically short of several key minerals. A
modern economy depends on thirteen basic raw materials. If it needs to
import more than half of one of these economists classify it as "import-
dependent." Twenty-five years ago this country was import-dependent on
only four of the thirteen: aluminum, manganese, nickel, and tin. Twenty-five
years from now specialists expect us to be import-dependent on all but
one of the basic thirteen—phosphorus.

The successful moon landings have encouraged many to believe that
no problem need any longer be considered insoluble. But where there's a
way there need not be a will. Social life, after all, resembles nature's
closed ecological system in which everything is connected to everything
else and nothing is really free of charge because getting something one
wants always involves giving up something else that one wants. As Peter
Schrag has pointed out, one can respond cheaply to the Environmental
Crisis "by lamenting the fix that science and technology have gotten us
into, but a bumper sticker proclaiming SAVE LAKE ERIE pasted barely a
foot above a smoky automobile exhaust is more an illustration of the
problem than a solution." [9]

Soon after a strong national consensus was formed during 1969–70,

[8] Norman Cousins, "Affluence and Effluence," *Saturday Review,* 2 May 1970,
p. 53. See also Wayne H. Davis, "Overpopulated America," *New Republic,* 10 January 1970, and the writings of Paul R. Ehrlich.

[9] Peter Schrag, "Life on a Dying Lake," *Saturday Review,* 20 September 1969,
p. 56.

that a crisis does exist and something must be done about it, it became clear that that "something" included selective weeding of deeply rooted habits, attitudes, and vested interests. Witness the screams of outrage when guidelines were proposed that would somewhat restrict automobile use within cities. Since then the inevitable backlash has been sweeping the nation, warning people against yielding to hysteria, because anything other than symptomatic relief seems stymied by insoluble dilemmas, for example: (1) Protection of the environment calls for measures to cut back on pollution, but full employment demands business expansion which will increase pollution. Moreover, antipollution regulations may put some factories out of business and many men out of work. Furthermore, how can the tremendous cost of cleaning up the environment be paid without an expanding economy with its attendant increase in pollution and the consumption of resources? (2) Present standards of living are threatened by the effects on the environment of the very things responsible for the living standards, e.g., consumption of our high productivity depends partly on deliberately building obsolescence into products and *not* repairing or recycling; packaging aggravates the problem of waste disposal but it also helps sell one product in competition with another; pesticides may have long-range harmful effects but in the short run they increase agricultural production. (3) To sell recycling to the people entails erasing the social stigma attached to junk and reusing what other people have discarded, and for recycling to succeed, long-standing tax incentives may have to be shifted from mining to salvaging—involved are vested interests. Furthermore, recovering a material from waste may drive its price down, and thus reduce the incentive to recover more of it. (4) How can pollution be reduced without also reducing individual and corporate liberty and states' rights? (5) Many people say that what we need is *more* technology, not less—new technology specially designed to clean up after itself. But for every problem technology solves it seems to create at least one new one. For example: (a) The new detergents replacing the phosphate-type have turned out to be so caustic that they poison anyone who is careless; (b) Recycling paper may actually increase pollution, because breaking down paper to reclaim its fibers involves using very harsh caustic acids which are then dumped into a water system; furthermore the ink and fillers removed from used paper must be deposited somewhere—usually into a river or sludge dump—and their removal from the paper fiber renders them no longer biodegradable, but totally inert; (c) New methods of recovering paper mill pollutants require huge amounts of extra electricity, which must be generated by either fossil-fueled plants that foul the air or nuclear plants that raise the temperature of rivers; (d) Shifting from landfill dumping to incineration merely shifts the pressure from one scarce resource (land) to another (clean air); (e) Likewise, aerating sewage to clean up the water aggravates the problem of air pollution; (f) Devices that reduce the hydrocarbons and carbon monoxide in car exhaust not only increase the consumption of scarce fuel, but also raise engine temperatures; the rise in temperature boosts the emission of nitrogen oxides, which then mix with air and convert to highly toxic nitrogen dioxide. One set of poisons exchanged for an even worse set! Are technological answers illusory?

"Man cannot live by ecology alone," complain critics of the ecology movement. They recognize that ecological thinking goes against the grain of Western civilization, challenging the very principles by which it has achieved power and glory. Ecology teaches, for instance, that human beings are prisoners of a colossal system of interacting organisms, food chains, and rhythmic cycles; the Judaic-Christian tradition, however, teaches that man is outside and above all that; nature exists primarily for men to conquer, and life should be perceived as a struggle against—not a joint venture with—nature. (According to the Book of Genesis, man was created in the image of God, who gave him "dominion over the fish of the sea, and over the birds of the air, and over the cattle, and over all the earth, and over every creeping thing that creepeth upon the earth.")

If we want to rescue the environment, ecologists advise us that we need to develop a new social ethic that gives the highest priority to harmony between man and nature—a new spirit of community that also embraces future generations of mankind, plants, and animals. The crisis tones of ecologists have panicked some people into making foolish, emotional tirades blaming pollution on science and technology in general, rather than on their own attitudes and value priorities. "We ought all to live closer to nature and stop interfering with it," they scold. Yet, the last thing these people want to do is to live closer to nature, when they realize what that means.

In addition, the study of ecology suggests that what the Environmental Crisis requires—and for that matter, all other social crises—is multidimensional thinking that simultaneously pays attention to connections going off in all directions, comprehending wholes as well as parts. However, Western nations measure their success in science and technology by the degree to which they have conquered nature, and attribute their success to the practice of thinking linearly in logical steps, concentrating on one thing at a time, isolating, simplifying, and, above all, specializing. (Jay Forrester of Massachusetts Institute of Technology maintains that the human mind is limited to linear reasoning and thus incapable of grasping total systems involving chain reactions and spirals in a state of flux, but the computer can do it if programmed with enough of the right data.)

Moreover, the principles of ecology rub Americans the wrong way by contradicting rules of mass production and many of the sacred values of the "frontier ethic." The frontier experience seemed to justify an assumption that, whereas time and labor are in limited supply and therefore must not be wasted, nature is endlessly bountiful; consequently, land is just another commodity to be consumed, a person should be free to use his land in any way he pleases, and it is more efficient to discard used things than to expend time and labor on repairs. Ecology, on the other hand, teaches that some resources, such as water and oxygen, are renewed only if nature is given enough time, and others, like minerals and topsoil, are practically nonrenewable; ecologists define land as a finite resource that is essential for the common welfare and, hence, something to be carefully husbanded; and as for discarding things because they have been used: ecologically speaking, wastes are liabilities only when they have not been cycled back into the system—pollutants are resources disguised as nuisances.

In addition to the ideal of equality, the frontier taught Americans to value quantity over quality; to measure progress according to quantitative growth in production, acquisition, and consumption; and to award high status to those who produce more or pioneer new ways to exploit the country's resources. In contrast, ecology teaches that infinite quantitative growth is impossible on a finite planet, and ecologists question the ethics of basing economic growth today on the exploitation of nonrenewable resources belonging to people in "developing" countries who are bound to miss them later when they reach a higher stage of industrialization. Consequently, they recommend dedicating ourselves to growth in the *quality* of life and concentrating on making things last longer, recycling, and going without.

Ever since the days of the frontier and unrestricted immigration, rapid expansion of an area's population has been taken as a sign of approval and a guarantee of rising economic values, whereas a stable population has been feared as a sign of decadence and a harbinger of economic stagnation. But studies of human ecology indicate that a low birthrate could do more than perhaps anything else to lower the temperatures of all three social crises—Urban, Rural, and Environmental. Computers at the Massachusetts Institute of Technology, programmed with a model of worldwide trends, have recently predicted a disastrous collapse of society within one hundred years if growth rates for population and industrial output are not stabilized soon. The sponsors of the study concede that such a task calls for a "Copernican revolution of the mind."

Still another fundamental part of American ideology attributable to the frontier is individualism, that is, putting the individual's welfare ahead of the common welfare. At least one ecologist, Garrett Hardin, calls this a tragedy. In explanation, he asks us to imagine a pasture open to all members of a village, like the "common" of an old New England town. Each herdsman comes to the same logical conclusion: it is to his personal advantage to keep adding animals to his herd even beyond the point where the meadow is being overgrazed and each cow becomes scrawny and her milk production drops, since the value of each cow accrues to him alone while the losses due to overgrazing are shared with all the other herdsmen. "Therein is the tragedy," writes Hardin.

Each man is locked into a system that compels him to increase his herd without limit—in a world that is limited. Ruin is the destination toward which all men rush, each pursuing his own best interest in a society that believes in the freedom of the commons. Freedom in a commons brings ruin to all.[10]

Hardin gives several examples of what might be called the "law of the commons" operating as a factor in environmental problems: federal officials who feel constant pressure from cattlemen who lease public land and want to increase the head count to the point of overgrazing; fish as a food source threatened by extinction as a result of the world's ocean fishing grounds being overfished by a few nations that have developed superior technology; the values sought by visitors to the National Parks being steadily eroded in a vicious circle by the increasing number of visitors attracted by these same values.

In a reverse way, the tragedy of the commons reappears in problems of pollution. Here it is not a question of taking something out of the commons, but of putting something in—sewage, or chemical, radioactive, and heat wastes into water; noxious and dangerous fumes into the air; and distracting and unpleasant advertising signs into the line of sight. The calculations of utility are much the same as before. The rational man finds that his share of the cost of the wastes he discharges into the commons is less than the cost of purifying his wastes before releasing them. Since this is true for everyone, we are locked into a system of "fouling our own nest," so long as we behave only as independent, rational, free-enterprisers. . . .

Our society is deeply committed to the welfare state, and hence is confronted with another aspect of the tragedy of the commons. In a welfare state, how shall we deal with the family, the religion, the race, or the class (or indeed any distinguishable and cohesive group) that adopts overbreeding as a policy to secure its own aggrandizement? To couple the concept of freedom to breed with the belief that everyone born has an equal right to the commons is to lock the world into a tragic course of action. . . .

The commons, if justifiable at all, is justifiable only under conditions of low-population density. As the human population has increased, the commons has had to be abandoned in one aspect after another.

First we abandoned the commons in food gathering, enclosing farmland and restricting pastures and hunting and fishing areas. These restrictions are still not complete throughout the world.

[10] Garrett Hardin, "The Tragedy of the Commons," *Science,* 13 December 1968, p. 1244. For an economist's analysis of a similar phenomenon, i.e., how conventional economic theory ignores the direct and indirect losses suffered by third persons or the general public as a result of private economic activities, see K. William Kapp, *The Social Costs of Private Enterprise* (New York: Schocken, 1971).

Somewhat later we saw that the commons as a place for waste disposal would also have to be abandoned. Restrictions on the disposal of domestic sewage are widely accepted in the Western world; we are still struggling to close the commons to pollution by automobiles, factories, insecticide sprayers, fertilizing operations, and atomic energy installations.

In a still more embryonic state is our recognition of the evils of the commons in matters of pleasure. There is almost no restriction on the propagation of sound waves in the public medium. The shopping public is assaulted with mindless music, without its consent. . . . Advertisers muddy the airwaves of radio and television and pollute the view of travelers. We are a long way from outlawing the commons in matters of pleasure. Is this because our Puritan inheritance makes us view pleasure as something of a sin, and pain (that is, the pollution of advertising) as the sign of virtue? [11]

In view of the sharp conflict between its principles and our traditional way of life, is it any wonder that some call ecology "the subversive science"?

What, then, is the likelihood that we will change our habits, attitudes, and values in time to rescue our environment? Our past behavior suggests that we will change in the nick of time—but only enough to survive, not enough to preserve the quality of our lives.

Perhaps the greatest obstacle to the rescue of the environment is man's own uncanny adaptability. "Modern man," as Dubos notes ruefully, "can adjust to environmental pollution, intense crowding, deficient or excessive diet, as well as to monotonous and ugly surroundings." And these adjustments are reinforced by the process of natural selection; so that the human beings who take most readily to regimentation, overcrowding, and esthetic privation rise to positions of leadership and also outbreed their less adaptable fellows. The real specter that pollution casts over man's future is not, perhaps, the extinction of Homo sapiens but his mutation into some human equivalent of the carp now lurking in Lake Erie's fetid depths, living off poison.[12]

In the first of the articles that follow, Barry Commoner shows how the principles of ecology apply to the case of California. In the second one, a troop of "Nader's Raiders" exposes the frontier ethic and the law of the commons at work in Savannah, Georgia.

The manner in which profit-hungry businessmen respond to criticism of industrial pollution reminds one ecologist of that old absurdity, " 'Shut

[11] Ibid., pp. 1245–48.
[12] *Newsweek,* 26 January 1970, p. 47.

up!' he explained." [13] But it is simplistic to reduce social problems and their remedies to "Who is to blame?" and "Throw the rascals out," instead of asking "What is wrong with the system?" and "How should it be reformed?" For we are all collectively responsible for the Environmental Crisis: "We have met the enemy, and they are us" [14]—as illustrated by the last two case studies, which suggest that confronting workers and residents with conclusive evidence that their health is being hurt by industrial pollution asks them to wrestle with prickly choices they would rather not touch.

[13] Bruce Wallace, *People, Their Needs, Environment, Ecology* (Englewood Cliffs, N.J.: Prentice-Hall, 1972), p. 162.
[14] The wording of the title and conclusion of this essay is borrowed from the possum in Walt Kelly's comic strip "Pogo," whose "We have met the enemy, and they are us," gave an original twist to the famous laconic report of Captain Oliver H. Perry, victor over a British fleet on Lake Erie in 1813: "We have met the enemy, and they are ours."

14

California

BARRY COMMONER

No one can escape the enormous fact that California has changed. What was once desert has become the most productive land in the world. The once-lonely mountain tops are crisscrossed with humming power lines. Powerful industries, from old ones like steel to the most modern aerospace and electronic operations, have been built. California has become one of the most fruitful, one of the richest places on the surface of the earth. This is all change, and it is good.

But there are other changes in California. Its vigorous growth has been achieved by many men and women who came to give their children a healthy place to live. Now, however, when school children in Los Angeles run out to the playing fields, they are confronted by the warning: "Do not exercise strenuously or breathe too deeply during heavy smog conditions." For the sunshine that once bathed the land in golden light has been blotted out by deadly smog. In a number of California towns the water supplies now contain levels of nitrate above the limit recommended by the U. S. Public Health Service; given to infants, nitrate can cause a fatal disorder,

Source: Barry Commoner, "Can We Survive?" *The Washington Monthly* (December 1969). Reprinted by permission of the author. Copyright © 1969 The Washington Monthly Co., 1028 Connecticut Ave. N.W., Washington, D.C. 20036.

methemoglobinemia, and pediatricians have recommended the use of bottled water for infant formulas. The natural resources of California, once a magnet that attracted thousands who sought a good life, now harbor threats to health. Beaches that once sparkled in the sun are polluted with oil and foul-smelling deposits. Rivers that once teemed with fish run sluggishly to the sea. The once famous crabs in San Francisco Bay are dying. Redwoods are toppling from the banks of eroding streams. All this, too, is change, and it is bad.

Thus, much of the good that has been produced in California, through the intelligence and hard work of its people, has been won at a terrible cost. That cost is the possible destruction of the very capital which has been invested to create the wealth of the state—its environment.

The environment makes up a huge, enormously complex living machine —an ecosystem—and every human activity depends on the integrity and proper functioning of that machine. Without the ecosystem's green plants, there would be no oxygen for smelters and furnaces, let alone to support human and animal life. Without the action of plants and animals in aquatic systems, there would be no pure water to supply agriculture, industry, and the cities. Without the biological processes that have gone on in the soil for thousands of years, there would be neither food crops, oil, nor coal. This machine is our biological capital, the basic apparatus on which our total productivity depends. If it is destroyed, agriculture and industry will come to naught; yet the greatest threats to the environmental system are due to agricultural and industrial activities. If the ecosystem is destroyed, man will go down with it; yet it is man who is destroying it. For in the eager search for the benefits of modern science and technology, we have become enticed into a nearly fatal illusion: that we have at last escaped from the dependence of man on the rest of nature. The truth is tragically different. We have become not less dependent on the balance of nature, but more dependent on it. Modern technology has so stressed the web of processes in the living environment at its most vulnerable points that there is little leeway left in the system. We are approaching the point of no return; our survival is at stake.

These are grim, alarming conclusions; but they are forced on us, I am convinced, by the evidence. Let us look at some of that evidence.

A good place to begin is the farm—on which so much of California's prosperity is based. The wealth created by agriculture is derived from the soil. In it we grow crops which convert inorganic materials—nitrogen, phosphorus, carbon, oxygen, and the other elements required by life—into organic materials—proteins, carbohydrates, fats, and vitamins—which comprise our food.

The soil, the plants that grow in it, the livestock raised on the land, and we ourselves are parts of a huge web of natural processes—endless, self-perpetuating cycles. Consider, for example, the behavior of nitrogen, an element of enormous nutritional importance, forming as it does the basis of proteins and other vital life substances. Most of the earth's available nitrogen is in the air, as nitrogen gas. This can enter the soil through nitrogen fixation, a process carried out by various bacteria, some of them living free in the soil and others associated with the roots of legumes such as clover. In nature, nitrogen also enters the soil from the wastes produced by animals. In both cases the nitrogen becomes incorporated into a complex organic material in the soil—humus. The humus slowly releases nitrogen through the action of soil microorganisms which finally convert it into nitrate. In turn, the nitrate is taken up by the roots of plants and is made into protein and other vital parts of the crop. In a natural situation the plant becomes food for animals, their wastes are returned to the soil, and the cycle is complete.

This cycle is an example of the biological capital that sustains us. How has this capital been used in California?

The huge success of agriculture in California is a matter of record; it forms the largest single element in the state's economy. To achieve this wealth a vast area in the center of the state has been transformed from a bare desert into the richest agricultural land in the nation. How has this been done? How has this transformation affected the continued usefulness of the soil system, especially the nitrogen cycle?

When the first farmers came to the San Joaquin Valley, they found fertile soil and sunshine; only water was needed to make the valley bloom. This was obtained first from local streams and later, increasingly, from wells which tapped the huge store of water that lay beneath the entire Central Valley. As the bountiful crops were taken, the soil, originally rich in nitrogen, became impoverished. To sustain crop productivity, inorganic nitrogen fertilizers were added to the soil. But with the loss of natural soil nitrogen, humus was depleted; as a result the soil became less porous, and less oxygen reached the roots, which were then less efficient in taking up the needed nutrients from the soil. The answer: more nitrogen fertilizer, for even if a smaller proportion is taken up by the crop, this can be overcome by using more fertilizer to begin with. California now uses more nitrogen fertilizer than any other state. . . .

One of the rules of environmental biology is: "Everything has to go somewhere," and we may ask: Where did the extra nitrate added to the soil, but not taken up by the crops, go? The answer is clear: The unused nitrate was carried down into the soil, accumulating at greater and greater depths as the water table fell due to the continual pumping of irrigation water.

With the water table falling, agriculture in the Central Valley was headed for disaster; recognizing this fact, the state constructed the Friant-

Kern Canal, which began to supply the valley with above-ground irrigation water beginning in 1951. Irrigation water must always be supplied to soil in amounts greater than that which is lost by evaporation; otherwise salts accumulate in the soil and the plants are killed. So, following the opening of the new canal, the valley water table began to rise toward its original level—carrying with it the long-accumulated nitrates in the soil.

Now there is another simple rule of environmental biology that is appropriate here: "Everything is connected to everything else." The valley towns soon learned this truth, as their drinking water supplies—which were taken from wells that tapped the rising level of underground water —began to show increasing concentrations of nitrate. In the 1950's, the Bureau of Sanitary Engineering of the California Department of Public Health began to analyze the nitrate content of city water supplies in the area. They had good reason for this action, for in July, 1950, an article in the *Journal of the American Water Works Association* had described 139 cases of infant methemoglobinemia in the United States identified since 1947; 14 cases were fatal; all were attributed to farm well water contaminated with more than 45 ppm of nitrate.

At first, only a few scattered instances of high nitrate levels were found in valley water supplies. However, a study of 800 wells in southern California counties in 1960 showed that 88 of them exceeded the 45 ppm limit; 188 wells had reached half that level. In that year, the U. S. Public Health Service recommended that a nitrate level of 45 ppm should not be exceeded, warning:

> Cases of infantile nitrate poisoning have been reported to arise from concentrations ranging from 66 to 1100 ppm. . . . Nitrate poisoning appears to be confined to infants during their first few months of life; adults drinking the same water are not affected, but breast-fed infants of mothers drinking such water may be poisoned. Cows drinking water containing nitrate may produce milk sufficiently high in nitrate to result in infant poisoning.

In Delano, a 1952 analysis showed only traces of nitrate in the city water supply; in 1966, analyses of three town wells obtained by the Delano Junior Chamber of Commerce showed nitrate levels of 70–78 ppm. In 1968, a study by the Water Resources Board, made in reply to a request by State Senator Walter W. Stiern, showed:

> Nitrate concentrations in groundwater underlying the vicinity of Delano are currently in excess of the limit . . . recommended by the U. S. Public Health Service. . . . Similar geologic and hydrologic

conditions occur in other areas of the San Joaquin Valley and the state generally.

So, agricultural wealth of the Central Valley has been gained, but at a cost that does not appear in the farmers' balance sheets—the general pollution of the state's huge underground water reserves with nitrate. Fortunately, there appear to be no reports of widespread acute infant methemoglobinemia in the area as yet. However, the effects of chronic exposure to nitrates are poorly understood. We do know that in animals nitrate may interfere with thyroid metabolism, reduce the availability of vitamin A, and cause abortions. Moreover, there is evidence that even small reductions in the oxygen available to a developing human fetus—which might occur when the mother is exposed to subcritical levels of nitrate—result in permanent damage to the brain. In sum, the success of agriculture in the Central Valley has been won at a cost which risks the health of the people.

Nor does the nitrogen problem end there. Much of the nitrogen fertilizer applied to the soil of the Central Valley finds its way into the San Joaquin River, which drains the irrigated fields. As a result, the river carries a huge load of nitrate into the San Francisco Bay-Delta area. Here the added nitrate intrudes on another environmental cycle—the self-purifying biological processes of natural waters—bringing in its wake a new round of environmental destruction. The excess nitrate—along with excess phosphate from agricultural drainage and municipal wastes—stimulates the growth of algae in the waters of the Bay, causing the massive green scums that have become so common in the area. Such heavy overgrowths of algae soon die off, releasing organic matter which overwhelms the biological purification processes that normally remove it. As a result, the natural balance is destroyed; the water loses its oxygen; fish die; the water becomes foul with putrefying material. In the cooler words of the Department of Interior report on the San Joaquin Master Drain, "Problems resulting from nutrient enrichment and associated periodic dissolved oxygen depression are numerous in the Bay-Delta area."

So the agricultural practices of the great Central Valley have overwhelmed the natural nitrogen cycle of the soil with massive amounts of fertilizer; once this cycle was broken, the rivers were contaminated with nitrate. Reaching the Bay-Delta area, the excess nitrate has destroyed the natural balance of the self-purifying processes in these waters, with the foul results that are only too well known to those who live in that once-sparkling natural area.

This much is known fact. But once the natural cycles of the Bay-Delta waters are disrupted, other biological disasters may soon follow. At the present time, in a number of regions of the Bay-Delta waters, the bacterial count exceeds the limit recommended by the California Department of Public Health for water contact sports. This may be due to the entry of too much untreated sewage. But experience with the waters of New York harbor suggests another, more ominous, possibility which connects this problem, too, to the drainage of nutrients from agricultural areas, as well as from treated sewage. In New York harbor, in the period 1948–1968, there has been a 10-20 fold increase in the bacterial count despite a marked *improvement* in the sewage treatment facilities that drain into the bay. Here too there has been an increase in nitrate and phosphate nutrients, in this case largely from treated sewage effluent. The possibility exists that bacteria, entering the water from sewage or the soil, are now able to *grow* in the enriched waters of the bay. If this should prove to be the case, changes in water quality such as those which have occurred in the Bay-Delta area may lead to new, quite unexpected, health hazards. The soil contains many microorganisms which cause disease in human beings when they are first allowed to grow in a nutrient medium. There is a danger, then, that as the Bay-Delta waters become laden with organic matter released by dying algae (resulting from overgrowths stimulated by agricultural and municipal wastes), disease-producing microorganisms may find conditions suitable for growth, resulting in outbreaks of hitherto unknown types of water-borne disease.

Nor does the nitrogen story quite end here. We now know that a good deal of the excess nitrogen added to the soil by intensive fertilization practices may be released to the air in the form of ammonia or nitrogen oxides. In the air, these materials are gradually converted to nitrate and carried back to the ground by rain. In 1957, a national study of the nitrate content of rainfall showed excessively high levels in three heavily fertilized regions: the Corn Belt, Texas, and the Central Valley of California. There is increasing evidence that nitrate dissolved in rain can carry enough nutrient into even remote mountain lakes to cause algal overgrowths and so pollute waters still largely free of the effects of human wastes. Recent pollution problems in Lake Tahoe may originate in this way.

I cite these details in order to make clear a profound and inescapable fact of life: that the environment is a vast system of interlocking connections—among the soil, the water, the air, plants, animals, and ourselves—which forms an endless, dynamically interacting web. This network is the product of millions of years of evolution; each of its connections has been tested against the trial of time to achieve a balance which is stable and long-lasting. But the balance, the fine fabric of physical, chemical, and biological interconnections in the environment, is a delicate one; it hangs together only as a whole. Tear into it in one place—such as the soil of the Central Valley—and the fabric begins to unravel, spreading chaos from the soil to the rivers, to the Bay, to remote mountain lakes, to the mother and her infant child. The great Central Valley has become rich with the fruits of the land, but at a cost which has already been felt across the breadth of the state and which is yet to be fully paid.

Nor do we yet know how the destructive process can be halted, or if indeed it can be. In Lake Erie, where the natural balance of the water system has already been largely overwhelmed by excessive nutrients, no one has yet been able to devise a scheme to restore its original condition. The Bay-Delta waters may suffer the same fate. The recently released Kaiser Engineers' report on the San Francisco Bay-Delta Water Quality Control Program predicts that the drainage of agricultural nutrients (nitrogen and phosphorus) from the San Joaquin will continue unabated for at least the next 50 years if present agricultural practices persist. The report proposes a system which, to control only the deleterious effects of the drainage in the Bay-Delta area, will cost about $5 billion in that period. And even at that cost the plan will only transfer the problem to the ocean—where the waste nutrients are to be discharged—which can only bring disaster to this last remaining natural resource, on which so many of our future hopes must rest.

The root of the problem remains in the soil, for if the disrupted balance is not restored there, its destructive effects will only spread into further reaches of the environment. Tragically, each year of continued over-fertilization of the soil may make recovery increasingly difficult. For example, we know that inorganic nitrogen nutrients stop the nitrogen-fixing activity of microorganisms and may eventually kill them off or at least encourage them to mutate into non-fixing forms. If the natural fertility of the soil is ever to be restored, we may have to rely heavily on these microbial agents; but this becomes less and less possible as we continue to use massive amounts of fertilizer. In effect, like a drug addict, we may become "hooked" on continued heavy nitrogen fertilization and so become inescapably locked into a self-destructive course.

This same tragic tale of environmental disaster can be told of another prominent feature of California agriculture—insecticides. One important aspect of the biological capital on which agricultural productivity depends is the network of ecological relationships that relate insect pests to the plants on which they feed, and to the other insects that, in turn, prey on the pests. These natural relations serve to keep pest populations in check. Pests which require a particular plant as food are kept in check by their inability to spread onto other plants; the other insects which parasitize and prey upon them exert important biological control over the pest population.

What has happened in attempts to control cotton pests—where the great bulk of synthetic insecticide is used in the United States—shows how we have destroyed these natural relations and have allowed the natural pest-regulating machinery to break down. The massive use of the new insecticides has controlled some of the pests that once attacked cotton. But now the cotton plants are being attacked instead by new insects that were never previously known as pests of cotton. Moreover, the new pests are becoming increasingly resistant to insecticide, through the natural biological process of selection, in the course of inheritance, of resistant types. In Texas cotton fields, for example, in 1963 it took 50 times as much DDT to control insect pests as it did in 1961. The tobacco budworm, which now attacks cotton, has been found to be nearly immune to methylparathion, the most powerful of the widely used modern insecticides.

California, too, has begun to experience environmental disaster from the intensive use of insecticides. Consider only a single recent example. In 1965 the rich cotton fields of the Imperial Valley were invaded by the pink bollworm from Arizona. The Department of Agriculture began an "eradication" program based on a fixed schedule of repeated, heavy, insecticide sprays. The pink bollworm was controlled (but by no means eradicated); however, the cotton plants were then attacked by other insects which had previously caused no appreciable damage—the beet army worm and the cotton leaf perforator. The insecticide had killed off insects that were natural enemies of the army worms and perforators, which had, in the meantime, become resistant to the sprays. Catastrophic losses resulted. The problem is now so serious that Imperial Valley farmers have proposed the elimination of cotton plantings for a year in order to kill off the new pests, which cannot survive a year without food.

California is beginning to experience the kind of insecticide-induced disaster already common in Latin American experience. In the Cañete Valley of Peru, for example, DDT was used for the first time in 1949 to control cotton pests. Yields increased—temporarily. For soon the number of insects attacking the cotton grew from 7 to 13 and several of them had become resistant to the insecticides. By 1965, the cotton yields had dropped to half their previous value, and despite 15–25 insecticide applications, pest control was impossible. Productivity was restored only when massive insecticide application was halted and biological control was reestablished by importing insects to attack the pests.

These instances are, again, a warning that present agricultural practices may be destroying the biological capital which is essential to agricultural productivity—in this case, the natural population of insects that attack insect pests and keep them under the control of a natural balance. Again, if the ecologically blind practice of massive insecticide treatment is allowed to continue, there is a danger of permanently losing the natural protective insects—and agriculture may become "hooked" on insecticides.

And here too we see disaster spreading through the environmental network. In 1969, the Food and Drug Administration seized two shipments of canned jack mackerel, an ocean fish originating from Terminal Island, Los Angeles, because of excessive residues of DDT and related insecticides. Insecticides draining off agricultural lands into the Bay-Delta area have caused levels of DDT which exceed the amount allowed by the FDA to appear in the bodies of striped bass and sturgeon. It is possible that the recent decline in San Francisco Bay crabs may be due to the same cause. Spreading through the food chain, DDT has begun to cause disastrous declines in the population of birds of prey, and there is some evidence that gulls are being affected as well. The latter would extend the web of disaster even further, for the gulls are vital in controlling waste in shoreline waters.

Now let me follow the track of environmental disaster from the farm to the cities of California. Again, nitrogen is a valuable guide, this time, surprisingly enough, to the smog problem. This problem originates with the production of nitrogen oxides by gasoline engines. Released to the air, these oxides, upon absorption of sunlight, react with waste hydrocarbon fuel to produce the noxious constituents of smog. This problem is the direct outcome of the technological *improvement* of gasoline engines: the development of the modern high-compression engine. Such engines operate at higher temperatures than older ones; at these elevated temperatures the oxygen and nitrogen of the air taken into the engine tend to combine rapidly, with the resultant production of nitrogen oxides. Once released into the air, nitrogen oxides are activated by sunlight. They then react with waste hydrocarbon fuel, forming eventually the notorious PAN—the toxic agent of the smog made famous by Los Angeles.

The present smog-control technique—reduction of waste fuel emission —by diminishing the interaction of nitrogen oxides with hydrocarbon wastes, enhances the level of airborne nitrogen oxides, which are themselves toxic substances. In the air, nitrogen oxides are readily converted to nitrates, which are then brought down by rain and snow to the land and surface waters. There they add to the growing burden of nitrogen fertilizer, which, as I have already indicated, is an important aspect of water pollution. What is surprising is the amount of nitrogen oxides that are generated by automotive traffic: more than one-third of the nitrogen contained in the fertilizer currently employed in U.S. farms. One calculation shows that farms in New Jersey receive about 25 pounds of nitrogen fertilizer per year (a significant amount in agricultural practice) from the trucks and cars that travel the New Jersey highways. Another recent study shows that in the heavily populated eastern section of the country, the nitrate content of local rainfall is proportional to the local rate of gasoline consumption.

Thus, the emergence of a new technology—the modern gasoline engine —is itself responsible for most of the smog problem and for an appreciable part of the pollution of surface waters with nitrate. And no one needs to be reminded that smog is a serious hazard to health. Again we see the endless web of environmental processes at work. Get the engines too hot —for the sake of generating the power needed to drive a huge car at destructive speeds—and you set off a chain of events that keeps kids off the playground, sends older people to a premature death, and, in passing, adds to the already excessive burden of water pollutants.

This is some of the tragic destruction that lies hidden in the great panorama of the changing California environment—costs to the people of the state that do not appear as entries in the balance sheets of industry and agriculture. These are some of the great debts which must be paid if the state's environment is to be saved from ultimate destruction. The debts are so embedded in every feature of the state's economy that it is almost impossible to calculate them. Their scale, at least, can be secured from the figure produced for the water quality-control system which will transfer the pollution problem of the Bay-Delta area to the ocean: $5 billion over 50 years, and continuing at $100 million a year.

At what cost can the smog that envelops Los Angeles be cleared up—as it surely must if the city is to survive? Start with the price of rolling back air pollution that risks the health and well-being of the citizens of the Bay area, the Peninsula, and San Diego. And do not neglect the damage already done by smog to the pine forests in the area of Lake Arrowhead. Nitrogen oxides have just been detected in Yosemite Park; what will it cost if the state's magnificent forests begin to die, unleashing enormous flood problems? How shall we reckon the cost of huge redwoods on the North Coast, which need for their secure footing the soil built up around their roots during annual floods, when these floods are stopped by the new dams and the trees begin to topple? How shall we determine the cost of the urban spread which has covered the richest soil in the state? What will it cost to restore this soil to agriculture when the state is forced to limit intensive, pollution-generating fertilization, and new lands have to be used to sustain food production? What is the price of those massive walls of concrete, those freeways, which slice across the land, disrupting drainage patterns and upsetting the delicate balance of forces that keeps the land from sliding into ravines? Against the value of the new real-estate developments on landfills in San Francisco Bay, calculate the cost of the resulting changes in tidal movements, which have decreased the dilution of the polluting nutrients by fresh water from the sea and have worsened the algal overgrowths. Or balance against the value of the offshore oil the cost of a constant risk of beach and ocean pollution until the offending wells are pumped dry. Finally, figure, if possible, what it will cost to restore the natural fertility of the soil in central California, to keep the nitrogen in the soil, where it belongs, and to develop a new, more mixed form of agriculture that will make it possible to get rid of most insecticides and make better use of the natural biological controls.

If the magnitude of the state's environmental problems is staggering, perhaps there is some consolation in the fact that California is not alone. Most of Lake Erie has been lost to pollution. In Illinois, every major river has been overburdened with fertilizer drainage and has lost its powers of self-purification. Automobile smog hangs like a pall over even Denver and Phoenix. Every major city is experiencing worsening air pollution. The entire nation is in the grip of the environmental crisis.

What is to be done? What *can* be done? Although we are, I believe, on a path which can only lead to self-destruction, I am also convinced that we have not yet passed the point of no return. We have time—perhaps a generation—in which to save the environment from the final effects of the violence we have already done to it, and to save ourselves from our own suicidal folly. But this is a very short time to achieve the massive environmental repair that is needed. We will need to start, now, on a new path. And the first action is to recognize how badly we have gone wrong in the use of the environment and to mobilize every available resource for the huge task of saving it. . . .

15

Savannah

JAMES M. FALLOWS

There are not many cities like Savannah left in this country, a fact that draws different responses from different people. Many young people leave, complaining that the town has no life. Other families move in to stay, saying that it is a good, calm place to raise children. Whatever its miscellaneous virtues or shortcomings, Savannah has a special, quite charming place in American culture. The relaxed pace of Southern towns is one aspect of it; but in that Savannah is no different from a hundred other Southern cities. The stately old houses are another part; but again, cities from Oxford, Mississippi, to Charlottesville, Virginia, have the same antebellum architectural heritage. Somehow, however, the mood of Savannah is distinct.

The city is not all history and old houses, of course. The plastic and neon of post-1950 America have made their mark here as elsewhere. On the outskirts south of town, the predictable cluster of 7–11 stores, burger stands, and shopping centers look the same as their counterparts in Anaheim, California, and Newton, Massachusetts. Savannah's suburbs have

Source: James M. Fallows, "Savannah" from *The Water Lords, A Ralph Nader Study Group Report* by James Fallows. Copyright © 1971 by The Center for Study of Responsive Law. Reprinted by permission of Grossman Publishers.

grown in the last ten years, and the plastic signs have followed. But so far, this influence has mercifully spared the heart of the city—the several square miles nearest the river, where the city first put down its roots and where it now retains its memories. In this area, Savannah not only preserves but still uses the relics of its past. The result of this harmonious acceptance of the old is a refreshing surprise for visitors accustomed to the dingy, bland, chaotic appearance of American cities from Pittsburgh to Atlanta to Houston. Parts of New Orleans retain the same antique flavor as Savannah, as do the older portions of San Francisco when the traffic calms down and the smog blows out to sea. Nearby Charleston, whose imposing old mansions loom over the waterfront, is probably Savannah's closest equivalent. . . .

Midway through the 1960's, Savannah began to pay serious attention to the aged houses that fill the downtown region. Instead of razing them for parking lots or skyscrapers, the city began to restore them. The work still goes on, but already rows and rows of graceful restored houses stand, looking much the same as they must have in the eighteenth and nineteenth centuries. Elaborate wrought-iron work (originally brought to Savannah as ballast for sailing ships) swirls down from many of the balconies and doorways. Less self-consciously than Williamsburg and other deliberate monuments, Savannah has successfully re-created a historic setting where modern people live and work. . . .

The houses, the fountains, the wrought iron would probably never have appeared in this corner of Georgia if a river had not run through Savannah. From the day Oglethorpe's boat sailed through the estuary and beached where the city is now built, Savannah's life has centered on the river. The city hall sits at the river's edge, looking out at what was once a spectacular stretch of water. Along the river front are the ruins of "Factor's Walk," the offices and wharves where cotton dealers once made their fortunes. Savannah's boats have carried different cargoes in the years since trading began, but the port has always been the core of the town's economic life. The people who made their money from the river also took their recreation there; swimming, boating, and fishing made the town a miniature paradise for many of its residents.

They had a good river to work with. Clear mountain streams from the forested Blue Ridge mountains in the Carolinas and upper Georgia run together to form it. For 300 miles, the Savannah is a large, forceful river, forming the boundary between South Carolina and Georgia. . . .

For a long time, from the founding of the city until the 1930's, the Savannah River served many needs of its community. No one user—commercial, recreational, or municipal—destroyed the river for the others. Cotton ships did not drive away the fishermen; pleasure boaters interfered with neither socialites nor merchants. If there was ever a model of balanced use of a natural resource, this was it. Much of the balance was accidental and, if the municipal sewage had been more voluminous, or if the industries then were as grossly polluting as the factories are now, the balance would have tipped many years earlier.

Like so many other aspects of Savannah life, the river's big change came in 1935, when the Union Bag Company (now Union Camp Corporation) brought its factory to town. There had been industry on the river before Union Bag; near the time of World War I, the Savannah Sugar Refinery built a factory several miles upstream from the city. But whatever pollutants it released—together with the untreated wastes from the city's sewers—were a relatively small concern compared to the torrent of filth that came from the paper mill. . . .

Upstream, at Union Camp, the normally muddy river gets a large dose of dark coffee-colored waste. For many yards downstream from the plant, the two kinds of water do not mix at all; the pollutant spreads out from the factory in a long, brown wedge. A line of foam runs along the edge of the pollutant and finally spreads out over the river when the mill wastes blend in.

As the river makes its way down through the city, it gives off the unmistakable odor of human excrement. This is no great surprise, for several large outfall pipes dump the untreated sewage of more than 100,000 people into the river. At times the water in front of City Hall literally boils as pockets of hydrogen sulfide and methane gas rise from the wastes on the river bed. The situation remains the same for several miles, until the river undergoes a final calamity as it passes the American Cyanamid factory. There, some 690,000 pounds of sulfuric acid flood into the river every day, killing fish and running into the marshes alongside of the river. The river water near the plant, often as caustic as concentrated laboratory acid, has seared the skin of small children who have unwittingly dangled their arms in the water. . . .

Although the chemical components of pulp mill wastes—wood sugars, bits of cellulose, natural wood adhesives called "lignins"—seem less obnoxious than sulfuric acid and human sewage, in Savannah they do much more damage to the river. More clearly than in most other areas, the blame for Savannah's pollution falls mainly on one source: the world's largest kraft paper mill, run by the Union Camp Corporation. . . .

Water Lords

This is a big mill, the biggest kraft paper plant in the world. The mill squats on the river outside Savannah's limits but still it thinks of itself as the social and moral leader of the city. Reading corporate publicity and counting up the Union Camp scholarships and charities, one would think this was a mill that took pride in its city and cared for its people.

If any mill could take the lead in ending pollution, this is it. With its massive production, Union Camp could absorb the costs more easily than its fledgling brothers. As the industrial giant of the lower Savannah, it could encourage other industries on the river to follow its lead. As the largest paper producer in the Southeast, it could help change the pattern of environmental neglect in the whole region.

But the bad example Union Camp has set appeals to the most recalcitrant elements of the paper industry. Faced with a set of legal requirements that were politely mild, Union Camp has made only the most grudging progress in cleaning the river. In the last five years, the company has consistently violated even the undemanding standards set by the state water control agency. Meanwhile, company representatives purport to be "concerned generally as responsible citizens with all aspects of the Savannah harbor pollution" and they bristle at the suggestion that their mill is not doing its best. . . .

In day-to-day life on the Savannah, Union Camp rarely faces direct questions about its environmental policy or its antipollution performance. The Savannahians who have learned to live with Union Camp's smoke, their dead water, and the company pay resigned themselves years ago to the mill's constant presence. Many of them claim not to notice even the smell, grossest evidence of Union Camp's existence. Because the people are resigned, they question the mill even less frequently than they question the skies that bring them heat and rain. This attitude naturally works to the mill's advantage; it spares Union Camp the need to develop a presentable, coherent policy on pollution control. Instead, mill officials learn a few phrases to insert in newspaper articles, and then they act on more deeply held beliefs. . . .

Vice president [John] Ray and manager [James] Lientz are both empowered to make decisions that can preserve or destroy thousands of acres of land and many miles of stream. We asked them what they were doing about Savannah's supply of drinkable ground water. What will happen, we asked Lientz, if heavy industrial pumping dries up the city's wells?

"I don't know," he answered. "I won't be here."

Later, in discussion with Ray, another [Nader report] project member explored the legal subtleties of the pollution issue. He asked Ray if there were any restrictions that Union Camp felt it could not abridge as it continued to deplete the ground water.

Ray was right on top of the problem: "I had my lawyers in Virginia research that," he said, "and they told us that we could suck the state of Virginia out through a hole in the ground, and there was nothing anyone could do about it.". . .

The Name of the Game: Profit-Ability

On a clear, mid-March day in 1968, scientists at Georgia's Marine Institute on Sapelo Island began what seemed to be another normal work day. Many years before, tobacco tycoon R. J. Reynolds had donated his estate on the island to the University of Georgia. Today, in the stables where Reynolds once raised race horses, scientists have set up laboratories for the study of marine life.

As students walked past one of the fountains Reynolds had built, however, a strang thing happened. The fountains, which had run for years on natural artesian water pressure, suddenly dried up. Several miles away in Riceboro, the Interstate Paper Company had turned on its huge underground pumps for the first time. The silence on Sapelo, according to Georgia's respected ecologist Eugene Odum, was "deafening."

What happened that day at Sapelo differs in two ways from what is now happening to much of coastal Georgia: it was more sudden, and it did relatively little harm. The supply of ground water that disappeared in one day from Sapelo is undergoing similar but more devastating attacks throughout coastal Georgia and in many other parts of the country. If there is one natural resource which we have more systematically mismanaged than our surface water, it is the invisible water system that runs beneath the ground. The same chronic shortsightedness, the same single-minded quest for profit, and the same refusal to think of consequences that have polluted our rivers and lakes now also threaten the ground water with great potential disaster.

Although ground water has not yet entered the standard vocabulary of environmental concern, it is one of our most important—and most threatened—resources. From a scientific viewpoint, it is impossible to think of ground water separately from the total network of rivers, lakes, and oceans that make up the world's water supply. Ground water is an integral part of the constant circulation of water through the air and ground; it is the subsurface reflection of the rivers that run above ground. . . .

As supplies of surface water become more heavily polluted and reach their limit as producers of usable water, we will turn more and more to the ground to find water.

Since we will continue to depend more and more heavily on ground water, the universal neglect with which we have treated our supply is all the more tragic. Ground water use in Savannah, for example, clearly shows this indifferent and gluttonous attitude. In the Georgia coastal area, where the ground water supply is uniquely plentiful, Savannah would seem to have all the water it could possible need for centuries to come. But because of insufficient information, nonexistent regulations, and poor understanding, farms, industries, and towns in the area all face the threat of a water famine.

In theory, the coastal plains of Georgia have such a huge supply of surface water—a phenomenal 25.7 billion gallons flow through their rivers
every day—that the region should not need a drop of ground water. Its
rivers have long been polluted, however, [so] that the region relies on
ground water for nearly all its water needs. Fortunately, the available
ground water is in plentiful supply; only the Pacific Northwest has more
underground water. But the supply has not been enough to withstand the
heavy loads that industrial pumps have put on it. The water level in the
whole coastal plain region has dropped drastically since the beginning of
the twentieth century. In several areas, the ultimate threat has come true:
salt water has oozed in from the sea to contaminate ground water supplies.
This is not a purely Southern problem; between 80 and 90 regions on the
Atlantic, Pacific, and Gulf coasts have all experienced the same disaster.
But its appearance in the water-rich Georgia coastal plain is more trou-
bling than in most other areas. . . .

Maps which show the amount of water decline leave no doubt about the
cause. On the maps, rings describe areas where the decline has been the
same, i.e., where the water level has fallen 10, 20, or 30 feet. All these
rings center around one bull's-eye; directly below the Union Camp well
field, the water has dropped to its deepest point. There, in what geologists
call a "cone of depression," the water level has fallen 150 feet since 1880,
to 120 feet below sea level. Even 15 miles away from the Union Camp
wells, the water level has dropped 50 feet. The influence of the Savannah
pumping stretches for miles, through many Georgia counties and up into
South Carolina. . . .

As Union Camp and other industrial pumpers continue to draw from
the cone of depression, they work a fundamental change in the aquifer.
The fresh water in the aquifer used to flow steadily out to sea. Now, because of the steady suction from one small area, the direction of the flow
has reversed and water flows from all directions toward the pumping point.
From the seaward edges, salt water begins to move in. The salt water can
come from two major sources: water from the sea water may flow into the
limestone that used to emit fresh water, or "connate" water—pockets of
salt water deposited in previous geologic ages—may move laterally toward
the pumping point. When salt water from either source enters the aquifer
under a well, the result is catastrophic and practically irreversible. The
well water becomes salty and unusable, and the well owner must go elsewhere for his water.

Already, the massive pull Savannah exerts on the aquifer has drawn salt
water into wells less than 50 miles away. Both Parris Island and Beaufort
in South Carolina have had to abandon their now salty wells. The cost of
finding new water has been painfully high; for Beaufort, a town much
smaller than Savannah, the price of a new water system was six million
dollars. Eighty miles south of Savannah, Brunswick is having ground water

problems of its own. In response to pumping by the city and its paper mills, connate salt water has entered the aquifer and contaminated water supplies. . . .

Hydrologists are not sure how long it will take the salt water to move under Savannah; some predict that the city has only ten years left, while others think supplies may hold out for 50 years or more. Nearly all agree, however, that salt water is on its way, and that if pumping continues at its current irrational rate, the city's wells will surely draw salt.

The day that happens, the city will start to pay a heavy price for its improvidence. With the ground water gone, the only other source of water will be the filthy Savannah. . . .

Of all the abuses it heaps on Savannah, Union Camp's arrogant assumption that it can use unlimited amounts of ground water is probably the worst. There is no good reason why Union Camp should take 27 mgd from the fragile aquifer. The Savannah River could supply huge amounts of treatable water and the cost of treatment would not be so great if Union Camp did not so grossly pollute it. But to minds shaped by Union Camp's annual slogan for the year 1970—The Name of the Game: PROFIT-ABILITY—it is easier and cheaper to use ground water. By continuing to draw on the ground water, the mill saves about $500,000 per year.

When all these values are toted up on the company balance sheet, the conclusion is obvious: take the ground water now, and worry about the consequences later. The $500,000 that Union Camp saves this way is a tiny drop in the corporate bucket—about one-tenth of 1 per cent of Union Camp's annual revenue. To get this last ounce of profit, the mill endangers the water supply of an entire region. But Union Camp has little to fear from salt water encroachment. When the ground water is finally depleted, it will have to use treated water, but since its machines can get along with water less pure than people need, its treatment costs would be far below those of Savannah. . . .

If either the city or its industries must give up ground water use, the city has a firmer claim to the resource which it uses to keep its citizens alive; the industries use it only to cut production costs. By allowing unlimited use of the aquifer, Savannahians are subsidizing cheap paper bags for nationwide customers. . . .

The Smell of Money

Some visitors to Savannah are first impressed by the city's gracious Southern charm, by its cobblestone roads and its trees dripping Spanish moss. Others first notice the graceful restored town houses with their wrought-iron railings and the potted flowers tumbling over them. The people of Savannah still own the charm, but the mood of Savannah is only one thing; the atmosphere is another. Union Camp and American Cyanamid, in their grim pursuit of profit at the city's expense, have taken away the ground water and the river, but their thievery does not stop there. They have taken the air. . . .

Although many American cities are plagued with foul air, there are relatively few where *smell* is an important part of the pollution. Savannah and the other towns that harbor kraft mills know that the distinctive stench —and the accompanying economic and physiological damage done by kraft pollution—are normal features of daily life.

It is difficult to describe the smell of a kraft mill to people lucky enough never to have been near one. The human nose is more sensitive to the two chemicals—hydrogen sulfide and methyl mercaptans—that make up the smell than to almost any other substances. It can detect these chemicals in the air in concentrations of two to three parts per billion. Scientists have speculated that the reason is evolutionary: long before there were paper mills, cave men learned to tell if meat was fresh or rotten by sniffing it for hydrogen sulfide. Whether or not the theory is true, it gives some idea of how repulsive the mill smell is.

The damage is more than merely aesthetic; it includes numerous hazards to property and health. . . .

The most complete list of kraft pollution dangers is from a government conference studying pollution in Vermont and upstate New York. Families who had lived for years in the shadow of International Paper's Ticonderoga, New York, mill came in with the following complaints:

upset stomach, nausea, headache, eye and respiratory irritation, aggravation of illness conditions, interference with sleep, reduction in appetite, offensive odors, discouragement to tourist trade, reduction in property rentals and loss of tenants, decrease in property values and sales of resort property, interference with comfortable enjoyment of property, damage to the community's reputation, and distraction to the conduct of school classes.

A resident of Lewiston, Idaho, where the Potlatch Forest mill makes its home, put the complex problems as simply as possible when he said, "I believe the horrible, rotten stench coming from the smokestacks of the Potlatch Pulp Mill here in Lewiston is killing me; I am afraid to remain here; I don't want my family or myself to die premature deaths." . . .

It is emotionally simple but scientifically very difficult to establish the direct relation between poisons in the air and victims on the ground. The casualties of air pollution appear slowly and undramatically. The human cost of a heavy day of kraft pulping may not show up for years, until a family loses its father sooner than normal, or when young men and women retire to sedentary lives years before they should. For many substances that fill the air, we still have no definite idea of the possible dangers. No scientist has yet had the time to see what 20-year exposure to contaminated air does to human bodies. All of us living now are serving as laboratory rats for a grim experiment, which no one is watching. . . .

Savannah's most measurably disturbing pollution problem is the disproportionately high amount of particulates in the air. Particulates are tiny bits of matter, never more than .0005 meters in diameter. Chemists have succeeded in determining only about 40 per cent of particulate composition. From what is known, however, it is clear that particulates inflict damage in two ways. The particles themselves lodge in the delicate linings of the lungs and respiratory tract, causing irritation and inflammation. The substances attached to the particulates are an additional danger. The particulates may combine with and carry sulfur oxides, various aerosols, insecticides like DDT, radioactive isotopes, or the obnoxious odor elements from various sources. By carrying these other compounds and releasing them inside human lungs, particulates greatly magnify the health hazards from other kinds of pollutants. . . .

Readings from a national air pollution survey show that Savannah's particulate level is in the running for the worst in the nation. Savannah constantly edges out such notoriously foul cities as New York and Los Angeles in its particulate pollution readings. Only towns like Steubenville, Ohio, or Charleston, West Virginia, with large, particulate-spewing mills nearby surpass Savannah.

The way Savannah's air hovers on the boundary between unsafe and lethal particulate concentrations is especially disturbing. Particulate levels in the poor, black housing developments near Union Camp are consistently twice as high as the Public Health Service's danger level. Data from British and American studies have shown that particulate levels much lower than those which usually prevail near Union Camp cause or aggravate many kinds of diseases. In downtown Savannah, the concentration is still well above the danger level. It is only in some of the newly developed, mainly white residential areas on Savannah's outskirts that particulate concentration reaches acceptable levels.

Most people who live near Union Camp realize that their area is aesthetically less pleasant than the suburbs, but few of them know that they may be sacrificing their lives to the mill.

16

Donora

CROSWELL BOWEN

Donora, Pennsylvania, is a steel mill town of 12,300 people, twenty-eight miles south of Pittsburgh. During the last five days of October, 1948, a heavy mixture of fog and smoke settled over the countryside, and by 11:30 Saturday night, October 30, seventeen persons were dead. The first died that morning. Four more, who became seriously ill at the time, died during the next two months. A government report later revealed that a total of 5,910 persons, 42.7 percent of the population, were made ill by the smog. Of those, 1,440, or 10.4 percent, were "severely affected."

Front-page stories drew a comparison between the Donora incident and what had taken place in the Meuse Valley in Belgium in 1930, when sixty persons died from a concentration of fog and smoke. Both places were located in heavily industrialized areas. News accounts suggested that the Donora disaster, like the Belgium one, was the result of a freak weather condition—what weather authorities called a "temperature inversion." A layer of warm air descended over Donora, which is located at the bottom of a river valley. This sealed in smoke from locomotives and factories, au-

Source: Croswell Bowen, "Donora Pennsylvania," *Atlantic Monthly* (November 1970). Copyright © 1970, by The Atlantic Monthly Company, Boston, Mass. Reprinted with permission of the Estate of Croswell Bowen and the publisher.

tomobile exhausts, and floating solid particles, probably fly ash. There was no wind to blow away this smog.

Two U.S. Steel installations were located in Donora—a zinc manufacturing plant and an enormous factory for forging iron from ore and making various steel products. The great open hearth furnaces used to burn night and day; they were back in full operation the week after the deaths.

Since the Smog

For a year after the disaster, U.S. Public Health officials conducted a study and issued a report on "The Unusual Smog Episode of October, 1948," as they termed it. But the incident at Donora was more or less forgotten until the late 1960s, when the country became aroused over the issue of pollution. Students of the air pollution problem began to see Donora as the Hiroshima of their particular area of concern.

Today, the visitor driving south to Donora from Pittsburgh on Route 88 travels through lush valleys of prosperous towns: Castle Shannon, Library, Finleyville. One passes farms where the farmer himself can do a little strip mining of soft coal on his own land to heat his house. Entering Donora, the bus driver points to the site of the U.S. Steel zinc mill, now known to be the chief offender in the 1948 smog. Dismantled in 1956, it was located at the northern end of the town which is spread out on the steep west bank of the Monongahela River. Across the river from the old zinc plant site, the east bank is partly devoid of vegetation, exposing bright tan clay. "It used to be all barren, nothing would grow there," a passenger remarks, "but it began to get green after the zinc plant went down." A Hercules Powder plant (which makes nitric acid) has replaced the zinc plant. Black smoke pours out of its chimney. Some of the stores are boarded up.

There used to be a sign on the road, as you entered Donora, which said: NEXT TO YOURS THE BEST TOWN IN THE U.S.A. Since the smog, the sign has been allowed to disintegrate. They now call their town HOME OF CHAMPIONS because Stan Musial, Arnold Galiffa, Bimbo Cecconi, and other great athletes came from here. . . . There is no record in the town, even in the obituaries of the local newspaper, the Donora *Herald American,* that any of the twenty-two dead suffocated to death from smog that weekend. There was no combined memorial service at the time nor since. There is no mass grave, no monument. . . .

Living with heavy dense smoke and fog was part of their way of life. They equated factory chimneys, sending forth smoke to the skies, with prosperity: "That smoke coming out of those stacks is bread and butter on our tables."

Steel men in Donora, like most steel men, were a proud lot, proud of their special skills. Wages in various job categories could go to $40 a day. There were three shifts to keep the plants going twenty-four hours a day. Men strolled with their lunchpails down the hillside from their homes and loitered at the factory gates an hour or so before starting time: "When I walked through those doors to go to work I just felt good. I loved my work. I knew my job. And I liked the guys."

"Your footprints"

The 1948 smog lasted over a long weekend. On Tuesday morning, October 27, smoke from the locomotives' stacks spilled down toward the ground. You could hardly see ahead to walk or drive. There was a sweetish smell in the air. (It was sulfur dioxide.) The smog left a layer of dust on porches, on the sidewalks and pavement: "You could see your footprints if you looked back. Tires left the marks of their treads in the streets." The town's eleven doctors were soon getting telephone calls; patients were having trouble breathing or felt as if they were coughing their lungs out. "Everything was black with gas and soot; you could even taste it," Dr. William Rongaus recalls. "The odd thing was that two days later some of the people whom I had treated while they were gasping for breath denied they had been ill."

John Turner, the tall, gaunt driver of the Donora Fire Department truck, can still hear the wailing sirens of ambulances taking people to hospitals in the neighboring towns. "I hauled oxygen tanks around the clock. We'd knock on doors to see if people were all right. You'd put a sheet over the head of somebody who couldn't breathe and then turn on the oxygen. Automobiles kept stalling. I thought something was wrong with the timing. Then we realized it was the lack of oxygen." . . .

No Change in the Process

"I can't conceive how our plant has anything to do with the condition. There has been no change in the process we use since 1915."
—Superintendent, American Steel and Wire Company, October, 1948.

News writers, photographers, air pollution authorities began arriving in Donora as word of the disaster spread in print and on the air. Dr. Clarence Mills, an air pollution expert from the University of Cincinnati, arrived to study the Donora smog. He said chronic damage had been done for years to the lungs of the people in the valley.

Sunday, October 31, rain and winds cleared away the smog. On Tuesday, most of the dead were buried. It was, the citizens recall, one of the most beautiful fall days they had ever seen. The zinc and steel mills resumed their operations. Now Donora people began to resent the cries of alarm. It was disloyal to Donora and, besides, the talk could drive away the mills. But Dr. Rongaus, who had been through a grueling experience ministering to the sick and dying, described the deaths as "murder . . . those who died could have been saved. Those who failed to get a second dose of adrenalin died. The smoke was a silent killer. Something murdered them. One more night and the death toll would have been one thousand and twenty instead of twenty."

Several men across the river in the town of Webster tried to get a valley lawyer to sue U.S. Steel on behalf of the smog victims and the families of the dead. But local lawyers hesitated to take the case, probably, as Al Kline of Webster thinks, because they were afraid of offending U.S. Steel. Finally a Pittsburgh lawyer was engaged. . . .

The Webster citizens were signed up easily, but most Donora people were reluctant to press the suit. The group in Webster insisted on trying to make people aware that smoke from the mills was at fault. . . . They organized and incorporated The Society For Better Living, sent out some forty press releases, and enlisted the help of air pollution authorities around the country.

When the U.S. Public Health people came to the valley to do a study, they were wined and dined by Al Kline, Abe Celapino, and others from Webster. "We tried to make them understand what had happened," Kline said recently, "but it didn't do any good. We still got a wishy-washy report. I think they were afraid of making U.S. Steel liable for damages."

The published report was not very enlightening or specific. It did say that weather had something to do with the smog, and that October was the "optimum" month for smog at Donora because of the frequency of "stagnant deep anti-cyclones." Illness from the smog was "essentially an irritation of the respiratory tract and other exposed mucous membranes, and varied in degree from mild to severe." The report discussed the existence in the air of fluoride, chloride, sulfur dioxide, hydrogen sulfide, sulfur trioxide, and other gases. But it did not "appear probable . . . that any one of these substances *by itself* [italics added] was capable of producing the syndrome [irritation of the respiratory tract]."

U.S. Steel, despite a virtual clearance by the Public Health Service report, decided to settle the Webster lawsuits out of court as a package deal for about $250,000. Four million dollars had been asked. The lawyers got a third, about $83,000. Families of the dead who sued got $5000 per fatality. Those made ill got $1000 apiece.

The Webster group met with Clifford Wood, president of American Steel and Wire, the U.S. Steel subsidiary. As Al Kline recalls, "He was extremely cordial, said he sympathized with us and would feel the same way if he lived in the Donora area. He was very impressive. Said they agreed smoke from the mills killed vegetation."

Forgetting

The crusade against smoke died out, and Donora entered the 1950s with increasing anxiety that all this talk about the smog would result in the mills leaving town. In 1957 U.S. Steel closed the zinc plant for good. People believed the company was angry because of the lawsuits and had concluded Donora was in danger of another smog. Many people viewed the tragedy as, literally, "an act of God." They argued: "Weren't the people who got sick or died all old people?" (Their ages ranged from fifty-two to eighty-four, and the mean age was sixty-five, according to the U.S. Public Health Service report.) "Wasn't the 'temperature inversion' a freak of nature?"

The companies denied rumors that the rest of the mills would leave town. But in 1960, the company discontinued making iron and steel in Donora and shut down two blast furnaces, thirteen open hearth furnaces, and five steel product mills. Seventeen hundred out of forty-four hundred workers were laid off. Now the town felt itself thoroughly doomed. The smog seemed to have cast a curse on the valley. Merchants were forced out of business, and many families left town. U.S. Steel did employ some of the Donora steel workers at its new Fairless Hills plant near Philadelphia three hundred miles away.

As it happened, U.S. Steel had tentative plans to phase out its Donora mills long before the 1948 smog. Already obsolete in the 1940s, they had been kept open owing to the demands of war production. The great coke-burning open hearth furnaces were obsolete. Oxygen and electric furnaces were the new things. Besides, Donora's steep hillside roads made truck access difficult, especially in winter. Rather than modernize an old plant, it was more economic to build new factories in new open space locations with planned housing conditions. Early in February, 1966, U.S. Steel officially announced the end of all its operations in Donora.

Although there was growing national concern about air pollution, the citizens of Donora immediately set about trying to persuade companies to build factories in their town. One of the objectives was to create jobs for young people. The Chamber of Commerce set up what it called Operation Native Son. There was a Society for a Green Donora. Trees, purchased from the state, were planted. Hercules Powder was one of the first plants to move in. A dozen or so followed. Smoke from factory chimneys again rose from the valley.

Donora refuses to pass ordinances designed to control smoke. It is argued that cars, buses, home and commercial heating systems, engines from locomotives and riverboats all are part of the air pollution problem. This view found support in the U.S. Public Health Service report. Reforms suggested in the report were adopted elsewhere in the valley, but not in Donora. The Weather Bureau instituted a system to warn of an impending temperature inversion or bad smog condition. Companies began installing air pollution devices. Wheeling-Pittsburgh Steel, in nearby Monessen, invested $4.8 million in such devices as an electrostatic precipitator and a graphite collection system. The company claimed a 70 percent reduction in dust fall. When a smog warning goes out, companies are told to cut back on production.

But people in Donora take a more traditional view. "Except for the lesson to be learned by other communities," a Donora *Herald American* editor wrote a few years ago, "this small Pennsylvania town could wish for nothing better than to have the world forget 'the Donora episode.' "

17

An Asbestos Town Struggles with a Killer

BRUCE PORTER

As company towns go, Manville, New Jersey (population: 15,000), has much to be thankful for. Besides deriving its livelihood from the 2,225 jobs provided by the Johns-Manville Company—the nation's largest manufacturer of asbestos products—the town enjoys a number of fringe benefits. In the late 1950s Johns-Manville donated $100,000 for a high school building. Over the past three years it has given another $100,000 to Somerset Hospital in nearby Somerville. The company has also picked up the bill for a large part of Manville's $125,000 worth of ambulance and rescue vehicles, and it has donated some $250,000 worth of pipe for the town's new sewage system. Town garbage is dumped at the company's refuse site, a service worth another $100,000 a year. On a smaller scale the company is an easy touch for everything from building materials for the new Veterans of Foreign Wars hall to the $10,000 needed for beer and hot dogs at the annual volunteer firemen's picnic.

But now, it turns out, Manville citizens have been paying a high price for such largess. The incidence of lung cancer among Johns-Manville em-

Source: Bruce Porter, "An Asbestos Town Struggles with a Killer," *Saturday Review,* 17 February 1973. Copyright 1973 by Saturday Review Co. Used with permission.

ployees is four times the national norm. Mesothelioma—a form of chest or abdominal cancer that accounts for only one out of every 10,000 deaths in the general population—has in the last eight years claimed the lives of at least fifty-eight Manville residents, most of them workers in the Johns-Manville plant. Asbestosis, or "white lung"—a severe scarring of the lungs caused by inhaling asbestos fibers over the course of many years—is another disease that plagues the company town. Beginning as a mere shortness of breath, asbestosis develops into a near paralysis that makes breathing and bodily movement increasingly difficult. In the end the victim's lungs function so marginally that, if the individual does not suffer death from respiratory illnesses such as pneumonia, he will eventually suffocate.

One Manville resident who is only too well acquainted with asbestosis is George Smith—"Smitty" to his friends—who moved to New Jersey twenty years ago from a Pennsylvania steel town. He was thirty-nine years old at the time, and he was active and healthy. "I was always off hunting or fishing," Smitty told me. "I couldn't stand not to be doing something, you know." A year ago last fall, after seventeen years of making asbestos-lined sewer pipe in the Johns-Manville factory, Smitty came down with asbestosis. "I didn't know what the hell it was," he recalled. "It was just a little shortness of breath, you know, and I'd always been as healthy as a horse all my life. The last doctor I'd seen was when I was born. At first I thought it was just something that would pass, but then it started getting worse and worse, until one day I came to work and I could barely move. I didn't think I'd make it through the day."

Smitty is now virtually immobile. Unable to work, he sits all day in the kitchen of the J & J Delicatessen across the street from the plant. At night Smitty hobbles back to his room above Mary's Tavern—a one-block journey that takes him nearly twenty minutes because he must stop to catch his breath every three steps. His body is thin and frail, and when he talks the words rattle out of his mouth in a series of hoarse belches. "Even if my friends would take me, I don't think I could fish anymore, because if I got a bite I couldn't do anything about it," Smitty said. "I'm finished. I can't work. I can't do anything. God help the man who ties up with anything like this."

While the effects of asbestos-related diseases are, in themselves, fearful, the prospect of the toll they may take in Manville in the near future is even more so. In the next few years, physicians who have studied the problem predict, the number of deaths resulting from asbestos-related diseases can be expected to reach near-epidemic proportions. This is so because the gestation period for asbestosis and mesothelioma ranges between twenty and forty years. Hence, workers who joined the plant in the late 1930s and 1940s are just now beginning to suffer the consequences. A study of 689 Johns-Manville employees that was released last May showed that out of seventy men and women who had worked at least twenty years in the plant's formerly very dusty textile division, some twenty-four of them, or 34 per cent, had died. This death rate is nearly triple that of a similar group in the general population.

"The next five or ten years are going to be rough in Manville," I was told by Dr. Irving J. Selikoff, director of the Environmental Sciences Laboratory at Mount Sinai Hospital in New York and the scientist who conducted the study, "because a lot of people are going to be dying, and so far no one knows what to do about it." Dr. Selikoff adds: "What is tragic is that this is a man-made disease. It is not a visitation from heaven. It was preventable. The serious situation that now exists is a record of failure on the part of us all—scientists, industry, and governmental authority. And industry is correct, in my opinion, in pointing out that what we're seeing now is a result of our mistakes in the past. Having said this, I would urge the most intense efforts to ensure that we do not continue to make these mistakes. Too many men and women have died of our blunders already."

Perhaps no other mineral is so woven into the fabric of American life as is asbestos. Impervious to heat and fibrous—it is the only mineral that can be woven into cloth—asbestos is spun into fireproof clothing and theater curtains, as well as into such household items as noncombustible drapes, rugs, pot holders, and ironing-board covers. Mixed into slurry, asbestos is sprayed onto girders and walls to provide new buildings with fireproof insulation. It is used in floor tiles, roofing felts, and in most plasterboards and wallboards. Asbestos is also an ingredient of plaster and stucco and of many paints and putties. This "mineral of a thousand uses"—an obsolete nickname: the present count stands at around 3,000 uses—is probably present in some form or other in every home, school, office building, and factory in the country. Used in brake linings and clutch facings, in mufflers and gaskets, in sealants and caulking, and extensively used in ships, asbestos is also a component of every modern vehicle, including space ships.

An estimated five million people—men and women employed in asbestos plants, insulation workers, construction workers, steamfitters, carpenters, tile setters, and the like—daily breathe in significant amounts of asbestos fibers. During World War II some 4.5 million Americans worked in the shipbuilding industry and were thus occupationally exposed to asbestos fibers. An estimated 3.25 million of these people are still alive. Medical scientists fear that the Seventies will bring the first big wave of asbestos-induced cancers among this segment of the population. . . .

Each time a car mechanic airhoses out a brake housing, he spreads asbestos fibers through his garage. Each time a do-it-yourself or professional carpenter saws up wallboard or plasterboard containing asbestos, he releases fibers into the air. So ubiquitous is asbestos that one tends to forget it is there at all. Last fall the New York City Department of Air Resources tested several brands of powdery papier-mâché mix widely used in elementary school, and found that some samples contained 50 per cent or more asbestos. . . .

Located some forty miles southwest of New York, Manville is a plain, predominantly Polish-American town built out on either side of a long main street punctuated by a single traffic light. Most of the houses that line the side streets are post-World War II bungalows and Cape Codders, each with its small front lawn and backyard. The tall factory stack and the sprawling complex of dingy old and spanking new buildings of the Johns-Manville plant dominate the scene.

I went to Manville, not because the asbestos plant there was Johns-Manville's biggest and longest established, but because the town's working population had been studied more closely than that of any other asbestos company town. I went also because I had read about the conditions that had long prevailed at the Manville plant, and which had been shown to be the cause of the local plague, and because I had heard of new policies that promised great, if late, improvement in those conditions. I saw Manville, New Jersey as a laboratory in which to study the phenomenon of a group of businessmen and industrial workers trying to cope with the painful discovery that their long-cherished means of livelihood has a lethal side to it. It is a phenomenon that, I suspect, has occurred, and will repeatedly occur, in the course of this century in which industrial progress always seems to outstrip man's knowledge of the full human consequences of such progress. For, once on the move, industry is usually too preoccupied to pause, look back, and help out. . . .

The health hazard posed by asbestos came home to Manville in 1963, when Dr. Maxwell Borow, a local physician, found that seventeen townsmen had died of mesothelioma within the span of three years. Four years later Borow asked Johns-Manville for $3,000 to finance a display to educate both workers and the medical profession at large on asbestos-related diseases; his request was turned down. Borow subsequently approached the workers' union, Local 800 of the United Papermakers and Paperworkers; the union organized the collection of the needed money.

Why had Johns-Manville declined to help out? "It was our opinion," Jack Solon, the corporation's vice-president in charge of environmental affairs, explained to me, "that in 1967 there was a need to learn more about mesothelioma before a relationship with asbestos could be affirmed or denied." Besides, Solon added, since 1950 the company had already spent some $2 to $3 million on new dust-control equipment and, as a result, considered the Manville plant a safe place to work in. Men and women who worked at the plant in the Fifties and Sixties, however, failed to notice that the new equipment made any appreciable difference. "There were times when the air was so thick with asbestos dust in some places that you couldn't even see," I was told by a textile division worker who has been with the company for thirty-two years. "Sometimes it was even impossible to breathe with a respirator because the filters would get so clogged with asbestos." (Respirators are generally unpopular among asbestos workers. The wearer sweats and his eyes smart. For workers who have cardiac or pulmonary problems, breathing through an ordinary respirator adds to the strain on their lungs and heart. Air-cooled respirators that supply air to the wearer are bulky and costly.)

Even outside the factory the air was frequently full of the potentially deadly fibers. In the Lost Valley section of town—an area downwind from the factory—the fiber fallout would get so thick that homeowners had to hose the stuff off their houses. Directly in front of the plant conditions were even worse. "When I'd direct traffic there," Sgt. George Kalman of the Manville police recalled, "there were days when it was like we were having snow flurries in July. I'd take off my hat, and it would be covered with this white dust."

Meanwhile, examinations by company doctors were carried out only once every two years—a schedule that was increased to once a year in 1972. Such infrequent checkups may have been sufficient to monitor a slowly developing case of asbestosis, but they were less useful as a means of catching a victim of a swiftly developing cancer, particularly mesothelioma, a disease that normally proves fatal six months to a year after the cancer shows up in X-ray pictures. (To jump from past decades to an illustration from the recent past: in December 1971 Danny Maciborski, a forty-nine-year-old ex-marine who had worked for Johns-Manville for thirty years, checked in at the company dispensary for his biennial physical and was given a clean bill of health. A few weeks later, however, he felt a strange sensation in his abdomen—as if his stomach were "getting bigger," as he put it—and went to see a private physician, who in turn sent him to Dr. Borow. Borow's tests showed that Maciborski had a malignant tumor of the membrane that lines the abdominal cavity—in other words, mesothelioma. "I knew what it was because everybody at the plant knows about asbestosis and mesothelioma now," Maciborski told a reporter for the *New York Post.* "I wasn't surprised or shocked about it . . . . I just asked [Dr. Borow], 'How long have I got?' " Maciborski died last September. He lasted as long as he did because he was willing to go to the doctor every two weeks to have up to eight quarts of fluid pumped out of his abdomen. Johns-Manville paid Maciborski's medical expenses, and, as provided by New Jersey state compensation laws, it is paying his widow $76 a week—a sum that will drop to $72 this June, when her eldest son will turn eighteen.)

Why, throughout the Fifties and Sixties, did men and women continue to work in the plant if conditions were so hazardous? The answer would seem to have as much to do with psychology as with economics. "It's funny," says Chester Raczkowski, a forty-one-year-old machinist and union shop steward at the plant, "but the only people who seem scared of this stuff come from outside the community." To Raczkowski, who has worked at the plant since he was eighteen, his job is a way of life that he is not about to give up just because of a few "scare stories" in the press. "You and I can work in a place for thirty-five years, and maybe you get cancer or something and I don't—who's to say? Dr. Borow says he's an expert on this mesothelioma or whatever it's called. How do I know? Maybe I'm fatalistic, but I'm a Catholic, and I figure you die when it's time to die." One thing Raczkowski does know is that he would find it difficult to leave his job at the Johns-Manville plant. As a first-class machinist, he earns $4.25 an hour, has a five-week vacation, and is entitled to a generous hospitalization program. "Where else could I get all these benefits?" Raczkowski asks.

Raczkowski's attitude—fatalism mixed with a sense of being pretty well off where he is—is one shared by the town's officials, most of whom work at the plant, too. Manville's mayor is a factory supervisor. A majority of the members of the local board of health, whose duties include seeing to it that the town's air is fit to breathe, are also employed by Johns-Manville. Last spring, when the town belatedly decided to ascertain whether asbestos fibers were still sifting down on Manville, it seemed only natural that the board should ask the company to do the monitoring. The air was found clean. . . .

PART IV

THE SPIRITUAL CRISIS

Introduction:
Coming Apart

There were, of course, the hippies—the long hair and love beads, the calculated unwashedness, the flagrant banners, the open lovemaking and disdain for the constraints of conventional society. In dramatic effect, both visual and vocal, these dominated a crowd whose members actually differed widely in physical appearance, in motivation, in political affiliation, in philosophy. The crowd included Yippies come to "do their thing," youngsters working for a political candidate, professional people with dissenting political views, anarchists and determined revolutionaries, motorcycle gangs, black activists, young thugs, police and secret service undercover agents. There were demonstrators waving the Viet Cong flag and the red flag of revolution and there were the simply curious who came to watch and, in many cases, became willing or unwilling participants.[1]

A large group of demonstrators walked in the street, chanting: "Hell no, we won't go!" and "Fuck the draft." They hurled insults at passing

[1] Daniel Walker, *Rights in Conflict* (New York: Bantam, 1968), pp. 3–4. What follows is a paraphrase of excerpts from pp. 6, 9–10, 194–95, 244, 248, 259–60, 272–73, 276.

pedestrians and when one answered back five of them charged onto the sidewalk, knocked him down, formed a circle around his fallen body, locked their arms together, and began to kick him viciously. When they tired of this they unlocked their arms and melted back into the crowd.

A female hippie confronted a policeman on duty, pulled up her skirt, and said, "You haven't had a piece in a long time." Egged on by a crowd, a blonde wearing a short red minidress made lewd sexual motions in front of a line of policemen. Earlier in that same general area a male youth had stripped bare and walked around carrying his clothes on a stick. Now, traffic along the broad avenue having been stopped by the demonstrators, many males in the crowd ran up and exposed their penises to car and bus passengers and passers-by, shouting "How would you like me to fuck your wife?" and "How would you like to fuck a man?" Others rocked some of the cars back and forth in an unsuccessful effort to tip them over.

Two police officers were trapped inside their patrol wagon. They submitted to being rocked violently by the mob for some time before the driver came out, swinging his club wildly and shouting. About ten people pulled him to the ground, and proceeded to "stomp" on him. The officer who had remained inside radioed that demonstrators were standing on the hood of his wagon and were preparing to smash the windshield with a baseball bat. His buddy, he added, was hanging on the door in a state of shock. The commander assured him that assistance was already on the way.

A Chicago attorney, wearing a suit and an "all-American crew cut," was accepted behind police lines while they waited for further orders. "As I wandered from group to group, those who were saying anything seemed obsessed with getting a 'Commie' or 'Hippie' and what they would do to them. . . . There was almost a circus air of anticipation. . . ."

A federal legal official accompanied a dozen policemen walking down a street. "Numerous people were watching us from their windows and balconies," he recalled later. "The police yelled profanities at them, taunting them to come down where the police would beat them up." They also stopped a number of people on the street, demanding identification and verbally abusing them.

A collection of screaming, frightened people jammed themselves against each other and the brick wall of a hotel, while police walked up and down spraying them with mace. Some pleaded with the police to tell them where they should move and allow them to move there. But the police began pulling individuals out of the crowd and clubbing them to the ground. Some of the people pressed hard against a big plate glass window of a lounge. With a sickening crack, the window shattered, and screaming men and women tumbled through, some cut badly by jagged glass. The police burst in after them, beating all those who looked to them like demonstrators, and yelling over and over, "We've got to clear this area." They were hitting with a vengeance and quite obviously with relish.

Several policemen on motorcycles trapped thirty or forty people against a railing along a ramp leading to an underground parking garage. The police charged their machines into the crowd, knocking several people down and forcing many others to jump over the railing. One officer, with a smile on his face and a fanatical look in his eyes, stood up on his three-wheel cycle, shouting, "Wahoo, wahoo," while trying to run down people on the sidewalk.

A priest who was in this crowd says he saw a teen-aged white boy standing on top of an automobile yelling something unidentifiable, when suddenly a policeman pulled him down and beat him several times with a nightstick. Other officers joined in and helped shove him into a police van. A well-dressed woman saw this incident and spoke angrily to a nearby police captain. As she spoke, another policeman came up from behind her and sprayed mace in her face and then clubbed her to the ground. He and two other policemen dragged her along the ground and threw her in the same paddy wagon.

It was shortly after 9:30 a.m. when two New York National Guard CH-34 Choctaw helicopters hedgehopped the 30-foot wall that rims the four sides of Attica state prison and assumed a hovering watch over the grimy fortress. The scene on the ground below was nightmarish in its sense of enveloping menace. Armed with homemade knives, spears and clubs, more than 1,200 rebellious convicts were holding 39 guards and other hostages in the debris-strewn courtyard of D block. All of the hostages were blindfolded and each had an inmate "executioner" at his side. . . . A group of the hostages had been put on display—knives held at their throats by their captors—a warning to the helicopter scouts of what would happen if the authorities stormed the convicts' bastion. . . .

At 9:46 a.m. the two Choctaws began dropping great clouds of incapacitating tear gas into the yard. At the same instant, state police sharpshooters with high-powered rifles began sniping from positions on the rooftops of the adjoining cellblocks. A small, special team of troopers and prison guards, responsible for the rescue of as many hostages as possible, dropped into D yard from catwalks atop the passageways leading out from neighboring cellblocks, firing shotguns and sidearms as they advanced. A larger, second strike force of troopers plunged through the dark tunnels leading from A and C Blocks and burst into D Yard, firing shotguns and high-powered rifles. Within the space of what one trooper described as a "handclap," the deadly fusillade faded away, and Attica had been resecured.[2]

These scenes of police being provoked and themselves rioting during the week of the Democratic Party convention in Chicago in 1968, and the insurrection at Attica state prison in 1971, ruthlessly suppressed when

[2] *Newsweek,* 27 September 1971, p. 25.

negotiations reached an impasse, illustrate what is involved in the Spiritual Crisis: on the one side a rebellion against the established power structure and conventional standards of behavior; on the other side a counterrebellion ferociously overreacting to what is perceived as a threat of revolution.

Two further examples are the Kent State Massacre and the Watergate Affair.

One weekend in May 1970, some students at Kent State University in Ohio set fire to the ROTC building and drove firemen away with a fusillade of rocks. As National Guardsmen rode into town they were also greeted with stones, but, using tear gas and bayonets, they quickly brought order to the campus and maintained a strict military rule for the rest of the weekend. The following Monday, around noon, the commander of the Guard unit ordered his men to form a skirmish line and disperse a crowd that had formed against his orders. As the Guardsmen fired canisters of tear gas they were showered with rocks and obscenities. After a while they retreated, followed closely by a small band of jeering students. Suddenly, some of the Guardsmen turned and fired their rifles indiscriminately—killing four students and wounding nine others.

In the wake of the shootings at Kent State, ordinarily docile student bodies all across the nation exploded in furious indignation and fear. Bullets against unarmed kids! What did it mean?

"Those kids got what was coming to them," declared many nonstudents, primarily among the older generation. "Students are getting away with too much these days and they should all be shot."

"Even your own son or daughter?"

"Yes," some parents actually replied, "if they don't follow orders."

Some 760 universities and colleges either closed down completely or came close to doing so, and students talked openly of revolution. Older citizens, outraged by what they were witnessing, began riding around at night with shotguns, threatening to shoot on sight any young people they spotted. Nomads, some of them on drugs and all of them looking like [the band of hippies that had murdered movie actress Sharon Tate and six others in California the year before], roamed the streets and gave substance to inchoate fears. Only those who were close to the scene, [and] talked to all three groups, appreciated how dangerously close to catastrophe this country came in those critical days.[3]

Stubbornly discounting C.I.A. investigations showing that the radical movements were homegrown responses to equally indigenous grievances, the Nixon administration persuaded itself that bombings, riots, and ambushed police meant that a leftist revolution was in the making in the

---

[3] James A. Michener, *Kent State: What Happened and Why* (Greenwich, Conn.: Fawcett, 1971), p. 7.

United States, supported by foreign funds and guerrilla training by way of Cuba and Algeria. Two years before, in contributing to Lyndon B. Johnson's decision to retire, the antiwar movement had demonstrated its power to break a President's authority. During that same year, the "events of May" in France had shown that it was possible for students to combine with workers and administer such a nasty shock to a government as popular as de Gaulle's as to cause it to lose its nerve and offer to let its legitimacy be decided by a referendum. Consequently, the Nixon administration viewed itself as an island defending majority rule against elite rule, besieged by sinister adversaries bent on violence and subversion. Dissent and protest were seen as signs of treasonous conspiracy. Instead of being punished as misdemeanants, hecklers and demonstrators deserved to be treated as enemy troops; they should be sought out and destroyed with the full arsenal of counterinsurgency weapons used in warfare.

Accordingly, during the summer of 1970 President Nixon approved a plan to set up a politically controlled secret police apparatus to supplement the F.B.I.'s gathering of domestic intelligence through electronic eavesdropping without court approval, the illegal opening and reading of mail, and "surreptitious entry," that is, breaking into homes and offices. Five days later, in response to vehement protests from the late F.B.I. director, J. Edgar Hoover, the President withdrew the plan, but, after the Pentagon Papers were leaked to the press the following year, he established a top-secret investigation unit operating out of the White House that apparently implemented parts of the previously aborted plan. Nicknamed the "plumbers" because of their mission to plug security leaks, this band of extralegal investigators and saboteurs committed a series of politically motivated wiretappings and burglaries during the next year, culminating finally in the Watergate break-in on June 17, 1972.

Ever since his Communist-hunting days in the Joseph McCarthy era, Richard Nixon had carried an obsession that his critics were out to destroy him. Therefore, he had deliberately staffed the White House with men who were fanatically devoted to him, although inexperienced in government. Besides their personal loyalty, each of his chief assistants had shown in hard-fought campaigns that he was adept at adversary politics and adapted to a tough world where victory was all. In short, the White House staff was dominated by sycophants whose loyalty to the President overrode their consciences—zealous amateurs who saw politics as a war with no holds barred, rather than professional politicians who recognized politics as a business or a game with rules, a game in which compromise and moderation were often necessary and in which there are limits to what the electorate will tolerate.

The men with whom Mr. Nixon surrounded himself during his first term tended to identify the nation's welfare with that of their leader. As they planned their strategy and tactics for the campaign of 1972, in an atmosphere bordering on paranoia, they were not only concerned about what they perceived to be a continuing threat of revolution, and anxious lest their chief be held responsible for losing the war in Vietnam; they were also dismayed by Republican losses in the 1970 election of congressmen and governors, and the steady drop in Nixon's ratings in the popularity polls. Thus, from their point of view, national security required their man's reelection in 1972 and justified any means to that end. Opposing presidential candidates were not to be treated as challengers under the rules of the two-party system but as would-be usurpers of the power that belonged to Richard Nixon for the sake of the nation.

Although by now these particular events—the Chicago police riot, Attica, Kent State, and Watergate—may seem to be no more than landmarks in history, together with other recent emotional jolts they have traumatized the nation. Furthermore, many of the stereotyped hates and fears that they brought to the surface persist to this day, scarcely diminished, though perhaps quiescent.

A few years ago, in diagnosing the sober mood of a people celebrating their national birthday, *Newsweek* decided that something ailed the American soul. None of the six prominent American historians independently consulted by the magazine's editors doubted that the country was in "some sort of trouble with itself." [4] Richard Hofstadter judged that "if there is any kind of civic experience that constitutes a crisis of the spirit, this crisis does go that deep." [5]

The term "Spiritual Crisis," then, refers to reverberations from a series of social earthquakes that have recently shaken the American spirit or cultural ethos. At its core is the spirit of rebellion. Several rebellions are going on simultaneously these days. They are interrelated but unsynchronized. A list of the major ones would probably include (1) the black rebellion, (2) the women's movement, (3) the counterculture, (4) the new left, (5) the alienation of workers, and (6) populism. In opposition to this rebellious potpourri is an amorphous counterrebellion (no less rebellious for being counter), an unorganized but massively powerful consensus that the present writer chooses to call the "backlash."

Like the other crises, this one involves inveterate social problems that have become inflamed, such as the racial and sexual caste systems, conflict between generations and between social classes, vigilante violence, moral justifications for war, and the problem of accomplishing drastic social reform without destroying the established democratic system. Even more than the other three crises, this one generates widespread anxiety over the future and shows signs of being a revolutionary turning point in American social history. In national politics it has been responsible for the underlying issues of the last two presidential elections. It seems to have dissolved most of the glue holding together the Democratic Party's previously winning coalition of labor unions and farmers, blacks and Southern whites, ethnics and intellectuals.

Social psychologists have isolated at least two root causes of rebel-

---

[4] "The Spirit of '70," *Newsweek,* 6 July 1970, p. 19.
[5] Richard Hofstadter, " 'The Age of Rubbish,' " ibid., p. 20.

liousness: (1) doubts regarding the legitimacy of authority and (2) a sense of injustice. Since legitimacy and justice are not objective facts, but instead are value judgments, both of these beliefs depend on how individuals or groups define or perceive their situation.

Let us examine these two major causes of the Spiritual Crisis one at a time; first, the erosion of authority's legitimacy. Authority is the established *right* to give orders and require obedience.

> It is authority that enables the jailor to hand to Socrates the cup of hemlock with the rueful but reasonable expectation that he will drink it; authority that enables the elders of the synagogue to execrate, curse, and cast out Spinoza with "all the maledictions written in the Book of the Law"; authority that permits a President of the United States to remove an imperious general from his commands. On less exalted levels it is authority that enables a vice-president to dictate to his secretary, a sales manager to assign territories to his salesmen, a personnel manager to employ and discharge workers, an umpire to banish a player from a baseball game, a policeman to arrest a citizen, and so on through innumerable examples.[6]

Authority differs from authoritarianism; the latter is forced to demand the respect that authority draws naturally to itself. Since it is a prerogative conferred by custom, law, or office, authority's power depends on neither rational persuasion nor physical compulsion, neither special competence nor charismatic leadership, but instead on faith in its legitimacy.

> Persons obey the rules of society when the groups with which they identify approve those who abide by the rules and disapprove those who violate them. Such expressions of approval and disapproval are forthcoming only if the group believes that the rule-making institutions are in fact entitled to rule—that is, are "legitimate." [7]

We tend to regard an authority as legitimate, that is, entitled to make rules, only as long as it arises necessarily from the performance of a particular function valued by our group. If school officials, for example, try to extend their authority to matters unconnected with what the students perceive as the school's proper functions, the issue of legitimacy is likely to be raised. Likewise, if the police are perceived as stretching their authority to cover personal behavior that does not threaten public order, safety, health, or decency, the legitimacy of their monopoly of force may come into question.

One sure sign of authority's loss of authority is the resurgence dur-

---

[6] Robert Bierstedt, *The Social Order*, 3rd ed. (New York: McGraw-Hill, 1970), p. 329.

[7] National Commission on the Causes and Prevention of Violence, *To Establish Justice, to Insure Domestic Tranquillity* (Washington: Government Printing Office, 1969), p. 42.

ing the past dozen years of vigilante groups, spanning the political spectrum from the Ku Klux Klan to the Weathermen. Another such sign is the return of large-scale civil violence after an absence of some thirty years. Still another is the emergence and growth of an antiwar protest movement among middle-class civilians, accompanied by a parallel demoralization in the United States Army.

Recent Harris polls indicate that during the past six years more than half of the American people have lost confidence in their elective officials and courts. Only about a quarter of them say they have much confidence in the Presidency, or the Congress, or even the Supreme Court. Eighty percent now believe that "most elected officials promise one thing at election time and do something different once in office," and about sixty percent (fifteen percent more than four years ago) think most politicians are in politics to make money for themselves and are not ashamed to take graft. According to another type of poll, politicians now rank nineteenth in public trust, on a list of twenty—just above used car salesmen. And the Gallup Poll reports that only one adult in four would want his son to enter politics, as opposed to one in three eight years ago. Moreover, voter alienation spans the entire ideological and political spectrum.

Conclusive evidence that traditional authority and conventional rules of behavior are being challenged may be seen in the flourishing of an alternative life-style commonly called the "counterculture." Warning that a "crisis of understanding" has developed between the generations, a presidential commission pointed to the spread of this subculture among college youth as "perhaps *the* basic contributing cause of campus unrest."

How can we account for the attraction of the counterculture and the spread of vigilantism, civil violence, and protest demonstrations? What forces and events have undermined the legitimacy of mainstream values and traditional authorities?

Since an authority is seen as entitled to rule only as long as it stays within the limits set by those who owe it obedience, any exposure of what is perceived as a betrayal of trust will annul its claim to legitimacy. Official lawlessness, lying, and hypocrisy are far worse than wrongdoing by ordinary citizens. When an authority breaks its own rules it undermines respect for itself, and it also chips away at respect for rules and authority in general. "If the government becomes a lawbreaker, it breeds contempt for law; it invites every man to become a law unto himself; it invites anarchy." (Justice Brandeis)

A depressingly long list could be made of what many people have perceived as official wrongdoing during recent decades, starting perhaps with the way in which victory was obtained over Japan by espousing what seemed later, to a generation never emotionally involved in that war, to be an evil as great as Nazi genocide; and continuing with the civil rights movement's exposure of official lawlessness that radicalized so many of the student idealists who participated in the movement, the hypocrisy of the North toward segregation in the South, the older generation's double standard in outlawing marijuana but not alcohol and tobacco, and the over-

reaction of authorities to rebelliousness, as exemplified by the way police rioted at the 1968 Democratic Convention, the way Attica was resecured, the way four students died at Kent State—aggravated by what
looked like a cover-up by the Department of Justice—plus many acts of
repression by the Nixon administration during its first term.

Perhaps more than any other combination of factors, the war in Vietnam, compounded by the "credibility gap" of two successive presidents,
has been responsible for the recent erosion of authority. That war differed from all previous wars in American experience in that the government was deliberately misleading the people about a war that was taking
their sons and digging into their pockets. According to the Pentagon Papers, calculated deception was justified by the Johnson administration as
the best way out of a situation in which they would be damned if they did
and damned if they didn't. Indeed, painful memories of the American people's extraordinary wrath over the loss of China to the Communists have
put each of the last five presidents, from Truman to Nixon, into a double
bind regarding Indochina: how to avoid losing that area, too, without
committing American ground troops to a land war in Asia? A large majority of the American people accepted the war in Vietnam as long as they
expected it to end fairly soon with only a minimum price paid on the
home front. But they became rebellious when the rug was pulled from
under these expectations by Hanoi's Tet offensive in February 1968. Light
was supposed to be showing "at the end of the tunnel" according to the
Pentagon, when the enemy nearly captured the United States Embassy in
the heart of Saigon. Most people turned against the war only when they
realized that victory was not going to be quick and easy, when domestic
prices began to inflate, and when the draft began reaching into the
homes of the middle class. Misjudging the nature of the contest, both the
Johnson and Nixon administrations tried to use military means to settle a
political conflict and technology to combat ideology. At first the end
seemed to justify the means, but eventually the means corrupted the end.
Having initially intervened to maintain the balance of power in Southeast
Asia and preserve American credibility in the eyes of other nations, our
armed forces ended up fighting primarily to save our President from the
disgrace of being "the first to lose a war." One result has been this country's painful reversal of roles, changing from a traditional haven for refugees from military conscription to a reason for exile in Canada, as illustrated by the following cases, the first being that of a young man named
Tom Lawrence: [8]

His girl is from San Francisco, and like hundreds of wives and
"chicks" she will shortly emigrate to begin a new life with her man
in exile. He wants to start a social-service center. He had finished
college in California and was going to a theological seminary, so

[8] The excerpt that follows is a composite from two different issues of *Newsweek,* 15 February 1971, pp. 29–30, and 17 January 1972, p. 23.

could have got a draft-exempt classification. But that would have been "copping out, just going along with the Selective Service system," he said.

"Dad wanted me to go into the Army, and Mom wanted me to go to jail, but I came up here because I really believe in freedom of speech, justice and equality, all the good things that are not practiced in America right now," he said.

"My best high-school friend came home from Vietnam with no arms and no legs," said Lawrence. "He spent the first six months at home crying. He said it wasn't worth it." . . .

Martin's mother was against his splitting and wanted him to take his medicine in jail. Many parents feel that way, but once their children have chosen exile, they generally give them monetary and moral support. "My parents are beautiful people," more than one kid told me. One said his father picked him up near the Army base from which he deserted, and drove him across the border.

Others are not so understanding. "My father called and said he knew who talked me into doing this—the Communists," a kid at Martin's hostel said with a bitter laugh. "My mother said she'd turn me in if she ever saw my face again," said an intense long-haired ex-marine. "My family wanted to disown me, but they found out it would cost too much in legal fees," said a Vietnam veteran with a Texas drawl. . . .

A University of Toronto psychiatrist, Dr. Saul Levine, treated 24 young exiles and interviewed another 60 for a paper on their problems. "They're racked with mixed feelings," he said. "It's a bloody stressful experience. You can't make a decision like that without saying 'what have I done to my family? Am I right?' Most of the ones with real problems don't have any parental support."

He personally knows of a half-dozen suicides. . . .

Al Finkel, a husky, jovial Temple University business grad who works with emotionally disturbed children in a Winnipeg social center, summed up what's unquestionably the consensus of the deserters and dodgers: "I loved America a long time, and in a way I still do. But right now it stinks. I wouldn't go back even if amnesty were declared. I'm kinda bitter, though, just on principle, because there ought to be room in the United States for people like me." . . .

A few [parents] who were furious with their own sons for taking off have since mellowed. Frank Machado, 68, is very nearly a quintessential Middle American, a retired California house painter and evangelist preacher. When his son, David, refused induction in 1965, the Machado household was bitterly divided along lines that were soon to become typical: father against son and mother. David was sentenced to three years in prison and, after his unsuccessful appeal, his mother drove him to the airport for a flight to Vancouver. Frank refused to give him any money.

But recently Frank has had second thoughts. "Now eight out of ten people I meet tell me the boys were right in running away to Canada," he says. "Everyone feels the war was wrong. I'm not so ashamed of what he's done any more. I'm not saying it was right. I'm an American born in this country and I feel you should help it, but maybe this war wasn't the right thing for us." And then, with a touch of pride, he adds, "My son was one of the first ones to go to Canada. I give the boy credit—he stood alone."

More than a few families have supported their sons whole-heartedly when they decided to leave for Canada, but none has done so more dramatically than the Lyle Walters of Fond du Lac, Wis. Lyle Jr. deserted in May 1969, when he got orders for Vietnam (he had applied for conscientious objector status but had been turned down). A little over a year later, the rest of the family—Lyle, 46, a former minister and college administrator, his wife, Alma, and their 20-year-old son Timothy—sold most of their furniture at auction and moved up to Blossom Park, an Ottawa suburb, to be near Lyle Jr. and his new Canadian wife. Their third son, Michael, joined them last year. "I think it was quite natural for us," says the senior Lyle who had been active with his wife in the antiwar movement and the McCarthy campaign, "I think we were basically disillusioned with the American dream."

Service in Vietnam disillusioned a great many more young men, who felt that

they had been plunged into a universe of meaningless death and evil; the war became for them "an exercise in survival rather than a defence of national vaues." The official justifications were quickly seen to be counterfeit. The men did not feel like noble warriors helping honest allies to repel foreign invaders; they felt they were invaders themselves, hired killers brought in to shore up a country of "thieves and whores". . . .

The enemy was unpredictable, elusive and often indistinguish-able from one's allies. Drawing on an old American racial adage, the men concluded "the only good gook is a dead gook." All Viet-namese became subhuman, potential scapegoats, victims whom one shot to keep death at arms' length.[9]

Many servicemen returned feeling that they had been used, manipu-lated, and cheated by their own military and political leaders, according to Dr. John Rosenberger, a psychiatrist who counseled a sample of them after their return to stateside duty. " 'But what they feared most of all was tarnishing the impeccability of America, which I suppose gave mean-ing to their sacrifices. And since they cannot bring themselves to do this,

[9] Richard Locke, Review of Robert Jay Lifton's *Home from the War, New York Times Book Review,* 24 June 1973, p. 23.

they often retreat into indifference—or else try to wipe from their memories what happened. The real tragedy of the war for them, and possibly for all of us, is that they don't feel the *tragedy* of the war,' " that is, how it is like a drama in which a noble protagonist is brought to ruin by the same qualities that make him heroic.[10]

Once you bloody a trusting people, once you take a loyal and believing population into an inexplicable war, once you tear apart the membrane that holds things together, you have set into motion as yet ill-defined forces that can no longer easily be contained. . . .

I met a field Marine who came home while his discharge was being processed. He had stepped on a land mine near Qui Nhon and lost his foot. He looked fifteen but in truth was a few months past nineteen. And he was upset. His mother and his girl friend refused to let him talk about the war. His former parochial school teachers in Chicago persisted in thinking of him as a hero.

Enlisting for him had been a natural act: "I joined the Marines because I wanted to go all the way with a fighting unit." Ever since he could remember, his mentors had insisted as with one voice that we have to "get the job done," that it was far better after all to fight "them" in distant deltas than in North America.

That was pre-Vietnam. Now the young Marine thinks somewhat differently. "I think any other war would've been worth my foot. But not this one. One day, someone has got to explain to me why I was there."

Or consider the statement of Captain Max Cleland, twenty-seven, a native of an Atlanta suburb, a triple amputee who lost both his arms and his right leg at Khe Sanh, and holds a Silver Star for gallantry in action: "To the devastating psychological effect of getting maimed, paralyzed, or in some way unable to re-enter American life as you left it, is the added psychological weight that it may not have been worth it; that the war may have been a cruel hoax, an American tragedy, that left a small minority of young American males holding the bag. These doubts go beyond just the individual involved. They affect his family, his friends, and many times his community." [11]

As Peter Schrag has suggested, Daniel Ellsberg may symbolize the extent to which the war in Vietnam alienated his generation of liberals (the middle generation, between the youth and their grandparents), who always in the past had been ready to obey the boss but "would never feel quite the same way about the boss again," because both the Johnson and Nixon administrations had betrayed their trust in a strong Presi-

[10] Quoted in Murray Polner, *No Victory Parades* (New York: Holt, Rinehart and Winston, 1971), p. 150.
[11] Ibid., pp. 160–61.

dency. Having grown up during the Great Depression and the Second World War—the last "good" war: their country had been attacked, and they were fighting against manifest evil—they had developed a nearly unshakable faith in the Executive branch.

It was the Congress that had been made up of isolationists and America Firsters; it was the Congress that had resisted foreign aid; it was always a recalcitrant legislature that stood in the way of a progressive President. . . . Because of Roosevelt, the President had become the heroic figure in a nation that our generation was raised to believe could do no wrong. Despite Eisenhower (whose major flaw, in the liberal view, was not misuse, but non-use of Executive powers) it was in the Presidency that progress resided. . . .

We learned a lot from the kids; *we* are the alienated people. The kids can't believe that we could ever have been so naive as to have once believed so deeply in the system.[12]

Faith in a strong, active President as a solver of social problems has been one of the main tenets of progressivism ever since the administration of Theodore Roosevelt at the turn of the century. But when it comes to homage and respect for presidential authority, one cannot distinguish between conservatives and liberals. In power and prestige the President of the United States resembles the British king of old, combining in himself the functions of the head of government as well as those of the head of state, the only major difference being that instead of inheriting his office the President is elected to it for a fixed term. Life in the White House is like that of a royal court; the President is surrounded by an almost reverential mystique and his staff so awed that they consider offering criticism or dissent, even relaying it from others, to be in shockingly poor taste. As a result, the American President tends to be as isolated and insulated from his constituents as a monarch from his subjects.

Yet the man who holds this exalted office is just a politician after all, usually ill-equipped for playing his nonpolitical role as head of state and a paragon of integrity. (Parliamentary systems avoid this double bind by separating the figurehead monarch or president who is head of state from the prime minister who functions as head of government, and requiring the latter to seek a new mandate from the people if a majority of his colleagues in the parliament lose confidence in him.) What happens in a system centered around monarchal authority when the legitimacy of that authority is undermined by unkingly behavior on the part of the incumbent? Then the American people are in deep trouble, with no good way out; impeachment, with or without conviction, has painful, far-reaching consequences, and so does following the lead of a crippled President.

The "credibility gap" of two presidents in a row, Lyndon Johnson

---

[12] Peter Schrag, "The Ellsberg Affair," *Saturday Review,* 13 November 1971, p. 38.

and Richard Nixon, tested the American system as never before. Can a leader lead a people while misleading them? Will the people give their consent to be governed after a President has misled and lied to them?

In 1960 a high altitude U-2 plane was shot down on a photographic spy mission 1200 miles inside the Soviet Union. President Eisenhower maintained it was a weather research plane that had lost its way near the Turkish border, until Chairman Khrushchev confronted him with the CIA pilot alive and talking. Eisenhower's public admission that he had lied cost him a chance to visit Russia and try to end the Cold War, but his offense was so isolated that it hardly affected his credibility with his own countrymen.

A pattern of clandestine acts of war, concealed from the American public and without the declaration of war from Congress that the United States Constitution requires, seems to have been started by the Kennedy administration. In 1961 the CIA carried out its ill-fated Bay of Pigs invasion of Cuba, and Adlai Stevenson, a man of celebrated international credibility, followed orders and lied about it to the United Nations as well as to the American public. At a later time, President Kennedy ordered American "advisers" to participate clandestinely in combat in Vietnam. During the Johnson administration, in 1964, the public was told that two American warships on "routine patrol" in the Tonkin Gulf off the coast of Vietnam had been under "continuous torpedo attack." Congress immediately voted the President a blank check for an undeclared war. But after 45,000 American soldiers had been killed, and over 300,000 wounded, Congress learned that the story was largely untrue—and so were many other stories circulated by the executive branch to cover up what it was really doing in Southeast Asia. The secretary of defense under President Nixon, for example, ordered the clandestine B-52 bombing of neutral Cambodia for fourteen months during 1969–70, and the secretary of state participated in the cover-up by assuring the Senate Foreign Relations Committee: "Cambodia is one country where we can say with complete assurance that our hands are clean and our hearts are pure."

This century's greatest political scandal so far is, undoubtedly, the multi-headed Watergate Affair. Whereas political corruption in the past has almost invariably centered on money—payoffs, bribes, kickbacks, etc. —Watergate was motivated by the desire to retain power. It was part of a conspiracy organized by the White House to pervert a national election, for reasons of ideology rather than greed, and as such it was a far greater threat to democracy than would be the theft of public property.

Respect for authority requires that the person holding authority stay within the bounds of the role expected by those who owe obedience: confidence and trust in Richard Nixon were deeply eroded even among his regular supporters when the Watergate cover-up was unraveled and the Nixon White House was revealed to have overstepped these bounds by treating its political opponents as if they were enemies of the nation, fighting them illegally with the techniques of war, and punishing them unethically with the power of the federal bureaucracy, e.g., harassing them with FBI investigations, selecting their tax returns for special auditing, and denying them federal contracts and grants. Some of the presidential assistants offered the excuse that they were merely giving law-breakers a dose of their own medicine, that their opponents included people who practiced civil disobedience against the government, deliberately breaking those laws that they considered unjust, and members of the New Left who believed in anarchism. But this is specious rationalization; illegal acts by citizens do not justify illegal retaliation by the government. When government officials indulge in illegal behavior they undermine respect for the very rules they are pledged to uphold. Besides, the means corrupt the end just as often as the end justifies the means.

Either President Nixon was completely unaware of the illegal and improper activities carried out under his authority by his closest subordinates, or else he knew about them but did not disapprove. If the first were true he would be guilty of gross incompetence, but if the second were the case he would be guilty of a felony. In either case, when the highest elected official in the land acts like an accused person taking the Fifth Amendment, refusing to give evidence that might decide the matter, he may be on solid legal ground, but the natural inference people make is that he does not do it because he dare not do it. Consequently, Richard Nixon lost the high moral ground to which the people sometimes need to be summoned by their leader.

However, if justice is ultimately seen to be done, proving that the office of the President is not above the law, and that the nation's head of state is indeed expected to set specially high standards of ethical and legal behavior, then the damage done to the system by the Nixon scandals will have been largely restored.

Of course, many other things besides official wrongdoing have gradually weakened the legitimacy of traditional values and authorities in recent years. It seems reasonable to suppose that most or all of the following have contributed: (1) The Peace Corps's discovery of what the United States looks like from outside. (2) The shock of rediscovering poverty and even hunger in the richest nation in the world. (3) The uncovering of affluence's hollowness and boredom. (4) The cumulative effects on the national psyche of the assassination of three irreplaceable leaders in the space of five years—John F. Kennedy, Martin Luther King, and Robert F. Kennedy. (One such murder might have been explained away as an isolated calamity unrelated to a people's inner life, but these three trip-hammer blows in quick succession left millions of Americans feeling personally thwarted and deeply ashamed of their country, many of them struggling for the first time with doubts about the superiority of the American way of life.) (5) The jolting rediscovery of the contrast between the American people's violent past and their historical vision of themselves as a latter-day chosen people. (6) The suspicion raised by the Environmental Crisis that our traditional faith in science, technology, and business may have been misplaced.

As previously stated, the other principal cause of the Spiritual Crisis, in addition to erosion of authority, is a sense of injustice, unfairness, or inequity.

Nothing so generates revolutionary currents at one extreme and sullen resentment at the other as does a government believed to be shot through with inequity. All revolutions in history have originated in perceptions of inequity, not, as is more commonly believed, in loss of individual freedom. Any power can, and generally will, be endured if only it is thought to affect all people equally. . . . A dictatorship *believed* to be equitable will be more welcome than a so-called popular government *believed* to be inequitable.[13]

A revolutionary state of mind commonly stems from being denied satisfaction of one or more basic needs. According to the psychologist Abraham Maslow, the needs basic to all human beings are not equally basic. In practice, we generally put our physical needs first, love and friendship second, dignity and self-respect third, and self-fulfillment or the realization of individual potential fourth. Not only are these needs basic, but they are perpetual. They are never finally fulfilled; life is spent pursuing them. Until our deaths we must eat and sleep, feel accepted by other people and worthy of their regard, and try to become whatever we sense we are capable of. Since these needs are ranked in a hierarchy, as soon as an individual feels assured of attaining the most important set he raises his sights to the next most important ones, newly confident that they are within reach.

People whose chief concerns are at the first two levels, physical and affectional, seldom rebel. Instead, it is those who already feel secure in satisfying these needs, and who, therefore, have raised their expectations to the higher levels of dignity and self-realization who are in a position to feel unjustly treated if they are now deprived of what they thought was coming next.

Feelings of relative deprivation are probably the most common reason for defining a situation as unjust. (The author of a book on why men rebel considers it "as fundamental to understanding civil strife as the law of gravity is to atmospheric physics.") If justice means receiving one's due, then an individual feels unjustly deprived to the extent that there is a gap between what he has and what he considers rightfully due him.

This is not a complicated way of making the simplistic and probably inaccurate statement that people are deprived and therefore angry if they have less than what they want. . . . People become most intensely discontented when they cannot get what they think they deserve, not just what they want in an ideal sense; and

[13] Robert Nisbet, "Vaseline Is No Cure for a Smallpox Epidemic," *Saturday Review*, 21 October 1972, p. 52.

when they feel they are making inadequate progress toward their goals, not whether they have actually attained them or not.[14]

Rebelliousness, then, often springs from frustrated expectations. According to James C. Davies's widely accepted theory of the inverted J-curve, a rebellion is most likely to occur if raised expectations are followed by a sudden reversal that frustrates these expectations and even threatens past progress. Revolts rarely occur when conditions are at their worst; rather, they typically spring from fears of losing ground only recently gained during a prolonged period of rising expectations combined with rising gratifications; and they are not led by the hopeless dregs of society but by people who have tasted success and feel they were on their way up until they were blocked.[15] (See Figure 1.)

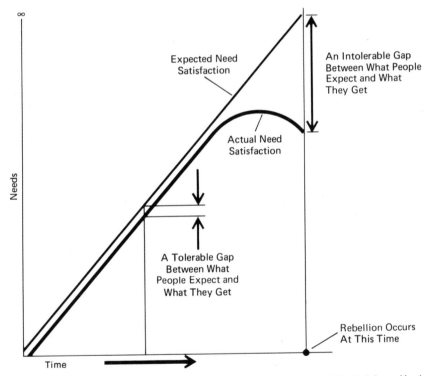

Figure 1. The J-Curve of Rising and Declining Satisfactions. Adapted from Hugh Davis Graham and Ted Robert Gurr, *Violence in America: Historical and Comparative Perspectives* (Washington: Government Printing Office, 1969), II, 548.

[14] Ted Robert Gurr, "A Comparative Study of Civil Strife," in *Violence in America: Historical and Comparative Perspectives,* eds. Hugh Davis Graham and Ted Robert Gurr (Washington: Government Printing Office, 1969), II, 463.
[15] See James C. Davies, "The J-Curve of Rising and Declining Satisfactions as a Cause of Some Great Revolutions and a Contained Rebellion," ibid., II, 547 ff.

If one's expectations rise much faster than one's achievements, and if these prospects are dashed, it is natural to react as if robbed or betrayed—even though what has been lost is only what one *expected* to have. It is therefore possible for improvements to keep boosting anticipations and cause some people to suffer more, rather than less, out of a sense of relative deprivation—as in the Urban Crisis, for example, according to Banfield:

> Improvements in performance, great as they have been, have not kept pace with rising expectations. In other words, although things have been getting better absolutely, they have been getting worse *relative to what we think they should be.* . . .
>
> Our urban problems are like the mechanical rabbit at the racetrack, which is set to keep just ahead of the dogs no matter how fast they may run. Our performance is better and better, but because we set our standards and expectations to keep ahead of performance, the problems are never any nearer to solution. Indeed, if standards and expectations rise *faster* than performance, the problems may get (relatively) worse as they get (absolutely) better.[16]

Banfield's reduction of the Urban Crisis to a vicious circle of expectations being constantly raised by success in realizing them has prompted Robert Nisbet into formulating a corollary to the Malthusian law of food supply and population:

> Whereas material benefits can rise in a social order only at arithmetical rate, expectations tend to rise geometrically. . . . [Therefore,] the whole complex we call "urban crisis" is not likely to be dealt with in such a way as to remove present tensions and sense of impending conflict, for the reason that while affluence does indeed rise, *the sense of relative deprivation* rises also, and at a faster rate.[17]

As people move to the suburbs they raise their expectations, and this makes them even more dissatisfied with the city to which they continue to commute for employment, shopping, and recreation. At the same time, suburban standards raise the expectations of those left behind in the core city, increasing *their* dissatisfaction, too. Theoretically, at least, we are locked into perpetual crisis.

The same vicious circle seems to be operating in the Spiritual Crisis. Since World War II, a mass movement has occurred to change people's

[16] Edward C. Banfield, *The Unheavenly City* (Boston: Little, Brown, 1970), pp. 19, 21.

[17] Robert Nisbet, "The Urban Crisis Revisited," *The Intercollegiate Review,* Vol. 7, Nos. 1–2, reprinted in George Ritzer, ed., *Issues, Debates and Controversies* (Boston: Allyn & Bacon, 1972), pp. 316–17.

expectations from working-class to middle-class, resulting in a general elevation of standards that make longstanding injustices and official hypocrisy appear to be getting worse even when, measured by a fixed standard, they may be getting better. National failings that were overlooked when most people were working-class may have become reasons for shame and indignation now that most are middle-class.[18]

Surely one of the signs that expectations have been raised by something like this process of "middle-classification" is the spread of a new concern for the quality of life. Another can be seen in the findings of market research that, although the typical American family has about one-third more to spend nowadays than ten years ago, even after adjusting for inflation, their expectations appear to have risen even faster. What they define as a necessity has changed; many people today, for instance, consider color television and air conditioners necessities. The general *standard* of living is rising faster than the individual family's *level* of living. This is a recipe for mass discontent—a domestic version of the worldwide "revolution of rising expectations."

Accelerated sociocultural change is creating a new awareness of alternatives all over the world, most dramatically in the countries that are still developing. Millions of people in tradition-centered societies are beginning to believe that they need not resign themselves, as their ancestors did, to lives shortened and dulled by poverty, hunger, and poor health. Their expectations have been inflated by changes in their lives such as their recent achievement of national independence; the infusion of foreign aid into their economy; their new appreciation of the benefits of modern technology—spread to even illiterate people by movies, radio, and television; and, most important of all, their new confidence in their ability to take care of their physical and affectional needs—at the bottom of Maslow's need hierarchy—leading to new demands for dignity and self-fulfillment for both the individual and the group. However, for a number of reasons, from the point of view of people lately awakened to the possibilities, achievement of these new goals seems painfully slow. They naturally react with rebellious impatience.

These two general causes of rebelliousness, then, erosion of authority and frustrated expectations, provide a framework for investigating what lies behind each of the rebellions that compose America's current crisis.

The black rebellion, that special identity crisis of a minority of black Americans, appears to be a reaction to the evaporation of faith, on the part of whites as well as blacks, in the legitimacy of traditional white supremacy (as illustrated by one of the case studies, "We Have Marched, We Have Cried, We Have Prayed"), and also to the frustration arising from expectations being kept out of reach by the very success of efforts to realize them.

[18] See Banfield, *Unheavenly City,* pp. 65–66, 252–54.

> The present friction in American race relations stems less from black Americans being "kept in their place" than from the fact that so many of them in the present generation have managed to work their way out of what has traditionally been "their place." [19]

The success of some raises the expectations of others. However, the presumption that equal opportunity would lead to equal results has been frustrated by the handicapping effects of past discrimination.

Moreover, a host of other hopes have been lifted up and later dashed, for example: that the passage of the most sweeping civil-rights legislation to come out of Congress since Reconstruction meant that equal status was just around the corner; that America could be turned around by laws and appeals to conscience; that black Americans would always be ahead of black Africans, at least; that salvation lay in migration to the "promised land" in the cities of the North, where there was no "color problem," and where even poor people had electricity, running water, and indoor toilets.

> It seems that Cousin Willie, in his lying haste, had neglected to tell the folks down home about one of the most important aspects of the promised land: it was a slum ghetto. There was a tremendous difference in the way life was lived up North. There were too many people full of hate and bitterness crowded into a dirty stinky, uncared-for closet-size section of a great city.
> Before the soreness of the cotton fields had left Mama's back, her knees were getting sore from scrubbing "Goldberg's" floor. Nevertheless, she was better off; she had gone from the fire into the frying pan.
> The children of these disillusioned colored pioneers inherited the total lot of their parents—the disappointments, the anger. To add to their misery, they had little hope of deliverance. For where does one run to when he's already in the promised land? [20]

And how does this first generation raised in the city cope with the suspicion that most white people have already corralled the glut of goodies pictured on television?

So, in spite of being better off in absolute terms than ever before, finally secure in their physical needs, many black Americans tend to feel relatively more deprived, and hence, angry, as remaining injustices, such as low status ascribed to all blacks and the failure of talented individuals to reach their biological potentials, seem more outrageous than ever.

Some of the angriest have turned away from assimilation and non-

[19] Raymond Mack, "Riot, Revolt, or Responsible Revolution: Of Reference Groups and Racism," *Sociological Quarterly,* Spring 1969, p. 151.
[20] Claude Brown, *Manchild in the Promised Land* (New York: Macmillan, 1965), pp. 7–8.

violence toward separatism and violence. This move does not necessarily represent a rejection of integration as an ultimate goal, since staging a walkout can be an effective short-term tactic on the way to eventual integration. As opposed to the traditional assimilation route to integration via the gradual absorption of "deserving" blacks one by one into white society, the separatist route calls for first organizing black people and then, from this position of strength, negotiating their acceptance *en masse* in a pluralistic society made up of interest groups and coalitions in peaceful but competitive coexistence with each other. (Black *nationalism* goes a step beyond separatism, envisioning the eventual geographic division of the United States into white and black nations.) The danger of the separatist tactic is that it may isolate black people in poverty-stricken enclaves, neither economically nor politically viable, and end up actually reinforcing racial stereotypes.

Eroded authority and frustrated expectations also fuel the engines of the women's movement, whose ideology and techniques have escalated the half-serious tug of war that used to be called the "battle of the sexes" into a real power struggle within families, political parties, businesses, schools, etc., destined perhaps "to eclipse the black civil rights struggle in the force of its resentment and the consequences of its demands." [21] Although the women's movement is almost as fragmented as Protestantism, two distinct groupings can be discerned, according to the priority allotted equality and liberty. The women's rights movement asks America to deliver to women the equal opportunity and political equality it promised to everyone long ago. Women's liberation, on the other hand, is much more disruptive of the status quo, for it questions the legitimacy of traditional male authority and aims at achieving independence from men. (A measure of its effectiveness may possibly be derived from the report of a private investigating firm in New York City that during the past twelve years the ratio of runaway wives to runaway husbands has jumped fantastically, from one in three hundred to one in two.) " 'The closest I've been able to come to what's wrong,' " declares one of the leaders of the movement,

> is that men have a greater sense of self than women have. Marriage is an aspect of men's lives, whereas it is the very center of most women's lives, the whole of their lives. It seemed to me that women felt they couldn't exist except in the eyes of men—that if a man wasn't looking at them or attending to them, then they just weren't there. [22]

Many women nowadays, particularly in the middle class, ask, "Is this all there is?" They have raised their expectations to levels three and four

---

[21] Lucy Komisar, "The New Feminism," *Saturday Review*, 21 February 1970, p. 27.

[22] Ibid., p. 28.

of Maslow's hierarchy of basic needs, dignity and self-fulfillment, in response to expanded affluence and education. Furthermore, as a result of increases in life expectancy and the ability to control unwanted births, they now have many more years of vigor left after bringing up the children. Many of those who have been socialized to give up natural desires for individual identity and achievement, and instead to submerge themselves in serving the needs and desires of husband, home, and children, reach middle age feeling empty and unfulfilled, frustrated by their low status as women (in occupational prestige tables where are the housewife and mother categories?) and sensing perhaps that during the past few decades the status of female occupations has been declining.

What triggered the revival of an old movement to challenge the legitimacy of male supremacy was female indignation over contradictions between the role reserved for them first in the civil-rights movement and later in the New Left, and expectations raised by the ideology of those movements. (Stokely Carmichael, for instance, declared that "the only position for women in SNCC is prone.") Furthermore, when black men in this country, under the influence of contemporary African models, began to redefine their situation as that of victims of white imperialism, with the urban ghetto corresponding to a colony, and when, consequently, under the banners of Black Power and Black Liberation, they rebelled against white leadership and domination of the movement in order to achieve self-respect and break with the Sambo stereotype, some white women began to apply similar analogies to their own situation.

As Caroline Bird puts it: [23]

> The movement began with bright, white girls from privileged homes who were free to join the student movement for Negro rights in college because they weren't pushed to marry well or earn money. When they went South for the movement, they found themselves identifying with the blacks more easily than the white boys. They knew how it felt to shut up; take a back seat; accept segregation, exclusion from clubs, restaurants, and meetings; lower their sights to work which was "realistically" open to them; cope with imputations of natural inferiority; and see themselves portrayed in print and picture as stereotypes rather than individuals.
>
> In 1967 it began to dawn on the girls who had gone into the radical movement full-time after graduation that they were toting coffee and typing, like office girls in business establishments. Those who had joined the movement to escape suburban domesticity found themselves making beds and washing dishes like their legally married mothers. Not taken seriously, refused an opportunity for more substantial participation, these movement women who were "feminists" concluded in 1968 that they couldn't really be liberated un-

[23] Caroline Bird, "The New Woman: Out to Finish What the Suffragette Started," *Think*, July/August 1970, pp. 9–11.

less they did it all by themselves, and while most hoped to rejoin men after their liberation, most excluded men (the Feminists of New York actually limit to one-third the number of members who may be formally or informally married).

Women's Liberation made its national debut in September 1968 by halting—if only for a few seconds—the television crowning of Miss America at Atlantic City. They picketed the contest with signs "Let's Judge Ourselves as People." They brought "freedom trash baskets" into which they proposed to dump hair curlers, false eyelashes, girdles, bras, and other devices for making themselves over into the standard sex object. They crowned a live sheep. They threw a stink bomb. They chanted, "We Shall Not Be Used." And some of them got arrested.

Women saw the point, even when they violently, and somewhat defensively, denied that they felt "used." The pageant had long made women feel uneasy, but few had verbalized or even admitted the discomfort they experienced at the spectacle of women parading in a competition to determine which one was most attractive to men. It was hard to say anything against a beauty contest without sounding envious or hostile. The rhetoric of revolution removes this embarrassment by making the notion that women are against each other a myth perpetrated by men to keep women from joining together against their "oppression."

The Miss America protest was a model of what the Communists used to call "agit-prop," or the art of making revolutionary capital out of a current event. . . .

Even more innovative is the solution Women's Lib has developed to the gut problems of any social action: how to recruit new members. The technique is "consciousness raising." A consciousness-raising session is informal, intimate. Ideally, a dozen or more women get together to talk about their experiences as *women,* to call to mind the little slights, frustrations and hangups they have put out of mind as inevitable.

There is, say the feminists, a well of anger hidden somewhere inside the gentlest women. Consciousness raising lets the genie out of the bottle. Once a woman admits to herself how she has been victimized, she can never go back to the Garden of Eden. She gets angrier and angrier and she infects the women around her. Every woman who admits she is a victim makes it that much harder for the next woman to pretend she isn't a victim. The anger feeds on itself, and it is contagious. That's what Women's Lib is all about. It is less a movement than a revolutionary state of mind. But is it, really, a revolution?

According to the article on Revolution in the *New Encyclopedia of Social Science,* revolutions are most likely to occur when the old order is breaking down, the despots are reforming themselves, the condition of the oppressed is improving, widening education has created a "revolution of expectations," and a war complicates the work of the ruling class. Read "men" for the powers that be, "women" for the oppressed, and paragraphs of the essay take on new and striking sense.

The old order, the patriarchal system *is* breaking down; more women are single or divorced, more wives are self-supporting, more children are born out of wedlock, more sex is extramarital. The despots *are* reforming themselves; more men, particularly younger men, treat women as companions rather than sex objects. The condition of women *is* improving, but perhaps not as fast as widening education is raising expectations. Finally, a war *is* distracting attention from domestic reforms that would improve the status of women, not the least of which is the establishment of publicly-supported child care centers. . . .

For all the similarities to classical revolutions, there is one great divide: women can't revolt against society in quite the same way that workers or blacks can revolt. Sex lines cut across class lines. As a bitter feminist has put it, women are the only oppressed class that lives with the master race. They cannot, like the black separatists, really secede from society. For the most part, men are part of the daily lives of even the most fire-breathing feminist.

What is actually happening, I think, is something that carries a wider meaning even than the status of women, trying as that status may be to those concerned about it. The notion of women as an oppressed group has surfaced in every revolution of modern history. The "demands" of the Congress to Unite Women would not have surprised Mary Wollstonecraft, who wrote *A Vindication of the Rights of Women* in 1792, the year they deposed Louis XVI. They would have delighted Elizabeth Cady Stanton, whose Seneca Falls "Declaration of Principles" demanded the vote for women at a time when the issue of slavery threatened the survival of the United States.

Women's Liberation is spreading because American society is in a comparable state of revolution. It reflects not only the revolt of the black separatists, whose rhetoric it follows so closely, but the general loss of credibility in all constituted authority—political, educational, intellectual, religious, even military.

Where will women come out? If previous revolutionary periods are any guide, the answer is: "Better—at least so far as their status as women is concerned." Beyond that, and just as importantly, the answer has to be: "No better than the society as a whole comes out."

One of the major factors determining how our society as a whole will come out is the influence of the counterculture. As already noted while explaining how doubts about the legitimacy of authority may cause rebelliousness, the counterculture is largely a response to what Ms. Bird has just called "the general loss of credibility in all constituted authority." But frustrated expectations may also be involved in the counterculture's origin and its current appeal to youth (See "The New Youth Culture," "Diana," and "Richie.")

The expectations particularly of middle-class youth have probably been raised by the quality of their suburban schooling, together with the hours of leisure and television-watching made possible by their parents' affluence. Reality, however, has disappointed many of them. For one thing, increasing educational requirements for employment in business and the professions, plus, during the years that the United States was engaged in the war in Vietnam, the desire to avoid the draft by going to college, have the effect of extending adolescent dependence on parents, postponing the adult status ordinarily achieved by employment and financial independence or marriage and parenthood.

The counterculture offers alternatives to people who want to rebel against traditionally American value priorities. Among other things, for example, it favors putting concern for the quality of life ahead of materialistic acquisitiveness, naturalness before artificiality, the appreciation of individual uniqueness above uniformity and standardization, and participatory democracy—not only the consent of the governed but also their involvement—in place of centralized power. Whereas the rebellions of blacks and women represent continuations of the old and familiar liberty-equality revolution that began in America and France two hundred years ago and then spread to the rest of the world, the counterculture is an attempt at a new revolution, a cultural and sociopsychological one for people who are ready to go beyond the first revolution because they have already achieved enough liberty, equality, and affluence. Consequently, the counterculture appeals particularly to youth of the upper and upper-middle classes, all of whose basic needs appear to have been "satisfaction-guaranteed."

It is natural for youth to strive for goals their parents regret not having reached. Thus, in their idealism, determined to avoid the pragmatic compromises that adulterate the examples set by adults and make them appear hypocritical, each generation tends to make overt what is covert or repressed in their parents' lives.[24]

> To be sure, the adult generation does proclaim its adherence to the traditional values of the Protestant Ethic: hard work, frugality, self-control, postponement of pleasure. . . .
>
> But, increasingly, those values have been outrun by events. . . . [Especially in the sybaritic suburbs] the children grow up at home in their mother's world, symbolized by the supermarket, the shopping center and goods to buy, to consume, to enjoy. In fact, American values are rapidly becoming spending rather than work,

[24] J. Anthony Lukas, *Don't Shoot—We Are Your Children!* (New York: Dell, 1971), pp. 423–24.

consumption rather than production, taking from life rather than shaping it.

The hippie drug culture is a dramatic sign of that shift—the covert theme in the older generation becoming overt in the younger. Drugs, at least marijuana and the hallucinogens, are associated not with action, production, achievement, and work, but with passivity, consumption, introspection, hedonism. They are literally consumed—swallowed, smoked, sniffed or injected. And they work their effect on the consumer—the reverse of the pioneer's shaping of his environment.

Today's adults, too, depend heavily on drugs—alcohol, tobacco, the amphetamines and barbiturates. But the values these drugs symbolize are still covert. When the father downs three martinis coming home on the club car he rarely admits to himself he is seeking pleasure; he says he needs the drinks to relax after a hard day's work and to recharge his batteries for the next day. When his son smokes marijuana he openly proclaims that he turns on for "kicks," or pleasure. One generation's forbidden fruit becomes the daily bread of the next.

In turn, this may influence the parents' and the older generation's view of youthful behavior. If the germ of that behavior is there —but suppressed—in the older generation, its uninhibited appearance in the young may stir up no little guilt in the parents. And guilt is rarely an aid to understanding or compassion. There is an old saying: "The most effective way to punish your parents is to imitate them"; if so, many parents today are being subtly tortured by their own children.

The counterculture's shift in priorities from production to consumption, from material success to creative satisfaction and social significance, and from regimentation to participatory democracy is echoed in an incipient rebellion of working-class youth usually referred to as either the problem of "worker alienation" or "the blue collar blues and the white collar woes." It first drew nationwide attention when young auto workers walked off their jobs in a new, highly automated plant at Lordstown, Ohio, in 1972, protesting that a work pace of 101 cars per hour was inhuman. Its salient symptoms include accelerating rates of absenteeism and turnover, isolated acts of sabotage and belligerency, and a major switch in union demands from the bread and butter issues with which they have been traditionally concerned to proposals for more individual control over working hours, the democratizing of discipline, more union control over working conditions affecting health and safety, and provision for earlier retirement. Investigations by social scientists have found signs of general unrest and increasing complaints about jobs being meaningless, too repetitive, and offering too little challenge and autonomy. Many workers question the quality of their lives, including the quality of the products they help make and the social need for them. They no longer accept authoritarian ways of doing things, but question management's right to say how a job should be done and demand the right to participate in decision-making.

". . . These kids have a different outlook on life [an old auto worker confided over a beer with a journalist]. They've never been broke the way we were, and they've got a hell-of-a-lot more schoolin'. You want to know somethin'—*they don't even know how to take the crap we took!". . .*

[And later at a steel mill in Chicago:] "Tommy—you've been out for two days. Don't you miss the bread?"

"I can get by. I rather have the time than the money."

"You know—if jobs stay tight, the company'll probably start cracking down hard.". . .

"They don't own me, man! If I want a day off, I take a day off. Nothin's gonna stop that!"

"What if they fire you?"

"Then let 'em fire me. I ain't seen 'em do it yet."

"Why not?"

" 'Cause the next guy who comes along is going to do the same thing I am." [25]

So far, this rebelliousness involves only a minority of factory and office workers, but its extent is hard to measure because it simmers below the surface. The workers' complaints are old and chronic ones that started with mass production generations ago. What is new is the rebellious attitude. The expectations of working-class youth have probably been raised by increased educational levels, the high wages and steady employment that they have experienced during their lifetime, plus the contagious influence of the counterculture, the black rebellion, and women's liberation—predictably, some have already raised the cry of "workers' liberation."

While the rebellion of alienated workers may still be in an incipient stage, that of alienated voters is on its way to being institutionalized. For the first time since the Great Depression, populism is being revived as a political movement. Populism is hard to define because it is not an ideology nor even a program; it is not much more than an emotional attitude —a deep distrust of the very powerful and the very rich, a free-floating suspicion that the nation is being plundered and manipulated for the benefit of a privileged few, and a conviction that the Common Man is being ignored by politicians in collusion with powerful corporations. (As a factor in American politics, such emotions date back to Andrew Jackson's time, but the word was coined in the election of 1892, when a third party, the People's [or Populist] Party, an alliance of rebellious farmers, miners, and factory workers offered a program of reforms which seemed at the

[25] Bennett Kremen, "No Pride in This Dust," *Dissent,* Winter 1972, pp. 24, 26.

time to be very radical, although most of them have since been put into law by members of the two major parties. The original Populist movement began in the 1880s in reaction to a farm depression—following a period of exuberant overinvestment—which undermined the farmers' faith in the Establishment of those days.)

Today's populists may be another domestic manifestation of the revolution of rising expectations. However, like yesterday's populists, they also feel betrayed by the Establishment, whose authority has been crippled by exposés of corruption in both politics and business, on top of factors previously mentioned as sapping the legitimacy of authority in general.

Observers seem to be in agreement that a belief is widespread that the tax system is rigged in favor of the "haves," penalizing those who work as opposed to those who live on capital, and that somehow or other a lot of people are escaping their fair share of the tax load. Over 20,000 individuals earning more than $20,000 in a recent year paid no federal tax whatever, including several hundred who earned between $200,000 and $1 million. Those earning in excess of $100,000 per year managed to avoid paying taxes on about $14 billion of their combined income. Five of the one hundred largest corporations paid no federal taxes at all, and another six paid less than ten percent of their earnings. The giant conglomerate, International Telephone & Telegraph Co., allegedly paid an effective tax rate of only five percent compared with an average of thirty-seven percent for all corporations. Lobbyists have arranged the passage of preferences that reduce the taxes paid by oil, steel, and timber industries, plus others having extensive operations abroad, to rates which are substantially lower than those of smaller businesses. Likewise with government subsidies: some of the biggest cotton growers, for example, evade congressional limits placed on subsidies by dividing up their farms among family members in order to qualify for the same total as before, or by leasing their cotton allotments to small farmers at rental rates high enough to recapture most of the subsidy. Such a system of privileges constitutes a welfare program that reverses the usual pattern, by giving huge payments to the super-rich but only pennies to the very poor and nothing to those in between. It sticks in the public conscience like a bone in the throat.

Another measure of populism's spread is a growing consumers' revolt, with factions led by Ralph Nader, former Oklahoma Senator Fred R. Harris, and others—potentially earth-shaking if ever united, for recent polls detect a sharp decline in public respect for business and a massive shift in people's confidence in competition and ethics as mechanisms for keeping prices fair.

Popular feelings of injustice are probably fed by frustration over inflation's robbery, felt most intensely by the working poor and the elderly whose retirement plans have been subverted, and by resentment about the way the national income is distributed, with the top fifth of the population getting fifteen times as much as the lowest fifth, and the top one percent getting twice as much as the bottom twenty percent. An aggravating factor may be the realization that opportunities to strike out on one's own and become one's own boss are disappearing:

Rural people hoped that they could become independent by saving up for a farm; factory workers, by going into business, perhaps opening a gas station or small workshop; and middle-class people, by entering the independent professions. Today these hopes have begun to disappear, for the family farm is economically obsolete, the small store cannot compete with the chain, and the independent professions now consist more and more of salaried employees.[26]

How far has the erosion of authority gone? Are established authorities about to collapse? Do the frustrated expectations of a militant minority of blacks, women, and youth—abetted by an assortment of new leftists, populists, and environmentalists—add up to a revolutionary situation?

At the present time a social revolution in the United States seems most unlikely. This country has, indeed, a tradition of violence and radicalism, but it is a tradition of individualistic rather than collectivistic radicalism, of anarchy and rioting rather than the seizure of power by a disciplined vanguard. Moreover, the "revolutionaries" are a mixed bag with very little in common ideologically. In fact, in many ways they are more in opposition to each other than to the Establishment. The concern of militant black students with reviving black ethnicity and group pride, for instance, seems irrelevant to the anticapitalistic aims of white radicals; black males who complain that they have been psychologically castrated by discrimination tend to be out of sympathy with women's movements; many underemployed blacks are afraid that enthusiasts for ecology may dampen business expansion and thus deprive them of a chance to improve their lot; and the life-style and objectives of Nader's Raiders and the consumer movement clash with those of the counterculture. In addition, the rebels are divided by class loyalties and attitudes—blacks, populists, and alienated workers tend to share the outlook of the bottom three classes, whereas feminists, counterculturalists, and new leftists tend to share the perspective of the top two. And finally, populists are themselves divided into radical and reactionary wings that largely cancel each other out. One of the most worrisome aspects of the new populist movement is that when a whole class of people feels unjustly treated and trapped it tends to become highly volatile—a source not only of revolution but also of reaction, capable of turning either "left" or "right" or even splitting in both directions, with some manning the barricades in the name of liberty and others supporting repression in the name of public order. In 1968 most populists voted for the third party candidate, George Wallace, who received 13.5 percent of the total votes cast; in 1972, with

[26] Herbert J. Gans, "The New Egalitarianism," *Saturday Review*, 6 May 1972, p. 44.

Wallace recuperating from an attempted assassination, their votes went to Richard Nixon.

But what makes a social revolution so improbable in the near future is the fact that the Common Man is opposed to it. Only about a tenth of the American people sympathized with the demonstrators beaten by the police outside the 1968 Democratic Convention. More than half of them blamed the Kent State killings on the students themselves.

In social life, as in nature, every action tends to provoke a reaction of some sort; consequently, it is not surprising that the Spiritual Crisis consists not only of rebellions but counterrebellions as well. For purposes of analysis, perhaps the latter may be reasonably grouped under a single banner, the "backlash," inasmuch as the same people tend to oppose all three of the main rebellions (the black rebellion, women's liberation, and the counterculture).

The backlash is a resistance movement. It is motivated by fears that things are changing too fast, so it tries to block further changes and reverse those that have already taken place. Its hard core consists of working-class and lower-middle-class whites of non-WASP background. A century ago, when these two classes were dominated by yeoman farmers of either Yankee or Southern stock, they were often referred to with respect as the "Common Man." Today's Comman Man, the ethnic, feels he has become the "Forgotten Man." Even though he is white and regularly employed, he may be the most alienated person in the country. He feels betrayed and trapped. He pays heavy taxes while the super-rich find loopholes and the very poor get welfare; his schools are integrated while the upper classes send their children to private schools; his new-won gains are threatened by racial competition, but the burden of social justice doesn't fall equally on other classes; his sons were drafted for service in Vietnam, while those of the affluent escaped at college.

His expectations have been foiled by the rebellions of the others. Just when he has finally begun to win, the others insist that the rules of the game be changed. He worked hard to achieve his present social position,

> but other groups in American society are demanding these positions as a matter of right. . . . [He] fought bravely to defend America in World War II and in the Korean War, and now it is being alleged that those who fight and die in wars are immoral or foolish. [He] lived according to the American ethic of sobriety and respectability, and now [he sees] on TV the spectacle of the drug smoking hippie at a rock festival. In other words, the white ethnic feels that he is being told that the rules no longer apply, that others are to achieve what he has achieved (frequently, it seems to him, with his picking up the tab) by doing exactly the opposite of what the rules prescribed.[27]

[27] Andrew N. Greeley, "The War and White Ethnic Groups: Turning Off 'The People,' " *The New Republic,* 27 June 1970, p. 15.

He does all the right things, obeys the law, goes to church and insists—usually—that his kids get a better education than he had. But the right things don't seem to be paying off. While he is making more than he ever made—perhaps more than he'd ever dreamed —he's still struggling while a lot of others—"them" (on welfare, in demonstrations, in the ghettos)—are getting most of the attention. . . .

Whatever law and order means, for example, to a man who feels his wife is unsafe on the street after dark or in the park at any time, or whose kids get shaken down in the school yard, it also means something like normality—the demand that everybody play it by the book, that cultural and social standards be somehow restored to their civics-book simplicity, that things shouldn't be as they are but as they were supposed to be. If there is a revolution in this country—a revolt in manners, standards of dress and obscenity, and, more important, in our official sense of what America is— there is also a counter-revolt. . . .

Suddenly the rules are changing—all the rules. If you protect your job for your own you may be called a bigot. At the same time it's perfectly acceptable to shout black power and to endorse it. What does it take to be a good American? *Give the black man a position because he is black, not because he necessarily works harder or does the job better.* What does it take to be a good American? Dress nicely, hold a job, be clean-cut, don't judge a man by the color of his skin or the country of his origin. What about the demands of Negroes, the long hair of the students, the dirty movies, the people who burn draft cards and American flags? Do you have to go out in the street with picket signs, do you have to burn the place down to get what you want? What does it take to be a good American? *This is a sick society, a racist society, we are fighting an immoral war.* ("I'm against the Vietnam war, too," says the truck driver in Brooklyn. "I see a good kid come home with half an arm and a leg in a brace up to here, and what's it all for? I was glad to see *my kid* flunk the Army physical. Still, somebody has to say no to these demonstrators and enforce the law.") What does it take to be a good American? [28]

"What does it take to be a good American?" As part of the aftermath of the Kent State killings by National Guardsmen, construction workers like Joe Kelly in New York City demonstrated their answer:

"When you were still up on Broadway you could hear the ruckus, the hollering. The peace demonstrators trying to outshout the construction workers. The construction workers hollering, 'U.S.A., all the way' and 'We're Number One.' And the peace dem-

[28] Peter Schrag, "The Forgotten American," *Harper's Magazine,* August 1969, pp. 28, 31.

onstrators screaming up there that the war was unjust and everything else, right by the Treasury Building on Broad Street there.

"There was just a lot of hollering and screaming going back and forth until whoever the individual was—oh, he was no spring chicken, he was 40, 45 years old—that spit on the flag. I was maybe four or five rows back in with the construction workers. I saw him make a gesture, you know, a forward motion. That was it. That was the spark that ignited the flame. It came out in the roar of the crowd. 'He spit on the flag! He spit on the flag!' And of course the construction worker got up there on top of the monument and he gave him a good whack and off came the guy's glasses and I guess he followed his glasses off the pedestal there.

"And then there just seemed to be a rush, a mob scene. The chant then was, 'Get the flags up on the steps where they belong. It's a Government building.' And they can say what they want about the New York Police Department, they coulda had the National Guard there with fixed bayonets and they would not have held the construction workers back then.

"When we first went up on the steps and the flags went up there, the whole group started singing 'God Bless America' and it damn near put a lump in your throat. It was really something. I could never say I was sorry I was there. You just had a very proud feeling. If I live to be 100, I don't think I'll ever see anything quite like that again."

Joe Kelly's big chin and right hand tremble as he is caught in the deep, remembered passions of that noontime on Friday, May 8. He is 31 years old, a brawny 6-feet-4, 210 pounds, with blue eyes and receding red hair under his yellow plastic construction helmet decorated with U. S. flag decals and "FOR GOD AND COUNTRY." . . .

During that long menacing midday several hundred construction workers, accused by reporters of using metal tools as weapons, were joined by office workers on a rampage through lower Manhattan. They beat up and injured 70 antiwar protestors and bystanders, including four policemen. With cries of "Kill the Commie bastards," "Lindsay's a Red," and "Love it or leave it," they surged up to City Hall. There they forced the flag, which had been lowered to half-staff in mourning for the four dead Kent State students, to be raised again. Then, provoked by peace banners, they stormed through Pace College across the street. It was a day that left New York shaken.[29]

Ironically, one group's challenging the legitimacy of the rules threatens to spoil another group's chances to get what has just come within its

---

[29] Richard Rogin, "Joe Kelly Has Reached His Boiling Point," *New York Times Magazine,* 28 June 1970, pp. 12–13.

grasp, and one group's reaction to its expectations being thwarted may place in jeopardy the expectations of another group. Plain jealousy plays a part too: "When is somebody going to look after me?" By now, action and reaction have evolved into a vicious circle: black militancy provokes white resistance, which in turn provokes black militancy.

"They may be poorer than a lot of white people, but not by very much. Anyway, what they don't get in money they more than gain in popularity these days. The papers have suddenly decided that the Negro is teacher's pet. Whatever he does good is wonderful, and we should clap. But if he does anything bad, it's our fault. I can't read the papers any more when they talk about the race thing. I'm sick of their editorials. All of a sudden they start giving us a lecture every day on how bad we are. They never used to care about anything, the Negro or anything else. Now they're so worried. And the same goes with the church. I'm as devout a Catholic as you'll find around. My brother is a priest, and I do more than go to church once a week. But I just can't take what some of our priests are saying these days. They're talking as if we did something wrong for being white. I don't understand it at all. Priests never used to talk about the Negro when I was a child. Now they talk to my kids about them all the time. I thought the church was supposed to stand for religion and eternal things. They shouldn't get themselves into every little fight that comes along. The same goes with the schools. I went to school here in Boston, and nobody was talking about Negroes and bussing us around. The Negroes were there in Roxbury, and we were here.

"Everybody can't live with you, can they? Everybody likes his own. But now even the school people tell us we have to have our kids with this kind and that kind of person, or else they will be hurt or something. Now, how am I supposed to believe everything all these people say? They weren't talking that way a few years ago. The governor wasn't either, nor the mayor. They're all just like cattle stampeding to sound like one another. The same with those people out in the suburbs. Suddenly they're interested in the Negro. They worked and worked to get away from him, of course, and get away from us, too. That's why they moved so far instead of staying here, where they *can* do something, if they mean so well. But no. They moved and now they're all ready to come back—but only to drive a few Negro kids out for a Sunday picnic. Who has to live with all this and pay for it in taxes and everything? Whose kids are pushed around? And who gets called 'prejudiced' and all the other sneery words? I've had enough of it. It's hypocrisy, right down the line. And we're the ones who get it; the final buck gets passed to us." [30]

[30] Robert Coles, *The South Goes North* (Boston: Little, Brown, 1971), pp. 274–75.

The Spiritual Crisis is essentially a conflict of values. Ethnics, in particular, vehemently defend traditional working-class priorities, such as respect for authority; loyalty to "my country—right or wrong"; "law and order"—above all, order—rather than "permissiveness" and "black violence"; neatness and cleanliness, as opposed to the deliberate slovenliness of hippies; material success and competition, rather than preferential quotas and reparations for past discrimination, or expansion of consciousness and creativity; work, not welfare; "machismo" and patriarchy, including the double standard in sexual morality, as opposed to sexual equality and occupational self-determination for women; and ethnic ties, involving the inviolability of ethnic "turf" and neighborhood schools, against school busing and scattered housing integration.

Theoretically, at least, the current stalemate between backlashers on the one side and blacks, feminists, counterculturalists, and radicalized youth on the other, can be turned into a revolutionary situation, after all, if something or somebody somehow were to unite rebellious ethnics with one or more of the rebel groups—most likely militant blacks.

A fighting family may just barely manage to hold together. The father may be unemployed and frequently drunk, the mother worn to a frazzle, the children quarrelsome as they displace the tensions generated by poverty and the frustrations of their fighting parents. The father, no longer able to provide for his family, may lose his authority within the family and strike out at those nearest to him. But when the landlord knocks on the door and announces that the rent must be paid by 10 o'clock tomorrow morning on pain of eviction, the family suddenly stops its own fighting, beats up the landlord, and throws him out on the street.

Such tension within the family is a microcosm of the tension within the national community; that is, among the individual members of the political society and among its conflicting regional, religious, racial, and socioeconomic groups. When the various segments of a deeply divided society suddenly sense that they all have the same enemy, the government, they can spontaneously unite for long enough to overthrow it. . . .

Marx to the contrary, revolutions are made not only by economically depressed classes and their leaders but by the joint effort of large numbers of those people in all social groups who are experiencing frustration of different basic needs. People deprived of career opportunities may join in revolt with people who have suffered indignities at the hands of employers, landlords, police, or military troops. They also may join with people who have suffered no indignities but are for the moment simply hungry.

The common characteristic of potential revolutionaries is that each of them individually senses the frustration of one or more basic needs and each is able to focus his frustration on the government. After this need frustration is generated, people begin to share their discontents and to work together. But preceding this joint action, there is no more conspiracy than there is among trees when they burst into flame during a forest fire.[31]

Revolutionaries feel the system is not worth reforming; it is best to start over again. New Left revolutionaries, for example, want to pull down the established order, no matter how, on the grounds that it is hypocritically undemocratic and illegitimate. They tend to believe in anarchism, the doctrine that all forms of authority should be abolished because they are inevitably oppressive, and in terrorism, the use of intimidation to achieve their ends and ultimately replace the rule of authority with the rule of terror. (Acts of terrorism do not mean that a revolution is under way. They are often a sign that a basis for revolution does not yet exist.) Although the terrorist policy of the Weathermen was never supported by more than two or three percent of the nation's students, it contributed disproportionately to provoking the backlash. At the present time, fortunately, the New Left revolutionary movement is splintered and quiescent, having been repudiated by both its student base and the "toiling masses" it saw itself championing.

However, most of today's rebels are not revolutionary, but reformist. Revolutionists consider reformers and reform movements to be their worst enemies, because successful reforms discharge a lot of the pent-up discontent needed to fuel their revolution. Nevertheless, reformers can be turned into revolutionists by being blocked in their efforts to bring about piecemeal, peaceful change. Therefore, the question of which way things will go in the future remains unsettled. It all depends on how repressive the backlash is and whether viable and attractive alternatives exist. The recent spread among adolescents and youths of the Jesus-cult and oriental mysticism, together with pseudosciences like palmistry, astrology, and witchcraft, may be a sign that revolutionary fervor has been rechanneled, at least temporarily, radicalized youth having realized that they lack the power to bring about the social changes they desire. Historically, faith in the possibility of human control of occult powers and the advent soon of the millennium, that is, a thousand-year period of justice and joy under the personal rule of Jesus Christ, has functioned as a popular nonviolent refuge from the psychological effects of feeling powerless amid rapid, drastic social change.

The revival of populism carries the potential for making revolutionary allies out of ethnics, blacks, and radical students.[32] However, the probability of its doing so is not great, judging by the absolute failure of George McGovern's efforts to exploit it in his 1972 campaign—even his

---

[31] James C. Davies, "The J-Curve as a Cause of Some Great Revolutions," in *Violence in America*, II, 548, 550.

[32] To glimpse the possibilities, see William Barry Furlong, "Profile of an Alienated Voter," *Saturday Review*, 29 July 1972, pp. 48 ff.

endorsement by the ethnics of Massachusetts being mainly a product of other factors, such as the influence of the Kennedys and the extraordinary effectiveness of the peace movement in that state.

The Spiritual Crisis boils down to a conflict between "them" and "us." Translated into the terminology of class warfare, this means it involves, on the one side, rebellious elements of the lower class loosely allied with rebellious elements of the upper-middle class ("them"), opposed on the other side by rebellious elements of the two classes in between, i.e., the working class and the lower-middle class ("us"). Rather than try to "bring the country together again" after 1968, and risk paradoxically creating a revolutionary alliance between ethnics and rebels, Richard Nixon and his aides chose to exploit the "them and us" psychology of the Spiritual Crisis and translate backlash fears into pro-Nixon votes in the 1972 election. As everyone knows, they succeeded in making yesterday's enemies—organized labor, particularly the "hard hats"—feel welcome in the Republican Party, loosening a landslide of "us" votes that buried "them" and their candidate.

Deliberately fomenting rebellion and counterrebellion in order to harvest votes may be expedient politics, but when it is finally exposed it further weakens authority in general. If events continue to erode the foundations of legitimate power, how will people be inclined to react? Human beings seem to abhor social disorder almost as much as nature abhors a vacuum. At some point, warns sociologist Robert Nisbet, they are apt to call in the raw power of a repressive police state.

> The most striking fact in the present period of revolutionary change is the quickened erosion of the traditional institutional authorities that for nearly a millennium have been Western man's principal sources of order and liberty. I am referring to the manifest decline of influence of the legal system, the church, family, local community, and, most recently and perhaps most ominously, of school and the university.

> There are some who see in the accelerating erosion of these authorities the beginning of a new and higher freedom of the individual. The fetters of constraint, it is said, are being struck off, leaving creative imagination free, as it has never been free before, to build a truly legitimate society. Far greater, however, is the number of those persons who see in this erosion, not the new shape of freedom, but the specters of social anarchy and moral chaos.

> I would be happy if I could join either of these groups in their perceptions. But I cannot. Nothing in history suggests to me the likelihood of either creative liberty or destructive license for very long in a population witnessing the dissolution of the social and moral authorities it has been accustomed to. I should say, rather, that what is inevitable in such circumstances is the rise of *power:* power that invades the vacuum left by receding social authority; power that tends to usurp even those areas of traditional authority

that have been left inviolate; power that becomes indistinguishable in a short time from organized and violent forces, whether of the police, the military, or the para-military.

The human mind cannot support moral chaos for very long. As more and more of the traditional authorities seem to come crashing down, or to be sapped and subverted, it begins to seek the security of organized power. The ordinary dependence on order becomes transformed into a relentless demand for order. And it is power, however ugly its occasional manifestations, that then takes over, that comes to seem to more and more persons the only refuge from anxiety and apprehension and perpetual disorder.

So was it in ancient Athens when, after the brilliant fifth century had ended in the disastrous Peloponnesian Wars, when intimations of dissolution were rife, the Athenians turned to despots, generals, and tyrants who could, it was thought, restore the fabric of authority. So was it in Rome after the deadly civil conflicts of the first century. So was it in Western Europe after the French Revolution had mobilized itself into the Terror—the better, it was thought by Jacobins and others, to destroy the final remnants of corrupt, traditional authority, thus freeing forever the natural virtue in man. What France got, as we know, was neither freedom nor virtue, but the police state of Napoleon; and what Western Europe got was an age of political reaction in which governments took on powers over human life never dreamed of by absolute monarchs of earlier centuries. And so was it in the Germany of a generation ago when, after a decade of spiritual, cultural, and material debauchery, of more and more aggressive assaults on the civil order by the political left, Germany got Nazism and Hitler; got these to the open satisfaction at the time of a large part of the German people, the secret satisfaction of many others, and, in due course, very close to the total satisfaction of all.[33]

Like some of its specific manifestations—rioting police and vigilante National Guardsmen, for instance—the backlash may be a far greater threat to traditional American ideals than the rebellions that provoke it. It is so hard to resist the temptation to overreact.

If political tyranny ever comes to America, it is likely to arrive not in the guise of some alien ideology such as Communism or Nazism but as a uniquely American way of preserving this country's traditional values. Instead of tyranny being the dramatic culmination of radical protest and revolution, it can come silently, slowly, like fog creeping in "on little cat feet."

The Watergate scandal is a profoundly sinister event because,

[33] Robert A. Nisbet, "The Twilight of Authority," *The Public Interest,* Spring 1969, pp. 3–4.

in so many of its aspects it reflects an authoritarian turn of mind and a ready willingness on the part of those at the highest levels of Government to subvert democratic values and practices. Tyranny was not yet a fact, but the drift toward tyranny, toward curtailing and impairing essential freedoms, was well under way until the Watergate scandal alerted the nation to the danger. That is what Senator Lowell Weicker, Connecticut Republican, had in mind when he referred on the opening day of the Senate hearings to the perpetrators of Watergate as men "who almost stole America."

What would constitute tyranny in the United States? It would involve reducing Congress to a peripheral role in making Government policy, discrediting the political opposition, suppressing the more aggressive forms of dissent, intimidating television, radio and the press, staffing the courts with one's own supporters, and centralizing all of the executive power in the hands of the President and his anonymous, totally dependent aides. During his [first term], President Nixon [made] discernible progress toward all of these objectives. . . .

A lively competition between the two major parties is at the heart of the American political experience. To rig that competition in an election year by trying to "frame" the chairman of the other party, by tapping the telephones, stealing the mail and "bugging" the offices of the opposition politicians, and by sabotaging the campaign activities of opposition candidates and collecting information to blackmail them—to try to rig the outcome of an American election in this despicable fashion is to subvert self-government. It is as subversive as the actions of any Communist agent or Ku Klux Klan lynch mob.

In his testimony before the Senate Watergate committee, Jeb Stuart Magruder explained the ethical basis of the Administration's actions on the grounds that public officials had become "somewhat inured" to illegal activity after years of contending with antiwar protesters who violated the law deliberately. But those who openly and peacefully violate the law in obedience to their conscience do so because they believe their moral witness will help society to change an unjust law or an unjust policy. Such protesters emulating Gandhi, Thoreau, Martin Luther King and other apostles of civil disobedience are prepared to go to jail for violating the law, even though they think the law is unjust.

Only revolutionaries who want to overthrow society commit violent or terroristic acts and then seek to escape capture and conviction. Civil disobedience casts up some difficult moral and legal questions, but it affords no pretext or justification for Government officials and politicians in the governing party to violate the law in secrecy and then cover their misdeeds with perjury. Such misdeeds are not acts of individual conscience; they are expressions of the gangster mentality that typifies every authoritarian political movement.[34]

The main sources of the Spiritual Crisis are illustrated by the case studies that follow. The first two show how the war in Vietnam soured the loyalty and pride of many Americans and helped undermine the credibility of government officials and military brass. They describe two of the events that made a moral issue out of United States involvement, stirring the American people at the time into a fit of emotional self-examination approaching hysteria: the My Lai massacre and the conviction of Lt. Calley. ("In Viet-Nam, at My Lai, America lost its innocence. We had thought that somehow, some way we were better than other people.") [35] Reactions to Calley's conviction also illustrate the point that rebellions and counterrebellions have identical psychological roots: eroded authority and a sense of injustice.

The next three cases show how feelings of injustice released by the erosion of authority make rebellion seem legitimate. The first is the angry testimony of a black barber-politician from Omaha, Nebraska. The other two dramatize what takes place in a "typical" women's consciousness-raising session—for example, the realization that females may be conditioned to fear success in competition with males—and some of the reactions of husbands after their wives' consciousness has been raised.

Although "The New Youth Culture" is an expository article rather than a case study, it is included here in order to meet a need for an explication of what is involved in the counterculture.

The radical New Left is illustrated by the case of Diana Oughton, showing how feelings of status inconsistency, relative deprivation, and injustice can convert privileged upper-middle-class youths into reformers, and how frustration can turn reformers into violent revolutionaries.

The last four articles illustrate the backlash. "Richie" is vividly dramatic, and it may be viewed as symbolic of the counterculture's drug abuse aspects and what many consider to be the nation's overreaction. Perhaps it is a typical example of drug addiction, but it is certainly not a typical case of parental reaction.

The two articles about the Kent State killings illustrate primarily the backlash against the counterculture. The first is an official version of what actually happened. But to understand the crowd behavior exhibited by some of the students, one should keep in mind that the social atmosphere at that particular time was supercharged with ugly emotions. Student expectations that the Nixon administration was gradually winding down both the war and the draft had been suddenly dashed when Ameri-

[34] "Subverting America" (editorial), *New York Times,* 17 June 1973, sec. 4, p. 14.

[35] Richard Hammer, *The Court-Martial of Lt. Calley* (New York: Coward, McCann & Geoghegan, 1971), p. 391.

can troops invaded Cambodia and widened the war. Students felt betrayed. To understand how the Guardsmen could either panic or turn into a lynch mob—taking the law into their own hands, judging guilt, and meting out punishment—one should recognize that they arrived already tired and grumpy from duty elsewhere and then were harassed and goaded by stones and threats, name-calling and obscene gestures; in addition, they may have felt that student activists deserved to be punished for burning down the R.O.T.C. building, blocking traffic, and breaking many store windows. Moreover, young men who had enlisted in the National Guard may have felt jealous and angry toward other young men who were wealthy and smart enough to avoid any kind of military service through student deferments, while those in the Guard had to take time away from their jobs and families, and suffer blows and harassment from privileged, precious kids whom they were not allowed to hurt in return. However, the chief thing that provoked the Guardsmen is suggested by the second article, a report of the reactions of local citizens and parents of students, revealing that fears and stereotyping of the new life-style lay behind the shooting.

The backlash against the black rebellion is illustrated by the last article, the case of "Bloody Attica." This is the story of black convicts who used the rhetoric of revolution to legitimatize an insurrection, claiming that they had been unjustly imprisoned for "political crimes," and the white authorities who accepted the prisoners' definition of the situation and chose to crush the revolution ruthlessly, indiscriminately firing into congested areas, killing or wounding 121 inmates and hostages. The raw power of the state government to put down an uprising was thus demonstrated, but the way in which it was used raised questions about its legitimacy. At the same time, the prisoners' claim that their only crime was that they were black tended to reinforce the stereotype that blacks have inferior moral standards. Recognition of the truth that crime is correlated with life-style rather than biological characteristics is not made any easier when black militants themselves either accept the equation that black equals crime or claim that black crime does not even exist because all black criminals are revolutionaries and all black prisoners are political prisoners.

18

One Morning in the War

RICHARD HAMMER

It was just about seven in the morning when the first shells began to rain on Xom Lang that March 16th. Those who were still at home—most of the people in the sub-hamlet, for it was still early and many of them were just beginning breakfast—quickly sought shelter in their family bunkers. Almost every house had its bunker dug into the ground nearby. The VC when they had arrived had forced the people to build them, and from friends in other hamlets they had heard enough tales to know that in case of a bombardment, a bunker was one of the few hopes of survival. So each family dug its own.

The shells continued to thud into the ground and explode, destroying houses and gouging deep craters for about twenty minutes. The artillery barrage marched up and down the hamlet and the area around it, preparing the landing zone for the troop-carrying helicopters. Overhead, helicopter gunships hovered without any opposition, pounding the hamlet and the ground around it with rockets and machine gun fire.

When the artillery finally stopped, there was a momentary silence, made

Source: Richard Hammer, *One Morning in the War* (New York: Coward, McCann & Geoghegan, Inc., 1970), pp. 118–38. Reprinted by permission of Coward, McCann & Geoghegan, Inc. Copyright © 1970 by Richard Hammer.

louder by the sudden absence of exploding high-explosives, and then the air filled with the ear-shattering clatter of the helicopters beginning to settle into the rice paddies and fields at the western edge of Xom Lang.

Captain Ernest Medina was in the lead chopper, watching the artillery and the gunships level Xom Lang. He "could see the smoke and flash of artillery" as the settlement was ripped apart. Then his helicopter settled into a paddy about a hundred and fifty meters west. Immediately the door gunners strafed the surrounding countryside with machine gun fire in case there happened to be VC waiting among the growing rice and brush.

As far as Medina could tell there was no return fire. "My instant impression," he says, "was that I didn't hear the familiar crackle of rifle bullets zinging over my head."

Accompanied by his radio operator and other company aides, Medina clambered down from the helicopter and rushed across the paddy to the edge of a small graveyard just at the edge of Xom Lang. Still there was no return fire, and all around him the other choppers were settling to the ground and the men of Company C were pouring through the doors, firing toward the houses as they emerged. It seemed to have occured to no one at that moment that the lack of return fire might mean that this was not the hamlet where the VC was centered, that this was not "Pinkville."

But Medina did note the lack of armed resistance. He radioed back to the tactical operations center at LZ Dottie that the landing had been smooth and that his men had come under no fire. "I reported the LZ is cold. Immediately thereafter the helicopter pilot broke in and reported, 'Negative, negative, negative. LZ is hot. You are receiving small arms fire.' "

This was the only report that morning of opposition. And it is more than likely that the pilot thought the firing of the American troops moving in toward Xom Lang indicated that small arms were being shot back from the settlement.

Though Medina could neither see nor hear any return fire from the houses, he quickly passed the word to the leaders of his three platoons, two of them blocking access to Xom Lang, or My Lai as the Americans had it on their maps, and to Calley's first platoon advancing on the settlement itself. "I told them to move with extreme caution and to return any fire."

Moving with that extreme caution and deliberation toward Xom Lang, the thirty-odd men of Calley's first platoon expected at any moment to come under intense fire they had been warned they would receive. They were tense, as though girding themselves to repel the bullets which would hit them. But there was only silence from Xom Lang.

As they approached the first houses, they broke into smaller units—squads and even smaller, just a few men separating and advancing on different targets. And from that moment on, no man saw all the action, saw all that happened. Each man's knowledge of the events of the next few hours that morning—as was the knowledge of those inside the settlement waiting for the Americans to arrive—was limited by his own immediate area of combat and vision, to his own particular ground inside and around Xom Lang and nearby Binh Dong. The events of those next hours, and particularly that next forty minutes, then, were necessarily episodic and chaotic; there was no order, no sequence, merely action and reaction, here and there and everywhere.

Any attempt, then, to describe what happened—on the basis of the recollections of the American soldiers as related to this reporter and others, and of Vietnamese reliving the carnage in conversations with me—can only, at best, attempt to reveal the chaos of the whole and the separateness of the small individual scenes.

With Sergeant Mitchell in the lead, five men of Charley Company descended from their chopper right outside the hamlet. They began moving toward the houses in a single line, Mitchell in the lead. Paul Meadlo remembers that "there was one man, a gook in a shelter, all huddled down in there, and the soldier called out and said there's a gook over here." Sergeant Mitchell brusquely gave the orders to shoot. "And so then the man was shot. So we moved on into the village."

"When the attack started," Sergeant Charles West recalls, "it couldn't have been stopped by anyone. We were mad and we had been told that the enemy was there and we were going in there to give them a fight for what they had done to our dead buddies."

Approaching Xom Lang, "we went in shooting," West says. "We'd shoot into the hootches and there were people running around. There were big craters in the village from the bombing. When I got there I saw some of the people, some of the women and kids all torn up."

"I was just coming to the first row of houses, with five or six other guys," says another member of the platoon, "when we heard this noise behind us. Everybody was scared and on edge, and keyed up, too, to kill, and somebody turned quick and snapped off a shot. We all turned and shot. And there was this big old water buffalo, I guess that's what it was, standing in the middle of this field behind us. Everybody was shooting at it and you could see little puffs jumping out where the bullets hit. It was like something in slow motion, and finally that cow just slumped down and collapsed." His face contorted by the remembrance, he adds, "Now it seems kind of funny, but it didn't then. And once the shooting started, I guess it affected everyone. From then on it was like nobody could stop. Everyone was just shooting at everything and anything, like the ammo wouldn't ever give out."

The contagion of slaughter was spreading throughout the platoon.

Combat photographer Ronald Haeberle and Army Correspondent Jay Roberts had requested permission to accompany a combat mission in order to get both pictures and a story of American soldiers in action. They had been assigned to Charley Company and to Calley's platoon. Leaving their helicopter with about ten or fifteen other soldiers, they came upon a cow being slaughtered, and then the picture turned sickeningly grisly. "Off to the right," Haeberle said, "a woman's form, a head appeared from some brush. All the other GI's started firing at her, aiming at her, firing at her over and over again."

The bullets riddled the woman's body. She slumped against a well pump in the middle of the rice paddy, her head caught between two of its poles. She was obviously already dead, but the infection, the hysteria was now ascendant. The men were oblivious to everything but slaughter. "They just kept shooting at her. You could see the bones flying in the air, chip by chip."

There were the sounds: the shots running into and over each other from inside the hamlet; it sounded as though everyone had his rifle on automatic, no one bothering to save ammunition by switching to single shot. And not drowned by the sharp bark of the rifles and duller thuds of grenades were screams; they sounded like women and children, but how can anyone tell in that kind of moment from a distance who is screaming?

Four or five Americans were outside the hamlet, moving along its perimeter. The job of their platoon was to seal it off and so prevent the VC inside from fleeing from Calley's men, to catch them in a pincer and slaughter them. Vernardo Simpson and these other soldiers were probing the bushes on the outskirts, delicately, searching for mines and bobby traps. As they neared the first group of houses, a man dressed in black pajamas —the dress convinced Simpson that he must be a VC even though black pajamas were traditional peasant dress—suddenly appeared from nowhere, from some bushes and began running toward the hamlet. A woman and child popped up from the same underbrush and started "running away from us toward some huts."

"Dong lai! Dong lai!" The Americans shouted after the Vietnamese. But they kept on running. Lieutenant Brooks, the leader of this second platoon, gave the orders to shoot. If these people did not stop on command, then they must necessarily be VC. "This is what I did," Simpson says. "I shot them, the lady and the little boy. He was about two years old."

A woman and a child? Why?

"I was reluctant, but I was following a direct order. If I didn't do this I could stand court martial for not following a direct order."

Before the day was over, Simpson says, he would have killed at least ten Vietnamese in Xom Lang.

With the number killed there, his total was about the average for each soldier.

When the shelling stopped, Pham Phon crept from the bunker near his hootch. About fifty meters away, he saw a small group of American soldiers. Poking his head back into the bunker, he told his wife and three children—two sons aged nine and four, and a seven-year-old daughter—to come up and walk slowly toward the Americans.

Like almost all Vietnamese in the hamlets around the country, Phon and his family had learned from the three previous American visits and from the tales told by refugees who had come to Xom Lang to seek shelter after their hamlets had been turned into battlegrounds and from tales carried by others from far away, just how to act when American troops arrived.

It was imperative not to run, either toward the Americans or away from them. If you ran, the Americans would think that you were VC, running away from them or running toward them with a grenade, and they would shoot.

It was imperative not to stay inside the house or the bunker. If you did, then the Americans would think you were VC hiding in ambush, and they would shoot or throw grenades into the house or bunker.

It was imperative to walk slowly toward the Americans, with hands in plain view, or to gather in small groups in some central spot and wait for the Americans to arrive—but never to gather in large groups, for then the Americans would think the group was VC waiting to fire. It was absolutely imperative to show only servility so that the Americans would know that you were not VC and had only peaceful intent.

So Phon and his family walked slowly toward the soldiers. The three children smiled and shouted, "Hello! Hello! Okay! Okay!"

Only this time, unlike the three previous American visitations, there were no answering grins, no gifts of candy and rations. The Americans pointed their rifles at the family and sternly ordered them to walk to the canal about a hundred meters away.

Inside the hamlet, the men of the first platoon were racing from house to house. They planted dynamite and explosive to the brick ones and blew them into dust. They set fires with their lighters to the thatched roofs and to the hootches, watched them flare into a ritual bonfire and then raced on to the next hootch. Some soldiers were pulling people from bunkers and out of the houses and herding them into groups. Some of the Vietnamese tried to run and were immediately shot. Others didn't seem to know what was happening, didn't understand what the Americans were doing or why. But most of them behaved as they had learned they must behave. Meekly they followed any order given.

Some of the groups were marched away in the direction of the canal, and those who straggled behind, could not keep up, were promptly shot.

There were soldiers standing outside the hootches, watching them burn, and as Vietnamese suddenly emerged from the pyres, would shoot them.

And through everything, through the sound of gunfire and through the crackling of flames, through the smoke that had begun to cover everything like a pall, came high-pitched screams of pain and terror, bewildered cries, pleading cries. All were ignored.

Michael Bernhardt remembers coming into the hamlet and seeing his fellow soldiers "doing a whole lot of shooting up. But none of it was incoming. I'd been around enough to tell that. I figured we were advancing on the village with fire power."

Inside the hamlet, Bernhardt "saw these guys doing strange things. They were doing it in three ways. They were setting fire to the hootches and huts and waiting for the people to come out and then shooting them. They were going in to the hootches and shooting them up. They were gathering people in groups and shooting them."

The raging fever in the other members of his platoon stunned and shocked Bernhardt. He watched one soldier shooting at everything he saw, blazing away indiscriminately and laughing hysterically as he kept pulling the trigger, kept his finger on the trigger until all the bullets in a clip were gone, then throwing away the clip and reloading and starting again. And laughing all the time. "He just couldn't stop. He thought it was funny, funny, funny."

Bernhardt says that he was sickened and appalled by what he was seeing, yet he felt helpless to do anything about it, helpless to do anything but stand and watch. "I found out," he told one reporter, "that an act like that, you know, murder for no reason, that could be done by just about anybody."

All through that bloody hour, Bernhardt kept his rifle in its sling, pointing toward the ground. He felt he had no reason to unsling it, no reason to aim it at anybody.

For Private Herbert Carter it was too much, a nightmare from which there seemed no awakening. "People began coming out of their hootches and the guys shot them and burned the hootches—or burned the hootches and then shot the people when they came out. Sometimes they would round up a bunch and shoot them together. It went on like that for what seemed like all day. Some of the guys seemed to be having a lot of fun. They were wisecracking and yelling, 'Chalk that one up for me.' "

When he could stand the sight no longer, Carter turned and stumbled out of the hamlet. He sat down under a tree and shot himself in the foot.

He was Charley Company's only casualty that morning.

When the first shells hurled their way into Xom Lang, Nguyen Thi Nien and her family took shelter in their bunker adjacent to their house. In the bunker with her were her eighty-year-old father-in-law, her sister and her sister's seven-year-old daughter, her own husband and their three children. They cowered in the bunker for a considerable length of time. Finally they heard steady rifle fire around them and American voices yelling: "VC di ra! VC di ra!"—VC, get out! VC, get out!

The family crawled slowly and carefully out of the bunker, making every effort to display no hostility. But once they were out they noticed that the Americans were still some distance away. Taking her youngest child, still a baby, in one arm and holding her second youngest by the hand, Nguyen Thi Nien started away, toward the rice paddies. She did not run, but walked on steadily. Her husband and oldest child started to follow her. But her sister and her sister's daughter hung back, then started in another direction. And her father-in-law turned and started back to the house.

"I am too old," she remembers him calling after her. "I can not keep up. You get out and I will stay here to keep the house."

There was almost no argument. "We told him," Nguyen Thi Nien says, "all right, you are too old. So you stay here and if the GI's arrive you ask them not to shoot you and not to burn the house."

The old man called that that was exactly what he intended to do. He would stand guard over the family home. But then Nguyen Thi Nien's husband decided that he could not leave his father alone in the house. He turned, sending the oldest child after his wife and the other children, and went back to his father. They stood outside the house for a brief moment arguing. The son trying to convince the old man to get out of the house and go with them to the paddies before the Americans arrived. The Americans were approaching and they could hear the clatter of shots, they could see the flames licking around other houses, and the smoke.

But the old man remained adamant. He was too old, he kept insisting. He could not make it to the paddy. He refused to leave, turning from his son and starting into the house.

The Americans were almost on them; the firing was all around them now. Nien realized that he could wait no longer. If he were to escape the approaching Americans—he realized by then that this was not a friendly visit, that the Americans were hostile this time and were shooting at everything—he would have to flee immediately.

About four hundred meters away, he saw his wife and three children just ducking into the rice paddies, safe. He started after them. Ahead of him, just a few feet, was an old woman, a nearby neighbor.

But suddenly [he says], five GI's were in front of me, about a hundred meters or so from me. The GI's saw us and started to shoot and the lady was killed. I was hit and so I lay down. Then I saw blood coming from my stomach and so I took a handkerchief and put it over my wound. I lay on the ground there for a little while and then I tried to get back to my house, to my old father and my sister-in-law and her child who must still be there. I could not walk very well and so I was crawling. On the way back to my house I saw five children and one father lying dead on the ground. When I reached my house, I saw it was on fire. Through the fire I could see the bodies of my old father, my sister-in-law and her child inside the house. Then I lost consciousness and I do not know anything more of what happened.

All around there was burning and explosions, shooting and the dead, the screams of the living and, beginning, the sweet smell of burning flesh in the hootches turned into funeral pyres. And, now and again, there was the awful hysterical laughter of one soldier or another. Some of the American faces had expressions which frightened and shocked their friends, those friends at least who emerged from the mass hysteria, which seemed to fill the entire company, long enough to look around them.

I was just coming into the middle of that ville [remembers one soldier, refusing to look around or to meet his questioner's eyes as he talks] and I saw this guy. He was one of my best friends in the company. But honest to Christ, at first I didn't even recognize him. He was kneeling on the ground, this absolutely incredible . . . I don't know what you'd call it, a smile or a snarl or something, but anyway, his whole face was distorted. He was covered with smoke, his face streaked with it, and it looked like there was blood on him, too. You couldn't tell, but there was blood everywhere. Anyway, he was kneeling there holding this grenade launcher, and he was launching grenades at the hootches. A couple of times he launched grenades at groups of people. The grenades would explode, you know, KA-PLOW, and then you'd see pieces of bodies flying around. Some of the groups were just piles of bodies. But I remember there was this one group a little distance away. Maybe there was ten people, most of them women and little kids, huddled all together and you could see they were really scared, they just couldn't seem to move. Anyway, he turns around toward them and lets fly with a grenade. It landed right in the middle of them. You could hear the screams and then the sound and then see the pieces of bodies scatter out, and the whole area just suddenly turned red like somebody had turned on a faucet. . . .

There is a well-documented theory of many psychiatrists that sex and violence are two aspects of the same emotion. And that sometimes violence will set loose uncontrollable erotic desires. It has happened often enough in civilized society during peacetime: the incidence of well-publicized sex murders is too well-known to even bother to comment on. If violence during peace can let loose erotic behavior, violence during war seems often to make such desires even less controllable. There had been evidence of this on patrols before. And there was evidence of it again in Xom Lang. The killing, the indiscriminate slaughter all around brought such emotions to the surface in some of the men in the platoon.

Jay Roberts and Ronald Haeberle moved about the havoc taking pictures. They came upon one group of Americans surrounding a small group of women, children and a teen-age girl. She was perhaps twelve or thirteen and was wearing the traditional peasant black pajamas. One of the Americans grabbed her by the shoulders while another began to try to strip the pajamas off her, pulling at the top of the blouse to undo it.

"Let's see what she's made of," one of the soldiers laughed.

Another moved close to her, laughing and pointing at her. "VC, boom-boom," he said. He was telling her in the GI patois that she was a whore for the VC, and indicating that if she did it for them why not for the Americans.

A third soldier examined her carefully and then turned to the others. "Jesus," he said, "I'm horny."

All around there were burning buildings and bodies and the sounds of firing and screams. But the Americans seemed totally oblivious to anything but the girl. They had almost stripped her when her mother rushed over and tried to help her escape. She clutched at the American soldiers, scratched them, clawed at their faces, screaming invectives at them. They pushed her off. One soldier slapped her across the face; another hit her in the stomach with his fist; a third kicked her in the behind, knocking her sprawling to the ground.

But the mother's actions had given the girl a chance to escape a little. She took shelter behind some of the other women in the group and tried to button the top of her blouse. Haeberle stepped in, knelt and took a picture of the scene.

Roberts remembers that at that moment, "when they noticed Ron, they left off and turned away as if everything was normal. Then a soldier asked, 'Well, what'll we do with 'em?'

" 'Kill 'em,' another answered.

"I heard an M-60 go off, a light machine gun, and when we turned all of them and the kids with them were dead."

Somewhere else in the hamlet another soldier says that he saw a buddy suddenly pull a small child out of a group of women. "She was just a little thing," he says. "She couldn't have been more than five or six."

What happened?

"He dragged her into one of these brick houses that hadn't been blown up yet."

And?

"I don't know. I didn't go inside with him. And I don't like to talk about it." He pauses for a few moments, looking away, and then he speaks in a muffled voice, toward the table. "He was in there maybe five, ten minutes. Then he comes out, turns around and throws a grenade into the house."

Another soldier says he saw a teen-age girl running across a rice paddy, trying to hide from an American who was chasing her. As he watched, he saw this American soldier aim with his rifle and shoot. The girl gave a cry and fell down. The soldier went after her and vanished into the paddy. A few minutes later there was another shot from the area and then the soldier walked back from the field into the hamlet.

Nguyen Thi Doc is over seventy, an ancient, stooped peasant woman with a stoic, expressionless face. Today she squats in misery in the doorway of the hootch she shares with a small grandson and a small granddaughter in the refugee camp across from Xom Lang.

On that March morning she was just beginning to make breakfast for her husband, her son, two daughters and nine grandchildren from three to sixteen. They were all gathered around her waiting for their rice. When the bombardment started, all took shelter in the bunker just outside the door. When the shells ceased, they emerged and went back into the house to eat.

A few minutes later Nguyen Thi Doc "heard the Americans come down from the sky." Within minutes they were at her doorway. Without saying a word, they began spraying the inside of the house with machine gun fire. Her husband, her son, her two daughters and seven of her grandchildren —the oldest seven—were killed immediately. Nguyen Thi Doc was shot in the arm; her five-year-old granddaughter was shot in the foot. Today it is scarred and shriveled and the child limps through the camp, often hiding from others. Only the youngest child, a little boy, escaped unharmed.

The Americans then set fire to the house. Somehow, Nguyen Thi Doc managed to get outside, taking her granddaughter and grandson with her, and from the yard they watched the house burn, inside of it the rest of her family.

Now she sits in the refugee camp, asking no questions why it happened. "I am too old," she says. "I have no idea why the GI's come and do this thing. The thing I must do is to make money to take care of these children. They have no one else. And I am too old. I just want to die."

Just outside the village there was a big pile of bodies. Jay Roberts sees this "really tiny kid—he only had a shirt on—nothing else. He came over to the people and held the hand of one of the dead. One of the GI's behind me dropped into a kneeling position thirty meters from this kid and killed him with a single shot."

Haeberle sees two small children, maybe four or five years old. "A guy with an M-16 fired at the first boy and the older boy fell over him to protect the smaller one. Then they fired six more shots. It was done very businesslike."

A small boy, three or four, suddenly appears from nowhere on the trail in front of a group of Americans. He is wounded in the arm. Michael Terry sees "the boy clutching his wounded arm with his other hand while the blood trickled between his fingers. He was staring around himself in shock and disbelief at what he saw. He just stood there with big eyes staring around like he didn't understand what was happening. Then the captain's radio operator put a burst of 16 into him."

When Paul Meadlo came into Xom Lang, Lieutenant Calley set him and some of the other men to work gathering the people together in groups in a central location. "There was about forty, forty-five people that we gathered in the center of the village," Meadlo told an interviewer. "And we placed them in there, and it was like a little island, right there in the center of the village."

The soldiers forced the people in the group to squat on the ground. "Lieutenant Calley came over and said, 'You know what to do with them, don't you?' And I said, 'Yes.' So I took it for granted he just wanted us to watch them. And he left and came back about ten or fifteen minutes later, and said, 'How come you ain't killed them yet?' And I told him that I didn't think he wanted us to kill them, that you just wanted us to guard them. He said, 'No, I want them dead.' "

At first Meadlo was surprised by the order—not shocked or horrified, but surprised. "But three, four guys heard it and then he stepped back about ten, fifteen feet, and he started shooting them. And he told me to start shooting. I poured about four clips into the group."

A clip is seventeen rounds. Meadlo fired sixty-eight rounds into this group of people. "I fired them on automatic," he said, "so you can't . . . you just spray the area on them and so you can't know how many you killed 'cause they were going fast. So I might have killed ten or fifteen of them."

One slaughter was over, but there was more to come, and the thirst for blood had become so contagious that no one thought anything about what he was doing. "We started to gather them up, more people," Meadlo says, "and we had about seven or eight people that we was gonna put into a hootch and we dropped a hand grenade in there with them."

Then Meadlo and several other soldiers took a group of civilians— almost exclusively women and children, some of the children still too young to walk—toward one of the two canals on the outskirts of Xom

Lang. "They had about seventy, seventy-five people all gathered up. So we threw ours in with them and Lieutenant Calley told me, he said, 'Meadlo, we got another job to do.' And so he walked over to the people and started pushing them off and started shooting."

Taking his cue from Calley, Meadlo and then the other members of this squad "started pushing them off and we started shooting them. So altogether we just pushed them all off and just started using automatics on them. And somebody told us to switch off to single shot so that we could save ammo. So we switched off to single shot and shot a few more rounds."

And all the time the Vietnamese at the canal were screaming and pleading with the Americans for mercy. . . .

Just as the slaughter at the canal began, Michael Terry happened to be passing by. "They had them in a group, standing over a ditch—just like a Nazi-type thing," he remembers. "One officer ordered a kid to machine gun everybody down. But the kid couldn't do it. He threw the machine gun down and the officer picked it up. I don't remember seeing any men in the ditch. Mostly women and kids."

Terry left for another part of the hamlet. Later he returned. Calley and his men had left by then and only a small group had stayed behind. Terry was at the canal, sitting on a mound eating some chow with William Doherty. As they were eating, the two noticed that "some of them were still breathing. They were pretty badly shot up. They weren't going to get any medical help, and so we shot them, shot maybe five of them."

In another part of Xom Lang, James Bergthold was moving just behind another soldier carrying a light machine gun. This soldier was moving from house to house, spraying in through the doors, not even looking where he was shooting. He came to one hootch, opened up and then strolled away. Bergthold stopped and looked in. An old man was writhing on the floor in pain, screaming, with large pieces of his legs shot away. Bergthold took his rifle and shot the old man. "Just to put him out of his misery."

All through Xom Lang and around it, the slaughter and the destruction continued endlessly, senselessly. Houses were blown apart and burned. Dead bodies were tossed into the pyres which had once been their homes, or they were left where they had fallen. Animals were slaughtered. Haeberle remembers one scene of a GI stabbing a cow over and over again with his bayonet while the blood spurted in all directions and other soldiers stood around watching and laughing and commenting on his technique. Dead animals and dead bodies were thrown down wells to pollute the water supply. And everywhere, it seemed, was Lieutenant Calley.

But for some Americans, at least, there was no joy in what was happening in Xom Lang, no glory and no victory. Haeberle saw one GI go over to a little boy who had been badly torn apart by a fusillade and with infinite tenderness cover him with a blanket.

And that night, when Nguyen Chi returned to the hamlet to seek her family, she found her three young sons still alive. When the first shells had fallen, the boys had taken their buffalo from the barn into the fields to hide it. At one point they raised their heads to see what was happening. Near them was an American soldier. He stared at them for a moment, then with great urgency motioned for them to duck again. No one is certain who this American was, but he may have been Pvt. Olson—like Bernhardt, he refused to shoot anyone that morning.

This chaotic dance of death was not enacted before an empty auditorium. There were spectators, an audience viewing the drama like ancient Romans at the martyrdom of the Christians. These spectators had a panoramic view.

There were the helicopters circling back and forth, hovering over Xom Lang, reconnoitering the area for signs of the VC and for information on what was going on below. The pilot of one of these choppers was Warrant Officer Hugh C. Thompson of Decatur, Georgia.

The gunner in this helicopter, Specialist Fourth Class Larry Colburn, says that as they were hovering low over one part of the hamlet, they "noticed people dead and wounded along the road and all through the village. There was an irrigation ditch full of bodies. We noticed that some people were still alive. We didn't know what had happened."

Thompson decided to drop down and evacuate some of the wounded. But the helicopter was already pretty full with his own crew, and so he radioed for the gunships to return and help lift the wounded civilians, mainly children, to safety. Then he spotted a group of about fifteen or a dozen children in the midst of the dead and the dying. "We went down," Colburn says, "and our crew chief brought out a little boy about two years old. He seemed in shock."

Huddled in a bunker a short distance away were about a dozen more children. Once again Thompson's radio operator called for the gunships to come in and help the children, ferry them to the nearest field hospital. As Thompson's helicopter lifted off, Colburn noticed that "there must have been about seventy-five or eighty people in a ditch—some dead, some wounded. I had never seen so many people dead in one place before." . . .

19

Judgment at Fort Benning

NEWSWEEK

He had been more than four months on trial and nearly two weeks awaiting judgment, and now First Lt. William Calley stood at last before the six officers of the jury, looking child-size and hot-faced and entirely too ordinary to be anybody's symbol of anything. He managed a slow, ragged salute, then gulped for air and trembled while the jury president read from a sheaf of white legal paper: "Lieutenant Calley, it is my duty . . . to inform you that the court . . . finds you . . . *guilty of premeditated murder* . . ." Calley's jaw went slack. His eyes fluttered. He stood rigidly through the rest of it, then forced another salute and sat down. The judgment of his brother Army officers was in: Calley had murdered at least 22 Vietnamese civilians at the hamlet called My Lai 4 just over three years ago. And so he became a symbol indeed: an outlaw soldier whose case embodied everything that was wrong with the war—and whose conviction fed the mounting pressures on President Nixon to speed it to an end.

Calley was a folk hero to some, a fall guy to others; it scarcely mattered which. The verdict, and the life sentence returned two days later, were massively unpopular, and their unpopularity made the judgment on Calley

Source: *Newsweek,* "Judgment at Fort Benning," 12 April 1971, pp. 27–29. Copyright Newsweek, Inc. 1971, reprinted by permission.

254

a first-magnitude political event. Doves argued that Calley was a scapegoat for war crimes at far higher levels of military and civilian authority; hawks even more clamorously argued that he was a martyr thrown to the wolves —or, rather, the doves. And both sides joined the public outcry. At the White House, clerks busily logged in an estimated 100,000 telegrams, 100 to 1 pro-Calley. Flags flapped at half-staff—spontaneously in many areas, by order of the governor in Indiana. Free-Calley resolutions dropped into hoppers in at least nine state legislatures. Draft boards quit en masse in communities scattered from Georgia to Connecticut to New Mexico. Local groups circulated pro-Calley petitions, held pro-Calley rallies, staged pro-Calley marches. Anti-war Viet vets showed their solidarity by trying to get themselves arrested. A Houston gun dealer put out a huge sign that said, FREE CALLEY OR TRY TRUMAN.

What happened in the streets was only the visible manifestation of a deep feeling that Calley got a raw deal—a psychic reaction to be placed alongside the 1968 Tet offensive and the 1970 Cambodia incursion among the traumata of an unhappy war. In a *Newsweek* poll conducted by The Gallup Organization, Americans disapproved the verdict and the sentence by about 8 to 1. Only a relative few doubted that what happened at My Lai was a crime. The far more general view was that such incidents were common—and the overwhelming conviction was that Calley was taking the rap for his superiors. . . .

[To defuse an increasingly volatile situation, President Nixon] took the unprecedented step of ordering Calley released from the Fort Benning stockade and returned to his quarters pending appeal; the move almost surely made it harder for Army reviewing authorities to sustain Calley's conviction—but it got a solid hand in the House, and as the *Newsweek* poll indicated, an enormous vote of approval from the nation. Two days later, he moved again to damp the continuing uproar—this time dispatching staff topsider John Ehrlichman to meet the press at an on-camera briefing and announce that the President himself would personally review the case before any sentence is carried out. . . .

Calley is an implausible figure to influence the course of history. The judgment on him was inevitable, given the weight of evidence against him —and his own admission on the stand that he had shot some My Lai villagers under his control. "I wish to God we could have found that this didn't happen," said one beleaguered juror in the aftermath. ". . . Soldiers don't do that. But they did." Yet Calley's very banality won him some sympathy: he is the classic cannon-fodder line lieutenant, and many Americans saw him as an underdog. And deeper still perhaps lay the fear that to convict him would be to acknowledge a larger community of shame—a community reaching far wider and higher than Calley and his Charlie Company at My Lai. The outcry was loudest not among doves who wanted to pursue the line of inquiry to generals and Presidents but among hawks who thought it should not have been opened at all. And it was their discontent that the senior Nixon men feared even more than the impatience of the doves. "If the war ends the way the Calley trial has ended—in disgrace, in shame, in a sense of guilt—the feeling would grow," said one, "that they've been taken, and there would be an enormous backlash."

The verdict revealed some of the potential. One night after the conviction, 100 protesters—mostly GI's from Fort Benning—marched from a rally in Columbus, Ga., to the post stockade chanting, "War is hell—free Calley!" MP's turned them back. In Louisiana, retired Maj. Gen. Raymond Hufft said he issued take-no-prisoners orders when he led a battalion across the Rhine in World War II—and "if the Germans had won, I would have been on trial at Nuremberg instead of them." Spiro Agnew told a Chicago Tribune interviewer that he wasn't talking about Calley, mind you, but he felt decisions in the stress of combat ought not to be subject to "Monday-morning quarterbacking." A Georgia American Legion post set out to collect a $100,000 defense appeal fund and 10 million petition signatures protesting his conviction. "There have been My Lais in every war," said Herbert Rainwater, national commander of the Veterans of Foreign Wars. "Now for the first time in our history we have tried a soldier for performing his duty."

Some of the reaction to the verdict was merely maudlin: "The Battle Hymn of Lieutenant Calley," sung by an Alabama vocal group called "C" Company, became an instant hit * and a Pasadena, Texas, radio station taped and played a bitter obituary for the Army, with the strains of "Onward, Christian Soldiers" soaring in the background.

And much reaction was plain angry. George Wallace asked Alabama Selective Service officials to see if they could suspend the draft in the state until Calley is pardoned (they can't), then went on to Columbus for a visit with Calley and a joint rally with Lt. Gov. Lester Maddox of Georgia. Georgia's Gov. Jimmy Carter proclaimed an "American Fighting Man's Day" . . . and asked citizens to drive with their auto headlights turned on. Audie Murphy, who killed 240 Germans in World War II, was "distressed and shocked." A Florida congressman proposed inviting Calley to address a joint session of Congress. A Georgia draft-board member offered to do a day at hard labor in Calley's place. And Robert Marasco, one of the eight Green Berets who were accused but not tried in the slaying of a suspected South Vietnamese double agent two years ago, was moved by the Calley verdict to "stand up and be counted" by admitting to a television inter-

---

* Sample lyrics: "My name is William Calley. I'm a soldier of this land. / I've tried to do my duty and to gain the upper hand . . ./ But they've made me out a villain . . . they have stamped me with a brand /. . . As we go marching on."

viewer that he had, with help, personally killed the agent on orders from the C.I.A. . . .

GI's stationed around the world reacted with almost uniform bitterness to the news, and so did a good many junior officers. Said an Sp/4 in Tokyo: "I don't care where you go in Vietnam, every gook you see is the enemy. A mama-san will pull a frag on you. Can you prosecute her for murder?" A first lieutenant at Fort Carson, Colo.: "If this is the way we're going to be honored on the battlefield, I'll never pull a trigger." A West Point shavetail, bound for Vietnam this summer from Fort Devens, Mass.: "The big point is—what's going to be a questionable order from now on? The hippie-generation people are in the Army now, and they're going to ask why for an order like 'Charge up the hill.' " A grunt who had just survived an enemy attack on Fire Base Mary Ann near Chu Lai: "Those dinks that hit us couldn't have been more than 14 or 15 years old. Calley was railroaded just because he did his job. In the boonies, man, it's self-defense. People back in the world don't understand."

20

We Have Marched, We Have Cried, We Have Prayed

ERNEST W. CHAMBERS

We have marched, we have cried, we have prayed . . . we have voted, we have petitioned, we have been good little boys and girls. We have gone out to Vietnam as doves and come back as hawks. We have done every possible thing to make this white man recognize us as human beings. And he refuses.

He teaches us in school about the American Revolution. Do you know that those people who you teach me in school are patriots, around Rhode Island, burned a British frigate because it was too active in cutting off what they felt were their "legitimate" smuggling activities? 1771 . . . The Gaspee was the name of the British ship. And do you know that those people in Virginia—who you teach me were patriots—did not condemn it? They praised this "patriotic" action, this blow struck for freedom.

George III was the King. The 13 American colonies were British Territories. They were extensions of the Mother Country, there for the purpose of Britain. A colony provides raw materials and then markets for the

Source: Ernest W. Chambers, "We Have Marched, We Have Cried, We Have Prayed," testimony given to National Advisory Commission on Civil Disorders, as quoted in *Ebony* (April 1968), pp. 29 ff.

258

Mother Country. You all know what colonialism is. We know what it is in *fact*, in America as black people.

You teach us that these colonies were not wrong when they spoke against George III and when Patrick Henry came out specifically against him and compared him to Caesar with his Brutus, somebody said, "Treason!" And he said, "If this is treason, make the most of it."

Then I look at what you're trying to do to Rap Brown and Stokely Carmichael—calling it sedition and treason. And saying if there isn't a law against them, there should be. Then you want to turn around and tell the world that these men couldn't speak like this if they didn't have freedom of speech . . . if they lived in Russia what would happen to them. Yet what you are saying, when you say a law should be passed against these men, is that Russia, in fact, has the right idea—and you'd better catch up with Russia and pass a law against these men so they cannot tell the truth.

Then there is a Freedom School in Tennessee which you want to say is teaching hatred because it tells black people that your ancestors brought us over on the Good Ship Jesus. You raped our women; you mutilated our men. You took away our dignity and our manhood. Any vestige of a culture, religion or language, you took away from us.

You can understand why Jews who were burned by the Nazis hate Germans, but you can't understand why black people who have been systematically murdered by the government and its agents—by private citizens, by the police department—you can't understand why they hate white people.

And you know what you want to do? And again we are learning all this in school, about how you reacted to the way people have done you—because in your background and history you have a Revolution, of which you are very proud. You celebrate July 4th as Independence Day because you stood up against the British Empire and told them to go to hell. Your ancestors committed treason, and you celebrate it now; and you were not treated nearly as badly as black people in this country.

As Malcolm X said, we're catching more hell than Patrick Henry ever saw or thought of. Patrick Henry wouldn't have been able to take it. You can understand Patrick Henry and make a hero out of him to me in school, but then you're going to turn around and condemn us when we use peaceable methods, like Father Groppi and other individuals, to get the rights that your Constitution promised us.

I didn't say being born or naturalized in this country was enough to make me a citizen. You said it. The Bill of Rights is yours. The civil rights bills are your bills. When the government itself violates the law, it brings the whole law into contempt.

A policeman is an object of contempt. A policeman is a paid and hired murderer. And you never find the policeman guilty of a crime, no matter what violence he commits against a black person. In Detroit, you were shooting "snipers." So you mounted a .50 caliber machine gun on a tank and shot into an apartment and killed a four-year-old "sniper." . . .

Yet you have the Mafia setting up headquarters outside of Cicero, Illinois—where the black people are not good enough to live—and taking out a charter of incorporation in Delaware; and you don't bring tanks and machine guns against the Mafia.

The Justice Department leases some of its offices from the Mafia.

And you want to talk about "respect for the law."

In history, they teach me how great Teddy Roosevelt was. Yet when he wanted a certain canal built—and he didn't have the authority, based on the way the laws are constructed in this country—you know what Teddy Roosevelt said? "Damn the law! Build the canal."

They taught me that in a white school.

And they taught me that Thomas Jefferson was a hero and a patriot because he wrote, "all men are created equal." And Thomas Jefferson was a slaveholder. And you want to teach my child that this man who would have enslaved him had he been alive in those days, is a hero to him?

Patrick Henry, who talked about freedom being so great that he would rather take death than enslavement, was a slaveholder himself.

Then George Washington—the President—"first in war, first in peace, first in the hearts of his countrymen," was a slaveholder.

And you want to teach my child that these are great men.

Then Abraham Lincoln, one of the most pious hypocrites of all time— and you can read from his own words where he said he had doubts whether black men were as well endowed as white people. Here is the only thing he would grant the black man: the right to eat the food that his hands produced. He was against slavery *morally;* but he said since he was the President, *officially* there was nothing he could do except what would benefit the Union. And his wanting to do what benefited the Union prevented him from carrying out what he, many stated, felt was his moral responsibility. Then you want to tell me about morality operating in this country—the "last stronghold of freedom."

The "free world"—the Statue of Liberty, "give me your tired, your poor, your hungry, those yearning to be free." And a black man who fought in every conflict that this country ever had—*that this country ever had*—the first blood spilled from the body of Crispus Attucks during the American Revolution.

Now I want to draw a parallel between what happened at the so-called Boston Massacre on Boston Common and what we do now. Here was Captain Preston with a detachment of British soldiers. And they had a right to be there because this was a colony. But the colonists felt oppressed because Boston was being occupied by a "foreign" force. So some of the citizens got together.

They didn't just sing *We Shall Overcome*. They didn't ask the soldiers: "Can we sit down here and pray to our God?" They got slabs of stone and snowballs and clubs and attacked the soldiers. When the soldiers fired into the crowd and killed seven people, the Americans called it a "massacre," and they say that was a great patriotic action by those people.

Yet black people doing ordinary, reasonable, peaceful things in this country are attacked by the police; and the police are praised for it. And you talk about giving the police more money and more power. You have got them as walking arsenals now—pistols, guns, clubs, saps; some of them carry knives, cattle prods, the new tear gas canister, high-powered rifles. They will be giving them hand grenades next. They can call in tanks with .50 caliber machine guns—in the United States of America. . . .

You know what you're going to tell *your* kid? George Washington, Patrick Henry, the great patriots—Benjamin Franklin discovered that lightning and electricity are synonymous. Everybody who ever did anything is white.

Here is what you are going to give my child. I am going to send him to school and teach him to respect authority. So here is a cracker teacher standing in front of my child making him listen to *Little Black Sambo*. See, that's the image the school gives him when he's young to teach him his "place." A caricature, wearing outlandish clothing that even the animals in the forest don't want to wear. His name is "Sambo." His mother's name is "Mumbo." And his father's name is "Jumbo." What are you telling him about family ties in America? That child does not have the same last name as either one of his parents. Since his parents have different last names, they are not even married.

All right. So he goes through the caricature like I did when I was a small child in grade school. And I don't forget these things. I wasn't born from the womb with the attitudes I have now. They were put in me by crackers. I sat through *Little Black Sambo*. And since I was the only black face in the room, I became Little Black Sambo. If my parents had taught me bad names to call the little cracker kids—and I use that term on purpose to try to get a message across to you—you don't like it. Well, how do you think we feel when an adult is going to take our child (we teach our child to respect that adult) and that adult gives these little white kids bad names to call him? Why don't you have Little Cracker Bohunk? Little Cracker Dago? Little Cracker Kike? You can't stand that. But yet you're going to take our little black children and expose them to this kind of ridicule, then not understand why we don't like it.

All right. He gets a little older, so he can't be Little Black Sambo because he's too old for that. So you turn to good old Mark Twain, one of your great writers. And the black child grows from Little Black Sambo into Nigger Jim. And the white kids read this stuff and they laugh at the black child; and he's got to sit there and take it. He is required to attend these schools by law, and this is what he gets.

All right. After he is Nigger Jim, he goes to high school and reads *Emperor Jones* written by Eugene O'Neill, who they are taught is a great playwright. And not only do they have to read it silently and master it, they've got to come to school and discuss orally about the "bush niggers." But still nothing about kikes. And nothing about dagos and spiks and wetbacks and bohunks and wops.

And then after he has passed through these degrading ages of the black man, and they have whipped the spirit out of him—after they have made him feel he's not fit to walk the earth and he always has to apologize to you for being here, then they crown him. They say, "I'm going to tell you what your grand-daddy had been; what your daddy had been; what you are going to be: Old Black Joe. And you know how Old Black Joe comes? With his head hanging low."

You tell us what you want to do to us and make of us. And this is the "educational process" which our children go through. And you wonder why they don't want to sit up in school.

And there is brutality in Omaha schools. A junior high school teacher had beaten, kicked and cut little black children. We took these children with their parents to the mayor's office. He would take no action. So in conjunction with his Human Relations Board director—a man named Homer Floyd who I think is one of the sharpest human relations men in the country; he's now in Topeka heading the Kansas Human Relations Commission—we went to the office of the city attorney with these parents who wanted to bring an action on behalf of their children. He was shown the injuries. There was a doctor named Johnson who photographed the injuries and was willing to testify in court as to the extent of them and the treatment he gave. And do you know the city attorney refused to accept the complaint and would not allow the parents to file charges against the teacher?

We contacted two lawyers, one's name is John Miller, the other Leo Eisenstatt—I mention the names because they are influential in Omaha —they contacted various members of the Omaha Board of Education and we sent written copies of the complaints to each individual member of the Board, to each individual member of the City Council, the mayor, the safety director, the chief of police and all of the cracker agencies which are so interested in teaching us about law and order and decency and democracy and respect—and not a bit of action was taken. This man was promoted from junior high to high school. And he now teaches in South High School. What do you think of that? . . .

You know why I don't mind telling you this stuff? Because you put us in jail for nothing. . . . If I go to jail, it's going to be for something; not like the last time about a year ago when I was standing on the steps of the barber shop where I work. I looked at a cracker cop and went to jail for "interfering with an officer" and "disturbing the peace." I have a transcript of the trial with me because you don't like to believe what we tell you. Then you want us to respect the police. "Help your police fight crime." To do that, we would have to fight the police because they, with Congress, are the greatest perpetrators of crime in this country.

You know what the police are mad about relative to Supreme Court decisions? They're upset because the Court says they have to respect the Fourth Amendment to the Constitution and other Constitutional guarantees of the people's freedom in a so-called democratic society. . . .

Now you don't know me, so maybe you don't want to kill me. You might just want me in jail. But you get me off the scene, and I'll multiply, because each time you handle one of us in this way, you show what you are. And you show the way you have to be dealt with. . . .

We have exhausted every means of getting redress, and it has not come. The police murdered a black boy named Eugene Nesbitt a year ago. He was against a fence. The cop was supposed to have been chasing him. His car—the tires had been shot off—hit a fence. A cop came up behind him, and from a distance of about nine feet, shot him in the back with a shotgun. Before the boy's body was cold, the safety director came out with a public statement and said the shooting was "regrettable" but "justified." There was no inquest. There was no autopsy. The cop was not relieved of duty pending an investigation. Nothing.

In March of this year, a 5'2" Negro youth was detained in the county jail. Five-foot-two. The following morning—there was a door frame six and a half feet high from which he was found hanging—with his belt, supposedly. There was nothing in the cell for him to stand on. Yet a 5'2" youth "committed suicide" in county jail. And again there was no investigation, but a whitewash. We are getting tired of having our people killed. . . .

One thing more. We have a mayor who . . . is on the board of Directors of what is known as Good Neighbor Homes. There is a Negro church with an Uncle Tom chicken-eatin' preacher for the pastor, who is fronting for the mayor's corporation; they are the sponsoring agency. Yet the mayor is on the board of Directors. The mayor's personal lawyer, Shafton, represents this group; and he is making that federal money which is put up for lawyer's fees. It is 221 (d) (3) housing. And this project was built in an area that is already overcrowded. And it is supposed to be for low-income people. Yet the rent starts at $115 a month. That is one of the mayor's interests.

He is also in charge of what is known as the Omaha Redevelopment Corporation (ORC)—and I have newspaper clippings on these things if you want to see them afterwards. They have about 45 houses in the ghetto which they have been buying up, his corporation. Now they have got some money under a federal program which is designed to help code enforcement and bring those houses up to standard.

Now at first they were tricky. They went into South Omaha and used some of this federal money. Then they went into the fringe of the Negro area to use some of this money. And then, the third time, it is called Project Pride, they went right into the area where between 30 and 33 of the mayor's corporation houses are located, and $40,000 in federal funds is being used there.

This same mayor asked me to review his Model City proposal because he needed what he called a "grass-roots" analysis. What he really needed was somebody who could make a hodgepodge look legitimate. But I am going to give him just what that thing deserves. It is justification for violent revolution in Omaha by black people.

We are late. If you read the admissions of the City of Omaha's application, you'll wonder why we Uncle Tom, handkerchief-head Negroes in Omaha haven't burned that city to the ground. This includes City Hall and everything else.

They admit that they don't give us the social services. We don't get the welfare attention. The buses don't give adequate service. The city itself doesn't clean the streets. There is inadequate garbage disposal. The police are poorly trained. They have bad, anti-Negro attitudes. All of this is presented. And you know why he did it? Because of the promise of the possibilities of getting some federal dollars. This made him admit crimes and flaws and shortcomings in the city which other considerations of morality never could.

We have been trying to bring these things to their attention for years, but they wouldn't acknowledge anything before. Then the federal government said "If you can show you have the imagination and you understand the causes of problems of the core cities, you can get some money." The mayor laid it all out, and there it is. And this is what I come from in Omaha, Nebraska.

You had better be glad—you see, some people there call me "militant." How can you call me "militant" when, in view of all these things I have mentioned to you, I haven't started a riot. I haven't burned a building. I haven't killed a cop.

You are looking at somebody who is more rational than any of you— or some of you—because some of you support the war in Vietnam, but you wouldn't support us if we burned down Omaha.

21

Raising Women's Consciousness

VIVIAN GORNICK

In a lower Manhattan office a legal secretary returns from her lunch hour, sinks into her seat and says miserably to a secretary at the next desk: "I don't know what's happening to me. A perfectly nice construction worker whistled and said, 'My, isn't *that* nice,' as I passed him and suddenly I felt this terrific anger pushing up in me. . . . I swear I wanted to *hit* him!"

At the same time, a thoughtful 40-year-old mother in a Maryland suburb is saying to a visiting relative over early afternoon coffee: "You know, I've been thinking lately, I'm every bit as smart as Harry, and yet he got the Ph.D. and I raised the girls. Mind you, I *wanted* to stay home. And yet, the thought of my two girls growing up and doing the same thing doesn't sit well with me at all. Not at all."

And in Toledo, Ohio, a factory worker turns to the next woman on the inspection belt and confides: "Last night I told Jim: 'I been working in the same factory as you 10 years now. We go in at the same time, come out

Source: Vivian Gornick, "Consciousness Female," *New York Times Magazine,* 10 January 1971, pp. 22ff. Copyright © 1971 by Vivian Gornick. Reprinted by permission of The Sterling Lord Agency.

the same time. But I do all the shopping, get the dinner, wash the dishes and on Sunday break my back down on the kitchen floor. I'm real tired of doin' all that. I want some help from you.' Well, he just laughed at me, see? Like he done every time I mentioned this before. But last night I wouldn't let up. I mean, I really *meant* it this time. And you know? I thought he was gonna let me have it. Looked mighty like he was gettin' ready to belt me one. But you know? I just didn't care! I wasn't gonna back down, come hell or high water. You'll just never believe it, he'd kill me if he knew I was tellin' you, he washed the dishes. First time in his entire life."

None of these women are feminists. None of them are members of the Women's Liberation Movement. None of them ever heard of consciousness-raising. And yet, each of them exhibits the symptomatic influence of this, the movement's most esoteric practice. Each of them, without specific awareness, is beginning to feel the effects of the consideration of woman's personal experience in a new light—a political light. Each of them is undergoing the mysterious behavioral twitches that indicate psychological alteration. Each of them is drawing on a linking network of feminist analysis and emotional upchucking that is beginning to suffuse the political-social air of American life today. Each of them, without ever having attended a consciousness-raising session, has had her consciousness raised.

Consciousness-raising is the name given to the feminist practice of examining one's personal experience in the light of sexism; i.e., that theory which explains woman's subordinate position in society as a result of a cultural decision to confer direct power on men and only indirect power on women.

Perceiving that woman's position in our society does indeed constitute that of a political class, and, secondly, that woman's "natural" domain is her feelings, and, thirdly, that testifying in a friendly and supportive atmosphere enables people to see that their experiences are often duplicated (thereby reducing their sense of isolation and increasing the desire to theorize as well as to confess), the radical feminists sensed quickly that a group of women sitting in a circle discussing their emotional experiences as though they were material for cultural analysis was political dynamite. Hence, through personal testimony and emotional analysis could the class consciousness of *women* be raised. . . .

The sessions consist mainly of women gathering once a week, sitting in a circle and speaking in turn, addressing themselves—almost entirely out of personal experience—to a topic that has been preselected. . . . [Such as] Love, Marriage, Sex, Work, Femininity, How I Came to Women's Liberation, Motherhood, Aging and Competition With Other Women. Additional subjects are developed as a particular group's specific interests and circumstances begin to surface. . . .

On the Upper West Side of Manhattan, in the vicinity of Columbia University, a group of women between the ages of 35 and 45 have been meeting regularly for six months. Emily R., an attractive 40-year-old divorcée in this group, says: "When I walked into the first meeting, and saw the *types* there, I said to myself: 'None of these broads have been through what I've been through. They couldn't possibly feel the way I feel.' Well, I'll tell you. None of them *have* been through what I've been through if you look at our experience superficially. But when you look a little *deeper* —the way we've been doing at these meetings—you see they've *all* been through what I've been through, and they all feel pretty much the way I feel. God, when I saw *that!* When I saw that what I always felt was my own personal hangup was as true for every other woman in that room as it was for me! Well, that's when *my* consciousness was raised."

What Emily R. speaks of is the phenomenon most often referred to in the movement, the flash of insight most directly responsible for the feminist leap in faith being made by hundreds of women everywhere—i.e., the intensely felt realization that what had always been taken for symptoms of personal unhappiness or dissatisfaction or frustration was so powerfully and so consistently duplicated among women that perhaps these symptoms could just as well be ascribed to *cultural* causes as to psychological ones. . . .

Early in the evening, on a crisp autumn night, a young woman in an apartment in the Gramercy Park section of Manhattan signed a letter, put it in an envelope, turned out the light over her desk, got her coat out of the hall closet, ran down two flights of stairs, hailed a taxi and headed west directly across the city. At the same time, on the Upper West Side, another woman, slightly older than the first, bent over a sleeping child, kissed his forehead, said goodnight to the babysitter, rode down 12 flights in an elevator, walked up to Broadway and disappeared into the downtown subway. Across town, on the Upper East Side, another woman tossed back a head of stylishly fixed hair, pulled on a beautiful pair of suede boots and left her tiny apartment, also heading down and across town. On the Lower East Side, in a fourth-floor tenement apartment, a woman five or six years younger than all the others combed out a tangled mop of black hair, clomped down the stairs in her Swedish clogs and started trudging west on St. Marks Place. In a number of other places all over Manhattan other women were also leaving their houses. When the last one finally walked into the Greenwich Village living room they were all headed for, there were 10 women in the room.

These women ranged in age from the late 20's to the middle 30's; in appearance, from attractive to very beautiful; in education, from bachelor's degrees to master's degrees; in marital status, from single to married to divorced to imminently separated; two were mothers. Their names were Veronica, Lucie, Diana, Marie, Laura, Jen, Sheila, Dolores, Marilyn and

Claire. Their occupations, respectively, were assistant television producer, graduate student, housewife, copywriter, journalist, unemployed actress, legal secretary, unemployed college dropout, schoolteacher and computer programmer.

They were not movement women; neither were they committed feminists; nor were they marked by an especial sense of social development or by personal neurosis. They were simply a rather ordinary group of women who were drawn out of some unresolved, barely articulated need to form a "woman's group." They were in their third month of meetings; they were now at Marie's house (next week they would meet at Laura's, and after that at Jen's, and so on down the line); the subject for discussion tonight was "Work."

The room was large, softly lit, comfortably furnished. After 10 or 15 minutes of laughing, chatting, note and book exchanging, the women arranged themselves in a circle, some on chairs, some on the couch, others on the floor. In the center of the circle was a low coffee table covered with a coffeepot, cups, sugar, milk, plates of cheese and bread, cookies and fruit. Marie suggested they begin, and turning to the woman on her right, who happened to be Dolores, asked if she would be the first.

Dolores (*the unemployed college dropout*): I guess that's okay. . . . I'd just as soon be the first . . . mainly because I hate to be the last. When I'm last, all I think about is, soon it will be *my* turn. (*She looked up nervously.*) You've no idea how I *hate* talking in public. (*There was a long pause; silence in the circle.*) . . . Work! God, what can I say? The whole question has always been absolute hell for me. . . . A lot of you have said your fathers ignored you when you were growing up and paid attention only to your brothers. Well, in my house it was just the opposite. I have two sisters, and my father always told me I was the smartest of all, that I was smarter than he was, and that I could do anything I wanted to do . . . but somehow, I don't really know *why,* everything I turned to came to nothing. After six years in analysis I still don't know *why.* (*She looked off into space for a moment and her eyes seemed to lose the train of her thought. Then she shook herself and went on.*) I've always drifted . . . just drifted. My parents never forced me to work. I needn't work even now. I had every opportunity to find out what I really wanted to do. But . . . nothing I did satisfied me, and I would just stop. . . . Or turn away. . . . Or go on a trip. I worked for a big company for a while. . . . Then my parents went to Paris and I just went with them. . . . I came back . . . went to school . . . was a researcher at Time-Life . . . drifted . . . got married . . . divorced . . . drifted. (*Her voice grew more halting.*) I feel my life is such *waste.* I'd like to write, I really would; I feel I'd be a good writer, but I don't know. I just can't get going. . . . My father is so disappointed in me. He keeps hoping I'll really do something. *Soon.* (*She shrugged her shoulders but her face was very quiet and pale, and her pain expressive. She happened to be one of the most beautiful women in the room.*)

Diana (the housewife): What do you think you will do?

Dolores (in a defiant burst): Try to get married!

Jen (the unemployed actress) and *Marie (the copywriter):* Oh, no!

Claire (the computer programmer): After all that! Haven't you learned yet? What on earth is marriage going to do for you? Who on earth could you marry? *Feeling* about yourself as you do? Who could save you from yourself? Because that's what you *want.*

Marilyn (the schoolteacher): That's right. It sounds like "It's just all too much to think out so I might as well get married."

Lucie (the graduate student): Getting married like that is *bound* to be a disaster.

Jen: And when you get married like that it's always to some creep you've convinced yourself is wonderful. So understanding. (*Dolores grew very red and very quiet through all this.*)

Sheila (the legal secretary): Stop jumping on her like that! I know *just* how she feels. . . . I was *really* raised to be a wife and a mother, and yet my father wanted me to do something with my education after he sent me to one of the best girls' schools in the East. Well, I didn't get married when I got out of school like half the girls I graduated with, and now seven years later I'm *still* not married. (*She stopped talking abruptly and looked off into the space in the center of the circle, her attention wandering as though she'd suddenly lost her way.*) I don't know how to describe it exactly, but I know just how Dolores feels about drifting. I've always worked, and yet something was always sort of confused inside me. I never really knew which way I wanted to go on a job: up, down, sideways. . . . I always thought it would be the most marvelous thing in the world to work for a really brilliant and important man. I never have. But I've worked for some good men and I've learned a lot from them. But (*her dark head came up two or three inches and she looked hesitantly around*) I don't know about the rest of you, but I've always wound up being propositioned by my bosses. It's a funny thing. As soon as I'd be doing really well, learning fast and taking on some genuine responsibility, like it would begin to excite them, and they'd make their move. When I refused, almost invariably they'd begin to *browbeat* me. I mean, they'd make my life miserable! And, of course, I'd retreat. . . . I'd get small and scared and take everything they were dishing out . . . and then I'd move on. I don't know, maybe something in my behavior was really asking for it, I honestly don't know anymore. . . .

Marie: There's a good chance you *were* asking for it. I work with

a lot of men and I don't get propositioned every other day. I am so absolutely straight no one *dares*. . . . They all think I am a dike.

Sheila (*plaintively*): Why is it like that, though? Why are men like
that? Is it something they have more of, this sexual need for ego gratification?
Are they made differently from us?

Jen (*placing her coffee cup on the floor beside her*): No! You've
just never learned to stand up for yourself! And goddammit, they *know* it,
and they play on it. Look, you all know I've been an actress for years.
Well, once, when I was pretty new in the business, I was playing opposite
this guy. He used to feel me up on the stage. All the *time*. I was scared. I
didn't know what to do. I'd say to the stage manager: That guy is feeling
me up. The stage manager would look at me like I was crazy, and shrug
his shoulders. Like: What can *I* do? Well, once I finally thought: I can't
stand this. And I bit him. Yes, I bit the bastard, I bit his
tongue while he was kissing me.

A Chorus of Voices: You *bit* him????

Jen (*with great dignity*): Yes, dammit, I bit him. And afterward he
said to me, "Why the hell did you do that?" And I said, "You know god-
dam well why I did that." And do you know? He respected me after that.
(*She laughed.*) Didn't *like* me very much. But he respected me. (*She looked
distracted for a moment.*) . . . I guess that *is* pretty funny. I mean, biting
someone's tongue during a love scene.

Veronica (*the assistant TV producer*): Yeah. Very funny.

Laura (*the journalist*): Listen, I've been thinking about something
Sheila said. That as soon as she began to get really good at her job her boss
would make a pass—and that would pretty much signal the end, right?
She'd refuse, he'd become an S.O.B., and she'd eventually leave. It's almost as if sex were being used to cut her down, or back, or in some way
stop her from rising. An *instinct* he, the boss, has—to sleep with her when
he feels her becoming really independent.

Lucie (*excitedly*): I'll buy that! Look, it's like Samson and Delilah
in reverse. *She* knew that sex would give her the opportunity to destroy his
strength. Women are famous for wanting to sleep with men in order to en-
slave them, right? That's the great myth, right? He's all spirit and mind,
she's all emotion and biological instinct. She uses this instinct with *cunning*
to even out the score, to get some power, to bring him down—through
sex. But, look at it another way. What are these guys always saying to us?
What are they always saying about women's liberation?—"All she needs is
a good ——." They say that *hopefully*. *Prayerfully*. They know. We *all*
know what all that "All she needs is a good——" stuff is all about.

Claire: This is ridiculous. Use your heads. Isn't a guy kind of
super if he wants to sleep with a woman who's becoming independent?

Marie: Yes, but not in business. There's something wrong every time, whenever sex is operating in business. It's always like a secret weapon, something you hit your opponent below the belt with.

Diana: God, you're all crazy! Sex is *fun.* Wherever it exists. It's warm and nice and it makes people feel good.

Dolores: That's a favorite pipe dream of yours, isn't it?

Sheila: It certainly doesn't seem like very much fun to me when I watch some secretary coming on to one of the lawyers when she wants a raise, then I see the expression on her face as she turns away.

Marie: God, that sounds like my mother when she wants something from my father!

Veronica (feebly): You people are beginning to make me feel *awful!* (*Everyone's head snapped in her direction.*)

Marie: Why?

Veronica: The way you're talking about using sex at work. As if it were so horrible. Well, I've *always* used a kind of sexy funniness to get what I want at work. What's wrong with that?

Lucie: What do you do?

Veronica: Well, if someone is being very stuffy and serious about business, I'll say something funny—I guess in a sexy way—to break up the atmosphere which sometimes gets *so* heavy. You know what I mean? Men can be so pretentious in business! And then, usually, I get what I want—while I'm being funny and cute, and they're laughing.

Diana (heatedly): Look, don't you see what you're *doing?*

Veronica (testily): No, I don't. What am I *doing?*

Diana (her hands moving agitatedly through the air before her): If there's some serious business going on you come in and say: Nothing to be afraid of, folks. Just frivolous, feminine little me. I'll tell a joke, wink my eye, do a little dance, and we'll all pretend nothing's really happening here.

Veronica: My God, I never thought of it like that.

Laura: It's like those apes. They did a study of apes in which they discovered that apes chatter and laugh and smile a lot to ward off aggression.

Marilyn: Just like women! Christ, aren't they always saying to us: *Smile!* Who tells a man to smile? And how often do you smile for no damned reason, right? It's so *natural* to start smiling as soon as you start talking to a man, isn't it?

Lucie: That's right! You're right! You know—God, it's amazing! —I began to think about this just the other day. I was walking down Fifth Avenue and a man in the doorway of a store said to me, "Whatsamatta, honey? Things can't be *that* bad." And I was startled because I wasn't feeling depressed or anything, and I couldn't figure out why he was saying that. So I looked, real fast, in the glass to see what my face looked like.

And it didn't look like anything. It was just a face at rest. I had just an ordinary, sort of thoughtful expression on my face. And he thought I was *depressed.* And, I couldn't help it, I said to myself: "Would he have said that to you if you were a man?" And I answered myself immediately: "No!"

Diana: That's it. That's really what they want. To keep us barefoot, pregnant, and *smiling.* Always sort of *begging,* you know? Just a little supplicating—at all times. And they get anxious if you stop smiling. Not because you're depressed. Because you're *thinking!*

Dolores: Oh, come on now. Surely, there are lots of men who have very similar kinds of manners? What about all the life-of-the-party types? All those clowns and regular guys?

Claire: Yes, what about them? You *never* take those guys seriously. You never think of the men of real power, the guys with serious intentions and real strength, acting that way, do you? And those are the ones with real responsibility. The others are the ones women laugh about in private, the ones who become our confidantes, not our lovers, the ones who are *just like ourselves.*

Sheila (quietly): You're right.

Lucie: And it's true, it really does undercut your seriousness, all that smiling.

Sheila (looking suddenly sad and very intent): And underscore your weakness.

Dolores: Yes, exactly. We smile because we feel at a loss, because we feel vulnerable. We don't quite know how to accomplish what we want to accomplish or how to navigate through life, so we act *feminine.* That's really what this is all about, isn't it? To be masculine is to take action, to be feminine is to smile. Be coy and cute and sexy—and maybe you'll become the big man's assistant. God, it's all so sad. . . .

Claire: I don't feel like *any* of you. Not a single one.

Dolores: What do you mean?

Claire: Let me tell you something. I have two sisters and a brother. My father was a passionately competitive man. He loved sports and he taught us all how to play, and he treated us all exactly as though we were his equals at it. I mean, he competed with us exactly as though we were 25 when we were 8. Everything: sailing, checkers, baseball, there was nothing he wouldn't compete in. When I was a kid I saw him send a line drive ball right into my sister's stomach, for God's sake. Sounds terrible, right? We loved it. All of us. And we thrived on it. For me, work is like everything else. *Competitive.* I get in there, do the best I can, compete ferociously against man, woman or machine. And I use whatever I have in the way of equipment: sex, brains, endurance. You name it, I use it. And if I lose I lose, and if I win I win. It's just doing it as well as I can that counts. And if I come up against discrimination as a woman, I just reinforce my attack. But the name of the game is competition.

(*Everyone stared at her, openmouthed, and suddenly everyone was talking at once; over each other's voices; at each other; to themselves; laughing; interrupting; generally exploding.*)

Laura (*dryly*): The American dream. Right before our eyes.

Diana (*tearfully*): Good God, Claire, that sounds awful!

Lucie (*amazed*): That's the kind of thing that's killing our men. In a sense, it's really why we're here.

Sheila (*mad*): Oh, that love of competition!

Marie (*astonished*): The whole idea of just *being* is completely lost in all this.

Jen (*outraged*): And to act *sexy* in order to compete! You degrade every woman alive!

Veronica (*interested*): In other words, Claire, you imply that if they give you what you want they get *you?*

Diana (*wistfully*): That notion of competition is everything we hate most in men, isn't it? It's responsible for the most brutalizing version of masculinity. We're in here trying to be men, right? Do we want to be men at their worst?

Lucie (*angrily*): For God's sake! We're in here trying to be *ourselves*. Whatever that turns out to be.

Marilyn (*with sudden authority*): I think you're wrong, all of you. You don't understand what Claire's really saying. (*Everyone stopped talking and looked at Marilyn.*) What Claire is really telling you is that her father taught her not how to win but how to lose. He didn't teach her to ride roughshod over other people. He taught her how to get up and walk away intact when other people rode roughshod over *her*. And he so loved the idea of teaching *that* to his children that he ignored the fact that she and her sisters were girls, and he taught it to them, anyway. (*Everyone took a moment to digest this.*)

Laura: I think Marilyn has a very good point there. That's exactly what Claire has inside her. She's the strongest person in this room, and we've all known it for a long time. She has the most integrated and most *separate* sense of herself of anyone I know. And I can see now that that probably has developed from her competitiveness. It's almost as though it provided the *proper* relation to other people, rather than no relation.

Sheila: Well, if that's true then her father performed a minor miracle.

Jen: You're not kidding. Knowing where *you* stand in relation to other people, what you're supposed to be doing, not because of what other people want of you but because of what you want for yourself . . . *know-*

ing what you want for yourself . . . that's everything, isn't it? . . . (*Outside, the bells in a nearby church tower struck midnight.*)

    Diana: Let's wrap it up, okay?

    Veronica (*reaching for her bag*): Where shall we meet next week?

    Marie: Wait a minute! Aren't we going to sum up? (*Everyone stopped in mid-leaving, and sank wearily back into her seat.*)

    Lucie: Well, one thing became very clear to me. Every one of us in some way has struggled with the idea of getting married in order to be relieved of the battle of finding and staying with good work.

    Diana: And every one of us who's actually done it has made a mess of it!

    Jen: And everyone who *hasn't* has made a mess of it!

    Veronica: But, look. The only one of us who's really worked well —with direction and purpose—is Claire. And we all jumped on her! (*Everyone was startled by this observation and no one spoke for a long moment.*)

    Marilyn (*bitterly*): We can't do it, we can't admire anyone who *does* do it, and we can't let it alone. . . .

    Jen (*softly*): That's not quite true. After all, we *were* able to see finally that there was virtue in Claire's position. And we *are* here, aren't we?

    Marie: That's right. Don't be so down. We're not 102 years old, are we? We're caught in a mess, damned if we do and damned if we don't. All right. That's exactly why we're here. To break the bind. (*On this note everyone took heart, brightened up and trooped out into the darkened Manhattan streets. Proof enough of being ready to do battle.*)

22

Some Husbands Talk About Their Liberated Wives

ROBERT E. GOULD

What is the effect of consciousness-raising on the husbands of wives who have had their consciousnesses raised? To answer this, I convened a meeting of the men whose wives are in the same consciousness-raising group as my wife.

This group of men and their wives may seem somewhat special: mostly Jewish, mostly professional and mostly successful—some unusually so.

It may also be unrepresentative that all the men and women save one have undergone previous psychotherapy experiences. Yet these people are typical of a certain segment of New York life and probably manifest many submerged feelings of society at large. Although more into psychotherapy and Women's Liberation than many other groups in our country, they are not really unrelated to them. The difference, I believe, is only one of degree and intensity—or possibly only one of timing. I think Women's Lib has already reached nearly every home on some level, sometimes without the inhabitants knowing it, often with their vigorous denials that it is there.

This group is special, then, because the wives have openly committed

Source: Robert E. Gould, "Some Husbands Talk About Their Liberated Wives," *New York Times Magazine*, 18 June 1972, pp. 10ff. © 1972 by The New York Times Company. Reprinted by permission.

themselves at least to the idea of change. And the husbands have had to respond if only by acknowledging that something about their marriage is already different. And ready or not, there may be a great deal more where that came from.

Another special characteristic, perhaps, is this group's basic attitude about marriage. Unlike many couples, they are not willing to settle for a bad bargain or an uneasy peace. Nor, like many others, are they willing to call it quits. They *want* their marriages—possibly enough to revise drastically the notion of what they want of marriage. The cost of such an overhaul has not been reckoned yet, but they do have a good idea that it will be high. I have a strong feeling that all of us are on the verge of great change, first in our thinking and then in our roles and lives. It has already begun. The group of men in this sample and their responses to the changing role of women may have relevance for many marriages and male-female relationships, where consciousness has not risen to this point—yet.

Bob [*psychiatrist and psychoanalyst; wife, Lois, is a writer; they have two children*]: I'm struck by how many of us in this room and our wives have been in some kind of therapy before. I wonder if, in a way, the need for the consciousness-raising group isn't a rather dramatic statement about how psychotherapy has failed to do its job. I see the women's group as a self-therapy group. Consciousness-raising, the term used for increasing self-awareness—the meaning and reason for your behavior and actions—is what therapy is all about. And I really feel that psychotherapy and psychoanalysis have paid too little attention to redefining the stereotyped male and female roles. The focus was too often on fitting the individuals into the roles. This is what is being picked up now because it is a crucial area. If your role is not a fulfilling one, you are not fulfilling your potential, and it is unlikely you will so long as we behave in role stereotypes for what is "masculine" and "feminine." . . .

Jerry [*actor; wife, Monica, is a TV producer*]: . . . I think you have a point. I think therapy has broken down somewhere along the line, for women, and I think in many cases for men, too, because I do definitely agree that what Monica is getting out of this "consciousness-raising" is group therapy. Nothing more, nothing less. . . .

Bob: What do our wives want of themselves—and of us? . . .

Arnold [*press agent; wife, Mary, is an advertising executive; they have one child*]: . . . I can recall shortly after my wife got involved deeply in Women's Lib, I was in my usual reclining chair reading the paper, and she was doing the dishes after a steak or roast beef or something very messy, and I said, "Oh, honey, let me do the broiler. . . ." She had done all the other dishes. So I did the broiler and when I came out she said, "Thank you, honey, that was nice of you." Then she said, "What the

———— am I saying thank you for? What am I so grateful for? I came home at 5:30 and cooked, served you, cleared and washed the dishes, and you came in and washed one broiler, and I say thank you! How about you doing *all* the dishes the rest of the week?" And she stormed out of the room. That was when it really came home to me. . . .

Clay [*engineer; wife, Sherry, stays at home with two young children but has begun to teach part-time*]: My wife has always been very dependent on me. Sherry doesn't drive; she isn't handy around the house. She also lets me take care of financial things—having been taught that a good wife lets her husband handle all of these so-called masculine functions. I think recently this has all been getting to her; she wants more independence. She wants to go back to some kind of creative work.

So I think the group is a very good influence for her now—just as an experience of being with other women who are working in that direction. . . . I feel good about her becoming more independent and wanting to do these things. On the other hand, I think I feel very threatened . . . at heart I like Sherry being dependent on me. I like her to say, "Clay, can you do this for me?" I like her to look up to me—old-fashioned as that is. . . .

Arnold: [The essence of what consciousness-raising is about is that] women are trying to change their role in society that is predetermined by a whole series of criteria that they don't particularly like because it keeps them down. Men in this context, as husbands of feminists, I have found, have to keep the politics going because it has to work both ways. When my wife says to me, "Damn it, that window has been broken for two weeks and you haven't done a thing," I say, "Don't call me 'boy.' " She has got to know that if she has a right to go out and leave me with the kids at night, then by the same token she has to pick up a hammer.

Alan [*freelance photographer; wife, Jenny, was a publicist for a large corporation; currently she is a full-time mother*]: I am all for that. . . . It's very valuable to be able to say to your wife, "You are playing a sexist role with me." It is very important to be able to say to your wife, "I think you're using just what you accuse me of using on you." I think that is one of the really positive aspects of this whole liberation skirmish. . . .

Bob: The point is giving up the so-called male role and the female role, so you can do things for each other solely on the basis of making the relationship work better. Then you don't have to get hung up with the politics at all. No one is going to like everything he has to do. I don't like to make the bed. Now if Lois says, "I don't like to make the bed either, I want to share this with you," I have no recourse really but to do it. I can say, "Damn it, I will not make the bed." She will have to make it then, because I know Lois; she is not yet ready to leave it unmade. So she will make it, but at too great a cost for me. She will resent making it and I will pay for it heavily in other ways, so I realize that my life would be better if I shared the bed-making chores. Also I would hope that the feeling I have for her happiness would make the nuisance work more acceptable to me. But I can't do that if I feel this is going to demean me as a man. This is what gets us hung up in male-female role rigidity and its unpleasant results. . . .

Arnold: There is an incredible amount of bull———— in the Feminist Movement. The first group my wife was in was composed mostly of writers or would-be writers, and they agreed at their first meeting that every one of them would be writing a great novel if it wasn't for the men who oppressed them, which was of course ridiculous. . . .

Bob: The trouble often with any movement when the people have been oppressed or discriminated against and suddenly become not only aware of it but also actively motivated toward changing it, is that the pendulum often swings to the other extreme. If their only role in life before was that of mother-wife-homemaker, then when they rebel, they're apt to begin by violently rejecting that role—even the rewarding parts—until they've explored all the other avenues that used to be closed. I think eventually that pendulum will swing back to the middle where bringing up children can be seen as okay, very creative and fulfilling in its own right for those who want to do it. But right now the question is still whether a woman truly has the *option* of bringing up babies or working or doing both. If so, the choice she makes may then truly reflect her innate capacities, desires, temperament; but if not, if there is still no free choice, then women still have that battle to win. . . .

Arnold: Can you point out an area where it has affected you that we haven't discussed? . . .

Bob: There is an area we haven't talked about—sex.

Arnold: It's all *they* talk about at meetings, though.

Dick [art director; wife, Nancy, is a magazine editor]: Really?

Arnold: Ninety per cent, I am sure.

Clay: That's what I hear. . . .

Arnold: Mary and I lived together quite a while before we were married, and we have been married now seven and a half years, and we have never had what one would call sexual problems in the sense where you would go for help; but the central problem, which I think is fairly characteristic, is what does one do if one partner wishes to and one doesn't? Now if the partner who wishes to is the woman and the one who doesn't is the man, that is a self-solving problem. There is just nothing you can do about it. So it may cause resentment, but it doesn't cause a fight, because there is nothing you can do. I mean if a guy just isn't going to get it up, you are not going to have sex. On the other hand, if the man wants to do it and the woman doesn't, that has always been a big problem in our house. It was a big problem. Since I consider myself a gentleman—in the true sense of the word: a gentle man—I would never pursue it. However, then my wife would feel very guilty, and then she would feel it incumbent upon her to seduce me to demonstrate that she changed her mind—to show me that she really wanted to do it. The whole scene of two people trying to be nice to each other, which ends up in a disaster, would occur. This was not frequent but when it happened it was very unpleasant, and I guess we would all agree the most unpleasant fights are about sex, because it is where we are all most vulnerable. In Women's Lib, Mary got the message: You have got the exact same sexual rights as your husband. And if he is not prepared to satisfy your desires when he doesn't feel like it, there is absolutely no reason in the world for you to satisfy his when you don't feel like it, and it is in a sense his obligation to make you feel like it if that is what his concern is. . . . We make love more often. It is better because she feels she can say no and that's it.

Bob: I think sex between two people can go downhill when there is poor communication. When the woman, as you say, serves the man and doesn't want to, resentment builds up and often never gets talked about, and this makes for lousy sex. Now with Women's Lib allowing women to be more honest about sex, it could be a lot better for all of us, even if it's still different from what it was when we were young, or single, or both. Sex can actually be much better after seven years of marriage, because you have worked out a lot of problems. And because you can at least talk about the others. . . .

Dick: One aspect of this which I feel most pessimistic about, and I don't see the prospect of it changing, is that most women still have one basic fantasy—the thing that turns them on the most—a fantasy in which they themselves are overpowered, raped, whatever. Is that a fair statement?

Arnold: As far as my wife goes, I would think so. If not overpowered, at least used totally impersonally.

Bob: Yes, I think that is one aspect but I do think that is the kind of sex women have fantasied who have not attained equality, or a feeling of equality in their own minds.

Dick: Here is my point. . . . I think it is a fairly universal woman's fantasy to be raped, to be used as a sexual object and so on. Now that being the case, as I assume it is, aren't women in the Movement in an odd position because their fantasies are totally at odds with their political feeling?

Bob: Yes, the fantasy is a common one and in part represents the only way a woman can permit herself to enjoy sex. This is because she has been brought up under the double standard that has been pervasive in our culture. Since "nice girls" hold back, being raped allows the woman to say, "It's not my fault I'm engaging in sex."

Dick: So say you try to respond, in effect, to both. Say during the day you try to respond to the political woman, and in bed you respond to the sexual-fantasy woman. But during the day perhaps you have been undercut; how do you keep from responding to *that* when you get the fantasy woman into bed that night?

Bob: The fantasy of wanting to be raped, taken that way, I think comes from the stereotyped role of women as passive, rather than active sexually; so if she is to enjoy sex it is not by being equal, assertive, and aggressive. It is by being raped. Remember when we were kids, at least when I was a kid, the girl could not say "I want to neck with you, I want to have sex with you." She would have to play coy, play passive; you would have to seduce her, half rape her, pushing her in the corner, and then she would think okay, now I have to give in, I can't fight any more, and she could then enjoy it. But she couldn't enjoy it otherwise. I don't think this is healthy sexual behavior; I think it was the only way she was able to enjoy sex without being married, because of the cultural stereotype. This is how she had to play it as a single girl, and when she gets to be married, the piece of paper doesn't change it that easily, so she still has fantasy rapes and all that. But I think what you call political, which I still call a form of group therapy, will allow the woman to say she can enjoy sex and engage in it fully, equally, actively, just as the man does, and the more she moves, the more control she has over her body, the more she is going to get out of it, and so on. When she eventually gets to the point of feeling it as well as saying it, that will be ideal; . . . .

His consciousness has to be raised too, for he has been just as victimized by the brainwashing, the stereotypes, as the woman. We had to be taught to be masculine, aggressive, masterful. . . .

Men have to learn to enjoy being passive at times, being tender, letting the woman take the lead in sex. When all that gets evened out then you really can hop around in bed in any position you want, playing any "role" you want just because it's fun and enjoyable and you are not anxious about playing or not playing the right one. . . .

Clay: Do you think this Women's Lib, this consciousness-raising is really going to help make sex a more equal situation? Make it better? Assuming that it is uneven now in a relationship?

Bob: Yes, I think that if Women's Lib works well, it will do this. Unless it's a lesbian group—whose policy is that sex between women is really better than sex with men. That kind of group is obviously not going to be helpful in direct man-woman relationships. . . .

Even if all we learned tonight were a few preliminary answers to the question of what the Women's Movement is doing to our lives, then I think this meeting was worthwhile. I think we at least began to see some of the changes—and maybe to anticipate the bigger ones that are ahead of us. I don't think we can see, yet, what that change is going to do to us. I do think we all admit feeling threatened, feeling anxious. And feeling sure that whatever happens next, our marriages aren't ever going to go back to the way they used to be.

23

The New Youth Culture

THE PRESIDENT'S COMMISSION ON CAMPUS UNREST

In early Western societies, the young were traditionally submissive to adults. Largely because adults retained great authority, the only way for the young to achieve wealth, power, and prestige was through a cooperative apprenticeship of some sort to the adult world. Thus, the young learned the traditional adult ways of living, and in time they grew up to become adults of the same sort as their parents, living in the same sort of world.

Advancing industrialism decisively changed this cooperative relationship between the generations. It produced new forms and new sources of wealth, power, and prestige, and these weakened traditional adult controls over the young. It removed production from the home and made it increasingly specialized; as a result, the young were increasingly removed from adult work places and could not directly observe or participate in adult work. Moreover, industrialism hastened the separation of education from the home, in consequence of which the young were concentrated together in places of formal education that were isolated from most adults. Thus, the young spent an increasing amount of time together, apart from their

Source: *The Report of the President's Commission on Campus Unrest* (Washington: Government Printing Office, 1970), pp. 61–69.

parents' home and work, in activities that were different from those of adults.

This shared and distinct experience among the young led to shared interests and problems, which led, in turn, to the development of distinct subcultures. As those subcultures developed, they provided support for any youth movement that was distinct from—or even directed against— the adult world.

A distinguishing characteristic of young people is their penchant for pure idealism. Society teaches youth to adhere to the basic values of the adult social system—equality, honesty, democracy, or whatever—in absolute terms. Throughout most of American history, the idealism of youth has been formed—and constrained—by the institutions of adult society. But during the 1960's, in response to an accumulation of social changes, the traditional American youth culture developed rapidly in the direction of an oppositional stance toward the institutions and ways of the adult world.

This subculture took its bearings from the notion of the autonomous, self-determining individual whose goal was to live with "authenticity," or in harmony with his inner penchants and instincts. It also found its identity in a rejection of the work ethic, materialism, and conventional social norms and pieties. Indeed, it rejected all institutional disciplines externally imposed upon the individual, and this set it at odds with much in American society.

Its aim was to liberate human consciousness and to enhance the quality of experience; it sought to replace the materialism, the self-denial, and the striving for achievement that characterized the existing society with a new emphasis on the expressive, the creative, the imaginative. The tools of the workaday institutional world—hierarchy, discipline, rules, self-interest, self-defense, power—it considered mad and tyrannical. It proclaimed instead the liberation of the individual to feel, to experience, to express whatever his unique humanity prompted. And its perceptions of the world grew ever more distant from the perceptions of the existing culture: what most called "justice" or "peace" or "accomplishment," the new culture envisioned as "enslavement" or "hysteria" or "meaninglessness." As this divergence of values and of vision proceeded, the new youth culture became increasingly oppositional.

And yet in its commitment to liberty and equality, it was very much in the mainstream of American tradition; what it doubted was that America had managed to live up to its national ideals. Over time, these doubts grew, and the youth culture became increasingly imbued with a sense of alienation and of opposition to the larger society.

No one who lives in contemporary America can be unaware of the surface manifestations of this new youth culture. Dress is highly distinctive;

emphasis is placed on heightened color and sound; the enjoyment of flow-ers and nature is given a high priority. The fullest ranges of sense and sen-sation are to be enjoyed each day through the cultivation of new experi-ences, through spiritualism, and through drugs. Life is sought to be made as simple, primitive, and "natural" as possible, as ritualized, for example, by nude bathing.

Social historians can find parallels to this culture in the past. One is re-minded of Bacchic cults in ancient Greece, or of the *Wandervoegel,* the wandering bands of German youths in the 19th century, or of primitive Christianity. Confidence is placed in revelation rather than cognition, in sensation rather than analysis, in the personal rather than the institutional. Emphasis is placed on living to the fullest extent, on the sacredness of life itself, and on the common mystery of all living things. The age-old vision of natural man, untrammeled and unscarred by the fetters of institutions, is seen again. It is not necessary to describe such movements as religious, but it is useful to recognize that they have elements in common with the waves of religious fervor that periodically have captivated the minds of men.

It is not difficult to compose a picture of contemporary America as it looks through the eyes of one whose premises are essentially those just de-scribed. Human life is all; but women and children are being killed in Vietnam by American forces. All living things are sacred; but American industry and technology are polluting the air and the streams and killing the birds and the fish. The individual should stand as an individual; but American society is organized into vast structures of unions, corporations, multiversities, and government bureaucracies. Personal regard for each human being and for the absolute equality of every human soul is a cate-gorical imperative; but American society continues to be characterized by racial injustice and discrimination. The senses and the instincts are to be trusted first; but American technology and its consequences are a monu-ment to rationalism. Life should be lived in communion with others, and each day's sunrise and sunset enjoyed to the fullest; American society ex-tols competition, the accumulation of goods, and the work ethic. Each man should be free to lead his own life in his own way; American organiza-tions and statute books are filled with regulations governing dress, sex, consumption, and the accreditation of study and of work, and many of these are enforced by armed police.

No coherent political decalogue has yet emerged. Yet in this new youth culture's political discussion there are echoes of Marxism, of peasant com-munalism, of Thoreau, of Rousseau, of the evangelical fervor of the aboli-tionists, of Gandhi, and of native American populism.

The new culture adherent believes he sees an America that has failed to achieve its social targets; that no longer cares about achieving them; that is thoroughly hypocritical in pretending to have achieved them and in pretending to care; and that is exporting death and oppression abroad through its military and corporate operations. He wishes desperately to recall America to its great traditional goals of true freedom and justice for every man. As he sees it, he wants to remake America in its own image. . . .

The dedicated practitioners of this emerging culture typically have little regard for the past experience of others. Indeed, they often exhibit a positive antagonism to the study of history. Believing that there is today, or will be tomorrow, a wholly new world, they see no special relevance in the past. Distrusting older generations, they distrust the motives of their historically based advice no less than they distrust the history written by older generations. The antirationalist thread in the new culture resists the careful empirical approach of history and denounces it as fraudulent. Indeed, this antirationalism and the urge for blunt directness often lead those of the new youth culture to view complexity as a disguise, to be impatient with learning the facts, and to demand simplistic solutions in one sentence.

Understandably, the new culture enthusiast has at best a lukewarm interest in free speech, majority opinion, and the rest of the tenets of liberal democracy as they are institutionalized today. He cannot have much regard for these things if he believes that American liberal democracy, with the consent and approval of the vast majority of its citizens, is pursuing values and policies that he sees as fundamentally immoral and apocalyptically destructive. Again in parallel with historical religious movements, the new culture advocate tends to be self-righteous, sanctimonious, contemptuous of those who have not yet shared his vision, and intolerant of their ideals.

Profoundly opposed to any kind of authority structure from within or without the movement and urgently pressing for direct personal participation by each individual, members of this new youth culture have a difficult time making collective decisions. They reveal a distinct intolerance in their refusal to listen to those outside the new culture and in their willingness to force others to their own views. They even show an elitist streak in their premise that the rest of the society must be brought to the policy positions which they believe are right.

At the same time, they try very hard, and with extraordinary patience, to give each of their fellows an opportunity to be heard and to participate directly in decision-making. The new culture decisional style is founded on the endless mass meeting at which there is no chairman and no agenda, and from which the crowd or parts of the crowd melt away or move off into actions. Such crowds are, of course, subject to easy manipulation by skillful agitators and sometimes become mobs. But it must also be recognized that large, loose, floating crowds represent for participants in the new youth culture the normal, friendly, natural way for human beings to come together equally, to communicate, and to decide what to do. Seen from this perspective, the reader may well imagine the general student response at Kent State to the governor's order that the National Guard disperse all assemblies, peaceful or otherwise.

Practitioners of the new youth culture do not announce their program because, at this time at least, the movement is not primarily concerned with programs; it is concerned with how one ought to live and what one ought to consider important in one's daily life. The new youth culture is still in the process of forming its values, programs, and life style; at this point, therefore, it is primarily a *stance.*

A parallel to religious history is again instructive. For many (not all) student activists and protestors, it is not really very important whether the protest tactics employed will actually contribute to the political end allegedly sought. What is important is that a protest be made—that the individual protestor, for his own internal salvation, stand up, declare the purity of his own heart, and take his stand. No student protestor throwing a rock through a laboratory window believes that it will stop the Indochina war, weapons research, or the advance of the feared technology—yet he throws it in a mood of defiant exultation—almost exaltation. He has taken his moral stance.

An important theme of this new culture is its oppositional relationship to the larger society, as is suggested by the fact that one of its leading theorists has called it a "counterculture." If the rest of the society wears short hair, the member of this youth culture wears his hair long. If others are clean, he is dirty. If others drink alcohol and illegalize marijuana, he denounces alcohol and smokes pot. If others work in large organizations with massively complex technology, he works alone and makes sandals by hand. If others live separated, he lives in a commune. If others are for the police and the judges, he is for the accused and the prisoner. In such ways, he declares himself an alien in a larger society with which he feels himself to be fundamentally at odds.

He will also resist when the forces of the outside society seek to impose its tenets upon him. He is likely to see police as the repressive minions of the outside culture imposing its law on him and on other students by force or death if necessary. He will likely try to urge others to join him in changing the society about him in the conviction that he is seeking to save that society from bringing about its own destruction. He is likely to have apocalyptic visions of impending doom of the whole social structure and the world. He is likely to have lost hope that society can be brought to change through its own procedures. And if his psychological makeup is of a particular kind, he may conclude that the only outlet for his feelings is violence and terrorism.

In recent years, some substantial number of students in the United States and abroad have come to hold views along these lines. It is also true that a very large fraction of American college students, probably a majority, could not be said to be participants in any significant aspect of this cultural posture except for its music. As for the rest of the students, they are distributed over the entire spectrum that ranges from no participation to full participation. A student may feel strongly about any one or more aspects of these views and wholly reject all the others. He may also subscribe wholeheartedly to many of the philosophic assertions implied while occupying any of hundreds of different possible positions on the questions of which tactics, procedures, and actions he considers to be morally justifiable. Generalizations here are more than usually false. . . .

But almost no college student today is unaffected by the new youth culture in some way. If he is not included, his roommate or sister or girlfriend is. If protest breaks out on his campus, he is confronted with a personal decision about his role in it. In the poetry, music, movies, and plays that students encounter, the themes of the new culture are recurrent. Even the student who finds older values more comfortable for himself will nevertheless protect and support vigorously the privilege of other students who prefer the new youth culture.

A vast majority of students are not complete adherents. But *no* significant group of students would join older generations in condemning those who are. And almost *all* students will condemn repressive efforts by the larger community to restrict or limit the life style, the art forms, and the nonviolent political manifestations of the new youth culture.

To most Americans, the development of the new youth culture is an unpleasant and often frightening phenomenon. And there is no doubt that the emergence of this student perspective has led to confrontations, injuries, and death. It is undeniable, too, that a tiny extreme fringe of fanatical devotees of the new culture have crossed the line over into outlawry and terrorism. There is a fearful and terrible irony here as, in the name of the law, the police and National Guard have killed students, and some students, under the new youth culture's banner of love and compassion, have turned to burning and bombing.

But the new youth culture itself is not a "problem" to which there is a "solution"; it is a mass social condition, a shift in basic cultural viewpoint. How long this emerging youth culture will last and what course its future development will take are open questions. But it does exist today, and it is the deeper cause of the emergence of the issues of race and war as objects of intense concern on the American campus.

24

Diana

THOMAS POWERS

Shortly before noon on Friday, March 6, 1970, an explosion tore through the front wall of a century-old red-brick townhouse on a quiet, tree-lined street in New York City. Within moments smoke began to pour from the building; a deep red glow in the dark interior was followed by flames. Visible against the red glow as people began to arrive were two young women—one of them completely naked, the other wearing only a pair of blue jeans—who had been momentarily trapped by falling debris.

Two men helped the women out of the building as chunks of brick and plaster crashed down around them. A woman who lived down the street gave her coat to one of the two and then led both of them, choking and covered with soot and dust, back to her own house. The two appeared unhurt, so the woman told them to use the shower, left some old clothes outside the bathroom door, and went back to the burning house to see if anyone else needed help. When she returned a few minutes later the two young women had already dressed and gone.

Fire trucks turned into Eleventh Street shortly after noon as two more

Source: Thomas Powers, *Diana: The Making of a Terrorist* (Boston: Houghton Mifflin Company, 1971), excerpted from the Bantam edition, pp. 1–142. Copyright © 1971 by Thomas Powers, reprinted by permission of the publisher, Houghton Mifflin Company.

explosions further weakened the townhouse at 18 West Eleventh Street. Attempts to search the building ended when the façade collapsed in a cloud of smoke, dust and fire. It was not until the flames were finally out, and a crane and other equipment had arrived later in the day, that efforts to search the building could be resumed. In the early evening, working in the glare of floodlights, firemen discovered the body of a short, solid, red-haired young man wearing blue jeans and a denim workshirt. He had been crushed to death. . . .

On Saturday, March 7, the day after the explosion, one of the two missing girls was identified as Cathlyn Platt Wilkerson, the daughter of a well-to-do advertising man, vacationing in the Caribbean at the time of the explosion, who owned the building. On Sunday, March 8, the dead man was identified as Ted Gold, a leader of the Students for a Democratic Society (SDS) chapter at Columbia University during the violent struggle there in the spring of 1968. Cathy Wilkerson had also been an SDS member and, it was reported, a member of the violent SDS faction called the Weathermen.

On Monday, March 9, detectives searching through the remains of the house found a pile of water-soaked SDS leaflets and then, on Tuesday, March 10, the badly mutilated body of a young woman was discovered near a workbench in the building's basement. That afternoon, while routinely searching through a huge pile of debris picked up by a power shovel, detectives found four lead pipes, each 12 inches in diameter, packed with dynamite.

The street was cleared, the bomb-removal truck was summoned and the search, with considerably greater caution, was continued. Before the day was over detectives found four cartons containing 57 sticks of dynamite, 30 blasting caps and some cheap alarm clocks with holes drilled in their faces for the attaching of wires. Assistant Chief Inspector Albert Seedman, in charge of the investigation, gave the first, and the simplest, explanation of what had happened: "The people in the house were obviously putting together the component parts of a bomb and they did something wrong."

That same Tuesday police found a credit card, library card and birth certificate belonging to Kathy Boudin, the daughter of Leonard B. Boudin, a lawyer well-known for his defense of political dissidents, including Dr. Benjamin Spock in 1968. It was suggested that Kathy might have been the second woman who disappeared the day of the explosion.

Early in the morning of Thursday, March 12, bombs exploded almost simultaneously in three corporate offices in New York City. A letter postmarked an hour before the explosions made it clear the explosion on West Eleventh Street was not going to be an isolated incident. In the days that followed thousands of false bomb scares were called in to the police. Dozens of major office buildings were emptied and searched. It was clear the bombers may have been few in number, but that thousands shared their hate for American society.

On Saturday, March 14, a third body, that of a young man, was found in the northeast corner of the basement near the spot where the woman's body had been discovered. On Monday, March 16, Cathy Wilkerson and Kathy Boudin failed to appear in court in Chicago, where they were facing charges stemming from a fight between police and the Weathermen on October 9, 1969.

On Sunday, March 15, detectives found a piece of flesh which turned out to be the tip of the little finger of someone's right hand. . . . The FBI identified the print as that of Diana Oughton, the oldest daughter of a long-established family in the small town of Dwight, Illinois, and, like Gold, Boudin and Wilkerson, long active in SDS. . . .

Newsmen quickly established the broad outlines of Diana's life: student at the Madeira School in Greenway, Virginia, and Bryn Mawr College, outside Philadelphia; two years in Guatemala, where the poverty had turned her toward radical politics; two years of teaching in an experimental school in Ann Arbor, Michigan; and finally a deepening involvement with SDS and the Weathermen. Her life seemed a symbol of the decade just ended, a progress from a privileged childhood to disenchantment with her country. American parents had long sensed their children turning against them; Diana's death seemed to mark the imminence of a final break. . . .

The sharpening conflict between the generations during the final years of the 1960s had frightened almost everybody; people sensed a dangerous potential for violence within America, an anger that might finally destroy the already-strained sense of trust and common commitment that holds a country together. Weatherman's open celebration of that potential, its exultation in random violence, its refusal to believe that anything, even outright fascism, could be worse than America as it already was, seemed just the sort of thing that might tip the United States over the brink of an abyss on which it had been balancing for a decade. The explosion on West Eleventh Street seemed an omen of provocations that no open society could survive. The United States began to be compared with France during the struggle over Algeria, and with the Weimar Republic during the last bitter days before Hitler came to power. . . .

Once Diana would have seemed to be among the best of her generation. Even more than the others, her life reflected a sense of having been blessed and a commitment to extend those blessings to others. But the bomb that killed her, wrapped in nail-studded tape, was a fact which could not be ignored. Something hard and even cruel had emerged from her idealism. A privileged child of the heart of the country, Diana had died with only one apparent purpose: to be among the country's executioners. Willfulness and frustrated idealism alone could not explain her final, chilling ambition.

Diana Oughton's first vision of America was formed during her childhood in Dwight, Illinois, a small town surrounded by the vast, flat farmland south of Chicago. Since the 1850s, Dwight has been dominated by three families, of which the Oughtons have always been one. It would be impossible to say which of the three is the *first* family of Dwight, but in January, 1942, when Diana was born, her family was probably the one most deeply rooted in the life, and the imagination, of the town. Previous generations of Oughtons had paved the streets of Dwight, built its waterworks, and donated land for the school and for the cemetery where Diana's grandparents were buried a mile and a half west of town.

One of Diana's great-grandfathers (on her father's side) founded Dwight's Keeley Institute, the first hospital successfully (and profitably) to treat alcoholism as a disease. . . . Another of Diana's great-grandfathers, William Boyce, founded the Boy Scouts of America.

In Dwight, the Oughton family holds that special position reserved for those who have been both blessed and cursed beyond the usual degree. . . .

Diana never accustomed herself to the special position enjoyed by the Oughtons in Dwight. In school the other children sometimes teased her by calling her "Miss Moneybags." When she was six she asked her nanny, Ruth Moreheart, "Ruthie, why do we have to be rich?" On another occasion, when money problems forced a girl friend to move away, Diana went to her father in tears and asked, "Why can't we be ordinary like them?" When she was a little older, Diana quietly wondered if her uniformly good marks in school had anything to do with the fact that several of her teachers rented houses from her father. . . .

[Diana spent the last three years of high school at Madeira, a girls' boarding school near Washington, D.C.] Madeira girls were trained to be the wives of the men who run the country. They were expected to learn how to hold up their end of serious conversations and to represent the best traditions of their class and to raise children who would do the same, but no one really expected them to *do* anything in life. . . .

In the fall of 1959, seventeen years old, Diana entered Bryn Mawr as a freshman, an open, generous girl with a talent for making friends and few pretensions. Bryn Mawr, like Madeira, prided itself (justifiably) on its serious academic tone, but, also like Madeira, basically reflected the upper-class background of its privileged students. . . .

Diana had arrived at Bryn Mawr a Midwestern Republican, which meant she was close to being a right-wing conservative in the eyes of most

of her friends at college. They were horrified to hear her criticize social security or defend Richard Nixon against John Kennedy in the 1960 presidential election. Gradually, however, Diana began to shed her Midwestern
political beliefs.

The year of Kennedy's election also marked the birth of the American
student movement in Greensboro, North Carolina, on February 1, when a
small group of black college students sat down at the lunch counter of a
five-and-ten and asked to be served. The sit-in movement which grew out
of that incident spread rapidly across the upper South and was paced by a
reawakening of political concern among white students in the North. The
end of the Eisenhower era, during which the country was run like a large
corporation, with an eye always on the ledger books, brought something
like a renaissance of social awareness to long-quiescent college campuses.
The apathetic "silent generation" of the 1950s was replaced by a new generation more concerned with the *rightness* of things than whether or not
the economy was in order and the social peace maintained. . . .

Diana majored in German at Bryn Mawr and spent her junior year at
the University of Munich [during which she] . . . traveled constantly,
worked sporadically, and spent long evenings in earnest social and political discussions with young Germans, not all of whom were grateful to
America for its victory in World War II or its domination of Europe
since. . . .

Despite a quickening sense of the social inequities in the world Diana
remained basically indifferent to politics. Like the rest of her generation,
she awakened first to matters of style—the chrome and fins on cars, the
shallowness of women's magazines, the sterility of life in the suburbs, the
banality of television. Only later were these criticisms to take on political
dimensions. . . .

During her last year Diana joined a special tutoring program for black
children with reading problems in Philadelphia's ghetto. The volunteers
were only supposed to tutor one child each but Diana, horrified to discover
that seventh graders could not read *at all,* soon had three. She took the
train into Philadelphia two nights a week.

That same year she read John Howard Griffin's *Black Like Me,* an account of a trip made by the author through the Deep South disguised as a
Negro. The widely read book marked a turning point in American attitudes toward racial problems. Coinciding with the struggle over school desegregation, Griffin's book suddenly revealed to white students that they
had been living a fiction: America was not the free and democratic country
which they had been taught about in school, but two nations, one of them
denied all the legal rights and material advantages enjoyed by the other.

Diana's experience among black people in Philadelphia, and in Cambridge, Maryland, where she worked in a voter-registration campaign, gave her a firsthand sense of the black man's situation in America. . . .

Diana had only one serious boy friend during her college years, a Princeton football player named John Henrich. . . . She liked Henrich but she didn't love him; when he asked her to marry him, she thought it over and realized that having to think it over meant she definitely did not want to get married. Henrich, like Bryn Mawr itself, was only an interlude.

Diana was in the process of changing as her senior year at Bryn Mawr came to an end. She was like a person with a nagging religious doubt, a sense that questions of overriding moral importance exist in the world. She had begun to reject worldly values and the proprieties of society; she sensed that most people put too much importance on the trivial things and too little on the important ones; she was sensitive about her *self*, vaguely aware that privilege made one somehow unworthy. She knew that America was far larger than Dwight, that the world she had known was only the complacent veneer of American life, that important things were wrong in the country, that honesty and sincerity and moral commitment were the qualities which gave size to people and ways of life.

Diana's friends only half-noticed these changes. They all knew she had given up two nights a week to tutor black children, but it never really occurred to them that having done so ought to have revealed something fundamental about her. Some people would get married; some would go on to graduate school; Diana might well go into social work: it was as simple as that. . . .

Nearly half the girls in Diana's class at Bryn Mawr went on to graduate school and most of the rest married or headed for New York to begin a career. Diana did not like academic life, New York or the idea of marriage, so she joined the Voluntary International Service Assignments (VISA) program run by the American Friends Service Committee and was assigned to Guatemala. The decision was made almost idly, from a mixture of idealism, a taste for adventure and the lack of anything better to do. . . .

The month-long VISA training program, during which she spent a week in New York's Spanish Harlem, and then the two years she spent in Guatemala, gradually exposed her to the reality of poverty, to the meanness of spirit, narrowmindedness and self-contempt which afflicted the poor more than the simple lack of things. . . .

The more Diana learned about the hard life of rural Guatemala, the more she reflected on the affluence of the United States. In Chichicastenango Americans seemed an alien presence, the fact of their wealth almost an insult to the impoverished Indians. A confusion emerged in her mind that lasted the rest of her life: she had rejected affluence (at first almost unconsciously) to work among the poor, but poverty, clearly, was nothing to be envied. She hated poverty but she hated affluence, too. Transistor radios struck a jarring note in the market, and yet the Indians wanted radios, cars, sewing machines and all the other doubtful (to Diana) benefits of modern life. . . .

By the spring of 1964 Diana's attitude toward Guatemala had begun to take on definition. The poverty had been immediately apparent, of course, but at first it had seemed as if the country itself were poor. Gradually it became apparent that only the lower classes within the country were poor, while the upper classes were very well off indeed. There was nothing startling about the presence of rich and poor in the world, but in Guatemala Diana began to see for the first time that the rich are afraid of the poor, and that the poor hate and envy the rich. . . .

Diana's recognition of the poverty of Guatemala and of the half-hidden war between rich and poor led to the formation of political opinions after she met Alan Howard, a Fulbright scholar living in Guatemala City. Howard, a graduate of Hamilton College from Newton, Massachusetts, was working on an experimental reading program in the federal prison. Long conversations with political prisoners had given him a decidedly cynical view of Guatemalan politics and a sense that traditional parliamentary methods would never end the inequities which divided the country. . . . Howard argued that the VISA program would never change Guatemala in fundamental ways. At best, he said, reformist programs like Diana's might help isolated individuals; at worst they would dilute the anger and desperation which alone could prompt the people to rise up and destroy the old system.

"You're only delaying the revolution," he told her.

Howard's was an old argument, but it was new to Diana. Her work in Chichicastenango seemed to confirm what he said. Sometimes she took pride in the men she had taught to read and in the classes they, in turn, had established in the outlying villages; but then she would think, so what? The country is still seventy per cent illiterate. When she talked with Guatemalans she found that many shared Howard's views: human poverty was not a fundamental thing, like poor soil or insufficient rain, but the product of a social system. Some people prospered under that system while others suffered. The only way to end the suffering was to replace the system. The idea was brutally simple, but it seemed to explain how the rich and the poor could exist side by side, and why something like war smoldered between them. Howard pointed to the experience of another American Fulbright scholar living in Guatemala. He had planned to spend a year studying the country's corporate structure but was finished almost as soon as he began: there was no corporate structure, only a handful of ruling families.

A Guatemalan friend told Diana the solution was as brutally simple as the problem. "What this country needs," he said, "is to line the fifty first families up against the white wall." . . .

When Diana had arrived in Guatemala she had been a liberal, believing the only way to make a better world was to identify the problems, and devise their solutions, one by one. Guatemala made her into a radical: she began to feel that things had to be changed all at once, or not at all. Step by step, she acquired a new sense of the world and its troubles, simple in outline but broad in its application: the name of the problem is capitalism, she concluded, and the name of the solution is socialism. She did not acquire her faith in a flash; it was a slow conversion, but nonetheless complete.

At the same time Diana began to feel that the United States, too, was playing a part in the half-submerged world struggle taking place around her. . . .

If reformism would perpetuate the status quo, then what was the purpose of the Peace Corps? Why did so much American economic aid seem to end up in the hands of the rich without affecting the lives of the poor? Why was the American military indirectly helping Guatemala to defeat the FAR guerrillas? Why did Americans—tourists, businessmen and government officials alike—seem to circulate almost exclusively in the upper classes of Guatemala? Diana's conclusions to these questions were basically two: that revolution was the only solution to injustice in Guatemala, and that the United States was actively working to prevent it from taking place. . . .

In September, 1966, Diana began teaching part-time at Ann Arbor's year-old Children's Community School (CCS), which occupied two basement rooms of the Friends Center on Hill Street. The school, established the previous fall by a woman named Toby Hendon, was based on the permissive principles developed by A. S. Neill at Summerhill. Children were allowed to do what they liked when they liked, on the premise that both teaching and learning were most successful when most spontaneous. Neill had concluded that humans were violent and competitive because of the way they were educated. If they were brought up to pursue things for their own sake, and were treated with understanding and love from the beginning, violent impulses would never have a chance to take root in their personalities. The Children's Community School, run largely by college students who felt their own educations had been dismal failures, pursued Neill's principles with a vengeance. . . .

The two years Diana worked at the school were among the happiest of her life. She and Bill [Ayers, the young director of the school] believed in the school and established an extraordinarily close relationship with the students. They spent weekends and holidays together. They felt they were a part of a new generation which was going to revitalize America. . . .

As an experiment, however, the school had mixed results. The children learned a lot of things they never would have learned in the Burns Park Elementary School, but they made almost no progress in reading, writing and arithmetic. . . .

Diana's two years with the school ended on a bitter note, partly because of the official harassment which had plagued the school from the beginning, but more importantly because of the rejection of the school by blacks. In its essence the conflict had been a simple one: Bill and Diana were committed to helping the black children, but rejected the terms on which the black parents wanted their children to be helped. . . .

The same dilemma which Diana had found in Guatemala reappeared at the Children's Community School. She rejected a system which denied its benefits to some of its citizens, but at the same time refused to admit the alleged benefits were truly worth having. Thus she was always most opposed to those she most wanted to help, since they were the most eager for the things she most detested.

It was a bitterly frustrating experience, but Diana and Bill were naturally unwilling to focus their bitterness on blacks who wanted their children to get ahead in life, or on parents who wanted their children to read, or on the children themselves. Instead they focused it on *the system,* those interlocking strands of American society which had created things as they were, and which had to be torn apart if that society were ever to be reconstructed after a different pattern. In this way Bill and Diana, like thousands of other young Americans, came to believe the oppressed could be saved only in spite of themselves, since part of their oppression lay in their desire to become like their oppressors. The oppressed were to be encouraged to struggle, but not to be allowed to decide what they were struggling for. . . .

The rush of politics swept up Diana and Bill Ayers in 1968 and they almost ceased to lead personal lives. Long associated with Voice-SDS in Ann Arbor in a casual sort of way, they found themselves in the front ranks of national SDS by the end of the year. . . .

Four major events transformed the American student movement in 1968, turning activists into self-proclaimed Marxist-Leninist revolutionaries. In chronological order, those events were the Vietcong's Tet offensive in January and February; the insurrection at Columbia University in April; the near-revolution in France in May; and the Democratic Convention in Chicago in August. Each of those events helped change the terms in which American radicals thought about their own situation. The Tet offensive dramatically ended the image of Vietnamese as the helpless victims of American power; the uprising at Columbia showed that resolute action could win overnight what patient organizing might fail to achieve in months; the May revolution in France proved that Western countries could be overthrown; the Democratic Convention seemed a sign that the American system was breaking down. At the beginning of 1968 Bill and Diana had assumed, like the vast majority of the radical movement, that American stability precluded any possibility of a genuine revolution. By the end of the year the country seemed bitterly divided and morally bankrupt. With the right kind of push, they felt, anything might happen. They were tired of waiting and they no longer had the slightest allegiance to democracy as they found it in America. . . .

Moralism ran through Weatherman theory like an infection: as whites, as Americans, as children of the upper classes they felt overprivileged. Their politics promised nothing to themselves, everything for others. Their selflessness was absolute. At the same time, however, they implicitly put themselves in a position to decide what was in the interests of the classes they wanted to help. . . .

In turning against society, however, the Weathermen were also turning against themselves, since it was their world which they considered to be the enemy. It was their country that was holding back the world revolution; it was their class which ruled the country; it was their own families who had raised them to take a place in the ruling class. The Weathermen felt they contained within themselves the seed of everything they opposed. Inside the organization, they turned savagely on each other and on themselves in an attempt to root out that seed. In Dwight, Diana had hated being rich; in Guatemala, she had hated being an American; in the Weathermen she finally came to hate herself. How else could she have tried so desperately to destroy everything that she was?

At Bryn Mawr and in Guatemala, Diana had begun by trying to help people in limited but concrete ways. By early 1970 she was preparing to dedicate herself to terrorism. . . .

On Monday, March 2, . . . in Keene, New Hampshire, a Weatherman purchased (for under $60) two 50-pound cases of dynamite from the New England Explosives Corporation. Sometime that week the dynamite, or at least part of it, was driven from Keene to New York where it was carried into the house at 18 West Eleventh Street. That week, also, Diana left Detroit for New York and joined the small group staying in the house while Cathy Wilkerson's father was in the Caribbean.

In the middle of the week, probably on Wednesday, Diana met Alan Howard. They talked about politics and, inevitably, the Weathermen. Diana admitted the Days of Rage had been a limited success, at best; that the Flint war council had achieved nothing useful; that the revolution was impossible without a mass base of support. Nevertheless, she said, building a Red Army was a necessary step and her role, personally, was to be one of its soldiers. "We have a lot to learn," she said. "We'll make mistakes."

Sometime on Friday morning Diana and a young man (later identified by the Weathermen as Terry Robbins) went down into the basement at 18 West Eleventh Street, where Cathy Wilkerson's father had built a workbench in an area he used for refinishing antiques. Using clocks, wire, batteries, detonating caps and dynamite, Diana and the young man began putting together bombs. A few minutes before noon, one of them attached a wire in the wrong place.

25

Richie

THOMAS THOMPSON

. . . They had been childhood sweethearts in Brooklyn on a row of
houses which Carol remembers as "like the ones you see at the beginning
of *All in the Family*." When people would ask later how they met, George
Diener would grin. "I was lazy," he would always say. "I fell for the girl
next door."

During their five-year courtship, Carol finished high school and became
a receptionist on Wall Street. But George dropped out and joined the
merchant marine at 16, hoping to catch a piece of the tail end of World
War II. He sailed the seas for seven years before Carol suggested—firmly
—that if he wanted her to marry him, he would have to settle down and
stay at home.

Carol was petite and red-haired and willful, like her Scotch and English
ancestors. She was proud of her family history and paid a genealogist to
trace her line back to a 16th-century Norman knight. George countered by
tracing his line, which went back, he said, only as far as a saloon in Ridge-
wood, N.J. about 1916. Carol also joined the DAR and hung the membership certificate on the living room wall. Efficient and good with money, she

Source: Thomas Thompson, "Richie," LIFE *Magazine,* 5 May 1972, pp. 59 ff. Copyright © 1972 Time Inc. Reprinted with permission.

paid the bills and kept up the cramped apartment they took in Queens.

George Diener was a muscular, compact fellow with thick and dark wavy hair. If you saw him in a bar, you would notice the U.S. flag tattoo on his strong arm, affixed there by a drunken tattooist in the Bowery when George was only 15. He had a Jimmy Cagney air about him. You would guess he had been a scrapper as a kid, maybe a welterweight boxer. He always seemed uneasy at rest. In conversations his eyes would dart about a room, his hands chopping the air. He was never one to sit at home on Sunday and watch the games. "I only like things that I can *do,*" he would say. Much more to his liking was a hike in the woods or a day of target practice at an indoor pistol range. He was a good enough marksman to be rated expert.

They named their first son George, after his father, but to distinguish between the two, the child quickly became known by his middle name, Richard. Soon he was Richie. He was a fine son, with a lusty cry and bright red hair. George Diener adored him.

When Richie was 2, George's new job as salesman for a food company required him to travel each day the far reaches of Long Island, from Huntington to Orient Point, stopping in on hundreds of grocery stores and restaurants, persuading them to stock his brands of coffees, teas and spices. He longed to move his wife and son from the congestion of a city apartment out into the land. . . .

George and Carol chose East Meadow in the heart of Nassau County, Long Island, once a place of potato farms but after World War II the definitive example of exploding suburbia. To the young couple who had grown up in Brooklyn, there was a delicious feel of newness about East Meadow. The houses were new and painted warm pastels, the people young and industrious and—like the Dieners—politically conservative. Policemen and firemen from the city were buying and moving in, and aircraft workers, and union men who took off their hard hats and turned to pruning rose bushes. East Meadow was 98 percent white. The sea was near, near enough to catch a breeze in summer. There seemed to be a boat in every other driveway. And everybody agreed the schools were excellent.

They lived for five years in the first house, and when a second son, Russell, appeared, it was time to move to a larger one. George had always wanted a basement to store his tools and do his home carpentry. On Longfellow Avenue, they found just the house, with a spacious wooded backyard and room for a pool.

Carol remembers that Richie was never happy in the new house. "There was only one other little boy on the block, and he moved away, and there were only girls around then." Richie was chubby and hated it when the girls called him "Fatty." He took refuge, found friends, in animals. Carol had had a Boston terrier named Boots who died when Richie was very small. He loved the dog so much that she bought another one for him, which he also named Boots. There followed a skunk, a rabbit, a crow, hamsters, gerbils, fish, alligators, a coati, even a boa constrictor that grew to five feet and suddenly vanished within the house. It was never found.

George encouraged his son's interest in animals. The father had always preached reverence for any form of life. "George wouldn't even let me step on a spider," said Carol. "He said spiders did more important work than people, and when I found one in the house I'd get Richie to pick it up and take it outside." When Richie wanted books on animals, his father bought them by the dozens. Richie became almost expert in animal diseases and he personally doctored all of his pets. The squirrels in his backyard would spring onto the new redwood deck and wait for their friend to feed them peanuts by hand when he got home from school.

Even when he lost his childhood fat and grew into a well-built lad of 5' 8", 145 pounds, with strong legs and a muscled chest, Richie had no interest in sports. George encouraged him to try wrestling, Carol suggested football and baseball. "But he always refused," his mother said. "He was so insecure. He told me that if he ever got on a team and made a mistake that caused his side to lose, he wouldn't be able to stand it."

Nevertheless, for the first 15 years of his life, Richie was a satisfying, average boy, very much a part of George's ordered life. The father recognized Richie's insecurity—but what 15-year-old is secure, anyway? He accepted his son's preference for animals over human friends, tolerated his periods of moodiness, his silences, his middling grades, his occasional breaking of midnight curfew on Saturdays. None of these particularly alarmed his parents: they seemed the classic problems of any adolescent.

When the first real trouble appeared . . . it was therefore as startling as a crack of lightning on a clear night. Twice Richie had been away to summer camp, but on this, his third session, Carol received a long-distance telephone call. Richie had become disruptive and belligerent with the counselors. And he had been caught smoking marijuana. Could his father come immediately and get him?

On the long drive back from the Adirondacks, George questioned his son. Richie said it was only "the first, maybe the second time" he had ever tried grass. "All the kids were doing it," he said. "Some brought it up, and others found it growing wild in the woods." He promised never to use it again.

The next year, when Richie was a junior in high school, his grades tumbled. He took the nature books and animal pictures that used to decorate his room and put them in his closet. "This is what my son used to be," his father said one day to a visitor, pointing to the forgotten books. "And this is what he is now." His arm swept the room in bewilderment.

Richie had transformed his room into a lair of the counterculture. Ticket stubs from rock concerts were pinned to the window ledge. Black light cast an eerie glow on replicas of rock stars. A game called "Feds 'n Heads" was pinned to the wall. When Richie lay in bed, he could look directly ahead at several bizarre and frightening drawings, grotesque demons, creatures with bulging eyes, hair tossed by electrical storms, hands of reptiles. One such creature sat in a bathtub of blood, holding a dagger.

Richie had discovered a tiny space, some six feet long, behind a panel at the back of his closet. He put a cheap mattress in it and took to lying there to escape his parents' calls. George found the secret place in May 1971 and decided to dismantle it. He came across a small cube of something brown wrapped in aluminum foil, neatly hidden behind a picture. "What is this?" he demanded of his son. Richie answered that it was hashish he was keeping for a friend. Then he said it was only mud that somebody was passing off as hashish. Whatever, George threw it out.

Not long after, Carol found a sandwich bag full of marijuana in Richie's room and threw that out too. This time the boy freely admitted that it was his. Moreover he was furious at his mother for what she had done. Carol tried to discuss the matter with him calmly. If he opposed her cigarette smoking, why did he smoke marijuana?

"Because the other kids do," he would say, or "Because I want to, that's why," or, shyly, almost a mumble, "Because it helps me talk to girls." Carol found a book in his room, *How to Talk to Girls*. Richie was undeniably shy. His longtime friend Sue Bernstein, whom he had dated since he was 14, said it took Richie three years to get up the courage to kiss her goodnight.

When Richie turned 16, the changes came faster. Carol and George learned that he had become a heavy user of marijuana and hash—and more, though they would not discover this for some time. He began staying out until 2 a.m. on weekends, two hours past his curfew. He told his parents never to enter his room, and if they did, there would be a yelling row. He rarely joined them for dinner. "I'm just not hungry," he would say, but Carol could see the haunting red eyes and hear his tongue tripping over the words, new profane words, that rushed out of the boy who had been so quiet so long.

Richie now had friends, disturbing ones. He began running with an East Meadow boy who was on probation for using marijuana and who was suspected of dealing in heroin. Ironically, Carol learned, Richie had met the boy on a Methodist Church retreat. For a time, Richie had been active in church, and he had been confirmed when he was 15. The new friend, whom we will call Eddie, tried to interest Richie in heroin. Apparently he refused. "Richie said he wasn't going to stick any needle in his body. No way," said one of the friends.

George discovered that he now could not talk to Richie without yelling at him, and the boy yelled back. When George ordered him not to see Eddie, and to be home at a certain hour, and to stop using foul language, Richie disobeyed every order. Finally George took his son to Family Court and charged him with being incorrigible. "I don't want him to have a police record, but he's only 16 and all the proceedings are secret," he told Carol. After the session in court, Richie suddenly changed. He found a summer job at Burger King and began saving money to buy a car. George Diener informed the court of his son's improvement and the case was dismissed.

Last October, a severe case of bronchitis developed into pneumonia and Richie stayed home from school for three weeks. He fell behind. He failed *every* subject the first quarter. Carol was upset because on his Scholastic Aptitude Tests for college he had scored well. When Richie returned to class in November, Carol received a call from the assistant principal. Richie was ill. Could she come and pick him up?

When Carol arrived at the assistant principal's office, Richie "was very talkative, his eyes were red and heavy. He was abusive," she told George that night. "He cursed me and everybody else." Carol talked privately that morning with the nurse. "Richie told me he took some pills on the school bus, but he insisted they were pills the doctor gave him for pneumonia," the nurse said. But her voice was skeptical.

"Do you think it was something else?" Carol asked.

The nurse nodded.

The "something else" was Seconal. The kids called them "downs" or "goofers" or "reds." With all the horror stories about heroin and speed, somehow Seconal has not received much attention. It is a powerful barbiturate, a mental depressant used as a sleeping pill. Tens of millions are manufactured every year in America. Marilyn Monroe died from an overdose of them. So have countless others. In the late 1960s, kids discovered that Seconals produced a quick and curious feeling, an hour of dreamy lethargy.

"If you become dependent upon Seconals," explains one New York doctor, "you actually *need* the drug to function, just as an alcoholic needs a drink first thing in the morning. Without Seconal, a dependent person becomes nervous, jittery, agitated. Withdrawal from Seconal is more severe than withdrawal from heroin." Because Seconal is a depressant which interferes with nervous transmissions from the central nervous system, it can so affect the brain's functions that one can become hostile and aggressive.

The market for Seconal thrives, particularly in high schools. A Nassau County narcotics officer said that the dangerous pills can be bought in the corridors or bathrooms or lunchrooms of "any school in this district, including parochial ones." They sell for prices ranging from 25 cents each to three for a dollar. "The kids like them because they are cheap, clean—no needles—and plentiful," said the New York doctor. "They don't think they are addictive. But God, are they ever. They don't think they are dangerous. I wish word could get around that at least six Long Island kids have died in the past year from Seconal abuse."

Last autumn, Richie began using Seconal heavily. He told one girl that he had a bottle of 100 pills, that he was tempted to sell them, but he thought he would keep them for his own use. "Why don't you stop doing drugs?" said the girl. "I can," answered Richie. "Anytime I want. I just don't want to stop right now."

No one could say for certain why Richie became so deeply involved with drugs. One "perhaps" was his being thrown into a massive high school with 3,000 students and wanting desperately to be accepted. When a shy, socially insecure youngster discovers that drug use will admit him to at least one circle, however pathetic that circle may be, the temptation can be great.

There were other signs that Richie was pleading, in his way, for status and friendships. He became an expert on rock music, not the standard Fillmore East pop groups, but obscure ones which Richie would "discover" and tell his friends about. He fretted constantly about his appearance. He took at least two showers a day and his clothes had to be clean and freshly pressed. Detesting his tight, curly red hair, Richie spent hours in front of the mirror attacking it. Finally he went to a barber and had it straightened. "Now it looks like a Brillo soap pad," he said in despair. He announced he was going to grow an Afro, which did not please his father.

His childhood nickname of "Fatty" was replaced by the time he was 17 with a new one, "The Kid." He hated this name so much that he once bloodied a friend's nose for calling him that. But when the fight was over, he invited the friend to come by his house anytime and listen to music. He told all his friends that. "Whenever the light in my room is on, that means come on in," he said. "I really mean it."

There were many signs that Richie was not totally comfortable in the drug world. He very carefully divided his friends into "straights" and "heads" and he never mingled the two. One of the straights, a boy who did not use drugs or even smoke pot, described this period of Richie's life: "We all knew Richie was doing drugs—a really heavy pill scene—but he'd never bring anything with him when he went out with us. He wouldn't take the chance of getting us busted along with him. I think he respected our way of life."

Once last summer Richie had arrived at Jones Beach with a group of "heads." A hundred yards away were two couples who were "straights."

Richie waved at the couples, then started walking toward them. But midway he stopped. He glanced back at his "head" friends, then looked forward toward the others. Finally he sat down on a dune mid-distance between them, not able to commit to either side.

By Christmas last, the rupture between George and his son became complete. They passed each other silently in the house. Occasionally anger would flash and they raged at one another. But George had decided that he could no longer deal with Richie. Perhaps Carol could achieve something. As long as she talked to the boy quietly, gently, he would listen. And promise. And go out and break his promise.

Late at night, George and Carol would lie in bed and search their lives for reasons. Carol assured her husband that it was not his fault. He had tried in his brusque, do-as-I-say way to interest Richie in scuba diving or in becoming a marine biologist. "What did I do wrong?" George would say, not content with his wife's murmurings. "What did I do wrong?" He had built up the walls of his life so that he knew exactly who he was, what he believed and where he belonged. That his son had no ambition, that his son lay in his room listening to loud music with confusing lyrics, that his son had covered his boyish face with a scraggly red beard and long shaggy red sideburns and was letting his hair grow in the directions of a windstorm was more than he could understand.

George was growing more and more politically conservative. He grouched often about welfare abuses, a "no-win" policy in Vietnam, and how " 'liberal' to me is a dirty word." It was not difficult for him to affix part of the blame for Richie's troubles on these villains. "It's this permissive liberalism," he told Carol. "The kids do just what they want because they know the courts won't punish them." Indeed, there had recently been a large narcotics raid on a house in the neighborhood which involved several arrests. But, George raged, "the pushers were back on the streets the next day." Carol agreed. She also felt Richie's school was partly to blame. "He has *three* free periods to do just what he wants," she said. "He can leave the campus or buy drugs or go into the bathroom and smoke pot. The teachers are afraid to go to the bathroom because they know what's going on in there."

On Christmas Eve, Richie was in his room and Carol went to call him. The house was full of relatives and it was time to open gifts. She opened his door and the smoke of marijuana assaulted her. "Put that out immediately," she said. "Everybody is waiting for you so we can open the presents." Richie shook his head. He would not join the family celebration. "I think he was so possessed of guilt," Carol told George later, "that he couldn't bear to face all those people who loved him. He couldn't let them see him stoned."

George Diener's ordinary dreams were being menaced in other areas.

The taxes on his house had originally been $300 a year. Now, in less than seven years, they had quadrupled. Even though George and Carol together earned $15,000 a year, there was rarely enough money for an evening out. Carol liked good restaurants, but the best George could normally do was hamburgers at McDonald's. Crime seemed to be encircling him. The house across the street was robbed, then one behind him, finally his own—in broad daylight. Because he worked part-time as a night security guard, George had a police permit for two pistols. One of them was taken by the afternoon burglar and the house was ransacked. Even though many of the parents in the Dieners' circle of friends knew their own children were using drugs, it was rarely discussed. Perhaps it should have been. District Attorney William Cahn publicly estimated that 75 percent of the youth in his county had at least experimented with marijuana and/or pills.

George worked ten hours at one job and often at another, he coached Little League baseball and was a committeeman with the Boy Scouts, but he had to come home from labor and civic endeavor to discover his own son stoned and red-eyed and mute. "Jesus God in Heaven, what's happening to us?" he would cry.

During one of their flashes of anger which was the only way they communicated anymore, George grew so exasperated that he snapped to Richie, "All right, son, you believe in the law of the streets. You believe strong is best. Put up your dukes."

Richie looked at his father in surprise: his hands were closed into fists. Richie picked up a piece of chain to defend himself. George, perhaps remembering his own Brooklyn street days, perhaps thinking he could "slap some sense into the boy," threw a roundhouse punch at his son. It exploded on his cheek. For days Richie had an angry, swollen bruise on his face. Later George apologized, but Richie did not accept it.

George began to suspect that his son was not only using drugs but selling them. He told Carol that the only way to find out for sure was to tap the family telephone. If his suspicions were true, he wanted to stop the business before it grew larger. Carol was reluctant at first—"How can we spy on our own child?" she said—but George insisted. He installed the bug secretly, but Richie found out and told his friends.

One girl friend remembers those days: "I'd call up Richie and I'd start off the conversation by saying, 'Hi there, Mr. Diener,' or 'Hello, Tape,' and we'd talk in code so he couldn't dig anything anyway."

But before Richie discovered the tap, George heard things that staggered him. His son seemed a budding expert at the art of "ripping off." The boy's telephone conversations with friends were peppered with requests to "front me," which George learned was a plea for enough money to buy, say, a half pound of marijuana which might cost as much as $100. Richie then broke it down into "nickels" and "dimes"—$5 and $10 sandwich bags—and sold it. Usually he sold an ounce that was either short-weighted or mixed with oregano.

George and Carol's younger son Russell was taking medication prescribed by a doctor, and Richie bragged on the telephone of stealing some of the pills and selling them to friends. He told one girl that his customers were "dumb kids, like only 13."

George also heard, on the tapped phone, that Richie was developing enemies who had discovered they were being cheated. "Richie told one contact that he was unable to sell a big batch of marijuana because he had ripped off so many customers that nobody trusted him anymore," George told Carol. "He says that people are out to get him, but he isn't worried because he will shoot them. Or stab them."

The police of Nassau County knew Richie was a marijuana user, but they did not know he was a large-scale dealer. "The pattern is typical," said one narcotics officer. "If a kid gets some grass, he sells it to friends at small profit and keeps his own use going. A lot of kids even *give* it away. It seems to be an element of social status, of making and keeping friends."

One day . . . Richie came home stoned, his eyes red, his speech fast but slurred. George challenged him once more. "I have done everything I know to do," said the father. "I have tried to reason with you, I have forbid you to see kids who take dope, I have asked you to stay home, I have taken you to Family Court, I have cried, I have told you I loved you, I have told you I'll do anything in my power to find you help. Your mother and I cannot talk to you anymore. So this is the way it's going to be. You're going to stay home Friday and Saturday nights if I have to lock you in your room."

Richie made a counterproposition. "I promise to stop doing drugs," he said slowly, "I really do promise . . . if, IF you'll let me go out with the kids on weekends and drink beer."

George answered quickly. "As much as I want you to stop taking drugs, I can't bargain with you. You're only 17, and I can't give you permission to go out and drink."

Richie began to yell. He shouted, as children so often do, "You don't love me! You don't understand me!"

"Of course we love you," Carol put in softly.

"You never even wanted me," Richie raged. "The only reason I'm here is that you two were fooling around one night. I didn't ask to be born."

George blew up. He hit his son in the mouth and blood gushed out. Richie took the blood from his mouth and flung it against the wall of the living room. While George watched the blood trickle down, Richie rushed out into the night.

Once again, George Diener took his son to Family Court, and this time Richie endured two sessions with a psychological counselor. After the second meeting, the counselor told Carol that he was going on a two-week vacation and when he returned, he would resume his work with Richie. "When the counselor returned," said Carol, "he called me and said he had been promoted, that another man would take over Richie's case. This new man would call me and make an appointment. I never heard from them again."

On Feb. 12, a Sunday, Richie was in a Walgreen's drugstore at the huge Roosevelt Field Shopping Center. The manager noticed him loitering near the drug counter and suspected him of shoplifting. He told Richie that he would have to stay until the police came to investigate. A punch-up occurred in which, according to the manager, Richie threw a display basket and a wooden table at him, tried to choke him with his necktie, and kicked him in the knee. The manager charged Richie with assault and a trial was set for Feb. 28. It was Richie's first arrest.

Two days later, Valentine's Day, George was working at home. The school called. Richie had been expelled for fighting and cursing at a teacher. George waited for his son to come home. He dreaded the confrontation. Richie pulled up in front of the house with a carload of friends. They noticed George's car in the driveway and hurriedly sped on. George knew that they would not come in with him as long as he was there, so he got into his car and drove away. Some time later he circled back and, sure enough, the boys were inside the house. George made a decision. He telephoned the police and asked them to raid his own son's room. "I thought that maybe if Richie was arrested, it would scare him out of it," he told Carol later.

When the police arrived and searched the room, there was no marijuana. The boys were only drinking. After the police had left, and after George had ordered the boys out, Richie began to scream at his father. George yelled back. It was the same ground they had gone over a hundred times before. Only this time Richie seized a pair of scissors (gold ones which his mother had once used to make elaborate Halloween costumes for him) and threatened to kill his father.

George checked his clenched fists and left the house. Richie called his mother at the junior high school where she worked in the cafeteria and sobbed into the telephone. "I must be crazy," he said. "I just tried to kill my father." Carol's mind raced. She figured this, at last, was Richie's cry for help. "You're not sick," she said. "You're just tired. Lie down on your bed and rest and I'll come home."

She telephoned a relative who put her in touch with a community health psychiatrist. The psychiatrist gave Richie a preliminary "screening" and told Carol that, yes, he would take the case, but that he would have to wait until the Walgreen incident was disposed of in court. Since that trial was only two weeks off, Carol felt the delay could be borne.

Toward the end of the week Richie had a conference with the principal of East Meadow High. If Richie agreed to stop using drugs and stop cutting classes he could come back on probation.

"The next week was almost miraculous," according to Carol. "Richie was a changed boy. He stayed in at night. He did his homework. He was sweet to me. He was our boy again. I think he realized this was his last chance. That Friday afternoon—I would learn later—a big shipment of drugs hit the school. Richie bought some pills. A lunchroom lady spotted him and some other kids and told them she was turning in their names to the office. Richie probably felt this was the end."

On Friday night, Feb. 25, Richie went to a Long Island bar called Ryan's which is popular with young people. In New York State, the legal drinking age is 18. Police raided Ryan's that night and checked ID cards. Richie had none. He and a few others were taken to the police station, questioned and released. This was Richie's second arrest.

On Saturday, Richie, oddly mute and peaceful, asked his mother to drive him to a girl friend's house. She agreed. Four hours later when he returned home, Carol suspected he had been smoking marijuana. But she said nothing. That night, Richie and two friends, two "straight" friends, went out and—for a few happy hours—played in the snow.

The next noon, Richie asked his mother if he could borrow the car. Carol had forbidden him use of the car but, as she remembers: "He had been acting so nice all week that I gave in. In fact, I made a bargain with him. 'If you stay this way,' I said, 'I'll give you my old car rather than trading it in on a new one as I had planned. You'll have to find a job to pay for the insurance.'" Carol watched as Richie happily left. She had always "lived with hope." She thought her lectures were getting through to him. Maybe.

Richie and a friend went to a local hamburger shop. As they left, Richie backed his mother's car into another one. There was negligible damage to both, but the other car's owner telephoned George and Carol. Assured that their son was not hurt, they waited for him to come home with an explanation. Richie had taken some Seconals. He pushed the car up to 60 mph on a quiet residential street in his neighborhood. Suddenly a tire blew out and the car bounced across the street, hit a station wagon, careened into a yard and knocked down a fence. Neither Richie nor his friend was hurt, but the car was destroyed.

George was summoned to the scene, and he told his son they would discuss the accident later. Richie went home while George stayed to discuss insurance matters with the police.

At 4 p.m. George and Carol sat down at the dining room table with Richie to talk about the accident. Carol had told George that it must be a calm meeting with no raised voices. But Richie seemed strangely remorseless. "You don't act the least bit sorry," said Carol. Finally she spoke sharply. "Don't you realize you just totaled my car? Besides that you could have killed somebody! You could have killed yourself!"

Richie raised his head and looked through the glass patio door to the yard. "Maybe that would have been even better," he said softly.

George remained silent during the dialogue. But he was shaking his head sadly. Richie noticed this. "That's right," the boy shouted, "shake your f---ing head."

Trying to avoid another scene, George rose and left. He went to his basement shop and began working on his salesman samples, sorting out broken packages and returns.

Richie and his mother continued to talk, but the boy kept jumping up and making telephone calls. Finally Richie went into his room, flipped on a rock tape, and shut the door. Carol took her younger son to a bowling alley and returned half an hour later. Richie came out of his room and his mother gasped. He was staggering. His eyes were red slits. He slurred his words. "What in God's name have you taken?" she cried. He confessed that he had taken four Seconals.

Ignoring her, Richie made a date on the telephone with a friend for 6:30. He hung up and shouted at Carol. "And don't go down in my room when I'm gone and look for pot."

"You're in no condition to go anywhere," said Carol. Richie began to walk past her. Suddenly he fell over a chair and onto the floor.

The two crashes—boy and chair—brought George racing up from the basement. Now Richie was standing up. He saw his father. "Did you tell the cops at the accident scene that I was on dope?" he cried.

George did not want to talk to the boy in this condition. He turned without speaking and started out. Richie ran after him. "Answer me! Answer me! I asked you a f---ing question," the boy shrieked, "and I want a f---ing answer!"

Richie's face was so contorted, his body so quivering with rage that George felt he and his wife were in physical danger, the kind that could not be handled with parental authority or even with fists. This was the last scene of the long painful drama and all the emotions were out. All reason was gone.

George went to his bedroom to get his pistol. The .32 was hidden behind a night stand. Weeks before, Carol had urged George to conceal it. She had been afraid that Richie would find the gun in a heated moment and use it on them as they slept. On the taped telephone calls, George had heard his son brag of being ready to shoot or stab any dissatisfied customer who was out to get him. And more than once Richie had shouted at George, "I'll get you . . ."

George tucked the .32 into his belt. He walked down the stairs into the basement.

Richie appeared on the stairs leading to the cellar. Unsteadily he made his way down. He saw an ice pick on a work bench and picked it up. When he was 15 feet from his father, Richie raised it and cried, once more, "I want an answer! Answer me!"

George's answer was to take the gun from his belt and to point it at his first-born son. Perhaps this would frighten him. Perhaps this would send him away.

Richie threw out his arms like a crucifix. "You've got your f---ing gun. Go ahead and use it." The boy walked slowly toward his father. When he was five feet away, the ice pick trembling in his hand, George cocked the .32. Richie stopped and flung out his arms once more. "Go ahead. . . . Shoot!"

Richie dropped his arms and somehow the ice pick fell to the floor. George lunged forward, grabbed his son by both shoulders, and kicked the ice pick into a corner. Carol had appeared by this time, paralyzed with fear. Richie broke loose from his father and rushed upstairs, shouting behind him, "I'm going up to get the scissors." He rushed past his mother. "Oh my God! What can we do?" Carol moaned.

"I don't know," George answered. "Maybe he won't come back down."

While they waited in the cellar, George and Carol could hear Richie rummaging in the kitchen above their heads. He pulled out a drawer too far and it crashed to the floor, utensils rattling about like hailstones on a metal roof.

Instantly the boy appeared at the head of the stairs with a steak knife in his raised hand. George pushed his wife behind him and faced his son. With each step he took down the stairs, Richie cried, "Shoot! Use your gun!"

George's finger trembled on the trigger. The frustrations of his life were suddenly telescoped. His seed had produced a son, but the son was no longer his. The son was a million miles away. The son was a child-man with a beard, with a knife, with obscenities on his lips, with drugs in his brain.

What God spared Abraham from doing to Isaac, what the makers of myth and literature could scarcely even imagine, George Diener at last did.

He fired.

The bullet tore directly into Richie's heart. He slumped backward onto the stair in a sitting position. He brought his young hands to his chest and he saw his blood. He was puzzled. He stood straight up and raised the knife again. Now its handle was soaked with the life draining from him.

Incredibly, George Diener fired again. This time the bullet went wide, screaming past his son and ripping a hole in the wall of the house that had been George's dream.

Richie sat down and toppled forward, down the stairs, onto the cement floor.

George grabbed Carol and pushed her up the stairs to the living room. He called the police and an emergency ambulance number.

He went back downstairs. Richie was quiet. He was not moving. George touched his throat. There was no pulse.

Slowly he dragged himself up the stairs.

George went to his wife and knelt beside her chair. "He's dead. I've killed our son. Can you ever forgive me?"

Then they sat and cried and waited for the police.

Several things quickly happened.

They carried out Richie's body in a canvas sack. An autopsy disclosed that his vital organs contained six times the amount of Seconal given by doctors in a therapeutic dose.

George was arrested and charged with murder, but he pleaded self-defense and the grand jury did not indict him. The police *did* want to know why George, an expert marksman, shot to kill, rather than to wound. "All I could think of was that if I only wounded the boy, he would come back and kill Carol and me," he answered. "There had been so many threats."

George vowed to lead a community war against drugs, in particular barbiturates.

The night before the funeral, many of Richie's friends went to the funeral home to pay their respects. George thanked most of them for coming, although he would not even speak to some he considered part of Richie's "head" crowd. In particular Eddie, who was sobbing almost hysterically. Carol was shocked to see that more than one of the young mourners came to the funeral parlor stoned.

When Richie's friends looked at him in the casket, they were stunned to see that his beard had been shaved off, his sideburns trimmed and raised, his hair neatly, forever cut. Sue Bernstein, his longtime friend, said that Richie looked "exactly the way he looked when I first met him, when he was 14, before the trouble started."

There was criticism of the barbering, but George dismissed it. "This is the way I wanted Richie to look," he said. And the father, at last, had his way.

Lately George has taken to going into Richie's room and shutting the door and stretching out on the bed. It is his way of getting through one sleepless midnight. There are others to come.

26

Kent State: How It Happened

THE PRESIDENT'S COMMISSION ON CAMPUS UNREST

Blanket Hill is a grassy knoll in the center of the campus of Kent State University, named by students who use it as a place to sun themselves in the day and to romance at night. From here, shortly after noon on a sunny spring day, a detachment of Ohio National Guardsmen, armed with World War II-vintage army rifles, fired a volley of at least 61 shots killing four college students and wounding nine.

Kent State University is a state-supported school with some 20,000 students, more than four-fifths of them graduates of Ohio high schools. Its main gate is only four blocks from the center of the business district of Kent, a city of some 30,000.

Compared with other American universities of its size, Kent State had enjoyed relative tranquility prior to May 1970, and its student population had generally been conservative or apolitical. Under state law, the university must accept any graduate of an accredited Ohio high school, and five out of six Kent State students are from Ohio, mostly from Cleveland and Akron, from the steel towns of Lorain and Youngstown, and from small rural towns. They are predominantly the children of middle-class families,

Source: *The Report of the President's Commission on Campus Unrest* (Washington: Government Printing Office, 1970).

both white collar and blue collar, and in the main go on to careers as teachers and as middle-level management in industry.

On the night of Thursday, April 30, President Richard M. Nixon announced that United States troops were being ordered into Cambodia.

Kent State President White did not hear President Nixon's speech. When his wife told him about it later, he had a "sinking feeling," he said. Downtown, in the North Water Street bar area, slogans denouncing the Cambodian action were being painted on walls. Many students viewed the move as a shocking reversal of President Nixon's announced policy of withdrawal from Vietnam and as an aggressive action which flouted widespread antiwar sentiment in the United States.

The first disturbance began Friday evening on North Water Street, a downtown area where six bars, popular with young people, are located. Some of these bars feature rock bands. The sale of 3.2 beer to persons 18 or older, and of liquor to 21 year olds, is legal in Kent. Because several surrounding counties prohibit the sale of beer or liquor, the Kent bars draw young people from as far as 50 miles away in addition to Kent State students.

May 1 was one of the first warm Friday nights of the spring. A sizable crowd of young people, some of whom were discussing Cambodia, gathered in and around the bars. About 11:00 p.m., they began to jeer passing police cars.

Kent's small police force had fewer than 10 men on duty when the disturbance began. Four of these men in two patrol cars were specifically assigned to North Water Street.

The crowd grew increasingly boisterous. They began to chant slogans, and a motorcycle gang called the "Chosen Few" performed some tricks with their bikes. Shortly before 11:30 p.m., someone threw a bottle at a passing police car. The Kent city police ceased efforts to patrol the street and waited for reinforcements from the day shift and from other law enforcement agencies.

Some of the crowd, which had grown to about 500, started a bonfire in the street. Soon the crowd blocked the street and began to stop motorists to ask their opinion about Cambodia.

One motorist accelerated when approached, narrowly missing people standing in the street. This incident, according to witnesses, angered bystanders. Shortly thereafter a false rumor that black students were "trashing" on campus circulated among the crowd.

Some demonstrators began to break store windows with rocks. A few items were stolen from the display windows of a shoe store and a jewelry store. A fertilizer spreader was taken from a hardware store and thrown through the window of a bank. In all, 47 windows in 15 establishments were broken, and two police officers were cut by thrown missiles.

At 12:30 a.m., after the trashing had begun, Kent Mayor LeRoy M. Satrom declared a state of emergency and ordered the bars closed. The assembled force of city police and sheriff's deputies then moved to clear the street, which became even more crowded as evicted patrons poured out of the bars.

Between 1:00 and 2:00 a.m., a force composed of 15 Kent city police and 15 Portage County deputies used tear gas to force the student crowd out of the downtown area, up East Main Street for several blocks, and back onto the campus through the main gate at Lincoln and East Main Streets.

City police, who would not enter the campus, and students faced each other over the border of the campus, and a virtual stand-off developed. A freak automobile accident on Main Street is generally credited with dispersing the crowd.

An electrical repairman was standing on his truck repairing a traffic light in front of Prentice Gate. A car hit the truck, knocking the scaffold from beneath the repairman and leaving him hanging onto the traffic light above the pavement. His odd predicament completely captured the attention of the crowd. They drifted away quietly after he was rescued.

Fifteen persons, all with Ohio addresses, were arrested that night, most of them on charges of disorderly conduct.

The disturbance on North Water Street angered and frightened many merchants and left the city administration fearful that it did not have enough manpower available to keep order. On the next day, these circumstances were to lead to the calling of the Ohio National Guard.

Many of the students who were in the crowd on North Water Street were there only because the bars were closed. Some were disgruntled because they had paid cover charges to hear rock bands and then had to leave before they felt they had had their money's worth.

The pattern established on Friday night was to recur throughout the weekend: There were disorderly incidents; authorities could not or did not respond in time to apprehend those responsible or to stop the incidents in their early stages; the disorder grew; the police action, when it came, involved bystanders as well as participants; and, finally, the students drew together in the conviction that they were being arbitrarily harassed.

The ROTC building was an obvious target. It was a two-story wooden structure—an old World War II-type Army barracks—and it looked easy to ignite. Many students saw it as evidence that the university supported the Vietnam war effort by maintaining a military training program on campus.

About 8:10 p.m. [Saturday evening], a few students began to throw rocks at the ROTC building. In a short while, flying rocks had broken some of the building's windows. A few in the crowd appeared to have brought bags of rocks to the scene. A group used an ash can as a battering ram to break in a window: some started throwing lighted railroad flares into and onto the building. A curtain caught fire. In the crowd, someone burned a miniature American flag. A student taking pictures was attacked and wrestled to the ground, and his film was taken and exposed. Professor Frank said that when he intervened in the student's behalf, he was grabbed from behind. Frank was saved from further attack only when recognized by one of his students. Finally, a young man dipped a cloth into the gasoline tank of a parked motorcycle. Another young man ignited it and set the building afire. The building began to burn about 8:45 p.m.

The mood of the part of the crowd nearest the ROTC building was one of anger. "I have never in my 17 years of teaching," said Frank, "seen a group of students as threatening or as arrogant or as bent on destruction as I saw and talked to that night." Faculty marshals did not intervene.

Many spectators behaved around the ROTC fire as though they were at a carnival. Only a dozen or so persons appeared to have made active efforts to set the building afire, and another two or three dozen threw stones, but many others cheered and shouted with glee as the building was destroyed and sat on the hills surrounding the Commons to watch the conflagration.

One student protested the burning of the ROTC building, telling his fellows, "You can't do this." He was shouted down. A faculty marshal who feared that the student was in danger of physical injury led him from the area.

About 9:00 p.m., a truck from the Kent fire department arrived. No police protection was provided. Members of the mob grabbed the hose from the firemen. They slashed and stabbed the hose with pocket knives, an ice pick, and a machete. They threw rocks at the firemen, who then withdrew.

When the building was burning furiously and live ammunition was exploding inside, the campus police appeared. The police fired tear gas at the crowd, which then left the ROTC building area and moved across the Commons to the tennis courts. Some students bent down the strong metal fence around the courts.

About 9:30 p.m., near the tennis courts, a small shed which was used to store archery equipment was set afire. Flames shot up from the shed and threatened nearby trees. Students hurried into buildings, filled wastebaskets with water, and put out the fire.

Aware of the turmoil on campus, Mayor Satrom had called General Del Corso's office at 8:35 p.m. to renew his request for troops.

At 9:30 p.m., Generals Del Corso and Canterbury arrived in Kent. As their troops were pulling into town, the flames from the burning ROTC building lit up the horizon.

The generals went to city hall and were briefed by Mayor Satrom. Del Corso then dispatched one detachment of guardsmen to prevent students from entering downtown Kent and sent another detachment to protect firemen who were returning to the burning building. As a Guard unit rode down East Main Street, it was stoned by persons hiding among trees.

The National Guard cleared the campus with dispatch, using tear gas freely. Some students had to spend the night in dormitories other than their own because the cleanup was so quick and emphatic.

When a group of faculty marshals wearing blue armbands attempted to identify themselves as guardsmen approached, the guardsmen knelt in a skirmish line and pointed rifles at them. Abandoning explanations, the marshals fled.

The university had made no effort beforehand to prepare the students for the possibility that the Guard might come to the campus. Administration officials had met with student leaders several times during the day, but the discussions were confined to the subject of dances and other diversionary social events. There was no discussion of what might happen if another disorder occurred—a subject administrators discussed only among themselves or with city officials.

President White and his wife were at the home of his sister-in-law in Mason City, Iowa, all day Saturday. After repeated telephone conversations Saturday morning with his aides in Kent, he called for the Kent State airplane to be sent to bring him back to his troubled campus. He took off for Ohio early Sunday morning.

As the ROTC building burned, the pattern of the previous night was repeated—authorities arrived at the scene of an incident too late to apprehend the participants, then swept up the bystanders and the participants together in their response. Students who had nothing to do with burning the building—who were not even in the area at the time of the fire—resented being gassed and ordered about by armed men. Many students returning to the campus on Sunday after a weekend at home were first surprised at the Guard's presence, then irritated when its orders interfered with their activities. Student resentment of the Guard continued to grow during the next two days.

At 10:00 a.m. Sunday, while Kent State President White was on his way home from Iowa by plane, Governor Rhodes arrived in Kent and held a news conference.

After referring to recent disturbances at two other Ohio universities, Governor Rhodes said:

We have the same groups going from one campus to the other and they use the universities state-supported by the state of Ohio as a sanctuary. And in this, they make definite plans of burning, destroying, and throwing rocks at police and at the National Guard and at the Highway Patrol.

"We are going to eradicate the problem," Governor Rhodes said. "We are not going to treat the symptoms."

Rhodes described the troublemakers as

> worse than the brown shirts and the communist element, and also the night-riders and the vigilantes. They are the worst type of people that we harbor in America. And I want to say this—they are not going to take over the campus and the campus now is going to be part of the county and the state of Ohio. It is no sanctuary for these people to burn buildings down of private citizens, of businesses in the community, then run into a sanctuary. It is over with in the state of Ohio.

Many persons felt that the governor had spoken firmly and forthrightly. Others felt that his remarks were inflammatory and worsened an already tense situation. Some, including many Kent students, believed the governor was hoping that his words and actions at Kent would win him additional votes in the primary election, to be held two days later, for nomination to the United States Senate.

After the governor departed, widespread uncertainty regarding rules, prohibitions, and proclamations remained. Many people were unsure about what was to be legal and what not, particularly with respect to rallies and demonstrations.

On Sunday afternoon, the campus was generally quiet, and many students felt the worst was over. Sightseers visited the ruins of the ROTC building, and some students conversed with guardsmen.

Students began gathering on the Commons about 8:00 p.m. The crowd was peaceful and included a group of coeds kicking a soccer ball around. But by 8:45 p.m., it had grown so large that campus police and the Highway Patrol suggested to Colonel Finley that the 1:00 a.m. campus curfew be cancelled and an immediate curfew imposed. As a result, shortly before 9:00 p.m., Major Jones read the Ohio Riot Act to the crowd on the Commons and gave them five minutes to disperse. When they did not, police proceeded to disperse them with tear gas. One group headed toward President White's house, another toward Prentice Gate.

The students were driven away from White's home by tear gas. At Prentice Gate, there was a more serious confrontation. A sizable crowd sat down in the intersection of Lincoln and Main, next to the gate, and asked to speak with Satrom and White about six demands: abolition of ROTC; removal of the Guard from campus by Monday night; lifting of the curfew; full amnesty for all persons arrested Saturday night; lower student tuition; and granting of any demand made by the BUS [Black United Students].

An unidentified young man who was permitted to use the police public address system told the crowd that Mayor Satrom was coming to discuss their demands and that efforts were being made to contact President White. (John Huffman, Matson's executive assistant, later said he had just told the young man specifically that White was not coming.) The young man said that if the students would move out of the street, the guardsmen at the scene would reciprocate by moving off campus. Both the Guard and the students did in fact withdraw slightly.

At 11:00 p.m., police were told that the two officials would not talk to the demonstrators. The Riot Act was read to the crowd, and Colonel Finley told them the curfew was in effect as of 11:00 p.m.

The students, previously nonviolent, became hostile. They felt that they had been double-crossed. They cursed the guardsmen and police and threw rocks at them. Tear gas was fired and the crowd ran back from the gate across the campus lawn.

During the confusion of the dispersal, two students were bayoneted and sustained minor cuts. Three guardsmen received cuts and bruises from thrown stones and a wrench.

With tear gas, guardsmen drove one group of about 300 young persons across the campus to the Tri-Towers dormitory area. A helicopter had been hovering over the Prentice Gate sit-in. Its spotlight illuminated the scene, following the students as they ran. Its wash increased the effectiveness of the gas along the ground. Among the fleeing Kent State students was Allison Krause.

Another group of students ran to the Rockwell Memorial Library, the building closest to the gate, and climbed through windows to get inside. A coed was reportedly bayoneted as she attempted to climb through a window. Some of the library windows were broken by rocks. The night guard locked the doors, sealing the students inside. They were later given a 45-minute grace period to leave the building and return to their dormitories.

Fifty-one persons were arrested Sunday night, most of them for curfew violations. This brought the total of arrests to more than 100 since the disturbances had begun.

Despite the day's promising start, the situation at Kent State had appreciably worsened by Sunday night. Students were more resentful of the Guard as a result of what they considered to be broken promises at Prentice Gate. The university was anxious to restore normal conditions, and law enforcement officers and guardsmen seemed to be growing more impatient with student curses, stones, and refusals to obey.

[On Monday,] as they lined up opposite students on the Commons shortly before noon, the three National Guard units involved in the Kent State shooting had had an average of three hours of sleep the night before.

Throughout the morning, guardsmen patrolled the campus without notable incident. About 11:00 a.m., students began gathering on the Commons, apparently for a variety of reasons. Some had heard vaguely that a rally would be held. Some came to protest the presence of the Guard. Some were simply curious, or had free time because their classes had been cancelled. Some students stopped by on their way to or from lunch or class. The Commons is a crossroads between several major university buildings.

Many students who described themselves as "straight," or conservative, later attributed their presence at the rally to a desire to protest against the National Guard. This attitude was reflected in the testimony of one Kent State coed before the Commission:

> I just couldn't believe that my campus had been taken over by Guards. You know, they said I couldn't cross the campus, they said we can't assemble on the campus. I stood on the Commons. I was watching the Guards and thinking, they are telling us to leave, but this is our campus, we belong here and they don't. That is why I stayed mostly.

This coed was gassed on the Commons, moved back over Blanket Hill to the Prentice Hall parking lot, and was within three feet of Allison Krause when Miss Krause was killed.

A Kent State policeman, Harold E. Rice, stood near the ROTC ruins and, using a bullhorn, ordered the students to disperse. It is doubtful that Rice was heard over the noise of the crowd. A jeep was brought up. Rice, a driver, and two Guard riflemen drove out across the Commons toward the crowd. Rice gave the dispersal order again.

The students responded with curses and stones. Some chanted "Pigs off campus" and "One, two, three, four, we don't want your fucking war." Rocks bounced off the jeep, and Rice said the occupants were hit several times.

At 11:58 a.m., as the jeep returned, Canterbury ordered the 96 men and seven officers to form a skirmish line, shoulder to shoulder, and to move out across the Commons toward the students. Each man's weapon was locked and loaded. Canterbury estimated the size of the crowd on the Commons at about 800; another 1,000 or more persons were sitting or milling about on the hills surrounding the Commons. His goal as he moved out was to disperse the crowd.

The guardsmen generally felt that the students, who had disobeyed numerous orders to disperse, were clearly in the wrong. The razing of the ROTC building had shown them that these noisy youths were capable of considerable destruction.

Many students felt that the campus was their "turf." Unclear about the authority vested in the Guard by the governor, or indifferent to it, some also felt that their constitutional right to free assembly was being infringed upon. As they saw it, they had been ordered to disperse at a time when no rocks had been thrown and no other violence had been committed. Many told interviewers later, "We weren't doing anything."

The guardsmen marched down the east slope of Blanket Hill, across an access road, and onto the football practice field, which is fenced in on three sides. The crowd parted to let them down the hill to the field and then reformed in two loose groups—one on Blanket Hill, above the football field, and the other in the Prentice Hall parking lot at the north end of the field. The crowd on the parking lot was unruly and threw many missiles at guardsmen on the football field. It was at this point that the shower of stones apparently became heaviest. Nearby construction projects provided an amply supply of rocks.

Tear gas canisters were still flying back and forth; after the Guard would shoot a canister, students sometimes would pick it up and lob it back at the guardsmen. In some cases, guardsmen would pick up the same canister and throw it at the students. Some among the crowd came to regard the situation as a game—"a tennis match" one called it—and cheered each exchange of tear gas canisters. Only a few students participated in this game, however. One of them was Jeffrey Glenn Miller. A few minutes later, Miller was fatally shot.

As the confrontation worsened, some students left the scene. Among those who departed was a student who had gone to the rally with a classmate, William Schroeder. Subsequently, Schroeder was killed.

While on the football field, about a dozen guardsmen knelt and pointed their weapons at the students in the Prentice Hall parking lot, apparently as a warning or a threatening gesture. Whether any shot was fired on the field is in dispute.

After the guardsmen had been on the football field for about 10 minutes, Canterbury concluded that his dispersal mission had been sufficiently accomplished. He ordered his troops to retrace their steps back up Blanket Hill. He also thought—wrongly—that his men had exhausted their supply of tear gas.

The Guard's march from Blanket Hill to the football field and back did not disperse the crowd and seems to have done little else than increase tension, subject guardsmen to needless abuse, and encourage the most violent and irresponsible elements in the crowd to harass the Guard further.

As the guardsmen withdrew from the field, many students thought either that they had run out of tear gas or that there was nothing more they could do in their strategically weak position. Many felt a sense of relief, believing all danger was over. Most expected the Guard to march back over Blanket Hill to the ROTC building.

Some students grew more aggressive. A small group of two to four dozen followed the Guard closely. Some came as close as 20 yards, shouting and jeering and darting back and forth.

Many witnesses said that during the Guard's return march the intensity of rock-throwing appeared to diminish. The witnesses also said that most rock-throwers remained so far away from the guardsmen that most of their stones fell short, but several guardsmen were hit and some rocks bounced off their helmets. Other student witnesses said the rock-throwing never slackened, and some say it grew heavier as the Guard mounted the hill.

Near the crest of Blanket Hill stands the Pagoda, a square bench made of 4-by-4 wooden beams and shaded by a concrete umbrella. The events which occurred as the Guard reached the Pagoda, turned, and fired on the students, are in bitter dispute.

Canterbury, Fassinger, and Jones—the three ranking officers on the hill —all said no order to fire was given.

Twenty-eight guardsmen have acknowledged firing from Blanket Hill. Four persons were killed and nine were wounded.

As the shooting began, students scattered and ran. In the parking lot behind Prentice Hall, where two were killed and two were wounded, students dove behind parked cars and attempted to flatten themselves on the pavement. On the slope east of Taylor Hall, where four were wounded, students scrambled behind a metal sculpture, rolled down the incline, or sought cover behind trees. The scene was one of pell-mell disorder and fright.

Many thought the guardsmen were firing blanks. When the shooting stopped and they rose and saw students bleeding, the first reaction of most was shock. Jeffrey Miller lay on the pavement of an access road, blood streaming from his mouth.

Then the crowd grew angry. They screamed and some called the guardsmen "murderers." Some tried to give first aid. One vainly attempted mouth-to-mouth resuscitation on Sandra Lee Scheuer, one of the fatalities. Knots of students gathered around those who had fallen.

[Dead or dying were:]

Sandra Lee Scheuer, 20, a junior, is believed to have been on her way to a 1:10 p.m. class in the Music and Speech Building when she was struck. She has not been identified in any available photographs as having attended the prohibited noon rally on the Commons.

Allison B. Krause, 19, a freshman, was among the group of students gathered on the Commons by the Victory Bell shortly before noon. After her death, small fragments of concrete and cinder block were found in the pockets of her jacket.

Jeffrey Glenn Miller, 20, a junior, was present in the crowd on the Commons when the dispersal order was given and made obscene gestures with his middle fingers at guardsmen. He also threw back a tear gas canister at the Guard while it was on the football practice field.

William K. Schroeder, 19, a sophomore, was an ROTC cadet. A photograph shows him retreating up Blanket Hill from the rally on the Commons, but he is not shown taking part in any of the harassment of the Guard.

At the moment of the firing, most of the nine wounded students were far beyond a range at which they could have presented any immediate physical threat to the Guard.

27

Kent State: The Reaction

JAMES A. MICHENER

. . . It seemed as if everybody in the Kent area suddenly wanted to unburden himself of resentments against young people, colleges and education which had been festering for years. The [local] paper had to reserve a full page, day after day for several weeks, for this violent outburst. . . . While the letter-writers were unburdening themselves in the local press, people on the street in Kent and Ravenna were being equally outspoken. The tone was set early by an esteemed Kent lawyer, who said in an interview with the Akron newspaper:

> We feel that the Guard did exactly what they are sent in to do: To keep law and order. Frankly, if I'd been faced with the same situation and had a submachine gun, there would not have been fourteen shot, there probably would have been 140 of them dead, and that's what they need.

Citizens less educated than this lawyer adopted the device of flashing their right hands in the air, thumb folded down and four fingers extended.

Source: James A. Michener, *Kent State—What Happened and Why* (New York: Random House, 1971), excerpted from the Fawcett edition, pp. 436–62. Copyright © 1971 by Random House, Inc. and The Reader's Digest Association, Inc. Reprinted by permission of Random House, Inc.

When a student asked what the sign meant, he was told, 'This time we got four of you bastards. Next time we'll get more.' . . . Many hideous things were said in these first weeks. It became almost common for people to say, 'They should have shot most of the professors, too.' . . .

When the flood of mail and speech had subsided, various persons began trying to decipher what the outburst had signified. These conclusions were suggested:

. . . The general population of Middle America was infuriated by what it saw happening to its universities and alienated by the presidents who administered them and the professors who taught in them. The average man downtown had little comprehension of what role a university ought to play in time of crisis or of its obligation to maintain discussion of all points of view; he was inclined to lash out at anyone who sought to change the university from what it had been when he was young. At Kent State some of the most vituperative comment came from alumni who rejected what their school had become.

. . . These people were outraged that the university had allowed young radicals like Jerry Rubin, Mark Rudd and Bernardine Dohrn to speak on its campus. They were infuriated that students used profanity to college officials and campus policemen. And they were deeply disturbed that young men who in all past generations had marched off obediently to war should be questioning the authority of the President of the United States to send them to their war. This theme, expressed in various ways, echoed throughout the letters.

. . . There was an honest longing for an old-fashioned college with old-fashioned problems. One citizen of Kent told a researcher, 'Why can't the kids come to college in the autumn the way they used to and worry about the things college kids always worried about: What fraternity to join? Where is the football rally going to be? Which of the coeds should I marry? Can I cut Professor Jackson's class one more time without his catching on? That's the way it used to be. What's all this moratorium stuff and the war in Vietnam? They can't do a damned thing about it.' This is a longing which is attacking all elements in our society; any change which offends it runs the risk of savage opposition.

. . . No one could talk with a cross section of the local population without discovering that they were truly frightened by the more disreputable young people they saw on the streets of their town. When the facts were isolated, it became evident that the troublemakers were not university students but casual and unattached hippies who had clustered around Kent as the place where the action was. One woman summarized the town's feeling: 'My husband expects me to keep our house clean and myself neat. I take pride in it, just as I take pride in his advancement in his work. It's what we got married for. Then I go downtown and see these hippies, barefooted, filthy, boasting about the ragged clothes they wear, elbowing me off my own streets, and using language I've never heard my husband speak. What am I to think? Have they taken over the world? Have we got to surrender Kent to them?' The visual appearance of the young was terrifying to many people, and no amount of reassurance could relax their fears. The notorious Manson trial in California had something to do with this, because on any afternoon in Kent you could spot two dozen characters who, judging by appearances, would have fitted right into the dramatis personae of that trial.

. . . There seemed to be no possibility of reconciliation between the life styles of the young and the old. There was a wide gap, with unbridgeable differences in dress, cleanliness, hair fashions, attitudes toward work, politics, music, religion, patriotism and sex. One woman who had children at Kent said, 'There is no single thing on which we can agree any longer . . . except maybe food. They still like my cooking.' There seems little inclination on the part of the young to modify their present styles to accommodate their elders. Seemingly endless conversations were held on this, with the young people stubbornly reiterating, 'No one is going to make me change. I'd give up any job in the world if it meant surrendering the way I want to live. I will never cop out.'

. . . Sex plays a much larger role in this than was once apparent. Older townspeople both despise and envy the sexual freedom enjoyed by the young, and this theme recurs in constant non-sequiturs. A businessman will be saying, 'The thing I can't stand is the way they dress,' but he will add, 'And it's disgusting the way the girls sleep around.' Or a Kent housewife will explain, 'I could tolerate them if they had any manners,' but she will conclude in a lower voice, 'And the way they sleep together in those dormitories!" At the time of the shooting, six or seven communes operated in Kent—not on campus—apparently without any great promiscuity but with an ebb and flow of partners, and rumors of these infuriated the townspeople who heard of them. Two reactions were customary: 'The university should expel them all' and 'They ought to be horsewhipped.' Sexual jealousy appears to be a very strong determinant of the manner in which a citizen will react to the younger generation which he sees enjoying itself in a manner forbidden to him when he was young.

. . . There was a strong tendency toward vigilantism running through the community after the shootings. One heard, from the more aggressive townspeople, much talk of 'shooting the hippies on sight,' and from the students, of 'shooting back at them next time.' On each side, there was open discussion of weaponry and covert movement of it. To an uninitiated outsider, this constant reference to violence was appalling, but very real. In the weeks immediately following the May killings, Kent was close to violence and persons of all categories appeared prepared for it. One heard from literally scores of young people that they would 'be afraid of coming through this town in long hair and on a motorcycle.' There were stories of citizens taking pot-shots at passing long-hairs and much discussion of 'the *Easy Rider* syndrome.' A young person would say, 'I'm not hung up on the *Easy Rider* syndrome, but I wouldn't be surprised to be greeted by a blast from a shotgun any day.' A leading businessman confided, 'I was aghast when I saw who had been appointed special deputies . . . with permission to carry rifles and shotguns at all times. Three fellows in their early twenties who two years ago were members of the town's worst motorcycle gang.' This tendency toward vigilantism had started when blacks began to run wild, particularly after the vendetta shooting of policemen in Cleveland, and was born out of real fear of the public pronouncement of black leaders as to how they were going to shoot up the community. That it should have received its major subsequent impetus from the deaths of four students was a dreadful irony; one had to remind people constantly as they talked about the coming show-down that it was the students who had died; they had not done the killing. One recurring verbalism haunted the mind that long summer: 'I suppose there's bound to be a shoot-out.'

. . . The attitude toward blacks was ambivalent. At least one letter-writer and many speakers referred to the exemplary restraint of black students during the uprising, and when attempts to blame them for the rioting did surface, they were quickly squelched. 'You've got to say this for the blacks,' began a frequent comment, 'they kept their noses clean this time.' But accompanying this, especially on the part of the students, came the ominous suggestion, 'They're biding their time.' It became an accepted part of the legend that the blacks were furious about the shooting, not because four whites were killed, but because they had planned to take over the Administration Building that day and felt co-opted by the precipitate white action. The shootings did nothing to add to the bad feeling already existing between the races, but it did nothing to alleviate it either.

. . . Some townspeople were plain fed up with students. Larry Smith, a serious graduate student, suffered painful proof: 'I had just bought this new windbreaker. Looked like leather but was really one of the new vinyls. I wore it downtown a couple of days after the shooting. Debi Moreland was along and needed some cigarettes, so I stopped in this little store where three scruffy-looking townies were lounging and one of them asked me, "You one of them smart college kids?" I nodded, bought the cigarettes and walked out. When we'd gone half a block Debi said, "I smell something burning," and I looked around but didn't see anything, so we walked on. Then she cried, "Larry! You're on fire!" I told her to stop kidding, but she started slapping at my new windbreaker, and I saw that my entire back was ablaze. One of the guys in the shop had lit it with a match.'

. . . Finally, one of the strongest impressions coming from both the letters and the speeches, and one that none of the people associated with this book could have anticipated, was the virulence of the attitudes expressed by women. Notice had been taken of the violent speech of the coeds and of the fact that they were often the ones who took the more extreme positions, and this appears to be a phenomenon across the United States. But the response from conservative women was even more emphatic. An undue proportion of the demands for more killing came from women; the most intransigent opposition to students came from them, and the harshest dismissal of the young. Some thought that this resulted from a real sense of fear. There were numerous cases in which mothers on downtown shopping trips would clutch their children defensively if hippies wandered by. There was also the shattering experience of suddenly turning a corner and finding oneself face to face with seven or eight totally disheveled members of a commune, the men dressed like Daniel Boone, the women barefoot and in long tattered dresses. Even strong men were taken aback by such unanticipated confrontations; women were terrified. There were other factors, too. It could not have been coincidence that so many women referred with a sense of hatred to the young girls who were appearing in town without bras; this became a fixation with many, and was apparently an intuitive reaction to a symbol: 'If I've had to wear a bra all my life, why can't she?' This overreaction of women might be considered humorous, except that, as we shall see in the next section, it produced a terrible consequence when it occurred not in women generically, but in specific mothers.

What the Students Heard

While the faculty members who remained in Kent were getting their daily dose of shock from the page of letters to the editor—many felt that the things they had taught and believed in all their lives were being destroyed—their students were undergoing an even more shattering experience.

It began, symbolically, at three o'clock Monday afternoon when Daniel Gardner, a stocky, well-behaved, short-haired young junior with good manners and a deferential manner of speaking, went to his car under police protection, and in obedience to orders, left the campus with some other students from New England and started the long drive back home. He had been in no way involved in either the shooting or the activities that had led up to them. If one had wanted to find a 'normal' Kent State student who had come there for an education, Gardner would have been a likely choice, but the killings had made him think that perhaps the students had had a raw deal, and he expected non-campus society to agree with him.

'After all, 30.06 bullets against a gang of unarmed kids . . . too much, man, too much.'

He began to learn the facts when he left the Ohio Turnpike to enter the Pennsylvania. When the ticket-taker saw the Kent State sticker on Gardner's car, he snarled, 'Those Guards should of shot all of you.' When Gardner stopped at a bar on the outskirts of Buffalo, the men inside refused to allow the young people entrance. 'We don't want commies in here.' And after Gardner had dropped off his passengers at various points en route and arrived at his home on Cape Cod, his neighbors told him, 'Anybody who defied the Guard, they ought to be shot.'

When Bob Hillegas reported to work at his part-time job with General Tire, in Akron, he found that the dominant opinion among his co-workers was that 'those kids got what was coming to them.' Men in the shop were circulating a petition condoning the use of any weapons deemed necessary in future campus outbreaks and exonerating the Guard in advance if deaths resulted. 'I refused to sign such an un-American document,' Hillegas says, 'and now I'm regarded as a total outsider. I tried arguing with them, but they said, "If they were on the hill they were guilty and they deserved to be shot. Next time if they don't do what the Guard says, they'll all get shot." '

Karen Bowes, the unusually beautiful wife of a graduate student in business administration and an unaggressive, soft-spoken girl with a good education, works in the office of a manufacturing plant at Aurora, twelve miles to the north. She was still shaken by the deaths when she reported to work on Tuesday morning, but became more so when she heard the reaction of her associates: 'At my job in the factory everyone, and I mean every person I came in touch with, said they wished the students had all been shot. I must have shown my shock because they went on to elaborate. "Any student who was on campus that day should have been shot down." When I tried to explain that my husband, for example, had not only a right but an obligation to be there as a student, they said, "He should have been shot. Students get away with too much and they should be shot." '

In various college towns throughout Ohio memorial services were held for the four dead students, but rarely without pickets. At the service in Toledo, women marched with signs reading:

> The Kent State four
> Should have studied more.

But one of the worst jolts came to the conservative fraternity men of the Sigma Chi house on East Main Street in the heart of town. On the front lawn the Sigma Chi's had some years ago erected a handsome Maltese

Cross, representing one of the arcane teachings of the secret society. Across its face someone had printed in spray paint a huge, ominous black 4. It would remain there throughout the summer, all attempts at erasing it proving futile. Who had done it, and for what reason, remained unknown.

It was difficult to find any student who escaped a harsh confrontation with public opinion, but those who were subjected to even greater blows were the ones whose own parents said, 'Everyone on the hill should have been shot,' and when reminded that their son or daughter was there too, added defiantly, 'Well, if you were there when the Guard warned you to stay away, you should have been shot, too.'

Of the four hundred students whom the researchers of this book interviewed in depth, a depressing number had been told by their own parents that it might have been a good thing if they had been shot. If one requires documentation of a generation gap, this statistic is so frightening that it requires both substantiation and explanation.

The working wife of one student reports: 'My mother lives back East, and when I told her of the tragedy, she said, "I read about it in the papers. It would have been a good thing if everyone on that hill had been shot." When I reminded her that her own son-in-law had been there, she said, "That doesn't change my mind." '

An ex-army student, with a good record in Vietnam, got the treatment: 'When I reported home my mother said, "It would have been a good thing if all those students had been shot." I cried, "Hey, Mom! That's me you're talking about," and she said, "It would have been better for the country if you had all been mowed down." '

But no case of parental rejection equals that of a family living in a small town near the Kentucky border with three good-looking, well-behaved, moderate sons at the university. Without any record of participation in protest, the boys found themselves inadvertently involved at the vortex: the middle son ended up standing beside one of the students who was shot (at a great distance from the firing); the youngest was arrested for trespass and his picture appeared in the hometown paper, to the embarrassment of his family. When the family spoke to one of our researchers, the conversation was so startling that more than usual care was taken to get it exactly as delivered.

Mother: Anyone who appears on the streets of a city like Kent with long hair, dirty clothes or barefooted deserves to be shot.

Researcher: Have I your permission to quote that?

Mother: You sure do. It would have been better if the Guard had shot the whole lot of them that morning.

Researcher: But you had three sons there.

Mother: If they didn't do what the Guards told them, they should have been mowed down.

Professor of psychology (listening in): Is long hair a justification for shooting someone?

Mother: Yes. We have got to clean up this nation. And we'll start with the long-hairs.

Professor: Would you permit one of your sons to be shot simply because he went barefooted?

Mother: Yes.

Professor: Where do you get such ideas?

Mother: I teach at the local high school.

Professor: You mean you are teaching your students such things?

Mother: Yes. I teach them the truth. That the lazy, the dirty, the ones you see walking the streets and doing nothing ought all to be shot.

Why would mothers say such things? First, as women they are honestly frightened by the radical changes that are modifying society and which they feel powerless to oppose. Second, they so completely reject the new life style that they are willing to approve death as a reasonable penalty for it. Third, the fact that the four were killed by a law enforcement agency proves that the victims merited punishment. Fourth, all these fears and emotions are intensified by the fact that the young against whom they react are their own children. Finally, it is only charitable to point out that many of the women spoke in temporary anger, expressing themselves more harshly than they intended.

Of course, as the summer progessed, many of the parents retreated from their first harsh judgments and backed down from their initial wish that 'many more students ought to have been shot.' Communication with children was reopened and in many cases an understanding was achieved.

But in hundreds of other cases young students caught a terrifying glimpse of what their parents really thought. For a moment the veil that properly exists between young and old was sundered and the former were shocked by what they saw. Reactions varied.

'I doubt that I'll ever bother to go home again,' several students reported.

'I'm going on to Canada,' three of the young people said. 'I've had it.'

'I don't suppose I'll ever be able to talk with my parents again,' was a frequent reaction.

More frightening was the repeated admission that this sequence of events had alienated the students not only from their parents but from all society as they had known it. It is tempting here to use names, for some of the very finest young people appearing in these pages told compelling tales of their alienation; and to follow their psychological development would be fascinating for the reader, but since it is likely that some of them may subsequently reconsider and find an acceptable place in our society, it would not be fair to have on record a judgment made in anger of a moment, even though they were willing that their names be used. . . .

A conservative biology major: 'I was considered a square. But when my parents talked the way they did I found that my entire sympathy lay with the students, so I guess you'd say I've been radicalized. If I am, they forced it on me.'

A coed now living in a commune: 'When I left home to return to school this fall, after spending only three weeks with my family, I was crying so hard, my parents couldn't understand it. What they didn't know was that I realized it was the last time I would ever be with them again. Everything I'd said, they looked down on, and I just don't have it in me to fight them on it. So I've left for good . . . left forever the kind of life they represent.'

History major with a 3.4 average: 'During the years of the sit-ins and peace rallies, my parents and I disagreed, but we respected each other's opinions. But after Kent, when I saw how so many people, including my parents, truly feared and hated students, I realized there was no middle ground. Now I'm working against everything my family has worked for, and I will fight them as long as necessary.'

Delightful, wisecracking apolitical junior: 'I was raised in what you might call a military-oriented family. My father had been in the army, and when I was young, my brother and I always played "war games." Now he's in the army, too, and is really gung-ho Vietnam, and I'm on the other side, working against his silly war. So the few times I do go home, the only way we can keep the peace is not to talk about anything the least bit political. What kind of situation is that, when you can't talk to your own family about the things that really bug you? If people don't start talking and listening soon, this whole thing is going to blow up.' . . .

Many readers may deride our contention that life style played an important role at Kent. Comparison should be made of two events which occurred in Ohio during a space of six months, one a riot at Kent State on a Friday night in May, the other a riot at Ohio State on a Saturday night in the following November.

At Kent 1,000 people were involved; at Ohio State, 40,000. At Kent the riot lasted about two hours; at Ohio State, twelve hours. At Kent some dozen business establishments were damaged, without looting; at Ohio State, about sixty, with some looting. At Kent no one suffered bodily harm; at Ohio State many did, including a student who was shot. At Kent about $10,000 worth of damage was done; at Ohio State, about $30,000.

By any index you choose, the Saturday night riot at Ohio State was three or four times more serious than the Friday night riot at Kent.

How, therefore, can one explain that Ohio went into a frenzy over the Kent riot and took the Ohio State disturbance in stride, without a strong reaction of any kind? At Kent the governor felt obliged to fly in and charge the participants with being worse than Brown Shirts; curfew was clamped down; vigilante groups were openly discussed; the National Guard was summoned with loaded rifles; four students were killed, nine others were wounded; and the university was closed down to general approval. At Ohio State none of these things happened.

For there was this significant difference. The Kent riot involved persons addicted to the new life style; it seemed to involve politics; and it was sensed as alien to our way of life. The Ohio State riot was conducted by persons who adhered to the older life style; it celebrated a football victory over Michigan, and it was recognized as a traditional part of our heritage. We knew how to handle it, how to jolly it along. Police were understanding in not attempting to break it up, and newspapers were jovial in cataloguing it as merely one more example of normal high jinks. This dual reaction of our establishment society—accept a football riot, punish a political one—is perhaps understandable and perhaps inevitable, but it highlights the necessity for explaining the nature of the new life style and those elements in it which lead to overreaction.

28

Bloody Attica

NEW YORK STATE SPECIAL COMMISSION ON ATTICA

Forty-three citizens of New York State died at Attica Correctional Facility between September 9 and 13, 1971. Thirty-nine of that number were killed and more than 80 others were wounded by gunfire during the 15 minutes it took the State Police to retake the prison on September 13. With the exception of Indian massacres in the late 19th century, the State Police assault which ended the four-day prison uprising was the bloodiest one-day encounter between Americans since the Civil War.

In attempting to answer the first major question presented by its mandate—why did Attica explode—the Commission was presented with no lack of explanations.

Correction personnel and some older inmates tended to take a conspiratorial view of the uprising, calling it the work of left-wing radicals and "troublemakers" among the inmate population and insisting that it was planned in advance.

No less pat are explanations found in the blossoming literature of the "prisoners' liberation" movement. Those partisans would be the last to dis-

Source: New York State Special Commission on Attica, *Attica: The Official Report* (New York: Bantam, 1972), excerpted from pp. 104–330. Some material has been transposed in order to amplify selected parts of the report's summary.

pute the conclusion that the uprising was spawned "for political reasons." But they would glorify the prison rebels as heroes and place the blame squarely on the political and economic system against which the uprising was, in their view, directed. "The realization is growing, especially in the black community," wrote one such advocate, "that prisoners are the real victims of this society. One must look outside the prisons for the criminals." According to that thesis, revolts such as Attica "will recur so long as men and women are put behind bars for disobeying the inhuman laws of the society and struggling against its inequities—that is, as long as capitalism remains intact."

Contrary to these popular views, the Attica uprising was neither a long-planned revolutionary plot nor a proletarian revolution against the capitalist system.

Attica happened at the end of a summer marked by mounting tensions between inmates and correction officers, but also by rising expectations and improving conditions. Attica was no longer the jim crow institution it was even in the early sixties. Prison discipline had become more relaxed. The courts had responded to inmates' complaints and begun to order limited reforms. And the new Commissioner had liberalized rules and was promising new programs, new facilities, and a new attitude, toward inmate problems.

But the new Attica was increasingly populated by a new kind of inmate. Attica, like most of our prisons, had become largely a black and Spanish-speaking ghetto, and the new inmate was shaped by the same experiences, expectations, and frustrations that culminated in eruptions in Watts, Detroit, Newark, and other American cities. The young inmate was conscious of the changes in attitudes in the black and Puerto Rican communities, on the campuses, in the churches, and in the antiwar movement. The increasing militancy of the black liberation movement had touched him. Names like Malcolm X, George Jackson, Eldridge Cleaver, Angela Davis had special meaning to him.

The new inmate came to Attica bitter and angry as the result of his experiences in the ghetto streets and in the morass of the criminal justice system. Very likely, he already did, or would soon, see himself as a "political prisoner"—a victim, not a criminal. For all its changes, Attica was still a prison, the very symbol of authoritarianism, and in the summer of 1971, it was caught up in an era of decline and rejection of authority.

Many inmates came to believe that they were "political prisoners," even though they had been convicted of crimes having no political motive or significance. They claimed that responsibility for their actions belonged not to them—but to a society which had failed to provide adequate housing, equal educational opportunities, and an equal opportunity to compete in American life. Believing themselves to be the victims, not the aggressors, they claimed that the public should concentrate its efforts on rehabilitation of society and not of them. To them, such prison programming and job training as existed did no more than prepare them for a submissive role in a racist and unfair society.

There were many men in Attica in 1971 who held the view that they were victims of society. They must be distinguished, however, from the small group who, like Samuel Melville, were totally committed to a firm political ideology of revolution. Melville had been convicted of bombing public buildings for political purposes. The bond between these two brands of self-proclaimed political prisoners was their common rejection of established authority and their denunciation as barbaric of the wages, programs, hygiene, medical care, censorship, and other conditions at Attica.

In contrast to this new breed of inmate were the older inmates—black, white, and Spanish-speaking—who had come to accept prison conditions: they made few demands upon the officials, proclaimed at most their innocence, but not society's guilt, kept their frustration and anger to themselves, and accepted the word of the guards as law. Many who were interviewed by the Commission expressed deep antagonism toward younger inmates who were not prepared to "do their own time," and insisted on defying authority.

The older inmate may have remembered when prison conditions were worse, but the improvements made no impression on the younger one. It did not matter to the younger inmate that he was not required to move in a lockstep shuffle; that he was not required to work 12 to 14 hours a day; that he had a makeshift handball court and a basketball hoop and television in his exercise yard; that there was a prison library and commissary for his use. To the young inmate, it was enough that he was still a faceless number in a silent formation of marching men; that he was assigned to meaningless, unpleasant work details for reasons of administrative efficiency having nothing to do with rehabilitation; that for many months of the year his exercise yard was buried in four feet of snow; that he was entitled to only one shower a week in all seasons of the year; that he was paid, on the average, 25¢ a day for his labor, half of which officials saved for his release, and was expected to buy his own cigarettes and toiletries from his wages; and that he saw a correction staff that did not include one black or Puerto Rican officer and that exhibited the same "remember your place and do as you're told" attitude that his people had been rebelling against for the last decade. The new inmate was not about to submit to these conditions simply because he had been convicted of a crime.

Attica's all-white correctional staff from rural western New York State was comfortable with inmates who "knew their place," but unprepared and untrained to deal with the new inmate, much less to understand him. Unused to seeing their authority challenged, officers felt threatened by the new inmate. Viewing the recent relaxations of rules and discipline, the intervention of the courts, and the new programs for inmates, they felt that their authority was being undermined by Albany and that their superiors were not backing them up. The officers became increasingly resentful and insecure. The result was, inevitably, daily confrontations between the new inmate and the old-style officer.

The Commission discussed the problem of the new inmate and the "political prisoner" with more than 200 of Attica's correction officers. Their responses varied from understanding to racist interpretations of inmates' complaints. But one theme stood out above all others and made any meaningful meeting of minds between inmates and correction officers almost impossible: "These men are not in here for missing Sunday School," said one officer. Another exclaimed, "No one comes here for just playing jacks on the sidewalk." An inmate's very presence at Attica was regarded as sufficient evidence that he had voluntarily forfeited, by his own actions, many of the rights the new inmate insists upon retaining. In speaking of the rights of prisoners, correction officers often turn the question to the rights of their victims. "They cry about their rights," correction officers say, "but what about the rights of their victims? Did they worry about the rights of the man they killed or the woman they raped?" The inmate who refused to regard himself only as a criminal simply could not relate in any meaningful, constructive manner with a prison staff that could not regard him as anything else.

Thus, correction officers frequently found themselves demanding adherence to rules which inmates would not accept. As the number of confrontations increased during this period, so did the intensity. An officer's orders to stop talking, for example, were first questioned, later ignored, and finally ridiculed.

Moreover, inmates challenged one of the oldest codes of the maximum security prison: "Do your *own* time." Inmates demanded the right to gather and form associations for religious and political purposes. Finding strength in numbers, many new inmates joined organizations which stressed ethnic identity, such as the Muslims, the Black Panthers, the Young Lords, and the Five Percenters.

"Now, one inmate's trouble was everybody's trouble," explained one officer. Although not overtly threatened, officers who singled out an inmate for discipline began to find themselves acutely and uncomfortably aware of the hostile glares of many inmates. Instead of retreating from a confrontation, inmates realized they could intimidate many officers simply by standing fast. They soon learned that they could communicate their hostility and their resentment and their unacceptance merely by their silent, ominous presence together. The politics of confrontation had come to prison.

The confrontations were accompanied by increasing societal awareness among inmates and the growth of organizations inside the institution determined to spread the consciousness and try to make changes. Groups such as the Muslims, Black Panthers, and Young Lords gained adherents and held meetings, but quarrels and rivalries among them and their leaders prevented them from coming together in concerted action.

Largely as the result of these groups' efforts, discussion groups began in the exercise yards. By the summer of 1971, an inmate-instructed sociology class in the school had become an informal forum for ideas about effecting change. There was, finally, a series of organized protest efforts at Attica in the months prior to September 1971. Some had moderate success, but others ended only in the discipline of participants. The reaction of the authorities became increasingly one of isolating and transferring suspected "ringleaders" and "troublemakers."

An inmate manifesto setting forth a series of moderate demands, and including a commitment to peaceful change, was sent to the Commissioner and the Governor in July 1971. The Commissioner responded with an acknowledgment and with a [promise to visit] Attica early in September. In the intervening eight weeks, tensions at Attica had continued to mount, culminating in a day of protest over the killing of George Jackson at San Quentin, during which few inmates ate at lunch and dinner and many wore black armbands. The inmates had demonstrated their ability and their willingness to act en masse, and there was now some talk about organizing a prisonwide sit-down strike. When Commissioner Oswald's visit produced nothing more than a taped speech promising future changes and asking for patience, the stage was set. No one really expected a violent take-over of the prison, but few at Attica thought the summer would pass without a major incident.

How It Happened

The initial explosion on Thursday, September 9, came in reaction to an incident the previous day which provoked anger and resentment among inmates in two companies in A block. A misunderstanding in the exercise yard on Wednesday afternoon led to an unusually intense confrontation between officers and inmates, during which a lieutenant was struck by an inmate. The officers were forced to back down, but that evening, two inmates were removed from their cells to HBZ, precipitating angry name-calling, hurling of objects from cells, and vows of revenge along the two galleries.

The following morning, uneasiness lingered on in one of the two companies, comprised largely of inmates considered "difficult" by the administration. An inmate who had been locked in his cell for throwing a soup can at an officer the previous evening was released from his cell by fellow inmates. After breakfast, a lieutenant who had been involved in the incident on Wednesday approached the company as it was lined up in A tunnel on its way back from breakfast. He intended to try to persuade the inmates to return to their cells, but as he reached them, he was attacked, and the uprising was underway.

After an initial outburst of chaotic violence, rebellious A block inmates regrouped and set upon the locked gate at Times Square, which separated A block from the rest of the institution. A defective weld, unknown to officers and inmates alike, broke and the gate gave way, giving the rioters access to the center square, and the keys which unlocked the gates in three directions. From Times Square, inmates from A block spread throughout the institution with little resistance, attacking officers, taking hostages, destroying property. As the rebellion reached other areas, some inmates joined in actively, but the majority tried to escape to secure areas, or were simply caught up in the tide.

The authorities were slow in responding, due largely to the absence of a riot control plan, the lack of available manpower, and an antiquated communications system. Connected with other parts of the prison only by single-line telephones, those in the administration building could not appreciate the full extent of the trouble, or summon help, until it was too late. By 10:30 A.M. the inmates had obtained control of four cellblocks and all of the yards and tunnels, and 1,281 inmates had gathered in D yard with over 40 hostages. Only then did the rudiments of organization begin to appear, with leaders of preexisting groups, inmates well versed in law, and other natural leaders among the inmates emerging as spokesmen. Most of those who took an active role in organizing the yard, drafting demands, and, later, negotiating with the state, had not been involved in the initial outbreak of violence and did not join in it when the rioters reached their area of the prison.

Was It Planned?

The Commission has found no evidence that the Attica uprising was planned, either by avowed revolutionaries or anyone else. All of the objective evidence, especially the course the uprising actually took, points in the other direction.

To begin with, if a take-over was planned, it would not have been planned to commence in an enclosed area, such as A tunnel, where access to the rest of the prison was presumably sealed off by iron gates. The mess halls or exercise yards, where there were concentrations of inmates, were more logical choices. The company which started the violence had just come from the mess hall, where hundreds of other inmates were present, had passed through Times Square, where the keys to four corridor gates were kept, and had seen the Times Square gates locked behind them, all without incident. A planned rebellion, even if the planning were limited to that company, would surely have been touched off before the moment the inmates were confined to A tunnel, with no immediately apparent avenue of escape and no guarantee of access to the rest of the institution.

No one could have anticipated that the Times Square gate would give way. Had it held, as everyone expected it would, the uprising would have been limited to A block and A yard—where at that hour fewer than 300 inmates and 10 correction officers were located. Before the gate broke, the A block rebels called to inmates trapped in other corridors to join in the uprising, but their entreaties fell on deaf ears.

Only after the totally fortuitous failure of the Times Square gate were the rebels able to get the keys to other gates and gain access to the metal shops, where they obtained tools, acetylene torches, and an electric truck for use in breaking through still more gates. Had an uprising been planned, inmates in other areas of the prison would surely have been alerted to begin hostile action before the rioters from A block reached their areas. In fact, however, no violence erupted, no damage was done, and no hostages were taken anywhere in the institution until inmates who had broken into Times Square arrived. Even then, most inmates just did their best to stay out of the way. Significantly, most of the inmates who were later to emerge as leaders and negotiators in D yard were not part of the first wave of violence and destruction.

The rioters did not take over the prison according to any rational plan. After the initial flare-up, before Times Square fell, there was a 10-minute lull during which A block inmates hurriedly gathered sports equipment and broom handles, broke up benches in A yard, and fashioned makeshift masks from bed sheets. During this lull, some inmates retrieved crude weapons from old hiding places. But the quick emergence of homemade weapons is no indication of advance planning, since inmates in prisons everywhere keep such weapons hidden for self-protection or "just in case."

After the violence had subsided and the hostages were taken, the inmates continued for at least an hour to act in a manner inconsistent with the idea that there were any preexisting plans. They raided the commissary and officers' mess in helter-skelter fashion, not at first stockpiling supplies or preserving them for future use. Before the commissary could be completely stripped of food, it was set on fire and destroyed. Once the metal shops were entered and over 20 hostages taken, fires were set and the inmates deserted the shops, leaving behind large quantities of volatile materials, tools, metal scraps, and machines that could be used for making weapons.

When the uprising broke out, only one correction officer and two civilians were on duty in the powerhouse, control of which would include the capacity of cutting off the electricity in the entire institution. Yet, inmates never made a concerted effort to take over the powerhouse. Even when they all reached D yard, there was a long period of chaos and internal bickering among inmates before organization emerged.

The lieutenant who had first been struck in A tunnel told the Commission that while he was hiding in an A block cell, he heard an inmate somewhere in A block shout, "Squad 1, go to your area, Squad 2, go to your area." To him, and others at Attica, this was a strong indication of preexisting inmate organization and planning. No similar reports were received from other sources and, in months of investigation, the Commission was never informed of the existence of the inmate "squads."

It is unclear exactly when the remark was heard, but it may well have been a considerable time after the initial flare-up, when the beginnings of inmate organization were emerging. Then, too, it is clear that tightly disciplined organizations, such as the Muslims, did exist at Attica and that they attempted soon after the uprising began to make some order out of the chaos. A group of Muslims, operating in A block, were responsible for protecting and releasing several injured officers that morning. Throughout the four-day uprising, the Muslims were always well disciplined and continued to protect the hostages from harm. The commands overheard by the lieutenant may well have been a part of that discipline. Standing alone, his report does not constitute persuasive evidence that the uprising was planned.

The Commissioner's Decision

[Commissioner of Correctional Services] Oswald had warned [Governor Nelson Rockefeller] in May 1971 that prison unrest was increasing "fomented and exacerbated by internal and external revolutionary political activities which were increasingly zeroing in on the criminal element in our society."

The Governor viewed the Attica rebellion as another step in an ominous world trend. As he told the Commission:

. . . one of the most recent and widely used techniques of modern-day revolutionaries has been the taking of political hostages and using the threat to kill them as blackmail to achieve unconditional demands and to gain wide public attention to further their revolutionary ends. I have followed these developments with great interest and considered that, if tolerated, they pose a serious threat to the ability of free government to preserve order and to protect the security of the individual citizen.

Therefore, I firmly believe that a duly elected official sworn to defend the constitution and the laws of the state and the nation would be betraying his trust to the people he serves if he were to sanction or condone such criminal act by negotiating under such circumstances.

In the handling of the Attica uprising, the Governor found that these views conflicted with his belief in delegation of responsibilities to the department heads he had selected. Despite his own convictions against negotiating with the holders of the hostages, the Governor chose not to overrule the man whom he had named and he supported Oswald's decision to attempt a negotiated settlement.

When Oswald informed the Governor that he was prepared to accept the 28 Points, the Governor backed him up with the assurance that he would recommend the legislation contemplated by the Points.

The Governor stood firm, however, on one matter—he told Commissioner Oswald that even if he had the power to grant amnesty, which he and his counsel agreed he did not have—he would not grant it as a matter of principle. The Governor drew a sharp distinction between amnesty, which he considered a "political" objective not negotiable with the holders of hostages, and penal reform promised in the 28 Points, which he testified Oswald "had in mind anyway."

Moreover, the Governor, with his concern that "revolutionaries" were playing a major role in the Attica uprising, concluded that [a personal visit to the scene by him] would be exploited by those "who were not interested in seeing the settlement or seeing a reform, but who wanted to drag this out, preserve the theater for worldwide coverage relating to revolutionary forces."

From the outset, the Governor perceived the Attica uprising as more than a prison riot. The uprising constituted an insurrection against the very authority of the state, and to tolerate it was to concede a loss of sovereignty over the rebels.

Sooner or later, the state's paramount interest in restoring order would have to be asserted. That point was really reached on Saturday night, when a settlement based on the 28 Points was rejected by the inmates. Despite the frantic efforts of Sunday, Oswald's attempt to avoid the use of force to end an uprising had, as the Governor testified, "proven to be a failure."

The decision to retake the prison was not a quixotic effort to rescue hostages in the midst of 1,200 inmates; it was a decisive reassertion of the state of its sovereignty and power. While all state officials were concerned about the safety of the hostages, they had finally reached the conclusion that, after four days of negotiations, the need to reassert the authority of the state over the rebels outweighed the risks of an assault.

Many inmates still believed, when the helicopters first appeared over D yard on Monday morning, that the balance of power was controlled by hostages, not guns. They failed to realize that once the state decided that the rebellion was no longer tolerable, the lives of the hostages were expendable.

Officially, the decision to commence the assault was made by Oswald, as the official in charge of all correctional facilities, and authorized and approved by the Governor. In fact, the decision was inevitable once the negotiations seemed hopeless.

THE CRISIS
OF CRISES

"One goes to other countries to see the past, the preserved remnants of history and ethnicity," recently wrote an Israeli journalist after spending many months exploring this country coast-to-coast by car. "But one comes to the United States—always, no matter how often—to see the future . . . a projection of what life in his own country will be like five, ten, twenty years from now."

Soon after he arrived, a woman on Long Island warned him, " 'You are going to find a lot of dissatisfaction around the country. The Government is giving everything to everybody, except to the working people. My husband says that in this country you must be very rich or very poor to make it. . . . I hope that in your country you'll manage to avoid all the problems we got ourselves into.' "

In New England a bartender complained to him, " 'We live in such lousy times. . . . Even during the Depression I don't remember people being so mean to each other. If you ever find out what is happening to us, please let me know.' "

At a drive-in hamburger stand in West Virginia, the carhop noticed his accent and asked where he came from. When he told her, she asked politely, " 'Is it as dirty over there as it is here?' "

In Arizona on a Navaho reservation, an Indian guide, dressed like a cowboy, responded to hearing where he was from by guessing it must be better there than here. " 'Why, isn't this a good country?' " asked the Israeli. The Indian turned and spat on the ground. " 'The hell it is,' " he said.[1]

Across the land, at various social levels and for different reasons, commentators sense a disappointment in America. For today we live surrounded by the wreckage of unrealistically high expectations, depressed by the suspicion that as a people we are not so special after all: our power may not be invincible, our resources may not be inexhaustible, and our heyday may not be ahead of us but already in the past.

The characteristically American vision of general prosperity acting like a detergent, emulsifying whatever may be nasty in our way of life, has proven to be a chimera; instead of alleviating our social problems, prosperity has aggravated them. The race with the Soviet Union to be the first to put a man on the moon has turned out to be irrelevant to our central concerns. While the rest of the world applauded the successful culmination of our decade-long push to beat the Russians, the American people as a whole acted distracted, strangely sad, and even a little bored.

Instead of uniting us against a common foe, a war abroad has divided us and helped undermine the legitimacy of our social institutions. (A philanthropist has granted a half million dollars to a university for research in how to reverse what he perceives as a massive erosion of public confidence "in the credibility of their leaders and virtually all of our institutions—the church, the schools, industry, banking and commerce, government, and communications media.") While the menace of foreign aggression has been losing much of its credibility, chronic internal conflicts have escalated into a major threat to the nation's security, as a set of mutually self-fulfilling prophecies of doom: anarchy⇌repression. An epidemic of rebellion and counterrebellion has spread distrust and anxiety and resentment throughout the land. "We have become more painfully conscious of what pulls us apart than what holds us together. . . . The flag itself, the very symbol of America's indivisibility, has become for some of her citizens a weapon of controversy." [2] Divisiveness has reached the point where some of the older generation are reminded of how a similar state of disunity among the French people during the 1930s caused their nation to disintegrate later under the pressures of World War II. Even some of the generals in the Pentagon say they are not as concerned about our ability to keep a balance of power in the world as they are about our ability to maintain a balance of trust among ourselves. Moreover, the percentage of Americans who say they would rather live in some other country has doubled during the past ten years, and every year an increasing percentage actually does emigrate.

We can no longer alibi that our social problems result from the social sciences being underdeveloped. We now have plenty of knowledge

[1] Ehud Yonay, "A Foreigner's America, From the Old Beginning to the New One," *New York Times,* 26 November 1972, sec. 10, pp. 1, 11.
[2] "The Spirit of '70," *Newsweek,* 6 July 1970, p. 19.

that is not being used. It isn't knowledge-power that we lack; it's will-power. In recent years the nation has been superbly served by presidential commissions to investigate crime, riots, violence, and campus unrest; yet the people seem unappreciative, and Congress hears no clear call to implement their recommendations. It can't be for lack of money. As a nation we claim to be the richest in the world—in material things, that is. To the extent that money alone can solve our problems, few doubt that we can afford to support massive programs on a crash basis, but many doubt that we are willing to tax ourselves that much.

We are rich and competent and anxious, but immobilized by a paralysis of the will. Some choose to call it the "crisis of confidence." Others refer to it as the "national malaise." [3] What is happening resembles an identity crisis on a national scale—a growing uncertainty about who we really are as a people, what we are becoming, and to what we should aspire; a turning inward, a moodiness—all in response to feeling overwhelmed by multiple crises that are interconnected, semipermanent, and simultaneous. Unfortunately, all four contemporary social crises, while themselves consisting of interlocking vicious circles, act at the same time as cogwheels in a greater spiraling system, feeding into each other and also back on themselves, making the current national situation unique in United States history—a supercrisis, a crisis of crises.

As long as the Rural Crisis persists, for example, coping with urban problems provides only temporary relief because it makes migration even more attractive; and as long as the Urban Crisis persists urban voters won't support rural rehabilitation.

For another example, fear of street crime, while playing a major role in the Urban Crisis, also contributes to rebelliousness by reducing mutual trust and undermining the legitimacy of the social order. "The fear of crimes of violence is not a simple fear of injury or death or even of all crimes of violence, but, at bottom, a fear of strangers. . . ." [4]

This fear of strangers has greatly impoverished the lives of many Americans, especially those who live in high-crime neighborhoods in large cities. People stay behind the locked doors of their homes rather than risk walking in the streets at night. Poor people spend money on taxis because they are afraid to walk or use public transportation. Sociable people are afraid to talk to those they do not know. In short, society is to an increasing extent suffering from what economists call "opportunity costs" as the result of fear of crime. For example, administrators and officials interviewed for the

[3] See Arthur M. Schlesinger, Jr., *The Crisis of Confidence* (Boston: Houghton Mifflin, 1969); Herbert J. Gans, "The American Malaise," *The New York Times Magazine,* 6 February 1972, pp. 16 ff.; Peter Schrag, "The Failure of Political Language," *Saturday Review,* 25 March 1972, p. 30.

[4] The President's Commission on Law Enforcement and Administration of Justice, *The Challenge of Crime in a Free Society* (Washington: Government Printing Office, 1967), p. 52.

Commission by the University of Michigan survey team, report that library use is decreasing because borrowers are afraid to come out at night. School officials told of parents not daring to attend PTA meetings in the evening, and park administrators pointed to unused recreation facilities. When many persons stay home, they are not availing themselves of the opportunities for pleasure and cultural enrichment offered in their communities, and they are not visiting their friends as frequently as they might. The general level of social interaction in the society is reduced.

When fear of crime becomes fear of the stranger the social order is further damaged. As the level of sociability and mutual trust is reduced, streets and public places can indeed become more dangerous. Not only will there be fewer people abroad but those who are abroad will manifest a fear of and a lack of concern for each other. The reported incidents of bystanders indifferent to cries for help are the logical consequence of a reduced sociability, mutual distrust and withdrawal.

However, the most dangerous aspect of a fear of strangers is its implication that the moral and social order of society are of doubtful trustworthiness and stability. Everyone is dependent on this order to instill in all members of society a respect for the persons and possessions of others. When it appears that there are more and more people who do not have this respect, the security that comes from living in an orderly and trustworthy society is undermined. The tendency of many people to think of crime in terms of increasing moral deterioration is an indication that they are losing their faith in their society. And so the costs of the fear of crime to the social order may ultimately be even greater than its psychological costs to individuals.

At the same time that fear of crime may contribute to the general erosion of authority, this same weakening of authority, combined with a sense of injustice, may aggravate the crime problem.

It seems likely (the data do not allow of very confident statements on any of these matters) that upper-working- and lower-middle-class persons are considerably more crime-prone than they were a generation or more ago. If this is really the case, the reason is not that the "wage" of crime has increased relative to other (honest) work. A more plausible explanation is that these classes have come to have less respect for authority, including the authority of the law. . . .

Other changes in public opinion have also made it easier for working- and lower-working-class people to commit crimes. Perhaps the most important of these changes is the wide acceptance during the 1960's of the view that individuals belonging to groups that have suffered injustice or are severely disadvantaged (for example, Negroes and the poor) have a kind of quasi-right to have their offenses against the law extenuated or even to have them regarded as political acts reflecting a morality "higher" than obedience to law. . . .

This feeling that victims of oppression have a kind of license to break the law was one of the conditions that made possible the major riots of 1964 and thereafter. . . . The riots and the public discussion that followed them (especially the Kerner Commission's verdict, endorsed by the sale of 1.3 million copies of its report, that "white racism" was mainly to blame) almost certainly made it easier for many Negroes to commit crimes that they would not otherwise have committed.[5]

Some of the rebelliousness of young urban blacks may be rooted in the Rural Crisis pressures that drove them north, as Dr. Gatch thinks: "They may prosper, but they can't forget how underprivileged and oppressed their people back home are. Their resentment is expressed in contempt for all whites, and there is enough of that resentment to breed revolution."

The Environmental Crisis may contribute to a general spirit of rebellion by making many people feel that their high expectations of the magic of technology and the benefits of limitless growth have been betrayed. They may have been expecting economic growth, for instance, to reduce unemployment and finance welfare services, but now it is blamed for much of the spoliation of the environment and the voracious consumption of natural resources. Suspicions about the safety of the food they eat—manufacturers' recall of everything from green bean casseroles and mushroom pizzas to tunafish and sauerkraut; a government ban on the synthetic hormone DES (diethylstilbestrol), for many years commonly fed to cattle and sheep to speed up their growth, on suspicion of producing cancer; warnings about possible contamination of clams and mussels by poisonous algae and sewage outflows; and calls for an all-out ban on nitrites and nitrates in bacon, hot dogs, and other processed meats—cause people to wonder if there is anything left that is safe to eat. Furthermore, a counterrebellion against the response to the Environmental Crisis is likely to balloon as the realization sinks in that saving the environment and raising the quality of life requires lowering the quantity of life, that is, the standards of consumption by which perhaps most people measure the quality of their lives.

And at the same time, the Spiritual Crisis exacerbates the other crises by working against any sense of community and by paralyzing the will to act. It may encourage a backlash against ecology, for instance:

Ultimately it seems that a serious program for saving the environment can depend on nothing other than authoritarianism, if only because the threat to the environment itself is announced to us not

[5] Edward C. Banfield, *The Unheavenly City* (Boston: Little, Brown, 1970), pp. 171–73.

directly yet but largely through authority. The problems of carbon dioxide in the atmosphere, radiation, eutrophication of water, scarcely affect our senses. We must be told of the dangers by authorities. . . .

Will young people continue to treasure a program for conserving the environment when they find that it pinches their equally treasured right to do exactly as they please? And that it derives from the very authority that, above all other sources of knowledge, they distrust? [6]

Social life, as previously pointed out, resembles nature's closed ecological system in which everything is connected to everything else and nothing is really free of charge because getting something one wants always involves giving up something else that one wants. The ways in which all four crises lock arms and support each other, added to the fact that each consists of hydra-headed problems that have persisted over several generations, suggest that none of them may be solvable. Jay Forrester of Massachusetts Institute of Technology maintains that intuitive and common sense solutions to social problems are bound to be wrong most of the time, because human minds are limited to "linear reasoning," that is, reasoning in direct lines, one at a time, between stationary causes and effects. Changing relationships between a pair of factors can be spelled out and grasped mentally, but our minds are unable to focus on total systems involving chain reactions and spirals, all in a state of flux. Forrester believes that computer technology can extend human capacities for grasping such complexities. Enormously complicated systems, with interactions so involved as to defy the best minds, can be modeled on a computer, and thus the consequences of proposed action can be foreseen. The use of computers in the past, for example, might have enabled planners and politicians to see the advantages of accomplishing school desegregation via black political power rather than via court orders implemented by the same people who previously enforced segregation, and to avoid the shortsightedness of replacing slums with public housing in the inner city at a time when employment opportunities were moving to the suburbs. Currently, a computerized model of the nation's health conditions might indicate that government funds put into nutrition and sanitation and full employment would raise health standards far more than spending the same money to expand medical schools, hospitals, and insurance coverage.

Social problems are so complex in themselves and so interrelated that the best remedies are often synergetic: either synchronizing the action of two or more remedies for the same problem or ameliorating two or more problems with the same remedy. Here again computers may help uncover the best combinations: fertilizing barren land, for instance, with

---

[6] Roger Starr, "This Is the Way the World Ends," *American Heritage,* October 1970, p. 101.

industrial wastes that would otherwise pollute rivers and lakes or composted garbage whose incineration would otherwise pollute the air; expanding mail deliveries to twice a day by hiring the unemployed as letter-carriers; hiring mothers on welfare to be live-in caretakers of schools and other public buildings, acting as an alarm system and deterrent to theft and vandalism; reducing poverty by turning the Army into a social welfare agency and a school system teaching the "3Rs" and skilled trades in competition with monopolistic unions.

It is clear that computers may indeed provide a useful service by predicting the social consequences of alternative policies, but it is also clear, as one considers implementing each of the above suggestions, that in the end human minds are left with the tasks of deciding which data to put into the computer and which course of action is the least objectionable among several that may all be very unsatisfactory. Are people more likely to heed disagreeable advice if it comes from a machine?

The fundamental reason that some social problems have persisted for generations is that they are not susceptible to technological remedies; instead their solution depends on changing the habits and attitudes and underlying value priorities of masses of people. The urgent tones of crisis characterizing discussions of environmental deterioration, for instance, stem not so much from its biological and technological aspects as from questions of social ethics requiring value judgments, e.g., what are our ethical obligations to future generations and to each other right now regarding how we use the earth's resources? Which should take priority when the common welfare conflicts with individual liberty? What should be done about consumption and growth as we move from an economy of abundance to one of scarcity? Likewise, the concern generated by each of the other crises arises from conflicts between high priority values: family versus corporate farming, the "them and us" polarization of both the Urban and Spiritual Crises, and so forth.

Along with just about everything else in our dynamic society, values and attitudes do undergo continuous change—albeit at a glacial rate most of the time. The chief agent of change is new experience. For example, the crash of the stock market and a decade of mass unemployment during the 1930s were new experiences which undoubtedly demoted values such as optimism and long-range thrift, self-reliance and hard work, private enterprise and laissez-faire, while promoting government intervention, economic security, and contraception. Back in 1957 the Sputnik launched by the U.S.S.R. produced a new experience of defeat in technology that shook up American priorities, at least temporarily. Our humbling experience in Indochina has thrown into question traditional assumptions about American invincibility and rectitude, and it has started a process of anguishing attitudinal change whose writhing can be felt throughout the country.

Deliberate attitudinal change on a massive scale is an enormous undertaking, and not much is known about how to go about doing it. Yet it has been accomplished many times in the past by a variety of social movements which have involved people in new experiences. In addition to the impact of the Great Depression, for instance, it took the labor movement, assisted by other social movements like progressivism and nativism, to gradually equalize the caste-like set of double standards against which organized labor struggled at the beginning of this century.

But social movements, once started, are difficult to steer or brake. They are a form of collective behavior, with a blundering, irrational life of their own, prone to counterproductive violence and foolishness. Moreover, they can be nullified by opponents mounting their own movements to resist attitudinal change.

Another way to generate the kind of experiences that cause people to rearrange their values and attitudes is suggested by an experiment conducted by sociologists at a summer camp for boys. Muzafer Sherif and his colleagues succeeded in deliberately creating conflict between two groups of boys and then restoring harmony by engineering a series of situations creating superordinate goals, i.e., "goals which have a compelling appeal for both [groups] but which neither could achieve without the other." [7] The magnetic effect of superordinate goals is demonstrated whenever a natural disaster like an earthquake or a flood creates a compelling need for people to pull together. "You care for the other guy when you need him," as Saul Alinsky used to say. True. But who would wish for another Pearl Harbor to pull this country together? And if you do bring conflicting groups together what is to keep them from finding a superordinate goal in the violent overthrow of the government?

To a significant extent attitudes can be changed indirectly by first changing overt behavior and then relying on a feedback process to cause people eventually to adjust their attitudes to fit the new conditions of their lives. To change attitudes, then, first change behavior. And to change behavior, reform the social institutions that set the examples and do the enforcing or conditioning. However, at this point one reaches what looks like a dead end with the question of how to achieve structural change democratically in opposition to the attitudes one hopes to change. Asking people to approve social reforms aimed at changing their attitudes is like asking rural legislators to vote for reapportionment knowing it will remove them from office. (It finally took court orders to accomplish that, remember.) Besides, the trouble with social reform is that it often has unintended consequences, creating new problems and aggravating old ones. Witness the miscarriage of many well-intentioned welfare programs such as urban renewal, farm supports, and minimum wage laws.

In other words, many of those who are concerned about the social crises simultaneously confronting this country feel trapped between the horns of a painful dilemma: at the same time that they concede the need for drastic social reform and attitudinal change they fear the unintended

[7] Muzafer Sherif, "Experiments in Group Conflict," *Scientific American*, November 1956, p. 57.

consequences of such changes. If sociocultural change is responsible in the first place for having fanned smoldering embers into crises, how can the remedy be more change? This paralyzing predicament is at the heart of the Crisis of Crises.

The Europeanization of America

"If you're not part of the solution, you're part of the problem," according to the popular saying coined by Eldridge Cleaver. But what if the solution is part of the problem? What if the cure is worse than the disease? What does one do if a problem turns out to be caused by unanticipated results of solutions to other problems? Could it be that some problems are *inherently* insoluble? For example, how does one separate good from evil when their relationship is symbiotic? Or escape unscathed from a double bind? Or tame a vicious circle? Is a problem solvable if its solution depends on changes in national character or subcultures? Can a whole nation or class be resocialized?

The idea that a problem may be insoluble is alien to American habits of thought. If at first we don't succeed, we believe we must try, try again. All problems can be solved, we assume, if only one tries hard enough; the impossible is supposed to take a little longer, that's all. With our traditional optimism and faith in human perfectibility, we tend to presume that, given sufficient determination and resolute collective action, any social problem can be first ameliorated and then eliminated. The evidence assembled in this book, however, suggests that some of our inveterate social problems may be as irreversible as an amputation, and all we can do about them is learn how an amputee copes. At best, perhaps, social crises composed of such problems can be merely reduced in temperature, or contained and managed until supporting conditions change or they work themselves out somehow. At worst, on the other hand, they may act together like an incurable and deadly infection, slowly and painfully destroying the society they inhabit.

Current social crises, on top of stalemates in Indochina and Korea, together with lingering memories of the Great Depression, may yet be sufficient to develop in us Americans the tragic sense of life—an understanding of how people with the best intentions can make the most dreadful mistakes and suffer the most terrible consequences; and a recognition that tomorrow will not inevitably be better than today, that the more things seem to change, the more they stay the same, that not every problem is soluble, nor every ill curable, nor every need answerable; in short, an end to innocence—the Europeanization of America.

For twenty years following World War II we told ourselves that our country was the leader of the "free world." We were not only the biggest and the strongest, with the largest GNP and the most ICBM's, but we honestly believed that we were also the most righteous. Today, a generation later, that self-image is badly tarnished, if not shattered, and much of the rest of the world sees less and less moral difference between us and their adversaries, whom we seem more and more to imitate.

But, to paraphrase the poet Archibald MacLeish, if we are not the liberty-loving people we once were, and if we have never been the humane and compassionate nation we believed we were, then who are we? We used to think that we were a great people; now we realize that all along we have been only a great power. "For most of our national existence," writes Arthur Schlesinger, Jr., "we have enjoyed a placid faith in our virtue and our invulnerability," secure in the conviction that we lived at the ethical center of the universe, but when so many of our pretensions collapsed during the 1960s we lost "our immunity to history." America's innocence is over, as Richard Hammer declares; we have "had to recognize that we were no better than anyone else, and in some ways, because of our arrogance and our technology, we might be a little worse than most." Europeans, who have been burned more often in the past than we by the mindlessness of war, the foolishness of strong leaders, and the backfire of moral crusades, long ago developed an almost instinctive appreciation of life as a tragedy.[8]

Like the Israeli journalist quoted at the start of this essay, Europeans have been coming to the United States for the past fifty years to see what life in their own country might be like someday in the near future. What foreigners have in mind primarily is business and technology, material living standards and the phenomenon of middle-classification. But when it comes to seeing themselves as tragic figures on the world scene, where everybody is right as in a Greek tragedy, and at the same time wrong as in the theater of the absurd, Europeans and the rest of the world, most particularly Israelis and Arabs, have always had much to teach Americans—that is, if such wisdom could be taught by anything other than experience.

Perhaps the example of Denmark shows that a people can be proud and happy with scaled-down dreams. During the early 1800s Denmark suffered a series of military defeats by various combinations of its neighbors and lost segment after segment of an empire built by centuries of conquest until a final humiliation occurred when provinces of the motherland were lost to Prussia. At this point, the Danes reacted to defeat of their imperialistic ambitions and attempts to uphold Danish traditions in a surprising reversal of character. Resolving to "win within what had been lost without," they began to concentrate on improving the quality of life in Denmark. A hundred years later, the results are manifest.

Our protective innocence lost, our proud pretensions collapsed, our beautiful self-image shattered—no wonder as a people we act as if in

---

[8] Archibald MacLeish, "A Great Power—Or a Great People?" *New York Times:* 19 November 1972, sect. 4, p. 11; Arthur M. Schlesinger, Jr., *The Crisis of Confidence* (New York: Bantam, 1969), p. ix; Richard Hammer, *The Court-Martial of Lt. Calley,* p. 393. Indebtedness is also acknowledged to articles by Peter Schrag, Leo Cherne, David Halberstam, Henry Steele Commager, and Charles W. Yost.

mourning for the untimely death of a loved one. Studies of how people cope with grief indicate that they normally go through three phases. First there is a state of shock, usually a mercifully short phase, followed by a period of mourning in which there is much "work" to do that is crucial to the mental health of survivors: a gradual breaking of one's ties to the person or thing irrevocably lost. Before the work of mourning is complete, the final stage usually begins: a gradual reinvestment in life by forming new ties with the living. As might be expected, we are not all in the same stage of grief for the nation these days. Some of us remain unaware of, or unwilling to concede, any loss, while others may have just gone into shock. Some of us are still in the process of talking ourselves into accepting the death of inherited illusions that we won't be able to bequeath, while others are already busy tentatively trying on new visions, more modest and mature this time. When most of us have completed this last stage, the Crisis of Crises should be over.

George Santayana, an American philosopher born and reared in Spain, raised the question some fifty years ago of what it might take to get Americans to reorder their priorities. "The American has never yet had to face the trials of Job . . ." he noted. "But if serious and irremediable tribulation ever overtook him, what would his attitude be? It is then that we should be able to discover whether materialism or idealism lies at the base of his character." [9]

It looks now as if we won't have to wait much longer to find out.

[9] George Santayana, *Character and Opinion in the United States* (New York: Doubleday Anchor, 1956), p. 116.

To Learn More...

ABOUT THE URBAN CRISIS

Banfield, Edward C. *The Unheavenly City*. Boston: Little, Brown, 1970.

Brown, Claude. *Manchild in the Promised Land*. New York: New American Library, 1965.

Clark, Kenneth. *Dark Ghetto*. New York: Harper & Row, 1965.

Conot, Robert. *Rivers of Blood, Years of Darkness*. New York: Bantam, 1967.

Gans, Herbert J. *The Urban Villagers*. New York: Free Press, 1965.

Glazer, Nathan, and Daniel P. Moynihan. *Beyond the Melting Pot*. 2nd edition. Cambridge: M.I.T. Press, 1970.

Jacobs, Paul. *Prelude to Riot*. New York: Random House, 1967.

Lewis, Oscar. *La Vida*. New York: Random House, 1966.

Liebow, Elliot. *Tally's Corner*. Boston: Little, Brown, 1967.

White, Morton and Lucia, eds. *The Intellectual Versus the City*. New York: New American Library, 1964.

Yablonsky, Lewis. *The Violent Gang*. Baltimore: Penguin, 1967.

ABOUT THE RURAL CRISIS

Bagdikian, Ben H. *In the Midst of Plenty.* New York: New American Library, 1964.

Caudill, Harry M. *Night Comes to the Cumberlands.* Boston: Little, Brown, 1963.

Coles, Robert. *Migrants, Sharecroppers, Mountaineers.* Boston: Little, Brown, 1971.

————. *The South Moves North.* Boston: Little, Brown, 1971.

————. *Still Hungry in America.* New York: New American Library, 1969.

Dunbar, Tony. *Our Land Too.* New York: Random House, 1972.

Good, Paul. *The American Serfs.* New York: Ballantine, 1968.

Harrington, Michael. *The Other America.* Baltimore: Penguin, 1963.

Weller, Jack E. *Yesterday's People.* Lexington: University of Kentucky Press, 1965.

ABOUT THE ENVIRONMENTAL CRISIS

Commoner, Barry. *The Closing Circle.* New York: Random House, 1971.

DeBell, Garrett, ed. *The Environmental Handbook.* New York: Ballantine, 1970.

Editors of *Fortune. The Environment.* New York: Harper & Row, 1970.

Ehrlich, Paul R. *The Population Bomb.* New York: Ballantine, 1968.

Graham, Frank, Jr. *Since Silent Spring.* Greenwich, Conn.: Fawcett, 1970.

Stewart, George R. *Not So Rich As You Think.* New York: New American Library, 1967.

Wise, William. *Killer Smog.* New York: Ballantine, 1970.

ABOUT THE SPIRITUAL CRISIS

Asinof, Eliot. *Craig and Joan.* New York: Dell, 1971.

Binzen, Peter. *Whitetown, U.S.A.* New York: Random House, 1970.

Cleaver, Eldridge. *Soul on Ice.* New York: Dell, 1968.

Coles, Robert, and John Erikson. *The Middle Americans.* Boston: Atlantic-Little, Brown, 1971.

Cowan, Paul. *The Making of an Un-American.* New York: Dell, 1970.

Cruse, Harold. *Rebellion or Revolution?* New York: Morrow, 1970.

Friedan, Betty. *The Feminine Mystique*. New York: Dell, 1963.

Goodman, Paul. *People or Personnel*. New York: Random House, 1968.

Hersh, Seymour M. *Cover-up*. New York: Random House, 1972.

Howe, Louise Kapp, ed. *The White Majority*. New York: Random House, 1970.

Jackson, George. *Soledad Brother*. New York: Bantam, 1970.

Keniston, Kenneth. *Young Radicals*. New York: Harcourt, Brace & World, 1968.

Killian, Lewis M. *The Impossible Revolution?* New York: Random House, 1968.

Lemon, Richard. *The Troubled American*. New York: Simon & Schuster, 1970.

Little, Malcolm. *The Autobiography of Malcolm X*. New York: Grove, 1965.

Lukas, J. Anthony. *Don't Shoot—We Are Your Children!* New York: Dell, 1971.

Michener, James A. *Kent State*. Greenwich, Conn.: Fawcett, 1971.

Morgan, Robin, ed. *Sisterhood Is Powerful*. New York: Random House, 1970.

Nelson, Truman. *The Right of Revolution*. Boston: Beacon, 1968.

Novak, Michael. *The Rise of the Unmeltable Ethnics*. New York: Macmillan, 1972.

Packard, Vance. *The Sexual Wilderness*. New York: Pocket Books, 1970.

Pettigrew, Thomas F. *Racially Separate or Together*. New York: McGraw-Hill, 1971.

Polner, Murray. *No Victory Parades*. New York: Holt, Rinehart & Winston, 1971.

Reich, Charles. *The Greening of America*. New York: Random House, 1970.

Roszak, Theodore. *The Making of a Counter Culture*. Garden City, N.Y.: Doubleday, 1969.

Skolnick, Jerome. *The Politics of Protest*. New York: Ballantine, 1970.

Slater, Philip E. *The Pursuit of Loneliness*. Boston: Beacon, 1970.

Tanner, Leslie B., ed. *The Women's Liberation Movement*. New York: New American Library, 1971.